DOCTORS IN THE GREAT WAR

DOCTORS IN THE GREAT WAR

Ian R. Whitehead

Pen & Sword
MILITARY

Published by Leo Cooper in 1999
and re-printed in this format in 2013 by

Pen & Sword Military
an imprint of
Pen & Sword Books Ltd
47 Church Street
Barnsley
South Yorkshire
S70 2AS

The right of Ian R. Whitehead to be identified as author of this work has
been asserted by him in accordance with the Copyright, Designs and
Patents Act 1988.

Copyright © Ian R. Whitehead, 1999, 2013

ISBN:-978-1-78346-174-5

Printed and bound in the UK by CPI Group (UK) Ltd, Croydon, CR0 4YY

Pen & Sword Books Ltd incorporates the Imprints of Pen & Sword Aviation,
Pen & Sword Family History, Pen & Sword Maritime, Pen & Sword Military, Pen
& Sword Discovery, Wharncliffe Local History, Wharncliffe True Crime,
Wharncliffe Transport, Pen & Sword Select, Pen & Sword Military Classics, Leo
Cooper, The Praetorian Press, Remember When, Seaforth Publishing
and Frontline Publishing.

For a complete list of Pen & Sword titles please contact
PEN & SWORD BOOKS LIMITED
47 Church Street, Barnsley, South Yorkshire, S70 2AS, England
E-mail: enquiries@pen-and-sword.co.uk
Website: www.pen-and-sword.co.uk

Contents

Acknowledgements

I wish to thank the staffs of the following libraries and archives for help given during the course of my research: the Bodleian Library; the Brotherton Library; the Imperial War Museum; Leeds University Medical Library; the Liddle Collection, University of Leeds; Nottingham University Medical Library; the Osler Club of London; the Public Record Office; the Library of the Royal College of Physicians (London); the Library of the Royal College of Surgeons (London); the Library of the Royal Military Academy, Sandhurst; the Wellcome Institute for the History of Medicine. Where relevant, I am also grateful to the above institutions for permission to quote material, and to reproduce photographs. I have sought to locate current holders of copyright for all material reproduced, but wish to express my apologies for any omissions in this respect.

I owe thanks to the British Academy, for funding my PhD research, which forms the basis of this book. I am also grateful to the Wellcome Trust for the award of a research grant; and to the University of Derby, for assistance with research expenses.

I am indebted to Hugh Cecil, who supervised my PhD thesis. I am particularly grateful to Hugh and his family, for making me welcome in their home, during my periods of study in London. My thanks also go to Peter Liddle for his advice and encouragement, and for his continued interest in my work. The trust which he placed in me, by allowing me free access to the Liddle Collection, is much appreciated. I am grateful to Gary Sheffield for arranging my visit to Sandhurst. I wish also to thank the following for their assistance and interest: Brian Bond; Roy Bridge; Roger Cooter; Mark Harrison; Edward Spiers; and my colleagues, past and present, at the University of Derby. In addition, I am grateful to the staff at Pen & Sword, for their assistance and efficiency.

I am particularly fortunate in my friends and family, and wish to thank them all for their continued interest and support. Above all, I wish to thank my parents, who have always encouraged me in my work, and who have given me so much more than words can convey.

Ian Whitehead,
Derby, January 1999.

Abbreviations

AAMC	Australian Army Medical Corps	CAMC	Canadian Army Medical Corps
ACI	Army Council Instruction	CCS	Casualty Clearing Station
ADGMS	Assistant Director General of Medical Services	CMP	Civil Medical Practitioner
		CMWC	Central Medical War Committee
ADMS	Assistant Director of Medical Services	CO	Commanding Officer
AHC	Army Hospital Corps	DADMS	Deputy Assistant Director of Medical Services
AMO	Administrative Medical Officer		
AMS	Army Medical Service	DDMS	Deputy Director of Medical Services
ARMW	Association of Registered Medical Women	DGAMS	Director General of the Army Medical Services
ASC	Army Service Corps		
BEF	British Expeditionary Force	DGMS	Director General of Medical Services
BJS	British Journal of Surgery	DGNATS	Director General of National Service
BMA	British Medical Association	DMS	Director of Medical Services
BMJ	British Medical Journal	DPH	Diploma in Public Health
BRCS	British Red Cross Society	EEF	Egyptian Expeditionary Force

EMJ	Edinburgh Medical Journal	NZAMC	New Zealand Army Medical Corps
FA	Field Ambulance	OTC	Officer Training Corps
GMC	General Medical Council	PMO	Principal Medical Officer
GMJ	Glasgow Medical Journal	PRO	Public Record Office
GRO	General Routine Order	QMAAC	Queen Mary's Army Auxiliary Corps
IWM	Imperial War Museum	QMG	Quarter Master General
JAMA	Journal of the American Medical Association	RAMC	Royal Army Medical Corps
JMWF	Journal of the Medical Women's Federation	RCS	Royal College of Surgeons
JRAMC	Journal of the Royal Army Medical Corps	RMO	Regimental Medical Officer
LC	Liddle Collection	SCCSC	Special Committee of Chairmen of Standing Committees
LGB	Local Government Board		
LMWC	Local Medical War Committee	SMO	Senior Medical Officer
MC	Military Cross	SMSEC	Scottish Medical Service Emergency Commission
MEF	Mediterranean Expeditionary Force		
MH	Ministry of Health	SR	Special Reserve
MJA	Medical Journal of Australia	SWH	Scottish Women's Hospitals
MO	Medical Officer	TF	Territorial Force
MOH	Medical Officer of Health	VAD	Voluntary Aid Detachment
MRC	Medical Research Committee	VC	Victoria Cross
		VD	Venereal Disease
MWF	Medical Women's Federation	WHC	Women's Hospital Corps
NSI	National Service Instruction	WIHM	Wellcome Institute for the History of Medicine
NYMJ	New York Medical Journal	WO	War Office

Appendices

Introduction

The expansion of the Royal Army Medical Corps (RAMC), to meet the needs of Britain's citizen army necessitated an unprecedented withdrawal of medical practitioners from civilian life. By 1918 over half of the nation's doctors were serving with the forces, mostly with the armies in France and Flanders. This book examines the issues raised by the Army's recruitment and employment of doctors. It addresses the tensions that arose between the Army's need for more doctors and the necessity of preserving adequate levels of civilian medical attendance. The purpose is to examine the utilization of doctors. The book does not investigate the impact of the War upon civilian health. Nor is it the intention to provide a comprehensive history of the RAMC during the War. The book does not cover the medical work of other organizations, such as the Red Cross, St John Ambulance or the Friends' Ambulance Units. Neither is there any consideration of the Naval Medical Service. The specific roles of nurses, medical orderlies and the like do not receive detailed coverage. The focus is upon the responsibilities and experiences of qualified medical practitioners. Given the geographical scope of the War, it is not practicable, within the confines of this book, to give adequate consideration to the medical history of all the theatres of conflict. It therefore concentrates upon the Western Front, although some contrasts are made with experiences elsewhere. The book is concerned with the British medical services, but it does recognize the universal character of the problems facing the medical profession in war. Thus, the British responses to issues such as shell shock, and the prevention of venereal diseases, are compared to the measures adopted by the medical services of other belligerent powers.

Co-operation between the medical profession and the Army was critical to the success of the medical arrangements. However, the profession's relationship with the military had a chequered history. Chapter 1 briefly examines the development of the military medical services, from 1854–1914, tracing the efforts by the British Medical Association (BMA) to improve the status of Medical Officers. There is consideration of the Crimean and Boer campaigns, highlighting the failure of the Army to recognize the importance of an efficient and authoritative medical service. The chapter discusses the factors that prevented most doctors from considering a career in the Army, and assesses the impact of the Edwardian army reforms on the military and professional standing of the RAMC.

The increasing calls of the Army upon the nation's medical manpower created a tension between military and civilian requirements. Chapter 2 discusses the problems of meeting these competing demands upon the profession, in the period of voluntary enlistment. It examines the factors that motivated doctors to volunteer. Attention is also given to doctors' concerns about the maintenance of adequate civilian medical provision, and to the fears of those serving abroad that their practices would fall prey to unscrupulous colleagues. The formation, by the profession, of war emergency committees, to oversee the mobilization of doctors, went some way to ease these concerns. In the summer of 1915, these committees were given sole responsibility for the recruitment of Medical Officers. They operated an enrolment scheme under which doctors attested their willingness to serve. It was the responsibility of local committees to decide whether an enrolled practitioner would best serve his country by becoming a military Medical Officer, or whether he ought to remain in civilian practice. These developments are placed in the context of the Government's gradual recognition that greater regulation of the nation's manpower was essential.

The passage of the Military Service Acts in 1916 marked the end of voluntarism for men under the age of forty-one. The medical profession, however, was treated as a separate case because of the need to strike a balance between civilian and military requirements. The voluntary enrolment scheme continued to be administered by the professional committees. Chapter 3 examines the increasing strain that was placed upon this system. It became evident that the voluntary scheme was incapable either of delivering sufficient Medical Officers to the Army, or of ensuring that doctors were adequately distributed throughout the UK, in accordance with the need to maintain satisfactory standards of civilian health care. The chapter explains why the system came close to collapse in 1917. An assessment is given of the impact, and veracity, of mounting accusations that the RAMC was making excessive demands on the profession, at the expense of civilian requirements.

Chapter 4 concerns itself with the position of medical students. It demonstrates that protecting the future supply of qualified practitioners became an increasingly important consideration in British manpower policy. The impact of the War on British medical education is discussed, including the opening up of the medical schools to female students.

The War appeared to offer great opportunities for medical women. The need to relieve male doctors for military service meant that women gained access to areas of medical practice that had previously been denied to them. Chapter 5 addresses these developments, and draws attention to the Army's failure to fully appreciate the potential contribution of women doctors. The War Office initially dismissed the idea of female Medical Officers. This chapter demonstrates that the medical work of women's voluntary organizations, such as the Scottish Women's Hospitals, forced the military authorities to reconsider their rejection of female doctors. However, it explains that throughout the War women remained in an iniquitous position inside the RAMC. The chapter concludes with an assessment of the War's long-term impact on the professional prospects of female practitioners.

Chapter 6 looks at the medical administration on the Western Front. It assesses the validity of contemporary claims that the Army's employment of doctors was wasteful. It evaluates the RAMC's ability to make effective use of doctors' specialist skills, and considers the role of the consultants who advised the Director General of the Medical Services in France. It also discusses doctors' concerns about the failure to promote Medical Officers on the basis of professional ability, and the resentment felt, by many temporary commissioned officers, at being unable to secure senior posts in the medical administration. Claims that unnecessary bureaucracy obstructed the work of Medical Officers and that the RAMC was obsessed with evacuating the wounded, at the expense of careful treatment, are also investigated.

Doctors were almost unique in being able to undertake military duties that were so closely related to their civilian work, and many believed that they would require little training. However, there were important differences in approach between civilian and military practice. Service in the RAMC involved a modification to the doctors' ethical code, with loyalty to the needs of the state taking precedence over those of the individual. Chapter 7 looks at the training of Medical Officers, highlighting the

3

limitations of doctors' civilian experiences as preparation for military medicine. It outlines the RAMC's gradual development of a system of instruction, both for initial training and to keep Medical Officers in touch with recent developments. It contends that the Army Medical Service (AMS) was slow to recognize the need for systematic training, and that it was not until the final year of the War that sufficient attention was paid to the importance of educating doctors about the various responsibilities of the military doctor.

Chapter 8 considers the work of Medical Officers at the various stages along the lines of evacuation. The chapter assesses the effectiveness of the evacuation procedures, on both medical and military grounds. Particular attention is given to developments in war surgery and the campaign against wound infection, in which the provision of immediate operative treatment at the Casualty Clearing Stations emerges as a significant factor. It also looks at the problems that confronted doctors, resulting from their status as non-combatants, within a military structure, and from their need to place military priorities at the forefront of arrangements for medical treatment. There is an examination of allegations that the work of doctors with forward units was undemanding of medical skill.

These issues are taken further in Chapter 9 which discusses the role of Medical Officers in maintaining the health and morale of the troops. This chapter highlights the increased status of sanitation and preventive medicine. It looks at the RAMC's success in defeating diseases that had formerly laid waste to armies, and also in responding to the 'new' diseases of war. The chapter demonstrates that the medical services played a considerable part in the victory of the British Army. However, several inefficiencies also become apparent. The RAMC was slow to respond to the issue of shell shock. Meanwhile on matters such as inoculation, which was not compulsory, and the prevention of VD, non-medical considerations were allowed to intervene. Nevertheless, the chapter argues that in its efforts to prevent and treat disease the AMS, in France, successfully combined its military responsibilities with the medical profession's humanitarian concerns.

The book demonstrates that doctors played a bigger part in the Great War, than in any previous conflict. To an extent, this reflected the scale of the contest. The withdrawal of a large proportion of the profession for military service ensured that the employment of doctors was an important aspect of manpower policy. But it also reflected an increasing recognition, in military circles, of medicine's vital contribution to the attainment of victory. Medicine had been called upon to deal with unexpected aspects of modern warfare, to develop new techniques for treatment and to place greater emphasis than ever before upon disease prevention. The conclusion offers an assessment of medicine's record on the Western Front in rising to these challenges. It also considers the longer-term implications of the War for the medical profession, and for the reputation and status of the RAMC.

Chapter 1

Doctors and the Army, 1854–1914: The Struggle for Recognition

The creation of the RAMC in 1898 marked a significant victory for the BMA in its fight to establish an efficient Army Medical Service, and to secure proper military status for army doctors. This chapter sets out to examine, briefly, the events that led to the formation of the RAMC, and its development thereafter, with a view to establishing the position of the medical service on the eve of the First World War.

It was the dismal performance of the medical arrangements during the Crimean War that had first awakened the BMA's[1] interest in army medical reform. The Army went to war in 1854 without a unified medical service, its personnel being divided horizontally. Each regiment had a surgeon, with an assistant, ranking respectively as Surgeon-Captain and Surgeon-Lieutenant. But there was also the Army Medical Department, the staff of which comprised a Director-General, four Inspectors-General, eleven Deputy-Inspectors and 163 officer-surgeons, distributed in garrisons worldwide.[2] The general readiness of the medical services for war left much to be desired. During the long interval of peace between the final victory over Napoleon's forces in 1815 and the outbreak of war in 1854, cuts in military expenditure had severely weakened the medical service. With the abolition of the Royal Wagon Train,[3] what little provision for ambulance transport that had existed was lost; whilst many of the lessons learnt regarding the treatment of wounds in battle were forgotten. Moreover, there had been no progress towards the establishment of a single body to administer the army hospitals; control was still

6

divided between the Army Medical Department and the Purveyor's Department.[4]

However, the central weakness of the service was the lack of authority and low status accorded to the Regimental Medical Officers. They had no direct control over the regimental troops and were without a support staff to collect the wounded and carry out orderly and nursing duties. An attempt was made to meet this latter deficiency through the formation of the Hospital Conveyance Corps, but, untrained, it proved a very ineffective solution.[5] In any case, the Medical Officers had no authority over the Conveyance Corps, and so their position was no better than under the existing arrangements whereby the regiments detailed men for nursing and orderly duty.[6]

The lack of authority conferred on Medical Officers was an expression of the prejudice against them which was widespread in military circles. They were not regarded as fellow officers, but merely as 'camp followers'; some regiments did not allow the Medical Officers to dine with the other officers in the mess, whilst the Medical Officer, no matter how long he had served was always subordinate to the most junior subaltern. In addition to social ostracism, the medical man also faced discrimination with regard to pay and the distribution of honours.

The doctor's pay was not on a par with that of other officers, and there were also expenses, related to his duties, that he had to meet out of his own pocket.[7] Meanwhile, despite the acts of gallantry performed by Medical Officers in the Crimea, military honours had largely been refused them,[8] although three surgeons did receive the Victoria Cross (VC).[9]

The lowly status of the Medical Officer was damaging in two respects. On the one hand, his lack of authority added to the inefficiency of the medical arrangements hampered any attempts he might make to improve the lot of the sick and wounded. On the other hand, it undermined morale within the service, and further discouraged young medical men from joining a service which was considered by the profession at large to have been passed over by the improvements in medical knowledge and practice.[10]

The inevitable result of this combination of administrative inefficiency and the impotence of the Medical Officers was a high incidence of disease during the Crimean campaign, and an organization incapable of responding to the task before it. Utter confusion was the result.[11] W.H. Russell, *The Times* correspondent in the Crimea, described the mismanagement of the medical services which could not even supply enough beds for the sick.[12] Provision of the most basic medicines and medical stores was also dangerously inadequate.[13] But most damning of all was the fact that had proper provision for sanitation been made, much of the disease that was destroying the British Army could easily have been avoided.

The Sanitary Commission, despatched to the Crimea in 1855, documented the sanitary defects of the Barrack Hospital, Scutari. The water supply was found to be contaminated; there were no covers for privies, and no means of flushing them. A sea of filth and wards filled with poisonous gases were the results of an overloaded sewage system. The Commissioners took in hand the cleaning up of the hospital, with positive results as regards the incidence of disease,[14] but the knowledge that so much disease could easily have been avoided fuelled growing public concern[15] regarding the performance of the military medical service.

Not for the last time, attempts were made to blame the Medical Officers themselves for the inadequacies of the AMS; accusations of army doctors neglecting their duty were carried in many of the daily newspapers. An enquiry held at Raglan's[16] headquarters, in the Crimea, seemed to authenticate such press claims.[17] The Association Medical Journal[18] sprang to the defence of the military doctors, blaming the hidebound Army Medical Department for the fact that little opportunity had been afforded Medical Officers to gain hospital experience during peacetime. It criticized the Army's reluctance to augment the ranks of the AMS with more experienced civil practitioners. Moreover, it was quite clear from Russell's reports that the devotion to duty of the Medical Officers was not in question; the problem was that there were too few of them to cope with the heavy load of work.[19]

Continued pressure from the BMA, and Florence Nightingale's crusading efforts on the issue of army sanitary reform, led to the appointment in 1857 of a Royal Commission, headed by Sidney Herbert. Its report a year later made several recommendations which were intended to ensure that the importance of sanitary science was recognized. It stressed the need for Medical Officers to be armed with sufficient knowledge and authority to enable them to take measures against preventable diseases, and so avoid a recurrence of the large-scale and unnecessary losses that had blighted the Army's performance during the Crimean campaign.[20]

Its recommendations on improving the status of Medical Officers were embodied in the Warrant of 1858 which granted them increased pay and equality of rank with the regimental officers. Although the position of the military doctor was still not perfect,[21] the Warrant was nevertheless looked upon as a significant step upwards for the military branch of the medical profession.

8

Other important advances resulting from the Report were the foundation of the new military hospital at Netley and the establishment of an Army Medical School.[22] At last, opportunities for improving scientific knowledge were being provided. The medical school both allowed for the education and specialist training of Medical Officers, and became a centre for research into military medicine and hygiene; many important discoveries in the field of tropical medicine were to follow.[23]

There was also the formation of the Army Hospital Corps (AHC), with the intention of providing high-quality personnel to carry out stretcher-bearer, orderly and nursing duties in the regimental, garrison and general hospitals.[24] And for the first time they were to be on a level status with the rest of the Army.[25]

Despite these improvements, however, the medical profession continued to take a disparaging view of army service, and recruitment continued to slide. Part of the reason lay in the fact that regimental officers, resenting the parity of status now enjoyed by Medical Officers, successfully neutralized the effects of the new warrant; a policy of slights and black-balling undermined the status of Medical Officers.[26] The War Office ignored the effects of depriving the Medical Officer of the necessary 'weight of a gentleman amongst gentlemen'[27] on his ability to carry out such essential functions as the maintenance of high standards of hygiene. Indeed, the War Office displayed a dangerously complacent attitude towards ensuring that careful sanitary provision could be made by Medical Officers, whilst hostile voices in Parliament were questioning the importance which Herbert's reforms had accorded to sanitation.[28] There was also hostility to the AHC because of the free access it would be allowed to regimental preserves, and this resulted in a whittling down of its powers.[29]

But, above all, the changes made did not approach the radical reorganization that was necessary to appease disgruntled Medical Officers. 'Fundamentally, it was still the same system: the army medical forces were entirely divided. The AHC had no officers; the Medical Officers, still attached to the regiments, but without authority in them, had no men. The Army Medical Department was an administrative office, separate from either of the executive branches of the medical service, and virtually incapable of exercising any influence over them.'[30]

Florence Nightingale warned of the consequences of not addressing the grievances of the Medical Officers, writing to Douglas Galton,[31] in 1863, 'You MUST do something for these doctors, or they will do for you – simply by not coming to you.'[32] However, her urgent calls for improvements in training, pay and conditions fell upon deaf ears. To a War Office seeking economies, the pay of Medical Officers proved an easy target. The War Office was unable to comprehend the fact that the cost of sickness in an army inadequately supplied with able medical practitioners would far out-weigh the cost of providing decent pay and attractive conditions for the military doctors.[33]

Throughout the 1860s the BMA continued the campaign for a thoroughgoing reform of the medical services, but with no success. It was not until the performance of the Prussian medical services in the 1870–1 conflict showed what could be achieved by a 'scientifically-trained and excellently-equipped'[34] medical department, that the War Office awoke to the need for change in the British system.

The year 1873 saw the reform of the regimental system by Cardwell, a reform long desired by Medical Officers but one carried out in a fashion that failed to stem the tide of Medical Officers leaving the service. Cardwell's reforms had disappointed because, although all doctors were now to be part of the Army Medical Department, a unified corps did not exist, and the Medical Officers were still without authority over the AHC.

Medical Officers' lack of authority combined with the failure of the AMS to keep pace with the opportunities available to doctors in civil life to make it increasingly difficult for the Army to recruit a sufficient number of medical recruits. The number of candidates coming forward for commissions became so few that competitive examinations ceased.[35] In 1878 the Thompson Committee concluded that substantial improvement in the pay and conditions of Medical Officers were essential: 'the time has fully come when the difficulty of obtaining Medical Officers for the Army must be met in a liberal and comprehensive spirit. Their services are indispensable, and are recognized practically in the civil community by handsome remuneration . . . [the Government] must supplement the certainty and the distinction of its service by pecuniary offers not seriously lower than those made by the civil community.'[36] As a result of the Thompson Report, the pay of Medical Officers was raised.

The question of giving greater authority to Medical Officers remained unresolved and came to the fore again during the Egyptian campaign of 1882. Criticism of the management of the AHC in Egypt led to an enquiry into its organization. The report which followed recommended that undivided control of hospitals be established, and that this control be vested in Medical Officers.[37] This recommendation was accepted and in 1884 a Royal Warrant brought a unified corps a stage closer: the Army Medical Department was renamed the Army Medical Staff, and its officers given command over the Medical Staff Corps (the former AHC).[38]

But the continued failure to address the question of bestowing full military rank upon Medical Officers meant that the discontent of the profession remained unassuaged. New urgency was given to the matter by the Warrant of 1887 which recognized only two kinds of rank, substantive and honorary, neither of which were held by Medical Officers.[39] The BMA led the medical schools in protest over this development and the result was a Departmental Committee,[40] which eventually compromised by bestowing compound titles[41] upon Medical Officers.[42] This combination of military and medical titles did not satisfy the profession and was a victory for those in the combatant branch who refused to recognize the right of Medical Officers to full military status.

In a letter of January 1891 the President of the Royal College of Physicians impressed upon the Secretary of State for War the necessity of granting full rank to Medical Officers. He argued that if they were to be able to carry out efficiently their duties of preventing disease and maintaining the health of the troops, they needed sufficient authority to ensure that adequate sanitary measures were adopted. He argued that this could best be achieved by the 'transformation of the whole Department into a Royal Army Medical Corps, in the granting of definite rank and title to all its officers, and in its organic incorporation into the general Army on the lines followed in the Royal Engineers'.[43] The War Office, however, was opposed to the idea of granting substantive rank to Medical Officers because it claimed that this would involve giving them military command in the field.[44] This claim was without foundation; the formation of an RAMC and the granting of full rank would merely have ensured that Medical Officers had sufficient power to carry out their duties. However, the attitude in the combatant service of those who regarded Medical Officers as just doctors was allowed to prevail. The War Office ignored the growing importance of an efficient medical service in modern warfare. It failed to appreciate that the medical branch needed to be consulted in preparation for a campaign, or to see that doctors required a clear understanding of military tactics and procedures if they were to execute their duties properly.

In the face of the War Office's refusal to act, the principal medical schools initiated a policy of boycotting the AMS,[45] which aimed at forcing the Government to grant full rank to Medical Officers. It was only in 1898, with the sympathetic Lord Lansdowne at the War Office, that the pressure of the medical profession finally achieved equality of rank within a unified corps.[46]

The formation of the RAMC was not, however, a complete victory for the medical profession, and it would seem an exaggeration to claim that 'the cloud had been lifted'[47] from the service. For substantial grievances over pay, leave and opportunities for study continued to blight the service, discouraged doctors from considering a career in the RAMC and caused the medical schools to maintain their boycott.[48] Indeed, medical students, if they considered a career in the Army at all, seemed more likely to opt for a combatant commission.[49] The result was a service which, on the eve of the South African War, was deficient in personnel and inadequately prepared for war.

Discussing the undermanning of the service in 1900 the British Medical Journal (BMJ) pointed out that the present strength of under 900 Medical Officers needed to be increased to at least 1,200 to be sure of providing adequate medical care.[50] In the meantime it was only the enthusiastic response of civil practitioners and medical students, to the calls for assistance,[51] that prevented a complete breakdown of the medical arrangements in South Africa.[52] The unprecedented scale of this civilian assistance was commented upon at the BMA's annual meeting at Cheltenham in August 1901:

> For the first time in our history the country has been largely represented by civilian surgeons in a great campaign. In the Crimean War a few were so employed, but in the present case civilian aid has not only been casual or occasional. Many hundreds of surgeons have left their peaceful practice at home and volunteered for service in the field to help their brethren of the RAMC.[53]

The medical corps in South Africa was also strengthened by the appointment of several distinguished medical men as consulting surgeons.[54] These men spoke highly of the manner in which their colleagues in the RAMC received them[55] and of the performance of the medical arrangements in South Africa. Frederick Treves (later Sir) described the organization of the medical services as 'sound and good' and assured readers of the BMJ that he 'left South Africa with the impression that nothing more could have been done to mitigate the suffering of the sick and wounded than had been done when a temperate regard for the circumstances of war was kept in mind'.[56]

However, the reports that Mr Burdett-Coutts had been sending back starkly contrasted with the praises doled out by Treves. Only six months into the War, Burdett-Coutts telegraphed Lord Wolseley, the Commander-in-Chief, concerning the lack of doctors, nurses and medical supplies.[57] Later, in one of many letters to The Times, he described the terrible conditions that men suffering from typhoid had to endure.[58]

Treves refuted the claims of Burdett-Coutts,[59] and the BMJ itself came to the defence of the medical organization, arguing that although the rate of sickness in South Africa was high, it was much less than in previous campaigns.[60] However, the fact was that had it not been for deficiencies in the AMS much of the disease could easily have been prevented. And, what is more, Treves knew this to be the case. For, as his biographer points out, Treves secretly acknowledged that the situation was one of complete disarray,[61] and despite their public stance, both he and MacCormac made efforts to distance themselves from the RAMC.[62]

Patriotism largely explains why Treves felt bound to cover up the inadequacies of the Army's medical provision.[63] However, once the War was over he no longer felt under this constraint and his evidence to the 1903 Royal Commission reiterated Burdett-Coutts's earlier statements regarding deficiencies in personnel, transport, medicine and equipment, and the general inefficiency of an administrative machine bound up with too much red tape.[64] Treves's wartime praise for the medical services also appears to have been motivated by a desire to defend the doctors against accusations of callousness and neglect.[65] But the devotion of individual Medical Officers never seems to have been in question. Burdett-Coutts made it plain that he thought it was the system that was at fault and not the Medical Officers. In Parliament he made the following statement:

> I have given every possible credit to the loyalty and devotion with which those who have had the care of the patients have acted, and I take this opportunity of expressing my deep regret that many – far too many of them – have lost their lives in the performance of their noble task.[66]

And, in a letter to *The Times*, published two days earlier, he had similarly recognized the bravery of the Medical Officers, whilst noting that this was not necessarily a sign that the service was efficient:

> The favourable note had been sounded from the first, from the plains of Colenso and other lesser battlefields where the splendid bravery of our Army doctors under fire seized and engrossed the public imagination. In that quality, indeed, the record of the RAMC shows no flaw; but it can no more provide a proper medical system in war than the bravery of our troops can supply tactics and strategy. When the talk is of 'perfect medical arrangements' it is only misleading to keep the attention fixed on acts of heroism in the field.[67]

The South African Hospitals Commission noted that, with few exceptions, the devotion to duty of the army doctors was worthy of the highest praise.[68] Even the German observers spoke of their work in complimentary terms.[69]

It was their sheer lack of numbers that had helped to prevent these devoted efforts of the Medical Officers from providing the adequate treatment that the troops in South Africa deserved.[70] But the War Office's neglect of recommendations made by the medical service, and the prejudices which Medical Officers had to contend with, were equally important in contributing to the medical disaster in South Africa.

Criticism has been made of the combatant branch of the Army for not recognizing the importance of ensuring that medical provision was maintained at the highest possible degree of efficiency, which circumstances permitted. General Sir George White, the commander of the forces at Ladysmith, never once visited the hospital there;[71] whilst General Roberts, who was later to betray a commendable understanding of the important part to be played in war by preventive medicine,[72] did not appear to recognize the necessity of removing incompetent Surgeons-General from their positions.[73]

A belief remained prevalent amongst combatant officers that the health of the men was beneath their interest.[74] This ensured that the necessity for good hygiene and sanitation continued to be ignored by the Army. For this state of affairs, the War Office must take full responsibility; far from attempting to educate army officers in the importance of careful sanitation, it was itself utterly disinterested. On the outbreak of war Sir William Foster had advised the War Office that specialist sanitary officers would be indispensable to efforts to preserve the health of the troops,[75] but the War Office failed to make any such appointments, ignoring all warnings about the importance of sanitation.

The attitude of the Army that nothing could be done to prevent men drinking contaminated water if they were thirsty,[76] and the ignorance of the men on matters of hygiene,[77] clearly demonstrated the folly of not paying heed to the advice of the medical profession. A programme of education was needed to fix in the minds of all ranks the relationship between high sanitary standards and disease prevention.

The lack of authority vested in Medical Officers prevented them from making sanitary improvements,[78] and their low status ensured that little notice was taken of their views:

All the senior officers, from the principal medical officer downwards, are impressed with a sort of feeling, first of all, that their service is looked at askance, that their branch is secondary; and, next, that they must not approach any General Commanding Officer, and certainly not if he has got a title, without their knees cluttering together with alarm and fright; they must not think of advising him that it really would be for the good of the Army if a camp was not pitched on a certain proposed site, because it is covered by stinking horses in various degrees of decomposition.[79]

Such a state of affairs can hardly have been healthy for morale within the RAMC, or conducive to the efficient conduct of preventive medicine. This dismal portrait of the Medical Officer's position within the Army did not, however, go unchallenged. It was argued that many commanding officers would be ready to take the advice of their Medical Officer on sanitary matters, and that few Medical Officers would feel constrained from proferring such advice.[80] But, whilst acknowledging that the views expressed above were probably those of an especially embittered Medical Officer, there is no doubt that suspicion and prejudice still obstructed the army doctor in his work.

Combatant officers appeared to have little confidence in the professional ability of the RAMC officers. Such doubts might appear to do the Medical Officers a great injustice, given the devotion to duty displayed by them during the South African campaign; but they did have a basis in fact. And, as the evidence of Treves to the Commission on the South African War showed, their brethren in the civil profession shared this lack of faith in the skill of the army doctors.[81] It is true that the unattractiveness of the unreformed medical service ensured that the candidates who came forward for commissions were not always of the best quality. On the whole, however, the criticisms were not so much a reflection upon the military doctors themselves but rather a condemnation of the Army's failure to give its doctors sufficient opportunity for professional improvement and advancement. Witnesses to the Commission were agreed upon the importance of allowing Medical Officers every opportunity 'to enlarge their professional experience'[82] and gain specialist skills through a wider availability of study leave. But it was recognized that to ensure the success of this policy, the underlying problem of an undermanned service needed to be tackled; otherwise Medical Officers would continue to be refused study leave on the grounds that they could not be spared.[83]

That the combatant branch did not appreciate the value of Medical Officers and their work is clear from the various grievances which doctors who were, or had been, serving in South Africa, communicated to the BMA. The pages of the BMJ teemed with complaints about the refusal of many combatant officers to call Medical Officers by their military titles; the failure to grant Medical Officers temporary local rank; the need to grant temporary commissions to civil surgeons; and the in-adequate pay and poor conditions accorded to the retired Medical Officers and civil practitioners who had volunteered their services in the Army's moment of need.[84]

But probably the clearest indication of the low esteem in which Medical Officers were held was the reluctance, in some quarters, to give due recognition to their countless acts of devotion and bravery. At one point there was an attempt to suggest that the VC could only be awarded to men serving in the combatant branch. The BMA, which at that time was anxious to secure recognition for the courage of Babtie and Douglas,[85] managed to obtain official assurances that the highest award, 'For Valour', was not the preserve of the combatants; the two men in question received their VCs. Nevertheless the BMJ was able to publish statistics that appeared to confirm a definite policy of discrimination against Medical Officers in the distribution of honours.[86] It is, however, difficult to quantify the extent of such discrimination, and it would be as well to bear in mind that only the Royal Artillery won a greater number of distinctions during the campaign.[87]

The performance of Britain's military organization during the Boer conflict had given rise to much public concern and criticism; it became apparent that a thoroughgoing reform of the Army was necessary.[88] And as the spotlight of reform fell on the Army as a whole, the medical services were to come in for particular attention; the process began of removing those grievances and deficiencies which the formation of the RAMC had failed to solve.

In 1901 the Royal Commission on South African Hospitals laid down the principal objectives of army medical reform. The Commission recommended the appointment of a committee to establish the best means of ensuring that:

> 1. The staff of the RAMC may be permanently enlarged and due provision may be made for its further necessary and speedy enlargement in times of great wars.
> 2. Inducements may be offered to ensure a continuous supply to the corps of sufficient men of good professional attainment; and
> 3. The men who have joined may be kept as a body thoroughly acquainted with the general progress made in professional subjects, and at a high professional standard of efficiency.[89]

The Government's response to the South African Hospitals Commission was Secretary of State Brodrick's appointment of an expert committee on army medical reform.[90] Response also came from the

BMA; a subcommittee of its Parliamentary Bills Committee investigated the matter and reported in April 1901.[91] Its recommendations were the result of inquiries made to the universities, colleges and medical schools in the UK, regarding the factors that deterred medical graduates from considering a career in the RAMC. From the replies received the general undermanning of the service emerged as the pivotal grievance: it was due to this that Medical Officers were overworked; that tours of duty were far longer than for combatant officers; that there was little opportunity for personal leave; and that study leave was virtually impossible. The latter point proved especially powerful in deterring able young candidates, for they would not enter a service which closeted doctors from developments in medical knowledge and so barred their way to professional advancement. Lack of study leave was regarded as the most damaging consequence of an undermanned service,[92] and, by deterring candidates, increased the problem of undermanning still further.

The survey revealed that if this vicious circle was to be broken, improvements in pay would have to be made; insufficient pay was at the heart of the unpopularity that caused the undermanning and so contributed to the many deficiencies in the service. Criticism was made of the War Office for ignoring the great rise in the market value of doctors which had taken place in the last thirty years or so. Consideration needed to be given to the fact that financial competition from civil life had become much greater since the outlawing of unqualified assistants. Also, increases in both the cost and length of medical education had reduced the numbers entering the profession, further pushing up their value and thus making it unlikely that they would consider a career that was so poorly paid. Better pay, especially for junior officers, on whom a greater cost fell, and for Medical Officers serving in India, where pay rates were far below those of other officers, was therefore essential.[93] Inadequate pay was a reflection of the continued low status of Medical Officers, which also had to be dealt with if sufficient numbers of able doctors were to be attracted into the RAMC. As a correspondent to the BMJ pointed out, it was 'useless . . . to expect men of superior education and training to enter a service in which they will be regarded and treated as "subordinates", "camp followers", and inferiors who are expected "just to do as they are told". Medical Officers, so far as my knowledge of them extends, simply claim to be treated as "gentlemen", on the same footing as their combatant brethren.'[94]

The BMA Report referred to concern felt within the medical schools regarding the failure to give due recognition to the Army rank of Medical Officers, and concluded that the 'Army status of Medical Officers should not be qualified, set aside, or rendered of no effect by General or Local Army orders, as seems still occasionally done'.[95] It also pointed out that the 'position of the Director-General himself, as well as of Honorary Physicians and Surgeons to His Majesty . . . are not defined or even recognized on State or Ceremonial occasions', with the recommendation that the Director-General of the Army Medical Service (DGAMS) should have a place on the Army Board and be given pay equal to that of other heads of department.[96] Such improvements in the status of Medical Officers, and of the DGAMS, would help to raise the RAMC to a position of influence and respect, comparable to that enjoyed by the German Army Medical Service,[97] and were essential to efficient medical provision.

The system of promotion was also in need of overhaul. Seniority promotion had been the norm, but, in order to make the RAMC an attractive career, the BMA felt that 'promotion should largely rest on professional and administrative merit'.[98] The granting of Brevet rank, as was available in the combatant branch, was seen as another way of making the service more attractive to able candidates:

> no advantage towards promotion accrues to a candidate who enters the Army Medical Service with very high qualifications. To remedy this serious defect we consider a system of Brevet promotion might be adopted, as in the combatant branches of the service, and that officers who distinguish themselves professionally, or on field service, should get Brevet promotion, with extra pay, remaining in the original position in their Corps list, as in other branches of the service. This would give officers so promoted extra pay, and seniority on mixed boards and committees, as well as a step towards further departmental promotion should they prove themselves worthy of it.
>
> In this manner, those who enter the service towards the limit of age, in consequence of, perhaps, remaining longer at their studies, or in the position of House-Surgeons, might have an opportunity of making up for time so lost before entry.[99]

The Report of Brodrick's committee[100] dealt with most of the issues that the BMA's Report had highlighted. The DGAMS was raised in status, being given a seat on the Army Board and the assistance of a Medical Advisory Board. Improvements were made in the scale of pay; provision was made for study leave and the establishment of a medical staff college; promotion was to be based on ability; and a system of Brevet promotion was introduced. However, the scheme as it stood was not without its faults; the excessive number of examinations to be passed by Medical Officers came in for particular criticism. Brodrick, to his credit, was responsive to the opinions expressed by the profession, and the new warrant made most of the alterations regarding examinations and terms of service that the BMA had recommended.[101]

Problems still remained. Professor Ogston's exceptions to the scheme[102] called attention to the failure to develop a sanitary organization, whilst deficiencies in Indian pay and undermanning still prevented the BMA from recommending a career in the service.[103] But the signs were that Brodrick's reforms were already having a positive effect on the undermanning; 1902 witnessed the first real competition for RAMC commissions for many years.[104] And combined with the improvements made in Indian pay in 1902[105] the BMA was able to declare the new scheme a success; the deluge of complaints had ceased.[106]

Brodrick's plans for reforming the Army at large had not, however, met with such approval; his ambitious and unrealistic strategy involved a massive increase in military spending and would have required the introduction of conscription to be successful. When a suitable opportunity presented itself,[107] Arnold-Foster replaced Brodrick; but his proposals proved equally unworkable.[108] What neither he nor Brodrick had realized was that before the Army could be reformed the War Office administration itself needed to be reconstituted.[109] It was left to the Esher Committee to tackle the chaotic state of the nation's military administration; the War Office was restructured, and a general staff system instituted.[110]

But Esher's scheme caused the medical profession some disquiet because the DGAMS was not given a seat on the new Army Council. Indeed, the initial Report made no mention of the medical services. The BMJ warned that without 'representation on the Army Council the medical service is relegated to a subordinate position which checks initiative, paralyses intelligent activity and tends to make the service shunned by the very men most fitted to make good officers'.[111] It was feared that this omission showed that complacency was already blotting out the 'terrible lessons of the South African War'.[112] The profession felt that the reorganization of the War Office was being too closely modelled on the Admiralty:

The analogy of the Board of Admiralty must not be pushed too far. In the first place, its constitution became fixed at a time when the science of hygiene had not yet come into being, and when sanitary administration was in its infancy. In the second place, the responsibilities for the prevention of disease in war which fall upon the medical service of the army are far more onerous, and the problems presented far more complex, than in the sister service. Finally, it is notorious that the absence from the Board of Admiralty of any representative of the medical department is a source of inconvenience, delay and inefficiency. To perpetuate in the Army Council this cause of inefficiency will be a retrograde step.'[13]

But, the BMA's demands for a representative of the AMS to sit on the Army Council were not met. This was not because the importance of preventive medicine was again being ignored. The third part of Esher's Report made it plain that 'too much importance cannot be attached to the Sanitary Service in peace and in war'.'[14] Rather, it was a consequence of the Committee's stated aim that the Council superintend, and not directly administer; experts who would be too immersed in detail were not wanted on the Council.'[15] Nor was the Council intended to be a representative body; if the principle of representation had been conceded, the idea of a small council deciding questions of military policy would have been lost.'[16] The BMA felt that having the DGAMS just below the Adjutant-General did not allow the medical service enough voice,'[17] a view which Esher himself was later to adopt. Nevertheless it would appear that medical opinion was given sufficient opportunity to make itself heard, and that the health of the troops was a principal concern of the Council:

> The Council as a whole is now responsible for the welfare of the soldier. It has full power over the whole range of military requirements and there should be no danger that sanitary considerations will be neglected. The Adjutant-General, as a Member of the Council, occupies a far stronger position than his predecessors, and will be able to represent effectively the medical needs of the personnel of the Army with which he is specially charged. Moreover, the Director-General, if necessary associated with a civilian representative of the Army Medical Services Advisory Board, should be summoned to the Council whenever his advice and specialist knowledge are required.'[18]

The year 1905 saw the reorganization of the field medical units; the Field Ambulance replaced the Bearer Company.'[19] The recommendations of the various Royal Commissions on the need for trained sanitary companies and a wider understanding of sanitary principles were, however, still awaiting a response.

The profession therefore made renewed efforts to press home the importance of ensuring high standards of hygiene, demonstrating how the Japanese had been able to keep the incidence of disease in their army to a minimum by the adoption of modern scientific practices.'[20] In

Haldane the medical world found a Secretary of State who recognized the importance of preventive medicine. His reform programme aimed at greater efficiency within an overall framework of economies on military spending;[121] he saw in sanitary science a means of achieving this end[122] by reducing unnecessary wastage, and allowing him to cut the amount of hospital accommodation maintained by the Army. Under his direction steps were taken to educate officers in health matters, a manual of army sanitation being produced. Schemes were also laid down for the formation of sanitary sections, both with regiments and in the lines of communication. These developments were welcomed by the BMJ which congratulated Haldane for embracing sanitary science:

> it is gratifying to the medical profession that hygiene, untaught in the schools, should find acceptance in the Army.[123]

Further initiatives on disease prevention were made, including the provision of clinical and bacteriological laboratories, which proved a stimulus to research and enabled the Corps to keep up-to-date with the latest scientific developments.

Undoubtedly the most significant step was the Army's acceptance of the value of anti-typhoid inoculation.[124] During the South African War, Almroth Wright's work on anti-typhoid inoculation had not been given a fair trial, an indifferent War Office and opposition from within the medical profession continually confronted him.[125] But, in the years between the end of the South African conflict and the outbreak of war in 1914, the War Office was persuaded of the efficacy of inoculation; trials in India provided clear evidence of its protective power. And, although never made compulsory during the War, Kitchener encouraged the inoculation of men due to be despatched.[126]

The cumulative effect of these various advances in preventive medicine was a dramatic reduction in losses from disease. The death rate had fallen from twenty per thousand in 1898 to eight per thousand in 1907; likewise, the number of discharges due to invaliding had fallen to eight per thousand in 1907, from nineteen per thousand in 1898.[127] This trend towards improved army health continued throughout the pre-war years. In 1912, Sir W.L. Gubbins, the DGAMS, pointed out that the result of these health improvements was 'equivalent to an annual addition of 6,164 men to its fighting strength'.[128] Here was unassailable evidence of the good that could be achieved when due weight was given to medical opinion.

When Haldane came into office in 1906 no progress had been made towards providing for the RAMC's 'further necessary and speedy enlargement in times of great wars',[129] and fears that the medical service was not ready to meet an emergency, should one arise, were mounting.[130] As it stood the Army Medical Reserve was of little use,[131] and, although there could be no doubt that civil practitioners would come forward in time of need, the BMA was keen to ensure that the War Office did not use this as an excuse for not tackling the question of organizing an adequate medical reserve.[132]

The failure to construct an adequate medical reserve was, however, not due to neglect of the Army's medical needs, but to the failure of Brodrick's and Arnold-Forster's schemes for reform. It was not until the passage of Haldane's Territorial and Reserve Forces Bill that reorganization of the auxiliary forces progressed: second-line support was provided by the Special Reserve, replacing the old Militia; the Volunteers were reconstituted as the Territorial Force;[133] and the formation of the Officer Training Corps (OTC) recognized the need to tackle the Army's deficiency in officers.[134]

With the Bill on the statute books, the task now, so far as the auxiliary medical services were concerned, was to ensure that the support of the medical profession was fully behind the scheme. In 1908, Keogh, the Director General of the Army Medical Service (DGAMS), stated that, 'in order to build up a citizen Military Medical Service, the medical profession as a whole, had to be consulted, no matter what opinion one might entertain regarding the possible and practicable limits of the scheme'.[135] Both Haldane and Keogh were anxious to avoid a repetition of previous confrontations. Haldane's proposals drew heavily upon a BMA blueprint for the creation of a single RAMC (Vols), encompassing all Medical Officers serving in the existing volunteer forces. This RAMC (Vols) was to provide the medical and sanitary service for the Territorials.[136]

The new corps was modelled upon the regular RAMC, although the regimental system was left in place, 'to meet special medical requirements',[137] and, as far as possible, the medical units were to be raised within the area covered by their particular territorial division. The existing bearer companies of the volunteer forces were reconstituted as field ambulances, in line with the regular forces, and stationary and general hospitals were to be organized; the intention was that these latter would be staffed by volunteers from the local civil hospital. Such local co-operation was also looked for in the field of preventive medicine; in time of war, members of the public health service were to be asked to pledge their advice and assistance should troops be concentrated in their locality.[138]

Keogh toured the country, [139] addressing medical meetings, in order to explain the organization of the new force, to enlist support, but above all, 'to consult . . . and to find out what the profession in the various centres was prepared to do'.[140] He found the profession fully 'aware of the necessity of acquiring special knowledge of military organization and administration',[141] and he welcomed the fact that, within its ranks, there was a growing 'body of men who saw clearly the need of making adequate provision for the expansion of the Regular Medical Service in war, and who, from purely patriotic motives, were devoting time and money to the study of military medical problems'.[142] Indeed, the profession was demanding that an adequate organization be established; never again should the expansion of the AMS be dependent upon civilian volunteers without any knowledge of military medical administration and lacking the requisite authority of a military commission.

Given this desire for action and the combination of Keogh's consultations with a scheme based largely on the BMA's own proposals, it is hardly surprising that the response from medical men was enthusiastic. The BMJ carried numerous reports in 1909 and 1910 of Territorial medical units rapidly approaching, or even reaching, their establishments.[143] Yet, after 1910, the enthusiasm waned and the gap between the number of RAMC (TF) officers serving and the number laid down in the estimates steadily widened;[144] by 1913 the shortfall was 379.[145] This was not, however, an expression of the kind of medical dissatisfaction with the Army that had for so long blighted the service, but rather it reflected the failure of the Territorial Army as a whole 'to match Haldane's unrealistic manpower targets or to sustain popularity after a waning of the invasion scare of 1909'.[146] Nor were these recruiting difficulties peculiar to the Territorial Force. In May 1914 the Regular Army was nearly 11,000 men short of its total establishment, whilst the Special Reserve was deficient by 13,699.[147] In fact, it must be seen as a tribute to the effectiveness of the army medical reforms in the pre-war decade that the average strength of RAMC officers in 1913 was only eighteen short of the establishment.[148]

Although lack of interest in military service[149] had precluded any notion of 'a nation in arms', we should be careful not to downgrade the achievement of Haldane's reforms. Considering the financial and recruiting restraints within which he worked,[150] he had probably created the best AMS that circumstances would allow. Of course, like the Army as a whole, its personnel were to prove insufficient for the task that was to befall it. Nevertheless, with the Regular RAMC nearly at full establishment, the problem of undermanning and all its consequent evils was, for the moment, consigned to the past.[151] Moreover, despite slow progress with the Special Reserve, the OTC had, by the outbreak of war, given military experience to some 1,900 medical students, thus providing a valuable source for expanding the ranks of RAMC officers.[152]

The establishment of the Royal Army Medical College, which finally transferred to its new building at Millbank in 1906, combined with greater opportunities for study leave to improve professional standards within the service. But the duties of a Medical Officer required a broader knowledge than a study of science alone could provide:

> For example, the work of officers of the RAMC includes the professional organisation of sanitary precautions, the collection of the sick and wounded, the compilation of records . . . certain arrangements in connection with the transportation of sick and wounded from the front, the discipline and maintenance of combatants under their charge, and the replenishment of medical and surgical requirements . . . they are as much concerned as officers of other units in the provision of food, clothing and other requirements to their men, in the care and management of transport allotted to them, in arranging their camps and movements, and fitting their units into their allotted places on the line of march.[153]

Measures were therefore taken to improve the training of Medical Officers in military matters. A syllabus of graduated training was drawn up, handbooks on field medical organization were published, lectures given, and in 1910 medical manoeuvres were inaugurated. These developments affected the RAMC as a whole, so that by 1914 a uniform system of training existed for the Regulars, Territorials, Special Reserve and the OTC, as well as the medical services in India and the Dominions.[154]

But most significant of all was the cumulative effect of Haldane's reforms; they completed the process of winning over the confidence of the medical profession in the Army. The reorganization of the auxiliary medical service was as important for the manner of its achievement as for its end result; Haldane and Keogh had clearly demonstrated that the War Office was now ready to listen to medical opinion. Also, with the promotion of sanitary discipline throughout all ranks of the Army, and the establishment of sanitary corps and commissions, the profession at last found itself with the means and conditions necessary to the success of its principal function – disease prevention.

A long battle by the BMA against the forces of prejudice and ignorance within the Army had thus come to an end. Medical Officers and their work had finally been accorded the status that their role deserved. The cloud had truly been lifted, and none too soon for the War Office and the nation; without the trust and goodwill of the BMA the task of organizing the medical profession for war might well have floundered, despite the patriotic response of medical practitioners to the nation's call.

Notes

1   On the outbreak of the Crimean War, the Association was still known as the Provincial Medical And Surgical Association, the change of name not taking place until 1855.
2   **Paul Vaughan,** *Doctors' Commons, a Short History of the British Medical Association,* Heinemann, 1959, p. 58.
3   **Peter Lovegrove,** *Not Least in the Crusade, a Short History of the Royal Army Medical Corps,* Aldershot, Gale & Polden, 1952, p. 8.
4   **Vaughan,** *Doctor's Commons,* p. 58
5   **Lovegrove,** *The Crusade,* p. 9.
6   **Vaughan,** *Doctors' Commons,* p. 60.
7   *Ibid.,* p. 59. The Medical Officer had to supply himself with a complete set of capital instruments; he had to purchase his own pocket case of minor instruments; and, if he was sick, he was expected to pay a fellow practitioner to deputize in his absence.
8   *Ibid.,* p. 73.
9   **Lovegrove,** *The Crusade,* p. 9.
10 The opportunities for doctors in England were particularly good, and this helps to explain why the number of Irish and Scottish doctors entering the AMS was disproportionately high, See **N.D. Lankford,** 'The Victorian Medical Profession and Military Practice: Army Doctors and National Origins', *Bulletin of the History of Medicine,* vol. 54, 1980, pp. 511–28. See Also **Vaughan,** *Doctor's Commons,* p. 60.
11 **Cecil Woodham-Smith,** *Florence Nightingale,* Constable, 1950, p. 169.
12 **Edward M. Spiers,** *The Army and Society 1815–1914,* Longman, 1980, p. 99.
13 **Lovegrove,** *The Crusade,* p. 9.
14 **Woodham-Smith,** *Nightingale,* p. 205.
15 **Jeanne L. Brand,** *Doctors and the State,* The John Hopkins Press, Baltimore, Maryland, 1965, p. 137.
16 Lord Raglan; commander of the forces in the Crimea.
17 **Vaughan,** *Doctors' Commons,* p. 63.
18 To become the *British Medical Journal* in 1857, after the Association's change of name.
19 **Vaughan,** *Doctors' Commons,* pp. 64–5.
20 **Lovegrove,** *The Crusade,* p. 12.
21 The seniority of Medical Officers counted for nothing in courts martial; and they were still denied the compliments paid to other officers by the garrison or regimental guard. **Vaughan,** *Doctor's Commons,* p. 77.
22 The Army Medical School was established at Fort Pitt in 1860, but moved to Netley three years later.
23 **Lovegrove,** *The Crusade,* pp. 12–14.

24 'The Army Medical Controversy', *British Medical Journal* (BMJ), 1901 (II), p. 33.

25 Lovegrove, *The Crusade*, p. 15.

26 **Surgeon-General J.B. Hamilton**, 'Reform in the Army Medical Service', BMJ, 1902 (II), p. 1033.

27 **Woodham-Smith**, *Nightingale*, p. 399.

28 *Ibid*, p. 403.

29 **Vaughan**, *Doctors' Commons*, p. 78.

30 *Ibid*, p. 82

31 Assistant Under-Secretary at the War Office.

32 **Woodham-Smith**, *Nightingale*, p. 399.

33 *Ibid.*

34 **Vaughan**, *Doctors' Commons*, p. 83.

35 'The Army Medical Controversy', BMJ, 1901 (II), p. 33.

36 'Report of the Committee to Enquire into the Causes which Tend to Prevent Sufficient Eligible Candidates from Coming Forward for the Army Medical Department', Cd.2200, 1878–79, XLIV, p. 25.

37 'Report of a Committee appointed by the Secretary of State for War to Enquire into the Organisation of the Army Hospital Corps, Hospital Management and Nursing in the Field and the Sea Transport of Sick and Wounded', Cd.3607, 1883, XVI, p. 29.

38 **Lovegrove**, *The Crusade*, p. 18.

39 'The Army Medical Controversy', BMJ, 1901 (II), p. 33.

40 'Report of the Committee Appointed to Enquire into the Pay, Status and Conditions of Service of Medical Officers of the Army and Navy', Cd. 5810, XVII, pp. 142–3.

41 For example, Surgeon-Lieutenant.

42 **Vaughan**, *Doctors' Commons*, p. 85.

43 Letter, dated 17 January 1891, from Sir Andrew Clark, Bart, M.D., F.R.S., to the Secretary of State for War, relative to the Status of Medical Officers of the Army; and the Secretary of State's Reply, dated 2 February 1891, Cd. 6282, 1890–1, L, pp. 585–7.

44 Further Correspondence relative to the Status of Medical Officers of the Army; the War Office to the President of the Royal College of Physicians, Cd. 6312, 1890–91, L, p. 599.

45 **Lovegrove**, *The Crusade*, p. 19.

46 **Vaughan**, *Doctors' Commons*, p. 86.

47 *Ibid*, p. 88.

48 **Stephen Trombley** cites an instance of a young medical man being discouraged from joining the RAMC, in his *Sir Frederick Treves: The Extraordinary Edwardian*, Routledge, 1989, pp. 122–3.

49 'British Medical Association, Provisional Report on, and Recommendations for, the Reorganisation of the Army Medical Service' (henceforth, The BMA Report), published in the BMJ, 1901 (I), Supplement, p. 1. The reply from St John's College, Cambridge, stated: 'That the University could not find any *alumnus* willing to be nominated for a commission in the RAMC, but found plenty, some of them medical graduates, for nomination to combatant commissions.'

50 Army Medical Establishments, BMJ 1900 (I), pp. 464–5.
51 'The Medical Profession And The War', BMJ, 1900 (I), pp. 33–4; An Appeal to the Younger Members of the Medical Profession, signed by Frederick T. Roberts, Edmund Owen, William Collingridge, William Duncan, J. Edward Squire, BMJ 1900 (I), p. 42.
52 Evidence of Kitchener, *Report of Commission Appointed to inquire into the Military preparations and other matters connected with the War in South Africa*, Cd.1789, 1904, XL, p. 349, (henceforth, Royal Commission on the South African War).
53 Sir William Thompson, 'Some Surgical Lessons from the Campaign in South Africa (Address in Surgery at the Annual Meeting of the British Medical Association at Cheltenham, July–August 1901)', BMJ, 1901 (II), p. 266.
54 The consulting surgeons in South Africa were: Sir William MacCormac, Mr Treves, Sir William Stokes, Mr Watson Cheyne, Mr Cheatle, Mr Kendell Foster and Mr Makins.
55 'Consulting Surgeons with the Forces in South Africa', BMJ, 1900(I), p. 150.
56 Frederick Treves, letter, BMJ, 1900 (I), pp. 1611–12.
57 Burdett-Coutts was *The Times* Correspondent on the sick and wounded in South Africa, and also MP for Westminster. See Telegram of Mr Burdett-Coutts to Lord Wolseley, Secretary of State for War, Cd.230, 1900, LVI, p. 784.
58 Burdett-Coutts, letter to *The Times* (dated Cape Town, May 29; entitled 'Our Wars and Our Wounded', June 27, 1900, p. 4.
59 Treves, letter, BMJ, 1900 (I), pp. 1611–12.
60 'Medical Arrangements in South Africa', BMJ, 1900 (I), p. 1611.
61 Trombley, *Treves*, p. 98.
62 *Ibid*, p. 103.
63 *Ibid*, p. 123.
64 Evidence of Treves, Royal Commission on the South African War, Cd.1791, 1904, XL, pp. 1–10.
65 Treves, letter, BMJ, 1900 (I), pp. 1611–12.
66 *Hansard*, Parliamentary Debates, Fourth Series, LXXXV, 29 June 1900, col.106.
67 Burdett-Coutts, letter to *The Times*, 27 June 1900.
68 'Report of the Royal Commission on the Care and Treatment of the Sick and Wounded in the Military Hospitals during the South African Campaign', Cd.453, 1901, XXIX, p. 17 (hereafter, Royal Commission on South African Hospitals).
69 Redmond McLaughlin, *The Royal Army Medical Corps*, Leo Cooper, 1972, pp. 26–7.
70 Royal Commission on the South African War, Cd.1789, 1904, XL, p. 111.
71 The Principal Medical Officer at the hospital was more concerned with petty matters of tidiness than the sufferings of the wounded, but White took no interest in the situation; Thomas Pakenham, *The Boer War*, Weidenfeld & Nicholson, 1979, pp. 354–5.
72 Evidence of Roberts, Royal Commission on South African Hospitals, Cd.454, 1901, XXIX, p. 577.

73 **Pakenham** criticises Roberts for leaving in place men in whom he had no confidence, *Boer War*, p. 383.

74 **John Laffin**, *Surgeons in the Field*, J.M. Dent & Sons Ltd., 1970, p. 200.

75 Correspondence between the Honourable Member for Ilkeston and the War Department in relation to Medical and Sanitary Arrangements at the Cape, Cd.279, 1900, XLIX, p. 257.

76 'The Prevention of Water Borne Disease in the Army', BMJ, 1903 (II), p. 604.

77 **Howard H. Tooth**, 'Enteric Fever in the Army in South Africa, with Remarks on Inoculation', BMJ, 1900 (II), p. 1368.

78 In a review of 'The Mortality Returns of the Field Force in South Africa for 1901', BMJ, 1902 (I), p. 167, it is observed that, 'Army medical officers already receive excellent sanitary training but they are hemmed in by restrictions which prevent them from carrying out reforms. They have insufficient administrative control, and it is not surprising therefore, that they should sometimes be inclined to lay greater stress on their medical and surgical than on their sanitary work.'

79 Royal Commission on the South African War, Cd.1789, 1904, XLI, p. 232.

80 Evidence of Lieutenant General Sir Charles Warren, Royal Commission on the South African War, Cd.1789, 1904, XLI, p. 233

81 Evidence of Treves, Royal Commission on the South African War, Cd.1791, 1904, XL, p. 7 and p. 10. His objections to military Medical Officers performing surgical operations in civil hospitals, and doubts about their ability to run a successful consultative practice, clearly demonstrated a lack of faith in his army colleagues.

82 Evidence of Colonel W. Johnston, Royal Commission on the South African War, Cd.1789, 1904, XL, p. 506. Professor A. Ogston made similar points, *Ibid*, p. 816.

83 Colonel W. Johnston, *Ibid*, p. 506.

84 See index of the BMJ, 1900–1903, under the headings **South African War** and **Army, British.**

85 'The Medical Service and the Victoria Cross' BMJ, 1900 (I), p. 593.

86 These figures revealed that there had been no recognition of the Medical Officers serving in the 4th and 5th Divisions, BMJ, 1901 (II), P. 444.

87 **Laffin**, *Surgeons in the Field*, p. 206.

88 **Spiers**, *Army and Society*, pp. 241–3.

89 'Summary of the Royal Commission on South African Hospitals', BMJ, 1901 (I), p. 236. For a full list of the Commission's recommendations see Royal Commission on South African Hospitals, Cd.453, 1901, XXIX, p. 75.

90 'The RAMC Expert Committee', BMJ, 1901 (II), p. 31.

91 'The BMA Report', BMJ, 1901 (I), Supplement, pp. 1–5.

92 See table of responses from the Universities, Colleges and Medical Schools, *Ibid*, p. 2.

93 *Ibid*, p. 3.

94 Letter, signed 'Retired', BMJ, 1901 (I), p. 1377.

95 'The BMA Report', BMJ, 1901 (II), p. 5.

96 *Ibid*.

97 'Sir William MacCormac on the Medical Arrangements in South Africa', BMJ, 1901 (I), pp. 715–16.

98 'The BMA Report', BMJ, 1901 (II), p. 1.

99 *Ibid*, p. 4.

100 'Report of the Committee on the Reorganisation of the Army Medical Service' (hereafter the Brodrick Report), Cd, 791, 1902, X, p. 131.

101 'The Reorganisation of the Army Medical Service', BMJ, 1902 (I), p. 221.

102 The Brodrick Report, p. 141.

103 'The New Army Medical Warrant', BMJ, 1902 (I), p. 788.

104 'The Military Medical Service', BMJ, 1902 (II), p. 145.

105 'Pay of RAMC Officers in India', BMJ, 1902 (II), p. 1975.

106 'Pay of RAMC Officers in India', BMJ, 1902 (II), p. 1975.

106 'The Medical Service of the Army', BMJ, 1903 (I), p. 1220.

107 Spiers, *Army and Society*, p. 252.

108 *Ibid*, p. 259.

109 Correlli Barnett, *Britain and Her Army 1509–1970*, Allen Lane, The Penguin Press, 1970, p. 359.

110 'Report of the War Office Reconstitution Committee', Cd.1932, 1968, 2002; 1904, VIII, p. 101, (hereafter known as the Esher Report).

111 'The Medical Service of the Army', BMJ, 1904 (I), p. 381.

112 'The Medical Service of the Army', BMJ, 1904 (I), p. 445.

113 Andrew Clark, Chairman of the Council of the BMA, letter to *The Times*, February 22, p. 14.

114 The Esher Report, Cd.2002, 1904, VIII, p. 166.

115 The Esher Report, Cd.1968, 1904, VIII, p. 128.

116 The Esher Report, Cd.2002, 1904, VIII, p. 166.

117 Ernest M. Little, *History of the British Medical Association 1832–1932*, British Medical Association, 1932, p. 156.

118 The Esher Report, Cd.2002, 1904, VIII, p. 166.

119 Lovegrove, *The Crusade*, pp. 32–3.

120 Sir Walter Foster, *Hansard* Parliamentary Debates, Fourth Series, CXLI, col.950; Report on the Medical Services in the Russo Japanese War written by Sir Ian Hamilton, dated 28/11/04, in the papers of Sir Charles Burtchaell, Wellcome Institute for the History of Medicine Contemporary Medical Archives, (henceforth W.I.H.M) RAMC 446.

121 In his 'Memorandum on Army Reorganisation,' Cd.2993, 1906, LXVII, p. 255, Haldane stated: 'The substance of these propositions is that increased economy and increased efficiency are no more in practice mutually exclusive conceptions than they are in logical theory.'

122 'The War Minister on Army Sanitation', BMJ, 1906 (II), p. 158.

123 *Ibid*.

124 It is stated in 'The Army Medical Department Report for the Year 1907', Cd.4057, 1908, LXIV, p. 603, that 'the use of anti-typhoid vaccine as a prophylactic has become more or less general throughout the Army. Arrangements are in force for the voluntary inoculation of all those who desire to benefit by its advantages, either at home or abroad, and a large number of voluntary

anti-typhoid inoculations have already been carried out among the troops in India, Egypt, South Africa, &c., with encouraging results.'

125 **Leonard Colebrooke,** *Almroth Wright: Provocative Doctor and Thinker,* Heinemann, 1954. Chapter Four, pp. 30–46, deals with Wright's development of the technique, and the opposition he came up against. 'Medical Society of London; Typhoid Fever in South Africa', BMJ, 1901 (II), p. 1342. This report documents Wright's disagreement with Elliot and Washburn regarding the effectiveness of inoculation, and is illustrative of the kind of opposition he had to overcome.

126 **Colebrooke,** *Almroth Wright,* p. 42.

127 Memorandum of the Secretary of State Relating to the Army Estimates for 1909–1910, Cd.4495, 1909, LI, p. 236.

128 Report on the Health of the Army for 1911, Cd.6287, 1912–13, LI, p. 259.

129 'Summary of the Royal Commission on South African Hospitals', BMJ, 1901 (I), p. 236.

130 'An Army Medical Reserve', BMJ, 1904 (II), pp. 1710–1711.

131 'The Volunteers and the Army Medical Reserve', BMJ, 1906 (I), p. 511.

132 'The Efficiency of the Army Medical Service', BMJ, 1905 (II), p. 447.

133 **Edward M. Spiers,** 'The Regular Army in 1914', in **Ian F.W. Beckett and Keith Simpson** (eds), *A Nation In Arms,* Manchester, Manchester University Press, 1985, p. 38.

134 Interim Report of the War Office Committee on the Provision of Officers (a) For Service with the Regular Army in War, and (b) for the Auxiliary Forces, Cd.3294, 1907, XLIX, p. 549. The Committee's terms of reference had asked it to consider ways of making up the deficiency of officers, especially with regard to the Auxiliary Forces; it saw the formation of the OTC as a means of meeting this need.

135 Report, dated 18 July 1908, by the Director General of the Army Medical Service, as to the progress made in constituting the Medical Service of the Territorial Force, Cd.4056, 1908, LXIV, p. 971.

136 'The Territorial Army and its Medical Corps', BMJ, 1907 (I), p. 518.

137 'The Medical Service of the Territorial Force', BMJ, 1907 (II), p. 1088.

138 Report, dated 18 July 1908, by the Director General of the Army Medical Service, *op. cit.,* pp. 972–4.

139 See BMJ, 1907 (II), pp. 1182, 1243, 1446, 1612, 1617, 1741, 1742, 1802.

140 'Note on Sir Alfred Keogh and the Territorial Army Medical Corps', BMJ, 1907 (II), p. 1271.

141 Report, dated 18 July 1908, *op. cit.,* p. 972.

142 *Ibid.* pp. 972–3.

143 BMJ, 1909 and 1910; see under Army, British, Territorial Force, in the index.

144 Annual Returns of the Territorial Force for 1908, Cd.4496, 1909, LI, p. 521; 1909, Cd.5017, 1910, LX, p. 781; 1910, Cd.5482, 1911, XLVI, p. 743; 1911, Cd.6066, 1912, LI, p. 691; 1912, Cd.6657, 1913, LI, p. 811.

145 Annual Return of the Territorial Force for 1913, Cd.7254, 1914, LII, p. 407.

146 **Ian Beckett,** 'The Nation In Arms 1914–18', in **Ian F.W. Beckett and Keith Simpson** (eds), *Nation in Arms,* p. 7.

147 Peter Simkins, *Kitchener's Army*, Manchester, Manchester University Press, 1988, pp. 18–20.
148 General Annual Report of the British Army for 1913, Cd.7252, 1914, LII, p. 267.
149 Spiers, *Army and Society*, pp. 280–1.
150 *Ibid*, p. 269.
151 By the early 1930s, however, there was again a shortage of Medical.Officers. Little, *History of BMA*, p. 157.
152 W.G. MacPherson, *Official History of the War – Medical Services, General History, I*, HMSO, 1921, p. 29.
153 *Royal Army Medical Corps Training*. HMSO, 1911, pp. 1–2.
154 MacPherson, *General History*, p. 39–40.

31

Chapter 2

The Medical Volunteers:
The Recruitment of Medical Officers
1914–1916

The profession's initial response to the War was dominated by individual effort, with doctors anxious to learn how best they might serve the national cause. Many doctors addressed their enquiries directly to the War Office, but others looked to the British Medical Association for advice. After consultations with the War Office the BMA explained that the Army's immediate need was for young doctors who would be willing to serve wherever required.[1] It was the duty of all such doctors to place their names upon a waiting list being compiled at the War Office, and then to await call-up, filling in their time by taking up resident hospital posts,[2] or acting as locum-tenentes.

The formation of the Scottish Medical Service Emergency Committee (SMSEC)[3] set the profession in Scotland more rapidly on the road to a collective response to the War than elsewhere in the UK. A memorandum, issued by the SMSEC, recommended various ways in which the profession might help to release young doctors for the Army. These included appeals to retired practitioners to relieve younger men, and to education authorities to allow school Medical Officers to give at least part of their time to general practice. It was also suggested that the visiting staffs of large hospitals should undertake a share of the work usually carried out by medical residents and clinical assistants, thus releasing these younger men for military service.[4]

The profession in Scotland responded positively to these recommendations. Numerous doctors, including some retired men, volunteered to take charge of single-handed practices in outlying areas, where the potential for a serious disruption of medical care was highest. On the advice of the Committee, a number of large hospitals and infirmaries had reduced their resident staffs, whilst doctors had made themselves available to minimize the disruption in the hospitals.[5]

That the release of all young doctors might prove incompatible with the maintenance of a safe level of civilian medical provision was apparent to the profession. Kitchener's dictum that those men engaged in work essential to the prosecution of the war effort should not enlist was felt to apply to a proportion of young doctors. But the Committee suggested that those young men who did remain in the UK could contribute by doing double work, and so relieving others for military service.

To the rest of the profession, however, the message was predominantly an echo of the current catchphrase, 'Business as Usual'. Attendance on the civil population was said to be just as valid a way of contributing to the nation's effort as enlisting with the Army,[6] and it was the course recommended to older men who were well established in practice.

J. Johnston Abraham offered his services to the War Office on the outbreak of war, but was refused because it was felt that, being in his thirties, he was too old for active service. He proved the War Office wrong by proceeding with a Red Cross unit to Serbia where he undertook difficult work fighting disease. Another experienced surgeon who proved that older men could make a valuable contribution at the front was H.S. Souttar.[7] Many doctors, rejected by the War Office on grounds of age, found employment with the Red Cross:

> At the outbreak of war, and for a considerable time after, there was no difficulty in obtaining all the medical men required.[8]

Once it became clear that Kitchener's predictions of a long war were not mere pessimism, the authorities at the War Office began to see the folly of turning away older doctors, who were demonstrably capable of performing military service. On his return from Serbia, the War Office engaged Abraham as a Lieutenant in the RAMC.[9] A large proportion of those who originally went abroad with the British Red Cross Society (BRCS) transferred their services to the RAMC, receiving temporary commissions. And, as the War progressed, a shortage of Medical Officers forced the War Office to raise the age limit for doctors on a number of occasions. This inevitably reduced the number and quality of candidates available to fill BRCS posts. The figures below show the decline in the number of doctors sent abroad by the Red Cross.[10]

YEAR	NUMBER OF DOCTORS SENT ABROAD	TOTAL
1914	108	108
1915	47	155
1916	44	199
1917	22	221
1918	15	236

Initially, however, the expectation of a short war led the War Office to believe that it could meet the Army's needs by relying on young medical volunteers; anxiety about obtaining a sufficient number of doctors was not yet evident. Indeed, in the early months, it is clear that the medical profession was far more concerned with minimizing the disruption of civilian medical provision than it was with ensuring an adequate supply of Medical Officers for the Army. In Scotland, practitioners were classified and their distribution throughout the country surveyed. Using this information a system of substitution to cover the practices of doctors leaving for military service was directed by local committees, appointed by the SMSEC.[11] South of the border the profession was slower in developing a central organization capable of adapting the profession to meet the war emergency; not until the formation of the Central Medical War Committee (CMWC) did England and Wales possess machinery on a par with that in Scotland.[12] Nevertheless, local divisions of the BMA in England did act to ensure that the work of those who left for active service was continued. In Exeter, a committee was appointed to organize and distribute the work of the practitioners absent on military duty, and arrangements were made for continuing the work of the Royal Devon and Exeter Hospital; similar arrangements were made elsewhere.[13]

A centralized organization in England and Wales might well have developed sooner had the War Office been more vigorous in pressing the medical profession to look at both sides of the equation; to organize itself in such a way as to be able to provide for the Army's future medical needs, as well as safeguarding civilian health care. This seems all the more likely when one considers the fact that proposals for just such an organization came from within the profession itself. The BMJ, in September 1914, published the following proposals:

[T]hat the central office of the [British Medical] Association should be responsible for dealing with correspondence, keeping a register of medical men available and of the direction in which their services can be used, and for furnishing information to those willing to render assistance to the country . . . if the organisation of the BMA were used in this manner, much time might be saved later on when more men are required for active service.[14]

But when the BMA followed up these suggestions and offered its machinery to the War Office, it met with a negative response.[15] The attitude of the War Office in rejecting the BMA's offer might appear incomprehensible, especially given the reports from Mons and the Aisne of an RAMC suffering from 'a great overtaxing of strength'; of doctors working for up to four days at a time; and of the urgent need for civilian medical practitioners to render assistance.[16]

Colonel Arthur Lee, who made a series of reports to Kitchener on the medical arrangements at the front, described the situation between the Mons retreat and the advance on the Aisne:

The RAMC staff at that time were undoubtedly overworked and overstrained. There were probably not enough Medical Officers in the first place, and many had been killed or wounded (I still doubt that there are enough to cope with the situation that may arise after the next heavy fighting and am of the opinion that more should be sent at once).[17]

[The] shortage of Medical Officers . . . is very apparent to the layman during these periods of great stress. It is difficult to get the RAMC staff to represent this – they seldom if ever complain and they work on until they drop from fatigue. But, apart from the fact that cases coming into the Clearing Hospitals have often to wait unnecessarily long before their wounds can be dressed, I have frequently seen Medical Officers who have been working for such prolonged periods, without sleep or proper food, that they are not in a fit condition to attend to serious cases. And yet, in the absence of anyone to relieve them, they are bound to go on and do so with admirable spirit. In view of the ceaseless fighting which characterises this campaign, I am convinced that a considerable addition to the prescribed establishment of Medical Officers is essential to provide adequate reliefs and to ensure that the wounded are treated as promptly as possible.[18]

Clearly, in the early months, the War Office failed to recognize that a shortage of doctors, both on the home front and with the Army abroad, was a serious possibility. The free flow of recruits suggested that military shortages could be plugged easily, and in the Commons, the Under Secretary of State for War informed the House that no shortage of doctors for the New Army was anticipated.[19] The War Office was short-sighted in not taking the opportunity to organize medical manpower more efficiently, but its failure to take decisive action cannot be considered in isolation; the Government as a whole, and most of the nation, had yet to appreciate fully the extent of the conflict. Once the scale of the task became more apparent in 1915 the War Office began to push for just the type of organization that it had been offered earlier, in September 1914.

Although not yet alive to the need for active co-operation with the BMA over the distribution of doctors, the military authorities did recognize the importance of retaining the BMA's confidence and support if sufficient Medical Officers were to be obtained. The improved relations with the BMA resulting from the Edwardian Army medical reforms now had to be consolidated; the Army had to show itself capable of responding to the concerns of the profession with tact and understanding.

Much anxiety had been expressed regarding the civil medical disruption likely to be caused by the mobilization of Territorial and reserve units, which involved the immediate withdrawal of 2,000 doctors from civil practice. The speed of their mobilization had taken a lot of these doctors by surprise:

> Many of the doctors attached to various units were not prepared, and did not-anticipate, that they would be called away from their practice at a moment's notice.[20]

As a result, they had insufficient time to arrange for locum-tenentes. Lieutenant Colonel A.H. Habgood recalls that the order to report within five days 'left little time to settle my affairs, arrange for the practice, get what I needed in the way of equipment and uniform'.[21] He was fortunate in that an older doctor, whose share in the practice he had recently taken over, agreed to return for the duration of his absence. Others, however, simply had to leave their practices unattended when they proceeded with their units to other parts of the country.

The War Office recognized that Territorials ought to be given time to settle their private affairs, and so a system of temporary release was authorized by the Army Council, which allowed officers to attend to matters bearing upon the public interest. It was also stated by the War Office that those Territorials with important duties at home, and therefore incapable of volunteering for duty abroad, should not be induced to do so, nor should they feel that their unavailability for foreign service required them to leave the Territorial Force.[22]

However, a Territorial Medical Officer complained that staff officers were taking little notice of these provisions:

[T]he brigade headquarters generally refuse the leave, occasionally granting it grudgingly as a special favour. I have, however, after a fight, now obtained four days' leave, but the permission is accompanied by instructions that I must proceed to take immediate steps to divest myself entirely of my civilian liabilities – apparently for quite an indefinite period – an understanding which I cannot and do not propose to attempt. Moreover, I was told by one of the headquarters staff officers on this occasion that as I was not a volunteer for foreign service I need expect no further leave whatsoever during the embodiment . . . the matter of granting leave . . . has been used and is being used as a lever to force Territorials to volunteer for foreign service.[23]

In order to remedy this unsatisfactory situation and allow doctors to make proper provision for the continuation of their practices, the SMSEC made representations to the Director General of the Army Medical Service (DGAMS). It was proposed to extend to general practitioners serving with the Territorial Force an arrangement similar to that for the à la suite medical staffs of the territorial general hospitals. This arrangement allowed these physicians and surgeons to attend to their ordinary hospital work and private patients, in addition to their military work.

In fact, it had already been conceded that general practitioners could attend to their civilian patients if their military duties allowed them the time. In a letter of 14 October 1914, the Deputy Director of Medical Services (DDMS) Scottish Command had given the Dundee Division of the BMA assurances that acceptance of commissions in the Field Ambulance Reserve Units need not involve a cessation of civil practice:

I see no reason why the Medical Officers who join the reserve unit of the Third Highland Field Ambulance (TF) should withdraw from all civil practice. The medical needs of the civil population must be attended. When not required for duty they can attend to their civil duties.[24]

This arrangement was commended to other districts as a way of resolving the conflict of duty between civilian and military service which many doctors were experiencing.

But for those doctors who mobilized with the Territorial Force in

August 1914, additional arrangements needed to be made if they were to be able to devote their spare time to their civilian patients. Since joining their units many of these doctors had found themselves in districts not within travelling distance of their practices, and the SMSEC pressed the War Office to instigate procedures which would enable Territorial Medical Officers to remain close to their practices. The War Office duly issued an order to the General Officer commanding of each of the Home Commands, which stated that:

> When a mobilised Territorial unit is moved from its own locality in Great Britain, the Medical Officers may be allowed:
> a) To effect exchanges . . . with Territorial Medical Officers in the new locality when possible.
> b) If the above is not feasible, the places of medical men not desiring to accompany their units may be taken by junior Medical Officers willing to take temporary commissions and serve with such units; the original Medical Officers being demobilised until the return of the units to their own localities, or until their services can be otherwise utilised there.[25]

The order also dealt with concerns over the position of Medical Officers serving with Territorial units passed for foreign service. The BMJ had expressed the hope that existing Territorial Medical Officers would be able to remain in the reserve Territorial battalions that were being formed, and their places taken with the units going abroad by doctors with fewer civil obligations to the local community[26] (presumably the young and recently qualified). The War Office order stated that in cases where 'a mobilised Territorial unit volunteers for imperial service abroad the Medical Officer will be given the option of accompanying it or of serving with the reserve unit raised for home service in its stead; vacancies in both units being filled up by junior Medical Officers with temporary commissions'.[27]

These arrangements for the Territorials, however, did nothing to ensure that the work of those doctors volunteering for temporary commissions in the RAMC would be continued. Captain J.H. Dible's experience at the War Office in August 1914 demonstrates that some volunteers were given equally little time to attend to their practices before being whisked off on military service. He and another volunteer, Wilson Smith, had gone to the War Office to offer their services. They were surprised when asked by a colonel to report to Harwich immediately:

> I know, for he had told me . . . that Wilson Smith had come up to town at some inconvenience and had made no arrangements for the carrying on of

his practice and the details of his domestic life. Like me he anticipated being enrolled and then being allowed to go back to the country and attend to these matters whilst waiting to be called up.[28]

Wilson Smith had tried to explain that he had matters to attend to, but the impatient colonel dismissed this hesitancy and demanded a commitment on the spot. This placed the doctor in a difficult position:

Poor Wilson Smith ... I knew what was going through his mind. Patriotism and his estimate of his country's need, struggling with the necessity of securing a locum, and explaining to his patients.[29]

After consideration, both men agreed to serve. But a situation in which doctors could be taken away from their practices, without adequately providing for continued attendance upon their civil patients, was clearly unsatisfactory.

The effect of this unregulated recruiting upon the nation's hospitals was equally unsatisfactory, as many began to experience a serious shortage of experienced staff. Captain M.S. Esler had hoped to join the RAMC in August 1914, like many of his friends and colleagues. But the house staff of Norwich Hospital where he held an appointment had been reduced to two inexperienced juniors. It could not continue to operate on this basis and so he agreed to stay on until they could fill the vacant posts.[30] To ensure adequate civilian hospital provision, however, required a system of medical recruitment that was capable of ensuring a balanced distribution of doctors between civilian and military service.

Without a system that could guarantee adequate medical care for the civilian population, it is understandable that many doctors continued to feel 'torn between two desires': to do their duty to their civilian patients, and a wish to contribute to the work of the RAMC.[31] Simple assurances from the War Office that civilian needs would not be disregarded were not enough; it was argued that doctors could not justifiably abandon their civilian work unless a more efficient organization for making use of available medical manpower existed. Moreover, although some doctors using this argument might simply have been seeking a respectable excuse for not volunteering, there is no evidence to support such speculation. It is clear, however, that doctors otherwise ready to join the RAMC were forced to think twice as a result of concern for civilian patients.

In August 1914, J.M. McLachlan had applied to the War Office for a commission, but receiving no reply he assumed that doctors were not required and took a locum job. Once he had taken up the post the War

Office contacted him with the offer of a commission, but he felt that he 'couldn't go and leave this practice with no one' and replied that he 'was extremely sorry . . . but must have sufficient notice so as to get another man to come here'.[32] Thus, if young medical men were not to be lost to the military, a system allowing for their rapid release from civil duties was essential.

By April 1915 the inability of the voluntary system to provide the degree of organization necessary for such a substitution scheme was becoming more widely recognized; only compulsory medical service, to mobilize the entire profession, could ensure that it was 'organised for civil and military service in such a way that the medical man could be utilised according to his physical and professional capacity'.[33] As the War progressed, the logic of this argument became ever more apparent, but, for the moment, the profession, the nation and especially Asquith's Liberal Government, were not ready to accept such a degree of compulsion. It seemed to be a matter of pride to the medical profession to do its utmost to make the voluntary system work, whilst the Government, still clinging to its laissez faire principles, was opposed to all forms of compulsion.

A more efficient organization of the profession was just as essential to the military medical service as it was to the civilian. The Army needed better knowledge about the supply and distribution of doctors if it was to be sure of obtaining sufficient Medical Officers to meet its growing requirements. At present it lacked information on the number of doctors available for military service, the kind of service that these doctors were capable of, and the qualifications that they held. In fact, the kind of information that the scheme proposed by the BMA in September 1914 would have provided. Sir Alfred Keogh's[34] appeal for recruits in March 1915[35] heralded a new sense of urgency in the War Office's approach to the question of providing sufficient Medical Officers for the RAMC. The need was becoming apparent for more effective co-operation with the civil medical profession, and in particular with the BMA, its principal representative.

Such co-operation was essential, in order to help dispel increasingly widespread rumours that the Army's employment of doctors was excessive and its distribution of them wasteful. Anxious to maintain the good relations with the civil profession which he had done so much to establish, Keogh stressed in his March appeal that the Army did 'not wish to denude the country of civil practitioners', but that every man who could 'arrange for his work to be done at home should come forward as early as possible to keep up an adequate supply of medical attendance to our armies in the field'.[36] However, the disquiet remained and so Keogh held a conference with the BMA's Special Committee of Chairmen of Standing Committees (SCCSC)[37] to discuss the Army's requirements and their civilian implications.

At this conference, on 1 April 1915, Keogh pointed out that any 'surplusage was transient and apparent only. There was a place for every one of these men to serve with units which would, sooner rather than later, be sent abroad. It was essential to distinguish between distribution in locality and the total number available. When everything that redistribution could effect was done, there still remained a most serious shortage of whole-time Medical Officers to serve with the troops wherever they might be sent.' He then proceeded to repeat his call for doctors to come forward for full-time service: those under forty for work abroad, and those over forty for home service. Those whose civilian obligations prevented them from taking up full-time commissions were asked to consider other ways of contributing, such as part-time work in military hospitals; attending the dependants of servicemen; or taking on the duties of doctors who had departed for military service.[38]

At the end of the conference the SCCSC decided to request that each of the Divisions and Branches of the BMA hold meetings, as soon as possible, to 'consider the appeal of the Army for whole-time or part-time services of more medical men, in the light of the explanations and additional information Sir Alfred Keogh had given'.[39]

A conference of the Scottish medical profession in May 1915 committed itself to obtaining 400 Medical Officers, and thus to meet the Army's need, before 7 July 1915. Every branch of the BMA in Scotland was instructed of its share of the 400, and requested to inform the SMSEC how many doctors from their area were already engaged on military service.[40] Newly qualified practitioners were to provide 100 of the recruits, and the demand on the rest of the profession was reduced to 280, to minimize the impact on the civil population. In distributing the burden of the call, the SMSEC took into account the nature of particular practices; sparsely populated areas, where amalgamation of adjoining practices would be difficult, faced lighter demands than more populous districts.[41] The co-operation of the SMSEC with the Army's demands and the positive response received from local branches, such as that in Aberdeen,[42] demonstrates that Keogh had been successful in retaining the confidence of the BMA.

He now sought to consolidate the position by transferring the responsibility for urging appeals upon the profession from the military authorities to the SCCSC.[43] The hope was that by giving a professional body this responsibility doctors would feel confident that the Army's demand for Medical Officers was not exceeding its requirements.

The early confusion which had caused doctors like J.M. McLachlan to be unsure of the Army's need for medical practitioners could be explained by the heavy workload which fell on the War Office in the opening months of the conflict. Eight months into the War, however, the continuing need to press the Army's requirements upon the profession is evident from the account of L.W. Batten. A recently qualified doctor, he recalled how in March 1915, when his resident hospital job ended, he could quite easily have obtained another post; being unclear about the Army's requirements, he did consider such a course. But because most of his contemporaries were in uniform, he considered it his duty to join up.[44] That young doctors remained confused about their duty to the nation, and hospitals ignorant of the need to release junior doctors for military service, makes plain the importance of the BMA's willingness to transmit the Army's requirements, via the BMJ, to the profession.

Some doctors had interpreted instances in which acceptance for whole-time service had not been immediately followed by employment to mean that the Army had all the Medical Officers it required. To prevent such a view having disastrous effects on medical recruiting, the BMJ explained that, in accepting such men, the War Office was providing for the future needs of the New Armies. But whilst these units were in the early stages of organization, it was felt better to leave these doctors to continue in civil practice until a place had been prepared for them. This was merely the War Office making wise use of medical manpower, and should not be allowed to disguise the Army's continuing need.[45]

Suspicion of the Army's employment of doctors remained, despite Keogh's explanation, and the BMJ set about persuading sceptics of the validity of military needs.[46] It dismissed reports that whole-time Medical Officers attached to units had little to do. The explanation for such cases was that these units were in training, awaiting despatch to the front; such units obviously needed a Medical Officer who should find more than enough work to do organizing and supervising sanitation, inoculating the men, educating them in personal hygiene and generally overseeing their physical well-being. Any Medical Officer who found time on his hands was not considered to be carrying out his duties to the full. The work of a battalion Medical Officer was in its nature dull and routine, especially when on home service, and it was this fact which led many to conclude that skilled medical practitioners were wasted in such a role. However, those who reached this conclusion had failed to understand the different requirements of the civilian and military medical services.

Moreover, it is clear that the War Office was exercising vigilance with regard to the economic use of medical manpower. In March 1915 proposals were made for a reduction in the number of Medical Officers serving on hospital ships;[47] and later the number of Medical Officers attached to Motor Ambulance Convoys was lowered from four to three, the surplus being employed elsewhere.[48] The War Office also issued instructions requesting Administrative Medical Officers to ensure that only necessary demands for medical reinforcements were made, so as to avoid alarming the civil profession:

> It is requested that all AMOs should carefully consider their requirements and that the duties of officers serving under their command should be so distributed as to prevent a surplus in any one station, and that no reinforcements should be demanded so long as present requirements and reasonable prospective needs are fully met.[49]

By mid-1915, with the development of trench warfare on the Western Front and the extension of the conflict to other fronts such as Mesopotamia and the Dardanelles, it is clear that the problem was not one of underuse of Medical Officers, but of ensuring a sufficient number to guarantee adequate care for the men. In August 1915 Sir A. Sloggett, DGMS with the BEF in France, recorded that the average monthly wastage in Medical Officers had been eighty for the previous four months. At the same time he expected to lose fifty-three temporary commissioned Medical Officers on the expiry of their one-year contracts. Meanwhile, drafts demanded for 23 July and 6 August had been diverted to the Dardanelles at the urgent request of the War Office. Thus, Sloggett concluded that even if drafts were to arrive, there would be a shortfall of approximately 100 Medical Officers below the proper number.[50]

Two months later Cuthbert Wallace, stressing the importance of the surgical work done at Casualty Clearing Stations (CCSs), pointed out the need for an increase in the number of Medical Officers attached to these units. And by the end of the year Sloggett argued that the shortage of Medical Officers was now such that the lowest working limit had been reached, and that another draft of 100 Medical Officers would be required before January 1916. It would thus appear that the utmost effort had been put into ensuring efficient utilization of medical manpower, and that the Army's continued demands for more Medical Officers were justified.[51]

Concern over the Army's employment of Medical Officers was not the only factor deterring practitioners from enlisting. The conditions of partnership agreements were tying many down:

> Partnership agreements . . . usually provide that the partnership shall not be dissolved, save by mutual consent, before the expiration of a certain number of years, and that a partner must not be absent himself from the practice without the consent of the other partner or partners.[52]

The violation of such agreements was punishable by expulsion from the partnership, and the loss of any capital invested therein. But it was argued that agreements designed for the protection of doctors in peacetime should not be allowed to prevent otherwise willing doctors from joining the RAMC:

> Members of the medical profession cannot live in watertight compartments, but, like every other section of the nation, must show their patriotism by subordinating personal and private interests in the national need . . . civilian doctors must be set to do military work where and when they are needed.[53]

The BMJ even pointed to the newly formed Coalition Government, as an example to the profession of the mood of self-sacrifice sweeping the nation, though one might wonder what doctors made of the idea that politicians were 'sinking their differences and personal ambitions'[54] to the greater good.

Many general practitioners, however, especially those who, prior to the War, had regarded public health physicians as a threat to their livelihood, were disinclined to respond to such patriotic calls, in the belief that Medical Officers of Health (MOsH) were hanging back.[55] Such accusations were unfair in two respects. First, they failed to recognize the valuable work undertaken by MOsH in assisting military sanitary officers attached to troops in the UK;[56] providing information on water supplies, overseeing conservancy arrangements, arranging hospital provision for infectious diseases, exchanging information on outbreaks of diseases and co-operating with the military authorities to ensure that every possible preventive measure was taken. Second, MOsH were constrained by the unwillingness of many local authorities to release them for military service. The Local Government Board (LGB) and the Poor Law Commissioners were called upon to remind local bodies that, in time of war, the civilian population would have to make some sacrifices. And that, consequently, no unnecessary difficulties should be

44

placed in the way of practitioners employed by them who wished to join the RAMC.[57]

The importance of releasing MOsH for military service was recognized at the provincial meeting of the Society of Medical Officers of Health held at Hereford on 5 June 1915. Lieutenant Colonel Herbert Jones, President of the Society, pointed out that MOsH were peculiarly suited to army work, having an especially important role to play in the prevention of disease and in teaching officers and men the principles of sanitation. All MOsH who could arrange for retired doctors or a local practitioner to continue their work were urged to place their services at the disposal of the Army.[58] The MOH for the rural district of Wirral was absent on military service from the outbreak of the War. Initially, he arranged for his work to be continued by the Assistant MO of the County, but when he was called away to another district arrangements were made for the appointment of a local practitioner who had knowledge of the district and experience in public health.[59] In September 1916 another district council, Penistone, was able to release its MOH for military service by appointing his father, an authority on public health, to take his place.[60] The arrangement was particularly advantageous to the MOH in question as the salary continued to be paid to him.

Those districts that felt that their MOH could not be spared could, at least, allow them to undertake some part-time military work. Dr F.C. Linton, the MOH of the Borough of Tunbridge Wells, could not be made available for general service; approval was given 'for a commission to be granted him in connection with work for troops in Tunbridge Wells, which he could undertake in addition to his work as MOH, School MO, Medical Attendant at the Isolation Hospital and Police Surgeon'.[61] Uckfield was another district where the MOH undertook military duties in conjunction with his civilian work. Here, the rural district council attempted to benefit from the situation; they proposed to reduce the salary of the MOH by the amount of his military pay. The LGB pointed out that this was not legal procedure and that, in any case, the additional military pay was largely eaten up in expenses.[62]

With the passing of the Military Service Acts in 1916, the LGB focussed its attention further upon ensuring that everything was being done to ensure the release of the largest possible number of MOsH of military age. In February and June 1916, the LGB circularized County and Borough Councils, Sanitary Authorities, Hospital Boards and Committees, and Boards of Guardians, requesting information on the number of doctors of military age, employed in public health work.[63] A form was distributed to all the various authorities which asked for the names of all men and women so employed; the nature of their duties; whether they were engaged in private practice; their age; what, if any, military work they had undertaken; and whether arrangements could be made for the discharge of their civil duties should they join the forces.[64] In analysing the position, the LGB hoped that authorities responsible for civil health would remember 'the special importance of maintaining the public health at the present time, but subject to this, they should be prepared to allow medical men of military age, who are in their service, to join the forces'.[65] Schemes were recommended by which the maximum number of men of military age could be released for service:

1. Combination of various officers, such as MOH, School MO, Assistant School MO, Tuberculosis Officer, Medical Superintendent of Isolation Hospital.
2. Obtaining the services of an officer holding one of the offices above in a neighbouring district.
3. Obtaining help from the County MOH or Assistant County MOH.
4. Employing a general practitioner over military age or a medical woman in any of the above capacities.
5. In the case of Tuberculosis Officers in Counties, further rearrangement or combination of tuberculosis dispensary districts.[66]

Having completed the LGB's circular, the Tunbridge Wells Health Committee responded to the military's need by releasing their MOH, Dr Linton, for service. Under the terms of the agreement, Dr Linton's salary was suspended for the duration of his absence, but the Borough undertook to make up the difference between his salary and his military pay, with a 'reasonable addition' to help cover his 'necessary extra household expenses'.[67] Arrangements were made with various general practitioners in the district over military age for the continuation of Dr Linton's work during his absence.[68]

Thus, it can be seen that MOsH were not hanging back. On the contrary, many were eager to join the forces. However, action needed to be taken to ensure that adequate arrangements were made for protecting standards of public health.

Another factor affecting the supply of Medical Officers was the potential threat to doctors' livelihoods which military service might involve; and, in particular, the belief that those doctors who stayed at home would benefit from the absence of others. At local level, the profession took action to protect the interests of those leaving for military service.[69] Arrangements were made for the remaining doctors to act as substitutes, keeping a separate account for the absentee's patients and refusing to attend them on his return.

A meeting of the profession in Exeter declared that it was the patriotic duty of all doctors remaining in the UK to protect the interests of their absent colleagues, and passed a motion that no one should be allowed to profit from the situation:

> work done for men on military service should entail no expense to them except that of out-of-pocket expenses.[70]

Wartime circumstances immediately increased the demand for locums as retired army practitioners, and those with Territorial commitments called to serve the military needed to make provision for their practices. Accusations soon began to appear in both the medical and lay press that locums were capitalizing upon this increased demand. It was claimed that unscrupulous doctors were 'cornering the income of the wives and families of professional colleagues',[71] and that many doctors were being discouraged from volunteering for military service because they could not afford the increased rates of pay for locums; in some cases this was now said to be as high as £12 12s.[72]

In Scotland the SMSEC acted quickly to curb excessive fees, setting a maximum fee of five guineas a week. The Scottish medical profession generally accepted this limitation and the SMSEC refused to approve any appointments where larger sums were involved.[73] Many doctors in England would have liked to see a similar restriction of locums' fees, but others felt that maximum fees would be undemocratic and against the principles of the open market.[74] Moreover, it was felt that the financial plight of those doctors who had departed for military service had been exaggerated:

> [The Doctor on active service] is receiving roughly £400 a year. He has an allowance for uniform, is kept by the Government and will receive a bonus of £60 at the end of his year's service. He therefore receives roughly £500 a year and has no expenses. With an efficient locum-tenens he risks nothing, and returns to his practice at the end of hostilities, full of his patriotism, uniform and rank.[75]

Doctors, in fact, were claimed to be in a far more favourable position than were businessmen, who, when they returned, would have to start from scratch. It was therefore felt by some to be unreasonable that 'if the law of supply and demand favours, for a few months, the reliable locum, they should be expected to place limits on their earnings';[76] this seemed especially so, given the fact that no corresponding limits were to be placed upon the fees of medical agents.[77]

Furthermore, it was claimed that the majority of locums' fees were nowhere near as excessive as they had been portrayed:

> Before the war broke out the fees for substitutes were mostly 5 and 6 guineas, the increase in a great measure being due to the extra amount of work involved and the higher incomes earned owing to the Insurance Act. When the war broke out a large number of those who had been acting as locumtenents [sic] at once offered their services, and were accepted and given commissions at a remuneration of roughly 7 guineas a week, and consequently the fees paid to those remaining automatically went up to about the same figure, and at the present time a large number of men unable from one cause or another to serve their country abroad are doing so by taking duty at home for those who have gone on active service, and at moderate fees. Personally, I have not come across a single instance of 12 guineas being paid, and my register shows that out of a list of over 600 engagements that have passed through my hands during the last 6 months (mostly war ones) no fewer than 300 have been at 6 guineas, 235 at 7 guineas, 16 at 8 guineas and the remainder at lower fees, on hospitality terms or other special reasons.[78]

Of course, it was admitted that there were some doctors ready to take advantage of the situation by demanding unjustifiably high fees. The writer of the above extract advised doctors that the best way to combat such individuals was simply to refuse to accept their terms;[79] but in a situation in which locums were in short supply, doctors did not always enjoy that luxury. Medical agents were well aware of this and were not hesitating to exploit the doctors' vulnerability:

> I was introduced to a medical man who was prepared to take over my work. The agent took his fee, and the working of my practice assured, I accepted a temporary commission. Since then the agent has repeatedly attempted to induce my locumtenent [sic] to give up my work and accept other locum work at a higher salary, with the result that in order to retain the services of my locumtenent [sic] it has been necessary to raise the salary to a figure which, had it originally been asked, would have prevented me from taking a commission. The action of the agency in the matter appears to me to be extremely questionable.[80]

For the level of fees to be fair to both the doctor and his locum-tenens, it was essential that the type, size and workload of a practice be taken into consideration. It was unrealistic to expect a Cumberland practice (like that where J.M. McLachlan was acting as locum), which consisted mostly of panel patients, and where the workload was relatively light, to offer locums the same kind of remuneration as other more lucrative, or more demanding, practices. Yet it appears that such was the expectation. Attempting to find a replacement for himself, so that he might join up, McLachlan had contacted a locum agency in London. He greeted their reply that the going rate for locums was around 6 or 7 guineas with disbelief.

> I don't think any man is worth as much – certainly not in this practice. £7. 7s would just about swamp the practice.[81]

The establishment of the CMWC did go some way towards ensuring that the fees demanded corresponded to the work being undertaken; the local committees which it set up were entrusted with the task of ensuring that financial arrangements were fair to all. But without a nationally enforced scheme for the distribution of doctors, it was always going to be difficult to prevent some individuals from turning the laws of supply and demand to their advantage.

Local schemes for distributing the work of practitioners absent on military service were being drawn up. These schemes were intended to reassure doctors that adequate civilian health care would be maintained; to ensure that the workload fell equally upon those doctors remaining at home; and to formalize the rather ad hoc financial agreements which doctors leaving with the Army had made, early in the War, with those undertaking to deputize for them. The medical profession in Dundee led the way, its arrangements becoming a model for other towns. The Dundee Emergency Medical Service established central consulting rooms where practitioners attended on a rotational basis, and settled reasonably equitable financial terms.[82] The system was financed by charging each absent panel practitioner 50 per cent of his panel credits, and absent non-panel practitioners 50 per cent of the accounts incurred by their patients. This arrangement was felt to be generous to those on military service, but justifiably so, given the risk to life and practice which they were enduring; and it was well received by those doing the work. Doctors operating the system were paid an hourly rate of 7s 6d an hour for work at the consulting rooms, whilst visits were paid on the basis of six visits being equivalent to an hour's work.[83]

The success of such local schemes in protecting the medical services of the towns concerned indicated the benefits that would accrue if a national scheme for regulating the distribution of doctors were to be operated.

The calls on the profession were already heavy and likely to be heavier in the future as the Army continued to appeal for doctors. Action was needed to ensure that the disruption caused by the withdrawal of doctors from civil life was kept to a minimum.

The situation was eased somewhat by drawing upon the medical personnel of the Empire. Australia, Canada and New Zealand all had efficient army medical services, modelled on the RAMC, which came to Britain's aid; and doctors in the Dominions volunteered enthusiastically to join either their own medical corps or the RAMC. Early in 1915 the British War Office approached the Australian Defence Department with a request for a hundred Medical Officers.[84] The 'Kitchener One Hundred' as it was dubbed received a favourable response; one of the volunteers recalls that most young doctors wanted to get involved in the War.[85] Australian doctors responded similarly to further calls for volunteers, and by mid-1915 28 per cent of the profession was serving at the front.[86] Meanwhile, a report in June of that year stated that the Canadian medical profession was providing care for between ten and eleven thousand patients.[87]

The British medical authorities hoped that colonial doctors, unable to undertake front-line work, might offer themselves for service with the British civilian population. Because their qualifications were registered under the Medical Act, doctors from Australia and New Zealand could offer their services immediately; special arrangements were also made recognizing the qualifications of Belgian doctors, sixty of whom were thus able to take up practice in Britain.[88] Canadian qualifications were not registrable in Britain, but the General Medical Council (GMC) made moves towards the establishment of medical reciprocity. Agreements were reached with each of the Canadian provinces individually, the process being completed in 1917 when Alberta and British Colombia passed legislation allowing reciprocity. This was followed by a similar arrangement between Britain and South Africa.[89] Thus the War hastened a long-cherished dream of the GMC, the medical confederation of the Empire. Doctors from all the Dominions could now take up practice in the mother country.

The Lancet had hoped that through the contribution of the Dominions 'the evils of shortage will be counteracted'.[90] But significant though these developments were, Britain could not rely upon assistance from the Empire to cover her medical needs. The supply of doctors in the Dominions was itself limited. In Australia the Melbourne Hospital was faced with serious staff shortages,[91] and concern began to be expressed about the diminution of doctors serving the civil population:

If the thinning of the ranks continues, a time must come when the profession in Australia will no longer be able to look after our own sick.[92]

The only adequate solution was for Britain to develop a more co-ordinated medical manpower policy. The voluntary system was incapable of ensuring that the distribution of doctors took account of civilian and military needs. And, as we have seen, its failure to resolve the concerns felt by many doctors meant that the voluntary principle was beginning to have counter-productive effects on medical recruiting. Practitioners capable of military service were not coming forward because they remained unconvinced that adequate provision was being made for their civilian patients. Meanwhile older doctors, and those with dependants, were especially reluctant to join up when they saw younger men still at home, apparently developing their medical careers. The voluntary system needed to be replaced by one capable of guaranteeing a minimum level of civil medical provision, and of convincing doctors that the burden of war service was being borne equitably.

Yet, despite these reservations, doctors had responded patriotically to the nation's call. Ten per cent of the profession enlisted during the opening months of the War,[93] and by July 1915, one quarter of the profession had joined up;[94] a response far in excess of that of the male labour force and one which reflected the higher proportion of enlistments from the professions as a whole.[95]

The motivation of medical volunteers resembled those that have been identified in the community as a whole.[96] Foremost amongst these was straightforward patriotism. Captain G.D. Fairley recalled that he 'had the great idea that [he] wanted to do everything he could for Scotland, Great Britain and the Empire' and he was keen to be in the front line because that was where the 'greatest danger' lay, and 'it was doing more for [his] country'.[97] He further expands on this sense of patriotic duty:

being young, keen and fit I felt that I should be at the front. I had no desire to use the War to better myself in the practice of my profession, and in particular in surgery, and despised those that did so. So I kept on agitating with the ADMS to be transferred to a Scottish infantry battalion at the front, and eventually this happened.[98]

His belief that it was the duty of young doctors to answer the nation's call, by serving with front-line units, is echoed in the account of Captain M.S. Esler. He believed that he would have learnt a great deal about medicine had he taken up an offer to do military work in the UK, but felt that it was his duty to join other men of his age at the front. In any case, he was keen to learn about things other than medicine:

> what I wanted to learn about was the conditions of warfare in the field, the comradeship in arms, what fear really was and how to overcome it, and whether I was man enough to take it, in fact, to learn about myself.[99]

Even though the risk to doctors was less than it was for others, it was a matter of pride for such men to be serving in the trenches. As Charles McKerrow told his wife: 'I certainly couldn't be anywhere else. I could not look you or anyone else in the face if I had sat in the receipt of custom all the war.'[100]

Doctors recognized that there was valuable work to do at home, but patriotism bred in many men the desire to risk their lives. One such was M.D. McKenzie:

> My life during the last three years [general practitioner] has been the happiest part of my life, although at times the work was too heavy. I have always wanted to get into the Army because I wanted to feel that I had offered my life for my country and whatever happens I shall be more glad than I can say that I have managed to help in this great struggle.[101]

The patriotism of doctors was accompanied by a strong humanitarian instinct; that doctors joined the RAMC demonstrates an awareness that they had a professional duty to treat and comfort the sick and wounded in the fighting forces. The President of the Royal College of Surgeons, in his 1915 address, pointed out that it was the patriotic duty of all newly qualified doctors to join up, but stressed that they would not 'find anywhere a more ennobling field for their energies and professional skills than in helping the gallant men who are daily facing death and mutilation'.[102]

Brigadier Sir John Boyd remembers wanting to marry his professional qualification with a desire to do his bit.[103] And Sir Geoffrey Keynes, who was keen to get away from his chief at St Bartholomew's Hospital, also felt a double motivation:

> War did not suggest unnamed horrors but to a young surgeon meant useful employment in his own profession while doing his bounden duty for his country.[104]

Other doctors were clearly excited by the adventure of military service:

> I left England filled with the anticipation of cutting off legs and arms upon the stricken field, amidst a hail of shrapnel and machine gun bullets.[105]

For those bored with their civilian work, military service offered the prospect of more interesting times. J.M. McLachlan was certainly keen to escape what he regarded as the dull routine of a panel practitioner.[106]

Such quests for adventure and eagerness to serve were given added vigour in the opening months by a fear that the War might be over before a man had the opportunity to do his bit. According to Harold Dearden, 'men sought [the privilege of service] with the ardour of lovers, convinced that delay would see the end of hostilities, and the frustration of their hopes'.[107] As another doctor recalled, 'the only question was how soon we could get away'.[108]

Of course, not all doctors were so eager to go off to war. Warwick Deeping, the well-established author, who himself served as a Medical Officer, depicted in his novel, *No Hero This*, a country doctor, settled in practice, who expresses a disinclination to serve:

> What is it that makes me shrink? Fear, yes, some fear, but of what? A doctor may never pass into the danger zone. On the other hand he may be with a battalion in the trenches. Fear of what? Death, mutilation, or of a strange new anonymous life full of alien faces, a kind of going back to school like some raw and sensitive child? Am I so old at 35 that I fear change, insecurity, the stripping of one's comfortable self on the edge of this sinister, dark sea?[109]

In such cases of reluctance, however, social pressure could be crucial; in Deeping's novel, the townspeople make it plain to the doctor that his duty lies with the Army. He is told at the local auxiliary hospital: 'We are very glad to have you, Dr Brent, until we can arrange for an older man to help . . . with the wards.' And when even his wife and his middle-aged partner begin to signal that he ought to enlist, he is persuaded.[110]

But whatever the reasons which impelled doctors to enlist and however favourable the response to the nation's call, relative to other sectors of the population, the patriotism of the profession could not disguise the dissatisfaction of a proportion of its members with the current system of recruiting, nor its inefficiency in providing for the nation's whole needs.

General awareness of the inadequacies of voluntarism was growing; for, just as the system was unable to strike a balance between civil and military needs, it was becoming equally clear that a more organized manpower policy would be required if the industries vital to Britain's war effort were not to be starved of skilled labour. In political circles there was increasing awareness of the need for a more efficient direction of the nation's manpower resources; the replacement of the Government's hands-off policy with compulsory service was essential, and a noticeable downturn in recruitment figures by mid-1915 merely served to highlight the point.

But Asquith's Liberal-dominated Coalition was not yet ready to bow to the inevitable; instead it was decided to give the voluntary system a final opportunity to succeed via the Derby scheme of attestation. This scheme used the information provided by the National Register to establish the identity of males not engaged in essential war work who were eligible for military service. They were then requested to attest their willingness to serve when called upon to do so. However, the scheme did not apply to the medical profession which had already begun to organize itself along similar lines.

In April 1915 the BMA's Metropolitan Counties Branch had appointed a War Emergency Committee in order to organize the profession to meet the civil and military medical requirements. One of the first acts of this committee was to draw up a register of all practitioners within its area, detailing their age, type of practice, qualifications, experience and any war work in which they were employed. Sir Alfred Keogh recognized the value of such information and requested that the BMA undertake a national registration of medical practitioners. At its Annual Representative Meeting on 23 July 1915, the BMA responded by accepting a proposal for the extension of the registration scheme from the Metropolitan Counties to the whole of England and Wales. A War Emergency Committee was appointed to co-ordinate the response of the profession to the War effort (on 15 October 1915 this committee renamed itself the Central Medical War Committee), and on 4 August it received official recognition from Keogh as the sole recruiting body for the profession in England and Wales. The SMSEC, which had also undertaken to register the profession, received similar recognition with respect to Scotland.

With its new responsibility for medical recruiting and the register of the profession completed, the CMWC began a scheme which proposed to enrol all men under forty years of age for full-time service, and arranged that after enrolment such men should be called up as required.

Particular effort was made to secure the release, for service abroad, of as many young doctors as possible. It was felt that there were still many individuals, in the civilian sector, who failed to recognize the urgency of the situation. The governing bodies of hospitals were reminded of the necessity of relieving from their duties all junior members of their resident and visiting staffs who were eligible for commissions in the RAMC. At the same time, in order to ensure that the most efficient use was made of the medical recruits obtained and of those already serving, the military authorities were advised against employing fit men of military age in the home military hospitals.[111]

When the Derby scheme was initiated in October 1915, a question mark was placed over the continued role of the professional committees. But given the success of their recruiting efforts, it was decided to allow them to continue. In November, Lord Derby extended his approval to the medical enrolment scheme, thus giving the medical committees the same responsibility for recruiting doctors as was vested in the local Recruiting Committee, with regard to the remainder of the population.[112]

To facilitate this work it had been necessary for the CMWC to improve local organization in England and Wales; throughout the country a total of 179 Local Medical War Committees (LMWCs) were established. These committees were closely based upon the existing divisional areas of the BMA, but not exclusively so, and encompassed the whole profession, regardless of membership of the Association.[113] It was the responsibility of the LMWCs to canvas medical men of forty-five years and under, the age limit set by the War Office for general service.

The CMWC was anxious to maintain a continuous supply of Medical Officers in order to meet the growing needs of the Army, and it was estimated that almost half of the profession would need to be in military service by mid-1916.[114] Eligible doctors were therefore urged to declare their willingness to serve and place themselves in the hands of the national and local committees, which were best placed to decide equitably in which direction a doctor's duty lay. The profession had been given a unique opportunity to organize itself and emphasis was placed upon the necessity of making the scheme work if compulsion was to be avoided:

> patriotism demands that every eligible man, whatever may be his views as to the value of his own work, should sign an application for a commission in the RAMC and hold himself in readiness to make every sacrifice in his power for his country, whenever it becomes plain that the holding up of his application is no longer justified by the nature of his employment in civil life. To talk about waiting until he is taken under the compulsion of conscription is unworthy of a member of the medical profession.[115]

The failure of the Derby scheme to provide an adequate supply of recruits finally forced the Government to accept the need for compulsion and resulted in the passage of the 1916 Military Service Acts, which made all men under the age of forty-one liable for service. Calling up all doctors of military age would, however, have severely disrupted civilian health care, and so, in order to ensure that a balance was maintained between civilian and military requirements, the voluntary enrolment scheme was retained.

Notes

1   'Volunteers for Medical Service with the Army', BMJ, 1914, (II), p. 343.
2   'The Duty of the Profession to the Army', BMJ, 1914, (II), p. 884.
3   The SMSEC was established by Dr J.R. Hamilton, see Currie, *The Mustering*, p. 5.
4   'Civil Medical Practice and the War', BMJ, 1915, (I), pp. 20-4; 'Civil Practitioners and War Needs', BMJ 1915, (I), pp. 29-30.
5   Currie, *The Mustering*, pp. 14, 17.
6   'Scotland – Medical Service Emergency Committee', BMJ 1914, (II), p. 485.
7   J. Johnston Abraham, *Surgeon's Journey*, Heinemann, 1958, ch. 10; H.S. Souttar, *A Surgeon In Belgium*, Edward Arnold, 1915.
8   *Reports by the Joint War Committee and the Joint War Finance Committee of the British Red Cross Society and The Order of St John of Jerusalem in England*, HMSO, 1921, p. 76.
9   Abraham, *Surgeon's Journey*, p. 153.
10   *Reports by the Joint War Committee and the Joint War Finance Committee of the British Red Cross Society and The Order of St John of Jerusalem in England*, HMSO, 1921, pp. 76-7.
11   Currie, *The Mustering*, pp. 8-10.
12   Winter, *The Great War*, p. 156.
13   'Medical Attendance on Patients of Practitioners on Military Duty', BMJ, 1914, (II), pp. 337-8.
14   'The Medical Service of the New Army', BMJ, 1914, (II), *Supplement*, p. 164.
15   'The Mustering of the Professional', BMJ, 1923, (I), p. 24.
16   'Need for an Extended Organisation', *The Times*, 13 October 1914, p. 4; F.S. Brereton, *The Great War and the RAMC*, Constable, 1919, p. 27.
17   WO 159/16, Public Record Office, Kew, (PRO), letters of Colonel Arthur Lee, MP, to Lord Kitchener, regarding medical arrangements in France. Letter no. 1, 12 October 1914.
18   WO 159/16, PRO, Lee to Kitchener, letter no. 3, 28 October 1914.
19   *Hansard*, Parliamentary Debates, Commons, Fifth Series, LXVIII, 1914, col. 779.
20   'Scarcity of Doctors in Civil Practice', *Glasgow Medical Journal* (GMJ), LXXXIII, 1915, p. 208.
21   Lieutenant Colonel A.H. Habgood, Imperial War Museum (IWM), Recollections, p. 3.
22   'The War and the Dislocation of Private Practice', *Lancet*, 1914 (II), p. 1120.
23   *Ibid.*
24   'Field Ambulance Officers and Civil Practice', BMJ, 1914, (II), p. 772.
25   'Civil Medical Practice and the War', BMJ, 1915, (I), p. 22.

26 'The Duty of the Profession to the Army', BMJ, 1914, (II), p. 884.

27 'Civil Medical Practice and the War', BMJ, 1915, (I), p. 22.

28 **Captain J.H. Dible**, IWM, Diary, p. 15.

29 *Ibid.*

30 **Captain M.S. Esler**, IWM, Recollections, p. 46.

31 'Hospital Residents and School Medical Officers' letter, Dr C.K. Toland, BMJ, 1915, (I), p. 611; 'Need For Local Organisation', letter Pro Patria, BMJ, 1915 (I), pp. 648–9.

32 **Captain J.M. McLachlan**, Liddle Collection, The University of Leeds (LC), Letters, Letter 181, 11/9/14.

33 'Compulsory Medical Service', letter, Dr H.E. Littledale, BMJ, 1915 (I), p. 685.

34 Sir Alfred Keogh who had retired became DGAMS at the War Office when Sir Arthur Sloggett, the DGAMS, went to France as DGMS with the BEF.

35 'The Need of the Army for More Medical Men', letter, Sir Alfred Keogh, BMJ, 1915 (I), p. 488.

36 *Ibid.*

37 Appointed by the BMA to oversee work arising from war conditions in England and Wales. See **Little**, *History of BMA*, p. 240.

38 'The Conference', BMJ, 1915 (I), pp. 646–7.

39 *Ibid.* p. 647.

40 **Currie**, *The Mustering*, pp. 26–7.

41 *Ibid.* pp. 35–6.

42 'Need of the Army for More Medical Men', BMJ, 1915 (I), p. 611.

43 **Little**, *History of BMA*, p. 241.

44 **Dr. L.W. Batten**, LC, letter to son, 18 March 1970, p. 1.

45 'The War and Partnership Agreements', BMJ, 1915 (I), p. 1013.

46 *Ibid.* pp. 1013–14.

47 WO 95/44, PRO, DGMS Diary, 1915, 18 March 1915.

48 WO 95/45, PRO, DGMS Diary, 1916, 8 February 1916.

49 WO 95/44, PRO, DGMS Diary, 1915, 24 November 1915.

50 WO 95/44, PRO, DGMS Diary, 1915, 9 August 1915.

51 WO 95/44, PRO, DGMS Diary, 1915, 1 October 1915; 6 December 1915.

52 'The War and Partnership Agreements', BMJ, 1915 (I), pp. 1013–14.

53 *Ibid.*

54 *Ibid.*

55 **Winter**, *The Great War*, p. 158.

56 MH 10/78, PRO, Local Government Board Circulars, 1914: circular 73, 21 August 1914, Officers of Local Authorities on Naval or Military Service; circular 83a, 31 August 1914, Co-operation Between Civil and Military Sanitary Services; circular 126, 21 October 1914, Sanitary Authorities, County Councils, Port Sanitary Authorities, Medical Officers of Health.

MH 10/79, PRO, Local Government Board Circulars, 1915: circular 44, 8 April 1915, letter from Army Council, commending the assistance given by public health authorities.

57 'Public Authorities and Medical Recruiting', BMJ, 1915 (II), Supplement, p. 193.

58 'Doctors and Military Service', BMJ, 1915 (I), p. 1056.

59 MH 48/17, PRO, Cheshire county Council, Joint Chester and Wirral Unions, Medical Officer of Health: Letter Wirral Rural District Council to LGB, 21 November 1914.

60 MH 48/273, PRO, Penistone Urban District Council, Medical Officer of Health: letter to LGB, 12 September 1916.

61 MH 48/314, PRO, Tunbridge Wells Borough, Medical Officer of Health: letter LGB to WO, 6 April 1915.

62 MH 48/140, PRO, Sussex (East) County Council, Medical Officer of Health: letter LGB to Uckfield Rural District Council, 31 August 1915.

63 MH 10/80, PRO, Local Government Board Circulars, 1916: circular 18, 18 February 1916, County Councils, Metropolitan Borough Councils, Sanitary Authorities, Joint Hospital Boards and Committees, Joint Committees for Appointing Medical Officers of Health.

64 Ibid. See also MH 48/314, PRO, Tunbridge Wells Borough, letter, 13 May 1916, Tunbridge Wells Education Department to LGB.

65 MH 10/80, PRO, Local Government Board Circulars, 1916: circular 18, 18 February 1916, County Councils, Metropolitan Borough Councils, Sanitary Authorities, Joint Hospital Boards and Committees, Joint Committees for Appointing Medical Officers of Health.

66 MH 10/80, PRO, Local Government Board Circulars, 1916: circular 71, 28 June 1916, County Councils, Metropolitan Borough Councils, Sanitary Authorities, Joint Hospital Boards and Committees, Joint Committees for Appointing Medical Officers of Health.

67 MH 48/314, PRO, Tunbridge Wells Borough, Resolution Passed by Health Committee, 5 July 1916.

68 MH 48/314, PRO, Tunbridge Wells Borough, Extract from the Minutes of a Meeting of the Health Committee, 23 October 1916.

69 'The Medical Profession at Home', BMJ, 1914 (II), p. 368.

70 'Medical Attendance on Patients of Practitioners on Military Duty, BMJ, 1914 (II), pp. 337–8.

71 'The Supply of Locumtenents', BMJ, 1914 (II), p. 345.

72 'Unpatriotic Doctors', letter, signed M.D., The Times, 14 April 1915, p. 9.

73 'Effects of War upon Civil Practice', GMJ, LXXXIII, 1915, p. 47.

74 'Unpatriotic Doctors', Letter, signed 'APIBUS SUAM MELLUM', BMJ, 1914 (II), p. 380.

75 'Unpatriotic Doctors', letter, signed 'MRCS, LRCP', The Times, 17 April 1915, p. 10.

76 'The Supply of Locumtenents', letter, received from 'D', BMJ, 1914 (II), p. 380.

77 'The Supply of Locumtenents', letter, received from 'Locum', BMJ, 1914 (II), p. 380.

78 'The Fees of Locumtenents', letter from Percival Turner, BMJ, 1915 (I), p. 742.

79 'The Fees of Locumtenents', letter from Percival Turner, Lancet, 1916 (I), p. 1234.

80 'Locum Fees', letter signed 'Temporary Lieutenant RAMC', BMJ, 1915 (I), p. 784.

81 J.M. McLachlan, LC, letter 267a, 13 January 1915.
82 'Emergency Medical Organisation in a Large City', BMJ, 1915 (I), p. 516. See also Currie, *The Mustering*, p. 13.
83 'The Dundee Central Bureau', BMJ, 1917 (I), Supplement, pp. 134–5.
84 'Doctors for the Front', *Medical Journal of Australia (MJA)*, 1915 (I), p. 218; see p. 421 for a list of the 'Kitchener One Hundred', and for a further appeal for doctors.
85 Dr C., Huxtable, LC, Tape recordings 641 & 617.
86 'More!' MJA, 1915 (I), p. 603.
87 'Canadian Army Medical Service', BMJ, 1915 (II), p. 70.
88 Minutes of the GMC, LII, 1915, Executive Committee, 22 January 1915, p. 75.
89 Minutes of the GMC, LIV, 1917, Presidential Address, 105 Session, 22 May 1917, p. 8.
90 'The War and the Supply of Medical Officers', *Lancet*, 1915 (I), p. 1190.
91 'The Shortage of Medical Officers in Hospitals', MJA, 1915 (I), pp. 128–9.
92 'More!' MJA, 1915 (I), p. 603.
93 Winter, *The Great War*, p. 155.
94 *Ibid*, p. 157
95 Simkins, *Kitchener's Army*, p. 110.
96 *Ibid*, chapter on 'Experience of Enlistment'.
97 Captain G.D. Fairley, LC, Tape recording 283.
98 Captain G.D. Fairley, LC, Diary, 20 August 1915, p. 6.
99 M.S. Esler, IWM, Recollections, p. 47.
100 Captain C.K. McKerrow, LC, Collected Letters, letter 14 October 1915, p. 22.
101 Captain M.D. MacKenzie, IWM, Letters, letter 25 June 1917.
102 'Royal College of Surgeons, President's Address', *The Irish Times*, 16 October 1915; in the papers of Captain E.C. Deane, LC.
103 Brigadier Sir John Boyd, LC, Tape-recording 463.
104 Sir Geoffrey Keynes, LC, A Doctor's War (held in Western Front Recollections), p. 183.
105 J.H. Dible, IWM, Diary, p. 9.
106 J.M. McLachlan, LC, letter 250, 20 December 1914.
107 H. Dearden, *Time And Chance*, Heinemann, 1940, p. 1.
108 Douglas McAlpine, LC, Typescript Recollections, p. 11.
109 Warwick Deeping, *No Hero This*, Cassell, 1936, p. 2.
110 *Ibid*, pp. 5–10.
111 'The War Emergency – The Appeal to the Profession', BMJ, 1915 (II), Supplement, pp. 113–14.
112 'Recruiting for the Naval and Military Medical Services', BMJ, 1915 (II), Supplement, pp. 213–14. See also Currie, *The Mustering*, p. 51.
113 Little, *History of BMA*, p. 242.
114 'A Classification for Medical Recruiting', BMJ, 1915 (II), p. 867–8.
115 *Ibid*.

Chapter 3

Medical Practitioners and Compulsory Service, 1916–1918

The Military Service Acts vested in the national organization of the medical profession the responsibility for selecting practitioners who could be spared from their civil work to serve as Medical Officers in the Army. In addition to the CMWC and the SMSEC, the national organization now also comprised the Committee of Reference appointed by the Royal Colleges of Physicians and of Surgeons 'to consider cases of doctors on the staffs of hospitals and medical schools in the Metropolis, and such other special cases in England and Wales' as were referred to it.[1]

To enable the committees 'to cope with the task of solving equitably and with due regard to the needs of the civil population the many difficult questions involved in the selection of doctors', they were recognized in the second Military Service Act as taking the place of local and other Tribunals, with regard to the hearing of doctors' appeals against military service.[2]

Under the terms of the Enrolment Scheme, the War Office guaranteed not to call up any doctor who enrolled himself as willing to accept a commission in the RAMC;[3] but medical practitioners who failed to enrol were liable to compulsory combatant service.[4] The Military Service Acts also affected the position of doctors already serving with the RAMC. Doctors holding a temporary commission in the RAMC were engaged on a contract lasting for twelve months, or until the end of the War, whichever was the sooner. At the expiry of this contract a Medical Officer had been free to return to his civil practice with no further obligation. But now a Medical Officer returning home became liable to compulsory service under the provision of the Acts, and had to enrol immediately to take advantage of the special arrangements made for the medical profession. It was hoped that doctors in this position would not be selected for a second period of service while others, equally eligible, had not done any service.[5] Medical Officers who wished their service to be continuous could, of course, simply re-engage on the expiry of their contracts.

For the Enrolment Scheme to work fairly required the voluntary co-operation of all doctors eligible for general service with the RAMC; the age limit for doctors had been raised to forty-five, but those over forty-one were not subject to the compulsory powers of the Military Service Acts. Professional pressure therefore continued to be exerted to ensure that all doctors of military age enrolled. A circular distributed by the Middlesex Insurance Committee fully endorsed the arrangements made by the CMWC to protect civilian health care, and went on to say:

> It is, of course, necessary that every doctor of military age (that is to say under 45) and physically fit should enrol with that Committee, when, after consultation with the local Medical War Committee, all arrangements will be made for the conduct of the departing practitioner's practice with the least possible inconvenience to his patients and the least possible loss to himself.[6]

In Scotland, the Enrolment Scheme commenced on 1 January 1916. The fact that by 15 January 75 per cent of the profession had responded demonstrates that the majority of doctors accepted the need for action, and were willing to co-operate.[7]

The professional committees recognized that the ease with which doctors could depart for military service depended upon the nature of their civil work. Those whose appointments carried a fixed rate of pay tended to have some degree of goodwill attached to their posts, which would be unaffected by their temporary absence on military service,[8] whereas those with private practices, especially in towns, were wholly dependent for goodwill on their continued personal attendance. The location of a practice could also cause difficulties; doctors in rural districts faced the problem of finding a substitute willing to take on their work. But the committees were anxious that these matters should not distract doctors from the urgent need to enrol.

From the outset the CMWC had assured doctors that full weight would be given to any difficulties which they might draw attention to on their enrolment forms,[9] whilst guidelines were issued to local committees on how to handle appeals and exemptions.[10] It was important that doctors should not attempt to judge their own circumstances, but rather that they should enrol and place their faith in the professional committees. Dr Cox,[11] at a Conference of Representatives of LMWCs held in Leeds, said:

> The fairness of the scheme lay largely in the fact that it was to be worked by the co-operation of local committees, which would bring to bear local knowledge, and a Central Committee, which could be relied upon to take a large and impartial view.[12]

If doctors failed to co-operate with the Enrolment Scheme, it would have been difficult to co-ordinate the response of medical practitioners throughout the country. The CMWC feared that some districts would become short of doctors whilst others continued to have an ample supply, with potentially dangerous consequences for certain sectors of the civilian population. To prevent the wider question of civilian needs being ignored, it was essential that doctors enrol. This is not to say that the Enrolment Scheme had always struck an even balance between civilian needs and medical interests. As stated, doctors in public posts could leave their work with less disruption to their own livelihoods than doctors in practice; but, by taking doctors engaged in public health work in preference to doctors in practice, a threat began to be posed to civilian health. However, pressure was brought to bear upon the CMWC and it began to look at the cases of all public health physicians individually, thus ensuring that safe levels of care were maintained.[13]

The role of doctors over military age and of those unfit for service was to facilitate the release for military service of enrolled practitioners; this meant registering with the CMWC their willingness to act as locums. Demand for locums was great, especially in rural districts, where doctors had particular difficulty finding substitutes.[14] Doctors excluded from military service could also help to relieve the strain on UK hospitals by taking up resident appointments; resident staffs had been greatly reduced by the need to release young doctors for the Army.[15]

Many fit doctors over military age resented the fact that they were barred from contributing to the national cause in a military capacity. Growing demands on the Army by mid-1916, however, caused the War Office to rethink the situation. It was decided to give whole-time, home service commissions to men between forty-five and fifty-five.[16] Men who accepted these home commissions would thus be freeing younger

Medical Officers for service abroad; in particular, the War Office wanted to release the large number of Territorial Force Medical Officers, whose pre-war training and practical experience would be invaluable at the front.

An address by the administrator of the Second Northern General Hospital (Leeds), Lieutenant Colonel Littlewood, emphasized that those who remained at home also had a duty to safeguard the interests of those on service 'so that those who are fortunate enough to return when they do so, will find they have not to begin professional life all over again.'[17]

Indeed, it was essential that doctors should not be deterred from enrolling by a fear that others might profit from their absence. To re-assure enrolled doctors that their public-spiritedness would not be taken advantage of by others, who did not enrol, the CMWC decided, in April 1916, that it would 'not proceed to call up practitioners under the Enrolment Scheme unless and until 75% of those medical men in England and Wales who, on January 5 1916, were of military age and not holding a commission have enrolled, or have, since that date, received a commission in His Majesty's forces or a letter of provisional acceptance'.[18]

From the beginning of the Enrolment Scheme, the profession had seen the necessity of action to prevent the poaching of an absentee's patients. Insurance Committees were requested to discourage the transfer of patients from a practitioner away on service, whilst the duty was impressed upon Panel Committees of preventing any practitioner taking on as a panel patient any insured person on the list of an absentee, until twelve months after the latter's return.[19] There was a moral obligation upon all doctors to recognize 'that the patients of every man who has left his practice to join the army are no longer available for increasing the connexion of the man who remains at home'.[20]

The CMWC had drawn up a circular pointing out the different methods by which an absentee's practice could be continued: neighbouring practitioners; or locums; or a bureau organized by colleagues. This circular laid down guidelines for settling questions such as the division of fees and the restoration of patients to the returning doctor;[21] it was the basis for the local arrangements made throughout the country. However, no formal legal agreement existed to cover the arrangements between absentees and deputies, and there were demands that the CMWC issue a model, legally binding, scheme. The Committee refused to do so on the grounds that no definitive scheme could meet the needs of every area. But it did endorse the idea of giving these practice arrangements a legal basis, and publicized a number of such agreements as examples to the profession of what had been done in certain areas. The first legally binding agreement to come to its attention was that drawn up in Holland, Lincolnshire (see Appendix A). The terms of the Holland agreement included provision for preventing the poaching of the absentee's patients:

> Each of the practitioners at home hereby promises and agrees with each of the practitioners on service that if any persons who are ordinarily patients of any of the practitioners on service shall consult him during the absence of such practitioner on service the practitioner at home will not attend such patients, or arrange for their being attended, except on the terms hereinafter mentioned, and further that he will refuse to act as the medical attendant of such persons on his own behalf from the date of the return of the practitioner on service until at least twelve calendar months have elapsed, and will in every way do all in his power to safeguard the interests of the practitioner on service in such patients, and to induce them to return to him when he resumes practice.[12]

The agreement also made arrangements for the division of fees between deputy and absentee, which was decided on the basis of the type of practice involved; and stated the steps to be taken in the event of the absentee's death on service (see Appendix A).

A legal scheme, drawn up in Wigan, also received the Committee's approval; it published this as a guide for the profession in other industrial areas (see Appendix A).

Despite such agreements, however, complaints about doctors who were disregarding the interests of their active service colleagues remained frequent. The medical correspondent in *The Times* highlighted the case of a doctor, typical of many which had come to his attention, whose practice had been steadily eroded:

> I had to leave my practice to my colleagues who promised to keep a note of all my patients consulting them, and forward me half the fees received. I have never received a single penny. When I placed the matter before the Branch President, BMA, he wrote to my nearest colleague with a view to his taking up the whole of my practice. The reply he received was to the effect that it was quite impossible, as his practice was increasing by leaps and bounds. In the meantime, by a curious coincidence, my own has disappeared.[13]

The CMWC was not blind to such cases of injustice. It reminded doctors who were 'not recognizing as fully as they should do their moral obligation to professional brethren who have undertaken military service' of their duty to 'cheerfully and generously' protect the interests of their absent colleagues.[24] To help them in this endeavour, attention was drawn to procedures designed to minimize the reduction in the patient lists of those who were away (see Appendix B). Recognition was also given to the role that the general public had to play in protecting the livelihoods of their doctors. Patients were ready to agree that it was the duty of their doctor to lend his services to the military, but once he had departed they frequently failed to comply with the arrangements made to protect his practice. When S.S. Greaves returned to his practice in Wakefield, after six years away in France, he found it virtually faded to nothing and his name almost unknown. It took a good deal of hard work after the War to restore the fortunes of the practice.[25]

This problem was especially acute in urban areas where the attachment between doctor and patient tended to be weaker. Appeals were therefore addressed by the CMWC to the public, asking them to co-operate with the arrangements made by LMWCs for the continuation of doctors' practices:

> While recognising the right of every person to consult any doctor he chooses, we appeal to all British citizens not to give up their usual medical attendant on account of his temporary absence on military duty, and to insured persons we appeal not to apply for transfer. . . . We hope that patients will inform the practitioner they may consult that their own doctor is absent on military service and that they intend to place themselves again under his care whenever the need arises after his return. The medical men who remain are willingly attending the patients of those absent on service on the distinct understanding that they shall not be asked to do so after the war. The public will assist these men greatly to fulfil this honourable understanding if it will observe the lines of conduct we have indicated.[26]

These calls, both to the profession and the public, to consider the interests of absent doctors, were echoed by the President of the GMC in his address to the 102nd session. He warned that any doctor who failed to work within the guidelines laid down by the CMWC would be 'regarded as dishonourable by his professional brethren of good repute and competency', and implied that punitive action would be taken against them.[27]

However, there were those who remained unconvinced of the CMWC's ability to effect any improvement to their situation. One doctor who had been on active service since the early months of the War was convinced that attempts by the Committee to safeguard the practices of absentees were futile. He believed that the Committee had overestimated the chivalrous nature of the profession and cited an example of the merce-nariness that, in his opinion, characterized the majority of the profession:

> One of my female relatives, whilst staying at a boarding house, found that by casually referring to me in general conversation she had aroused the curiosity of a medical honeymoon couple as to the locality of my deserted practice. Apparently they looked upon it as derelict and possibly a good find.[28]

He was also dismissive of the CMWC's appeals to the loyalty of the public, which, he argued, assumed that the average member of the lay community possessed 'the morals of high class biblical characters'. It was impossible to regard patients as chattel, and nothing the CMWC might do would halt the frequency with which many patients, especially in poorer districts, changed doctor. This continued movement of patients between practices meant that any attempt to safeguard the livelihoods of absent doctors was fraught with complications:

> [E]ven friendly colleagues often forget to ask a newcomer if he has been previously attended by the absentee, whilst naturally they never dream of putting the question to one of their old patients who return to the fold after an unaccountable absence of several years. Another factor not allowed for by the Committee is that many of the patients think that they get better treatment at first than at second hand, and therefore not only seldom volunteer the information, but often deliberately conceal it.[29]

Meanwhile, doctors serving with the colours continued to complain that their practices were being bled dry by unscrupulous colleagues. Middle-aged doctors felt particularly aggrieved. Young men who had taken commissions would be able to face the future with confidence, having gained experience and prestige, but the doctor in middle life who, having forsaken civil responsibilities and family obligations and answered the military call, faced financial ruin. Young, newly qualified men would be able to obtain posts easily, giving them a very ample income, from which they would be able to purchase practices after the War. On the other hand, doctors settled in practice and with families, received only the same level of army pay as their younger brethren, yet faced far greater outgoings and with practices no longer capable of helping them make ends meet:

> Ask any of us how the practice at home is faring and the reply will be the same. The indifference of the public, the carelessness and in some cases

uncrupulousness of his colleagues at home, have made the horizon of the future dark with care.[10]

On top of all this it was galling for Medical Officers, invalided out of the service, to find that men of military age were seemingly monopolizing medical posts. One such returning Medical Officer complained:

At one special hospital . . . there are two house surgeons, senior and junior, while to cap it all an athletic young gentleman is acting as clinical assistant. . . . I applied for a public health appointment to one of the London boroughs. . . . What was my surprise to find that five of the six candidates up were of military age and apparently in the pink of condition, while the man who did get the post already held a similar appointment at the same salary, except that it was in the country and he preferred being in the town.[31]

Accusations of profiteering were also directed against doctors in the lower grades of medical fitness. If they were capable of working up to twelve hours a day and, in the words of Dr J. Clarke, 'piling up riches for themselves',[32] then surely they should be fit enough to undertake some work for the nation; this might include hospital work, at home or abroad, which would release older men for locum work.

It is certainly the case that the burden of war service was not borne equally. Whilst many ordinary general practitioners, absent on military service, would return to greatly reduced practices, top doctors stood to profit from the War. Many had been employed under the system of staffing the Territorial Force General Hospitals with à la suite officers of high standing in the community. These à la suite officers were entitled to wear uniform, were given commissioned rank and drew army pay. Yet the amount of military work they did was often minimal and they were still able to retain their private practices.[33] In contrast, general practitioners employed as Civil Medical Practitioners (CMPs) in military hospitals were poorly treated: their contract was terminable at a day's notice; their pay stopped if illness forced them off duty; they had no rank or uniform and so people were not aware that they were serving their country; they were not entitled to a gratuity; and they got no assistance with railway travel unlike their commissioned colleagues.[34]

Similar grievances were felt by Territorial and Special Reserve (SR) Medical Officers who, compared to doctors holding temporary commissions, were at a disadvantage as regards pay, allowances and gratuities. Understandably there was resentment that those who had patriotically offered their services, prior to the War, were rewarded with inferior conditions of service:

> The main thing that the present war has impressed on us is Don't join any reserve force in time of peace, because when your country needs you it will give you better conditions, higher rank, and more pay if you have done nothing before.[35]

The sense of injustice was heightened further when it became clear that doctors who refused to enrol were (on being conscripted) to be *punished* by serving under the *same* conditions as the Territorial and SR officers.[36]

It was also more difficult for Territorial and SR officers to protect their civil interests. They had been called up immediately, for the duration of the War, and consequently had little time to attend to their private affairs. Those on temporary commissions generally had more time to make arrangements, and had the option (after the termination of the twelve months contract) to return to their practices. Pressure grew for the reservists to be given equal treatment with the temporary officers, the BMA taking a leading role in the campaign. A committee of enquiry was established to look into the grievances of the reservists, and its principal recommendation was that:

> Officers of the Royal Army Medical Corps, Territorial Force and Special Reserve who joined before the war should be put on a level with temporarily commissioned contract officers as regards pay, allowances and gratuities where they would gain thereby.[37]

This was in line with the BMA's position, but the Army Council negated the proposal, claiming that Territorial and SR officers received the same pay as Regulars. In fact, Regulars were at an advantage over the reservists. There seems no justification for the Government's insistence on maintaining the division between the reservists and the contract officers. Some disparities were bound to occur, given the rapid expansion of the RAMC, but more action could have been taken to rectify the situation. The War Office's failure to act was to damage its reputation with the profession, making it difficult for the RAMC to meet its postwar recruitment targets.

Many civilian doctors serving with the military clearly had good reason to be dissatisfied with their conditions of service. It has also been suggested that their civilian interests were under threat. Contemporary accusations of widespread profiteering have received scholarly support. According to Frank Honigsbaum those schemes that were designed to safeguard practices 'nearly all foundered on the rock of medical greed'.[38] There undoubtedly were those in the profession who sought to benefit from the absence of their colleagues, but it would not be right to attribute the entire wartime losses of doctors on military service to the greed of their fellow practitioners. In fact, it seems safe to say that the general body of the profession did its utmost to minimize the disruption caused to the livelihoods of the absentees. In 1918, a report on central surgeries being run in Scotland and the Midlands highlighted the success of these schemes in protecting the interests of panel practitioners. However, the vicissitudes of patients and the fact that no new patients were added to practice lists during the War (to make up for losses due to death and movements out of the area) made it difficult to prevent some degree of financial loss in private practice.[39] J.E. Mitchell was not surprised when, at the end of his first year on military service, his practice was faced with losses of £600.[40]

When looking at the question of medical profiteering, it is therefore essential that we retain a sense of proportion. It is likely that only the cases of dissatisfied doctors came to the public attention; those content with their lot were probably less motivated to write to the correspondence columns. Moreover, although the system for carrying on the work of absent doctors was not perfect, it would seem that the majority of the profession were willing to try and make it work. The fact that by April 1916, 90 per cent of the profession had enrolled under the CMWC's scheme[41] is demonstrative of the public spiritedness that, in general, characterized the profession. It ought also to be recognized that the strain of civil work told heavily upon many of those who remained at home.

One doctor, passed unfit for military service, defended such as himself from the attacks of Dr Clarke:

> Before war broke out I was working as hard as my health permitted, and was making a decent income fairly comfortably. Since war broke out I have had to work even longer hours, endeavouring to cope with the increase of work entailed by the loss of colleagues. As a result my health broke down last year, and I was on the sick list for four months. I did not pile up riches last year, and even if I had not broken down my income would have been less than normal because so much of the work done was at half rates and one's own fully paid work had to suffer for the sake of one's colleagues.[42]

Indeed, this doctor argued that if the tales from Medical Officers at the front of a lack of work were to be believed, he would gladly give up civil practice for work in a military hospital.[43] And a Croydon doctor was so overworked that when told by a policeman that he would be summoned for having only one light on the front of his car, he replied that he hoped he would be sent to prison because it would give him a rest.[44]

The BMJ received numerous complaints from civil practitioners regarding the heavy workload that they had to bear, in contrast to the light duties of Medical Officers attached to barracks in the UK. It was felt that the War Office ought to show more concern for overworked civil practitioners, and co-operate with the civil authorities to ensure a more economical use of medical manpower. There was certainly a case for allowing doctors attached to barracks the opportunity to undertake some civilian work, and thus relieve the burden on their colleagues.[45]

The increasing burden of civil work was falling especially hard on older men,[46] many of whom broke down under the strain of carrying on two or three practices. Deeping's picture of an elderly doctor who is left to run a practice single-handed, without a break, is seemingly typical of the experience of many such practitioners; he is aged by the experience, his health is broken and he is reduced to a state of irritability and depression.[47] Medical Officers who had partners or relatives left at home, working under these difficult conditions, were well aware that home practice was not a bed of roses. One doctor was so concerned when his father was left to run the practice on his own that he tried to obtain leave to help him out. His detailing to Italy made this impossible,[48] but another Medical Officer, M.S. Esler, was successful in obtaining leave to relieve his father.[49]

Although doctors at home were doing more work, it did not necessarily follow that they were all earning increasing amounts of money; in many instances it was the doctors on active service who were in a better financial position. Henry Gervis, who spent the first three years of the War with the Second Eastern General Hospital at Brighton, found that he was much better off financially when he was transferred overseas. And this increase in earnings was accompanied by a lighter workload; in England he had been combining heavy hospital duties with a dwindling, though still demanding, private practice.[50]

Claims that men of military age were monopolizing hospital and public health posts were not without foundation. In August 1916 Dr M. Whiting wrote of two young opthalmic surgeons who had obtained civil posts that they would not have got if the patriotism of others had not cleared the field.[51] However, they were combed out under the Military Service Acts. Given the high enrolment rate and a policy that sought to ensure that all doctors under forty-five served overseas, the number under military age who were opportunistically advancing themselves must not be exaggerated.

Furthermore, to prevent those doctors who remained at home from advancing themselves professionally, the central committees urged that no permanent medical appointments be made in the Public Health and School Medical Services.[52] Such appointments were seen as unfair to the absent practitioners, nor were they felt to be in the best interests of the public; appointments made in a time of restricted competition did not ensure that the best individuals were being recruited. In January 1916 the LGB had therefore decided to limit the duration of appointments as MOsH to the period of the War.[53]

In Ireland, where the Military Service Acts did not apply, there was the added difficulty of preventing young doctors, fit for military service, from holding such appointments. The LGB for Ireland issued a circular to the Boards of Guardians requesting them to refrain from filling Poor Law medical posts, but to make temporary arrangements until the conclusion of the War.[54] On a number of occasions, however, Boards of Guardians in Ireland attempted to question the right of the LGB to challenge appointments, simply on the grounds that the doctor chosen was eligible for military service.[55] Was the Irish medical profession not pulling its weight? One Territorial Captain certainly thought not:

> The absence of conscription in Ireland leaves it open to young Irish practitioners to profit by the military service of English, Scottish and Welsh doctors, and set up practice in the homes of the absentees to their obvious hurt.[56]

A letter from the CMWC to the Honorary Secretary of the Irish Medical War Committee, however, suggests that despite the lack of any compulsion, Irish doctors were not hanging back:

> [W]e should like to take this opportunity of offering our congratulations to your Irish Medical War Committee on the steady flow of volunteers it is securing.[57]

In answer to further appeals, this favourable response continued. And whilst some Boards of Guardians had been obstinate in attempting to oppose the LGB's ruling, the majority did comply.[58]

Just because concerns over practices did not seriously undermine the Enrolment Scheme, does not mean that doctors were not worried about the effects of the War on their livelihoods. Doctors who had given up their civil work to serve the Army, in the certain knowledge that they would incur financial loss, deserved reassuring that everything possible

71

was being done to limit the cost to their careers. Despite the best efforts of the professional committees to safeguard their interests, nagging doubts about the care of their practices were bound to persist for as long as an element of voluntarism remained in the recruiting scheme.

The Manchester Medical War Committee had been operating a system for providing recruits for the RAMC, conserving practices and co-ordinating civil work. The scheme had succeeded, thanks to the co-operation of 80 per cent of doctors in the area, but the Committee concluded 'that even that large percentage is insufficient to meet the national need, and that the secret of success can only lie in compelling the laggards to do what the majority of the profession is eager to do on its own initiative'[59] (see Appendix C). The growing difficulties facing such local committees, in their endeavour to provide doctors for the civil and military services, and at the same time protect the professional interests of practitioners, caused the CMWC to address the question of medical mobilization. At a meeting in December 1916, it accepted 'the principle of mobilisation of the medical profession apart from any question of general mobilization of the whole community, so that every individual whose name is on the Medical Register should be held bound to give such service as he is competent to give, when called upon to do so'.[60] A similar resolution was passed by the SMSEC.

However, there were those in the profession who remained opposed to the idea of compulsion. Many felt it wrong that the medical profession should be treated differently to the rest of the nation in the matter of mobilization. But they failed to recognize the special position of the medical profession, with its equally important civilian and military duties. Moreover, because of its dual responsibilities the profession had throughout the War been treated differently with regard to military service, having been granted the privilege of co-ordinating its own manpower resources. Surely, it was too late now to start complaining about distinctions.

In any case, according to Dr William Thornely, doctors ought to have had nothing to fear from compulsion; it merely represented a more efficient way of carrying out their commitments to the civil and military services, and to their absent colleagues:

Why should compulsion be looked upon, as it appears to be, as something of which to be ashamed? It is compulsion only for those who would shirk their proper responsibilities; for the rest it is merely just an equitable organ-isation, and would, I am convinced, be warmly welcomed by the majority of the profession.[61]

Many in the profession, however, feared that mobilization would be the first step towards a post-war salaried Service. Indeed, there were those who hoped and believed that, after a brief trial of a nationalized service, neither the profession nor the nation would wish to return to the old system.[62] Calls for a salaried service were led by the medical correspondent of *The Times*, who argued that it would be the most equitable way of ensuring the future financial security of doctors absent on service.[63] It is certainly the case that dwindling receipts from their depleted practices convinced many doctors, previously hostile to a salaried service, that it was the only option likely to guarantee them a steady income on their return to civil life. Meanwhile, those already favourable to a salaried service became even more enthusiastic as a result of their war experiences. H.J.B. Fry spent his spare time (whilst at the front) developing a scheme for transforming the RAMC into a national medical service, and read a paper on the subject to a divisional medical society.[64]

However, what was seen as the excessive bureaucracy of the RAMC led others in the profession to fear that the same would be true of a civilian salaried service. And, despite anxieties about their financial security, it would appear that the majority of doctors in the Army were opposed to a salaried service.[65] Certainly, the BMA's support for mobilization of the profession did not represent a change of attitude. It regarded itself as the principal protector of the interests of individual general practitioners. After the War it successfully fought to prevent a salaried service being established.[66]

Nevertheless, whatever qualms sections of the profession might have felt about the possible implications of medical mobilization, the majority recognized that it was the only means of ensuring efficient distribution of medical personnel. The professional committees therefore proceeded to draw up a scheme, in consultation with the Director General of National Service, for the compulsory mobilization of doctors. At the beginning of 1917, however, the Government was still not prepared to sanction compulsion for the civil profession.[67]

Given that the Asquith Coalition had already endorsed the principle of compulsory national service, it might appear surprising that Lloyd George's new administration, which claimed to stand for a more vigorous prosecution of the War, did not adopt the CMWC's scheme. However, the Lloyd George Government did not effect any immediate improvement in British manpower policy; concern about growing war weariness and the prospect of labour unrest caused the Cabinet to hold back from civilian compulsion. Neville Chamberlain, the Director General of

National Service, headed a department that lacked the power to co-ordinate the nation's manpower requirements, and was limited to the administration of a voluntary mobilization scheme. The failure to endorse the CMWC's proposal was therefore a reflection of the continued lack of co-ordination in British manpower policy as a whole.[68]

The War Office's lack of control over the auxiliary military hospitals, which were administered by a variety of voluntary bodies, was clear evidence of the need for greater central co-ordination. Criticism was centred on the overlap of function between the multiplicity of small VAD and private hospitals and the consequent waste of medical personnel.[69] The system whereby top consultants were paid full-time salaries for a nominal amount of work, whilst still being able to retain their private patients, was unfair and wasteful. Responding to pressure for equitable treatment of doctors and a more efficient use of medical manpower, the War Office terminated the employment of part-time doctors in the military hospitals. Doctors from the USA replaced them. Some understandable ill-feeling was caused by the abrupt manner in which the War Office dispensed with the services of part-time doctors,[70] but the motivation for the policy was commendable. The release of part-time consultants would leave them free to undertake full-time duties in either a military or civil capacity. However, the practice of employing part-time consultants continued in hospitals not controlled by the War Office.[71]

In March 1918 the Committee of Reference produced a memorandum pointing out the need for a reorganization of hospital staffs. It recommended grouping of hospitals and the transfer of staffs, but pointed out that as this would 'involve the closing of certain hospitals and the diversion of others from the objects for which they were instituted, it is difficult to see how any voluntary arrangement can be arrived at without prolonged negotiations including complicated financial considerations'.[72] Moreover, it doubted whether individual hospitals would admit the need for reorganization. Thus, to guarantee that the hospitals were making the most economical use of medical men, compulsory mobilization was essential.

Of course, the limited availability of doctors meant that compulsory mobilization would have made little impact upon the supply of Medical Officers to the Army. But by showing a commitment to a more efficient direction of medical manpower it would have done a great deal to convince doubters that everything possible was being done to reduce inequality of sacrifice within the profession. Mobilization was also essential to allay continuing and growing fears that the Army's use of Medical

Officers was wasteful and totally lacking in consideration of civilian needs. Critics argued that the Army was employing far more doctors than it could possibly need:

[The DGAMS] says that under his present methods an army of 4,000,000 will require 15,000 doctors. That will leave only 15,000 for the care of 40,000,000 civilians, including the wounded and invalided who are sent home to civilian hospitals from the front.[73]

Sir Wilmot Herringham, who served with the forces as a consulting physician, recognized that the proportion with the Army was bound to be excessive, but believed that 'it is easy to see that the number is necessary, and that the reason why so many are required is that a sick or wounded soldier cannot be treated in one place by one man, but has to be carried down the line in successive stages, at each of which he must be ensured adequate care and attention'.[74] Clearly, those who criticized the scale of the RAMC's employment of doctors had failed to take account of the special circumstances of military medicine. However this would not suit them as an explanation of the situation; they believed that there was an administrative fault and that better management techniques needed to be adopted if wasteful deployment of doctors was to be avoided. Mobilization would have checked growing concern over the distribution of doctors between the civil and military spheres, but, as it was, complaints continued to be made that the Army was employing too many doctors for too little work.

An article in the BMJ, by a Medical Officer in charge of an infantry battalion, pointed out that it was 'no answer to say that there are too many Medical Officers'[75] simply because moments of slackness occurred at varying and spasmodic intervals. It was short-sighted in the extreme not to recognize the reality that a military operation 'cannot slide along with the even smoothness and regularity of a business concern'.[76]

Nevertheless, many Medical Officers failed to come to terms with inactivity as an inevitable consequence of the ebb and flow of war. They believed that their light workload was evidence of an overstaffed service. One such officer gave details of his experience to the BMJ:

I have now just completed my year, and if I had to do all the work that I have done in that time again I could easily fit it into one month and have plenty of time for recreation or study.

It can be no question of my having fallen on a soft job as I've done practically every sort of job in my time, both at home and in France, with the

75

exception of work in a C.C.S., where I believe the Medical Officers generally overworked.[77]

Another doctor wrote home:

I am in my sixth month now and really during this time I have done less . . . work than I managed to fit in during a week at home. I have yet to find out where the scarcity of doctors comes in.[78]

In particular, it was felt that the position of Regimental Medical Officers (RMOs) was too undemanding of medical skill to merit the employment of a qualified practitioner:

Even with the best intentions and the greatest keenness – sanitation, lectures to men and officers – it is difficult to spin the work out for more than an hour or two each day. Loafing about and trying to be amused is our usual lot day after day. Only during a push for the short time that one's own regiment is engaged does our work ever approach the amount done by an average general practitioner in busy practice very day.[79]

Writing of doctors who claimed that regimental work occupied them for no more than a couple of hours a day, Sir Wilmot Herringham said, 'I have no hesitation in saying that such officers did not know their duty.'[80] And, as we shall see in a later chapter, there was no doubting the important role which the RMO had to play in maintaining the health and morale of the troops under his charge. Doctors who complained of inefficient use of medical manpower were probably having difficulty adjusting to a war situation; used to busy civil practices, they could not understand how periods of inactivity could mean anything other than a sign of oversupply. The inquiries of a BMJ correspondent revealed that the general opinion in France took the opposite view, that the medical staff there 'has been numerically low as is compatible with efficiency, and that at busy times many of its members have been very hardworked, in some instances overworked'.[81]

The CMWC felt that those who questioned the Army's employment of medical men at home were being equally short-sighted. The necessity of maintaining a reserve from which the Army could draw when required was pressed upon the profession. Not to employ doctors until their full-time services were required was considered an unrealistic policy, which ignored the fact that Medical Officers, just like their combatant colleagues, benefited from some preliminary military training.

Doctors were assured by the CMWC that the Army's requests for

Medical Officers were made after full consideration of the need for economy. It stood by its 1916 statement to the effect that:

> the responsibility must rest upon the military authorities, who would be blamed if at any given time it were found that there were not sufficient Medical Officers, and the Committee does not consider that it is wise or patriotic to question the decision of the military authorities.[82]

Writing in September 1915, Captain C.K. McKerrow demonstrated a similar faith in the ability of the War Office to judge the situation: 'they have asked for a third of all able-bodied doctors under 40, so there is little doubt we are needed'.[83] Indeed, there is every indication that this faith in the War Office was not misplaced. Action was taken to reduce the excessive employment of Medical Officers in some of the home military hospitals,[84] and to ensure that only men over military age were thus employed.[85] Also, doctors serving in the combatant branches were given the opportunity to transfer to the RAMC; in January 1915, Captain Duncan of the Fifth Black Watch applied for a transfer to medical work.[86] Where this provision can be criticized is in its voluntarism, as it was only later in the War that men were actually seconded from combatant service.[87] Nevertheless, that it existed at all is evidence that the War Office was aware of the need to make better use of medical manpower.

Furthermore, given the demands which the War was making on the RAMC, there seems no grounds for saying that the continued calls being made upon the civil profession were excessive. During the 1916 Somme campaign alone the RAMC lost 400 doctors killed and wounded, leading to a shortage.[88] Nor was this shortage confined to the Western Front; in Salonika, in November 1916, a deficiency of sixty-one Medical Officers was reported, and the problem remained into 1917.[89] Moreover, it should be emphasized that the numbers which the War Office was attempting to maintain were not the pre-war establishments, but the minimum necessary to safeguard the health of the men. In February 1917 the War Office informed the Director of Medical Services (DMS) in Mesopotamia, that 'the supply of Medical Officers is now insufficient to meet all demands. Demands should be based on the minimum working number, allowing a 10% margin for casualties, and considering requirements for hospital river transport'.[90] Already, when calculating the provisions for the coming hot season, the DMS had recognized the futility of creating new hospital formations which would require additional Medical Officers.[91] Indeed, the DMS produced a memorandum advocating a reduction in the number of Medical Officers by combining

British and Indian Field Ambulances (FAs) into a smaller number of uniform units.[92]

Despite the efforts of the RAMC to keep its demands to a minimum, the confidence with which, in March 1917,[93] the BMJ had reiterated assurances about the War Office's good intentions was shattered in April of that year, by the War Office's own clumsiness. As a result of Germany's adoption of a submarine campaign against hospital ships, Lord Derby notified the profession of a decision to increase the number of hospitals in the various theatres of war. To implement this policy it was decided that all doctors under forty-one should immediately be called up.[94]

Thus the statutory power of the professional committees to regulate the supply of doctors to the Army and ensure that a balance was maintained between civilian and military requirements was completely disregarded. The CMWC responded with a memorandum deeply critical of the Government's action; it pointed out that 'the immediate calling up of all doctors under 41 for military service effected by the War Office must inflict grave injury on the civil community in many parts of the country, particularly in the industrial areas upon which so much depends', and concluded that 'nothing short of a Government decision to maintain the complete continuance of the requisite scrutiny will suffice to avert great danger'.[95]

The high-handed attitude of the War Office in not discussing the call-up with the profession caused it to forfeit a good deal of the profession's goodwill and trust; it had helped to validate claims that the military's demands for Medical Officers were excessive and failed to consider civilian needs.

In the face of professional protests the War Office reversed its decision, and Dr T. Jenner Verral, Chairman of the CMWC, in praising this decision, felt that no lasting bitterness between the War Office and the Committee had resulted.[96] But from this point on it is clear that growing suspicion throughout the profession of the War Office's demands began to affect the Committee itself; the concern of the Committee was increasingly diverted from recruiting towards maintaining a safe level of civilian medical provision. Nor was it only from within the medical profession that such concerns were expressed. Sir William Robertson argued that around 75 per cent of a nation's war effort depended on non-military factors;[97] therefore any nation which failed to give due regard to the welfare of its civilian population did so at its peril.

Fears that certain areas were becoming seriously depleted of medical practitioners, and the increasingly heavy strain falling on those who remained at home, combined in mounting pressure upon the Army to reassess its uses of medical manpower. Moreover, without compulsory mobilization of the profession it was becoming virtually impossible to supply the Army's need and yet preserve civilian health care. As a result, in August 1917 the CMWC had to inform the War Office that the supply of Medical Officers for the Army had been exhausted.[98]

This combination of factors led to the appointment of a Commission of Inquiry into the Army Medical Service[99] to determine what, if any, economies could be made by the military. On the whole its conclusions were favourable,[100] but it did recommend some economies such as the reduction in the number of Medical Officers with an infantry FA from eight to seven and with cavalry FAs from six to five. It also called for the reduction of the staff of Convalescent Depots and for fewer doctors to be employed on Ambulance Trains.[101]

It would appear that administrative changes were adopted as a result of this report[102] and 200 nursing sisters were specially trained as anaesthetists; their employment in 1918 released a corresponding number of Medical Officers for service at the front.[103] In May 1918 the War Office was informed of proposals to reduce the number of Medical Officers by two per FA; efficiency could be maintained by granting commissions as Second Lieutenants to NCOs with the necessary experience.[104] But the War Office, in deciding not to publish the report, ignored one of its principal recommendations: that there be greater collaboration and exchange of information between the civil and military authorities. In so doing the War Office missed a valuable opportunity to allay the fears of medical men; continued calls for publication of the report throughout 1918 demonstrated that suspicion of the military remained strong.[105]

In March 1918 the National Health Insurance Committee expressed fears that the continued demands of the Army would lead to a dangerous depletion of doctors in the industrial towns. Prior to the War, the concentration of doctors under forty-one was said to be higher in these towns than in the country generally, and so any further calling up was likely to fall heavily upon these areas. The Committee argued that the profession and the public could not be expected to quietly accept further civilian sacrifices without an independent, authoritative demonstration that the Army was making efficient use of the 13,284 doctors currently on active service.[106]

Dissatisfaction with the recruitment machinery was not confined to the medical profession. The failure of Chamberlain's National Service Department and its reconstitution as the Ministry of National Service was followed by an investigation into the new standards of physical fitness being applied by military medical boards under the Military Service

79

(Review of Exceptions) Act. Much criticism had been directed by ex-servicemen's associations and the labour movement towards the new regulations and their suspicion aroused by the activities of the military authorities. As a result of this inquiry it was decided to place recruiting under civil control by transferring the responsibility to the Ministry of National Service.[107]

Thus, on 1 November 1917, Sir Auckland Geddes, the Minister of National Service, took over responsibility for medical manpower. The Ministry of National Service continued to work through the professional committees, but relieved of ultimate responsibility, these now became freer in their criticisms and more defensive of civil interests. Indeed, throughout the last year of the War, the professional bodies, whilst supporting the Ministry in its efforts to obtain sufficient Medical Officers, remained convinced that the Army could exercise greater economy and doubtful about its cries of shortage. The Army's failure to respond to frequent requests for the publication of the report on medical establishments did nothing to discourage such beliefs.[108]

In fact, throughout 1917, the Army had continued to suffer from a shortage of doctors. The Adjutant General informed the War Office, in October of that year that there was a serious shortage of Medical Officers serving with the Army in France, both in the field and on the lines of communication. On top of a shortage of 382 Medical Officers on the lines of communication, there was a need for 152 to replace casualties.[109] The drain on medical manpower was increased by the despatch of a force to assist the Italians at the end of 1917. The DDMS XIII Corps recorded that the transfer of Medical Officers to the 48th Division, which was part of the force sent to Italy, had led to difficulties in the 47th and 81st Divisions. The shortage caused the DDMS to reduce the number of Medical Officers sent from the XIII Corps to the newly opened RAMC School of Instruction. And on 14 November he informed the DMS First Army that the shortages could not be made good by redistribution within the Corps.[110]

The inability of the bases and lines of communication in France to re-inforce the field units, combined with the deployment of medical units in Italy, heightened the RAMC's concern with economy. In October 1917 the DMS First Army had stressed that there should be 'no multiplicity of institutions for treating sick as it wastes Medical Officers. The ADMS and DDMS are to make every effort to keep all Medical Officers employed on a full day's work'.[111] However, actual reductions in the number of Medical Officers employed were difficult. The arrival of American Medical Officers did help to ease the situation a little; the

DDMS XIII Corps was able to replace nine RAMC officers detailed for duty in India and Mesopotamia with Americans.[112]

As the Army's need for medical reinforcements grew, it became increasingly concerned with the need to retain the trained Medical Officers already on service. The DGMS in France noted that in the three months August to October 1916 the RAMC had lost 142 Medical Officers due to men refusing to renew their annual contracts; he argued that everything possible should be done to discourage this unnecessary wastage.[113] In Egypt, the DMS felt that if contract-expired Medical Officers were made aware of the importance of their continued service, most would be willing to sign on again. Meanwhile, those who remained unwilling were made aware of the fact that under the Military Service Acts they might be sent back to Egypt immediately upon returning home; signing on again would thus avoid a long, dangerous and probably point-less voyage. Using these arguments the ADMS Alexandria was able to persuade a number of Medical Officers to renew their contracts.[114] Similarly, in November 1916, the DMS Mesopotamia had issued a circular letter asking that Medical Officers 'consider carefully the ques-tion whether they are acting to the best of their ability when requesting to return home'.[115]

By the end of 1917, however, the right of Medical Officers to refuse to renew their annual contracts was coming into question. At a con-ference on the shortage of Medical Officers, Keogh pointed out the inefficiencies of the contract system:

1) The annual contract limits gravely the powers of administrative medical officers to move Temporary Commissioned officers overseas in the same way as regular and Territorial Force officers. In many cases four months travelling, for example to Mesopotamia, is necessary.

2) The annual contract is expensive in both money and manpower and it causes recurring disturbance of medical arrangements for the Army and civilian population. This disturbance gives rise to much adverse comment by civilian members of the medical profession. In the last six months 730 Temporary Commissions had been relinquished.[116]

As a result, in December 1917 it was decided that 'in future, every officer of military age relinquishing his commission on expiration of the annual contract will at once be called up for the duration of the War and for such additional period of demobilization as may be necessary. This in no way affects the right of every medical practitioner to appeal to one or other of the three statutory professional committees . . . [but] no appeal is likely to be successful unless the appellant can bring forward a strong case based upon the medical needs of a particular locality or upon reasons of urgent private or public importance.' Medical Officers were urged not to relinquish their contracts unless they were certain that their appeals would be successful.[117]

With the opening of the German offensive in 1918 the situation became critical. Sir T. Goodwin, who replaced Keogh as DGAMS at the War Office in March of that year,[118] informed the Minister of National Service: 'We are getting urgent demands from France for more medical men. The minimum working establishment in France is at present 501 below strength and we have now, at a request from France, 221 Medical Officers prepared to leave at an hour's notice, this exhausts our available supply and we are not in a position to supply urgent demands from East Africa, Mesopotamia and Salonika.' Indeed, given the crisis in France, only demands from that front were currently receiving a response; forces elsewhere were asked to reconsider their positions and to keep their demands to a minimum.[119] Some assistance came from Italy, where the DMS decided to send thirty Medical Officers to reinforce units in France.[120]

In a bid to solve the crisis, the following letter was sent to practitioners who had already seen service in the RAMC:

> I am directed by the CMWC to inform you that they have received information from the Ministry of National Service that medical men (both surgeons and other practitioners) who have had experience with HM's Forces are urgently needed for immediate service in the RAMC in France.
>
> As you have had the experience, the Committee hope you will volunteer at once for this service, and immediately indicate your willingness to do so to this Committee, assuming for the moment that the civil needs do not preclude all possibility of your leaving your work at present.
>
> The Ministry of National Service has undertaken that the case of any doctor now responding to this appeal who may desire on personal grounds to return home or whose presence at home becomes greatly needed for the civil requirements, shall be reviewed by the Ministry of National Service at the close of the present crisis – in any case not later than six months from now – with a view to his being then released unless the Ministry of National Service, after considering the military and civil necessities at the time on consultation with the CMWC, decides that this is impossible.[121]

The response to this appeal was poor: only twenty-seven men answered the call.[122] The response might well have been better had there been a guarantee that service would be limited to the duration of the present crisis. As a result of this failure, a more radical approach was now adopted.

In April 1918, Parliament reacted to the general manpower crisis by passing a Military Service Act, which extended conscription to all men below fifty-one. The age for doctors, however, was raised to fifty-five. It was realized that in some districts, such as munitions areas, fit doctors were as necessary as in the trenches, but that in some residential districts there were numbers of older doctors who were really excess to requirements. By raising the age for military service it was hoped that these older doctors would be able to relieve younger men in the Base Hospitals and set them free for front-line work. If adequate levels of civilian health care were to be maintained, there was also a need for these older doctors to act as substitutes in areas where medical practitioners were scarce. Appeals for older doctors to move to areas of need had met with some response. But in order to ensure that a sufficient number was obtained, it was decided to introduce civil compulsion for the medical profession.

For the rest of the population, the Government had held back from introducing civil compulsion; it feared that outright industrial conscription would provoke serious labour unrest. Instead, the Government co-operated with the Trade Union Advisory Committee in promoting voluntary enrolment, and this provided a satisfactory system of labour distribution. Certain sections of the medical profession complained that it was unfair to treat doctors separately from the rest of the nation as regards conscription. Sir Donald MacAlister, President of the GMC, though recognizing that the situation was far from favourable, nevertheless felt that 'we shall do well to accept it as an honour that, as we are capable of a unique form of service to the state, so we are charged with a heavier responsibility than others'.[123] In any case the CMWC had already approved the idea of mobilizing the whole profession. Thus, under the Military Service (Medical Practitioners) Regulations, the Ministry of National Service and the professional committees were given the power to direct all doctors of military age found fit for service to practice in districts where the need for medical men was great.

Momentum towards compulsory mobilization of the civil profession was now virtually unstoppable; proposals were made for the redistribution and concentration of civil practice[124] to ensure the most efficient use of medical personnel. And by the summer of 1918 the CMWC had finalized plans for a system of compulsory medical transfer.[125] There can be little doubt that these proposals would have brought Britain to the verge of a wartime national health service that might have laid the foundations for a full-scale reorganization of medical care in the post-war years. Germany's defeat in the autumn, however, meant that they never had to be put into practice.

Mobilization of the profession represented the most efficient way of balancing military and civil needs and at the same time securing the interests of doctors themselves. This is not to say that the recruiting machinery, as it had developed prior to mobilization, had completely failed in these goals. There was never a breakdown in either the Army or civilian medical services, whilst it must be accepted that little more could have been done to protect doctors' personal interests. But the continuation of an element of voluntarism and the lack of complete central direction of the profession made it inevitable that complaints of abuses, of profiteering and Army wastefulness would arise. Moreover, had mobilization not been introduced, a breakdown in medical services might well have occurred; undoubtedly so, had the War continued through the winter of 1918, and the nation had to face the influenza epidemic without an effective scheme for the distribution of doctors.

Already, the influenza epidemic had begun to place a heavy strain on both the civil and military services. In the Army the shortage of Medical Officers was exacerbated by the increased workload caused by the epidemic, and the fact that many Medical Officers themselves were lost to the disease. In Mesopotamia the shortage of Medical Officers consequent upon the epidemic led to a curtailment of pathological work in the hospitals at Baghdad, and a reduction in the number of officers per FA.[126]

Meanwhile, in the UK the depleted medical service was facing a crisis. According to one doctor, the medical situation in Hull was 'completely out of hand'.[127] And in Stockport many of the doctors went down with influenza, so that there was great difficulty in carrying on the medical work. The situation was so bad that the doctors serving on the National Service Medical Board in Stockport were having difficulty in coping with the work of their private practices. It was thus decided, in November 1918, to close down the Stockport Board for a week; similar steps were taken elsewhere.[128]

Assistance was also given by the War Office, which circularized commands, requesting that wherever possible military doctors be allowed to assist their civilian colleagues.[129] Changes in court martial procedure also gave Medical Officers the chance to assist the civilian population. Previously, Medical Officers, like all commissioned officers dismissed the service for misdemeanour, were immediately called up for military service in the ranks. However, in the case of Medical Officers this process was delayed to allow them time to satisfy the professional committees that they could be of advantage in civil employment.[130]

With the cessation of hostilities, efforts were made to relieve the civilian profession by rapidly demobilizing Medical Officers. On 23 November 1918 the BMJ reported that although only a small number could be released in the near future it was hoped that they would reduce the pressure on the civil profession in areas where there was a substantial risk of a breakdown in medical care.[131] Such measures, combined with the vigilance which the professional committees had exercised over the Army's recruitment demands since 1917, and the War Office's own efforts to secure economy, helped to prevent a breakdown in civil medical attendance. Even so there were many, like the cases reported in *The Times* on 15 July 1918,[132] who were unable to obtain medical care due to the shortage of doctors. Had the War continued into the winter of 1918–1919, there can be little doubt that the civil and military medical services would have been hard pressed to provide adequate care without a scheme for complete mobilization of the profession.

If mobilization had been introduced when the CMWC first presented its scheme to the Government, the souring of relations between the medical profession and the War Office might well have been avoided. Early in the War the influence of Sir Alfred Keogh and the links between the civil and military branches of the profession helped to ensure that there was an awareness of the need for civil-military co-operation. However, as the drain on medical manpower became more acute, goodwill alone could not prevent growing suspicion that the Army's employment of doctors was extravagant. On the whole, these suspicions appear to have been unfounded, but when in 1917 the War Office called up all doctors of military age, it demonstrated the lack of co-ordination in British manpower policy. The idea that the Army should have first call on the nation's manpower still dominated; mobilization was necessary to ensure a more balanced policy.

The Lloyd George Coalition supposedly embodied a more efficient manpower policy yet it brought little immediate change, shying away from civil compulsion. We can forgive the hesitancy as far as the general population was concerned; industrial conscription would have been difficult to implement and involved delicate political and industrial relations questions. In the case of the medical profession the delay is less easy to understand. The supply of doctors was a question of equal importance to the home and fighting fronts and the present system of distribution was proving inadequate. The profession, having recognized this, had made plain its willingness to operate a scheme of civil compulsion; and in the professional committees the machinery already existed with which it could be implemented. It would appear that only the hesitancy of the new, vigorous Lloyd George Coalition stood in the way of a more rapid improvement in the system of distributing medical manpower.

Notes

1   'Memorandum – the National Organisation of the Medical Profession in Relation to the Needs of HM Forces and of the Civil Population and to the Military Service Acts', BMJ, 1916 (I), Supplement, p. 142.
2   *Ibid.* p. 143.
3   'The Army Council and Medical Recruiting', BMJ, 1916 (I), p. 102.
4   'Under Forty-One and Unenrolled', BMJ, 1916 (I), p. 824.
5   'The Position of Medical Men under the Military Service Acts', BMJ, 1916 (I), p. 798.
6   'The Insurance Commissioners and Medical Recruiting', BMJ, 1916 (I), p. 212.
7   Currie, *The Mustering*, pp. 59; 64.
8   M.H. 10/78, Local Government Board Circular, 1914: circular 73, 21 August 1914.
9   'The War Emergency', BMJ, 1915 (II), p. 409.
10 'A Classification for Medical Recruiting', BMJ, 1915 (II), pp. 867–8.
11 Secretary of the BMA and Medical Secretary of the CMWC.
12 'Conference of Representatives of Local War Committees – Leeds', BMJ, 1916 (I), pp. 49–50.
13 Winter, *The Great War*, p. 162.
14 'The Supply of Medical Officers', letter, Chas. W. Smeeton, BMJ, 1915 (II), p. 421.
15 'The War Emergency Committee', BMJ, 1915 (II), p. 446.
16 'Commissions for Men Between 45 and 55', BMJ, 1916 (I), p. 860.
17 'The War Emergency', BMJ, 1915 (II), pp. 137–8.
18 'Medical War Committees – England and Wales', BMJ, 1916 (I), Supplement, p. 61.
19 'The War Emergency Committee', BMJ, 1915 (II), p. 446.
20 'Two Score and Five to Three Score and Ten', BMJ, 1916 (I), p. 135.
21 'Local Arrangements for the Conduct of Practices', BMJ, 1915 (II), Supplement, p. 130.
22 'Protection of Practices of Medical Men on Active Service', BMJ, 1916 (II), Supplement, p. 29.
23 'State Medical Service: a Reply and Facts about War Doctors – Medical Correspondent', *The Times*, 28 November 1916, p. 7.
24 'Central Medical War Committee – Safeguarding the Practices of Men on Active Service', BMJ, 1916 (II), p. 141.
25 Lieutenant Colonel S.S. Greaves, IWM, Papers, Biography, p. 8.
26 'Patients of Doctors on Service – an Appeal for Loyalty', letter from Medical War Service Emergency Committee, *The Times*, 24 September 1915, p. 5.
27 Minutes of the GMC, LII, 1915, Presidential Address, 102 Session, p. 44.
28 'Safeguarding the Practices of Men on Active Service', letter, Francis Heathesly (No. 3 Medical Board, Manchester), BMJ, 1916 (II), p. 781.

29 *Ibid.*
30 'The Future of the Medical Profession', letter Captain TF, BMJ, 1917 (I), p. 102.
31 'Recruiting for the Naval and Military Medical Services – The Plea for Compulsion', letter, Captain RAMC, BMJ, 1916 (I), Supplement, p. 109.
32 'Mobilisation of the Profession', letter J. Clarke, BMJ, 1917 (I), p. 176.
33 Brian Abel-Smith, *The Hospitals 1800–1948*, Heinemann, 1964, p. 270.
34 'Civil Surgeons in Military Hospitals', letter received from C.S., BMJ, 1918 (I), p. 40.
35 'Territorial and Special Reserve Officers', BMJ, 1917 (I), pp. 657–8.
36 'Medical Officers, Special Reserve and Territorial', letter from A Saturday afternoon (RAMC TF) soldier, BMJ, 1916 (I), p. 899.
37 Second Report of the Committee on Promotion of Officers in the Special Reserve, New Armies, and Territorial Force, together with a Note by the Army Council. Promotion and Pay of Officers of the Royal Army Medical Corps, Special Reserve and Territorial Force. Cmd. 8643, 1917–18, IV, p. 622.
38 Frank Honigsbaum, *The Division in British Medicine*, Kogan Page, 1979, p. 81.
39 NATS 1/842, PRO, Report on Central Surgeries, CMWC – Local Arrangements Subcommittee, Report by Dr Richmond and Dr Pearse on Medical Bureau, 13 July 1918.
40 Dr J.E. Mitchell, LC, Letters, letter 10 August 1917.
41 'Recruiting for the Naval and Military Medical Services – Scottish Medical Service Emergency Committee', BMJ, 1916 (I), Supplement, p. 65.
42 'Mobilisation of the Profession', letter, signed SCARIFIED, BMJ, 1917 (I), p. 245.
43 *Ibid.*
44 *The Times*, 6 November 1918, p. 3.
45 'Army and Civil Co-operation for Medical Economy', letters, BMJ, 1917 (I), pp. 701; 786.
46 Currie, *The Mustering*, p. 193.
47 Deeping, *No Hero This*, p. 412.
48 Dr G. Moore, LC, Letters, letter to father, 12 March 1917; letter to sister, 19 December 1917.
49 M.S. Esler, IWM, Recollections, p. 59.
50 Henry Gervis, *Arms and the Doctor*, Daniel 1920, pp. 16; 38.
51 M. Whiting, LC, Letters, letter to father, 18 August 1916.
52 M.H. 10/78, PRO, Local Government Board Circulars, 1914: circular 73, 21 August 1914, Officers of Local Authorities on Naval or Military Service.
53 'Public Health Appointments During the War', BMJ, 1918 (I), p. 299.
54 'Circular by Local Government Board to Boards of Guardians (Ireland)', BMJ, 1916 (I), p. 2.
55 'The Local Government Board in Ireland', BMJ, 1916 (I), pp. 9; 14. 'Medical Officers of Military Age', BMJ, 1917 (I), pp. 100; 207. 'Dispensary Doctors of Military Age', BMJ, 1917 (I), p. 276. 'Ireland', BMJ, 1917 (I), p. 377. 'Local Employment of Unfit Doctors of Military Age', BMJ, 1917 (I), pp. 408; 526.
56 'The Future of the Medical Profession', letter from TF, BMJ, 1917 (I), p.102.

57 'The Irish Medical Profession and the War', letter from Maurice R.J. Hayes, Hon. Sec. Irish Medical War Committee, BMJ, 1916 (II), p. 888.

58 'The Irish Medical Profession and the War', BMJ, 1917 (I), pp. 891–2.

59 'Mobilisation of the Profession – Manchester Report on the Need for Compulsion', BMJ, 1917 (I), Supplement, p. 9.

60 'Voluntary Mobilisation of the Profession', BMJ, 1916 (II), p. 909.

61 'Recruiting for the Naval and Military Medical Services – The Plea for Compulsion', letter from William Thorneley, BMJ, 1916 (I), Supplement, p. 109.

62 'Mobilisation of the Profession', letter from Ferdinand Rees, BMJ, 1916 (II), p. 917.

63 'State Medical Service: a Reply and Facts about War Doctors', The Times, 28 November 1916, p. 7; 'A Civil Medical Corps – How to Avoid Waste of Doctors', The Times, 9 February 1917, p. 3.

64 H.J.B. Fry, LC, Diary, 22 July 1917; 20 August 1917.

65 Honigsbaum, The Division in Medicine, p. 82.

66 Ibid.; see Chapter 8, Doctors Resist Salary, pp. 79–89.

67 Little, History of BMA, p. 246.

68 For a detailed discussion of British manpower policy during the War see Keith Grieves, The Politics of Manpower, Manchester, Manchester University Press, 1988.

69 'Army and Civil Medical Economies', BMJ, 1917 (I), pp. 621–2; 'Military Hospital Economies', BMJ, 1917 (I), p. 813; Abel-Smith, 'The Hospitals', p. 264.

70 'American Doctors for England – BMA Criticism of War Office Action', The Times, 14 September 1917, p. 3.; 'American Doctors for English Hospitals – A War Office Explanation', The Times, 17 September 1917, p. 5; 'Substitution in Hospitals – Medical View of the New War Office Policy', The Times, 18 September, 1917, p. 3; 'The American Doctors – First Arrivals Being Drafted to British Hospitals', The Times, 20 September 1917, p. 3; 'Civilian Doctors Protest – Lord Derby on the Three Days Notice', The Times, 19 October 1917, p. 3.

71 Abel-Smith, The Hospitals, p. 270.

72 NATS 1/837, PRO, Reports on Voluntary Substitution in the Medical Profession. Letter from F.G. Hallett (Secretary of the Committee of Referenced) to the Ministry of National Service, 8 March 1918.

73 'The Supply of Doctors', The Times, 7 January 1916, p. 9.

74 Sir Wilmot Herringham, Physician in France, Edward Arnold, 1919, pp. 96–7.

75 'The Army Medical Service – by a Medical Officer in Charge of an Infantry Battalion', BMJ, 1916 (II), p. 528.

76 Ibid.

77 'Mobilisation of the Profession', letter from MCI, BMJ, 1917 (I), p. 32.

78 J.E. Mitchell, LC, letter, 7 August 1917.

79 'Mobilisation of the Profession', letter from Regimental MO, BMJ, 1917 (I), p. 63.

80 Herringham, Physician in France, p. 97.

81 'Some Impressions of a Civilian at the Western Front', BMJ, 1916 (II), p. 502.

82 'Question of More Economical Use of Medical Men in Military Service', BMJ, 1916 (I), p. 26.

83 C.K. McKerrow, LC, letter, 29 September 1915, p. 15.
84 WO 293/2, PRO, War Office Instructions, January–June 1915: instruction 250, 29 January 1915, RAMC Officers for the E.F. and arrangements for the performance of Medical Duties at home.
85 WO 293/3, PRO, War Office Instructions, July–December 1915: instruction 336, 27 August 1915, Medical men of military age not to be employed in War Hospitals.
86 WO 95/44, PRO, DGMS Diary, 1915, 21 January 1915.
87 Captain W.J.F.Mayne, IWM, Diary, 1918, 30 November 1918.
88 *Hansard*, Parliamentary Debates, Lords, Fifth Series, XXIV, 1917, col. 844.
89 WO 95/4772, PRO, DMS Salonika Army, Diary, September–December 1916, 30 November 1916. WO 95/4773, PRO, DMS, Salonika Army, Diary, 1917, 6 January 1917; 20 January 1917; 27 January 1917; 6 April 1917; 19 April 1917.
90 WO 95/4979, PRO, DMS, Mesopotamia, Diary, January–June 1917, 16 February 1917.
91 WO 95/4976, PRO, DMS, Mesopotamia, Diary, January–June 1917, 4 February 1917.
92 WO 95/4976, PRO, DMS, Mesopotamia, Diary, January–June 1917, 26 February 1917.
93 'The Medical Service of the Army', BMJ, 1917 (I), pp. 399–400.
94 'War Office Call on all Medical Men Under 41', BMJ, 1917 (I), Supplement, p. 67.
95 'Memorandum by the Central Medical War Committee', BMJ, 1917 (I), p. 551.
96 'The Association and the War', BMJ, 1917 (II), Supplement, p. 24.
97 Field Marshal Sir William Robertson, CIGS 1915–1918. See *Army and Civil Co-operation for Medical Economy*, BMJ, 1917 (I), p. 652.
98 'Medical Officers for the Army: Exhaustion of the Supply', BMJ, 1917 (II), Supplement, p. 35.
99 Commission on Medical Establishments in France.
100 'Report of Commission on Medical Establishments in France', WIHM., RAMC 1165, pp. 5–6.
101 *Ibid.* pp. 117–23.
102 'Economy in Military Medical Service', BMJ, 1918 (II), Supplement, p. 19.
103 W.G. MacPherson, *Official History of the War – Medical Services, Surgery of the War*, I, HMSO, 1922, p. 178.
104 WO 95/47, PRO, DGMS Diary, 1918. Letter from Field Marshal, C-in-C., State at the War Office, 18 May 1918.
105 NATS 1/745, PRO, Synopsis of Memorandum on the Estimated Requirements of HM's Forces in Respect of Medical Officers during 1918, p. 3.
106 NATS 1/833, PRO, Medical Officers For Army, Navy and Air Services, letter from National Health Insurance Commissioners to the Ministry of National Service, containing a document on the Question of Further Withdrawal of Doctors from Civil Medical Practice for Recruitment of AMS, pp. 2–4.
107 Grieves, *Politics of Manpower*, pp. 152; 205. Little, *History of BMA*, p. 248.
108 'Medical Practitioners under the Military Service Act', BMJ, 1918 (I), p. 702.
109 WO 95/45, PRO, DGMS Diary, 1917, 16 October 1917.

110 **WO 95/903**, PRO, DDMS, 13 Corps, Diary, January–December 1917, 11 November 1917; 12 November 1917; 14 November 1917.

111 **WO 95/903**, PRO, DDMS, 13 Corps, Diary, January–December 1917, 15 October 1917.

112 **WO 95/903**, PRO, DDMS, 13 Corps, Diary, January–December 1917, 13 September 1917.

113 **WO 95/45**, PRO, DGMS Diary, 1916, 14 November 1916.

114 **Colonel T.B. Beach**, ADMS in Alexandria, WIHM., RAMC 248, Diary, 5 May 1917; 9 May 1917; 10 May 1917; 11 May 1917; 23 May 1917.

115 **WO 95/4975**, PRO, DMS Mesopotamia, Diary, September 1915–December 1916, 15 November 1916: circular letter on shortage of Medical Officers.

116 **NATS 1/723**, PRO, Conference at Office of DGMS 20 November 1917, Précis of: Difficulties in the Provision of Officers for the Work of AMS.

117 **NATS 1/821**, PRO, Medical Men – Reorganisation of Supply, (IB) Suggested alteration in draft of letter from DGMS December 1917.

118 **MacPherson**, *General History*, I, p. 65.

119 **NATS 1/833**, PRO, Medical Officers for Army, Navy and Air Services, letter DGMS Goodwin to Minister of National Service, 22 March 1918.

120 **WO 95/4198**, PRO, DMS Italy, Diary, 25 March 1918.

121 **NATS 1/833**, PRO, Medical Officers for Army, Navy and Air Services; Draft (approved) of letter to be sent by Central Professional Committees to selected practitioners who have already served, 27 March 1918.

122 **Winter**, *The Great War*, p. 170.

123 Minutes of the GMC, LV, 1918, President's Address, 107 session, 28 May 1918, p. 7.

124 *Ibid.*

125 **Winter**, *The Great War*, p. 172. **Little**, *History of BMA*, p. 250.

126 **WO 95/4977**, PRO, DMS Mesopotamia, Diary, July–December 1918, 20 October 1918; 25 November 1918.

127 **Maurice Jacobs**, *Reflections of a General Practitioner*, Johnson, 1965, pp. 81–2.

128 **NATS 1/797**, PRO, Influenza Epidemic – Instructions to Regions to Liberate Medical Practitioners from Recruiting Boards to Assist Civilian Work where Necessary. Letter to Ministry of National Service from Commissioner of Medical Services, North Western Region, 9 November 1918. Letter from Chief Commissioner of Medical Services, Ministry of National Service, to the Town Clerk of Leicester.

129 **NATS 1/179**, PRO, Interdepartmental Agreement Re Supply of Medical Men for Government Service. Medical Services Interdepartmental Committee, minutes of meeting, 6 November 1918.

130 **NATS 1/843**, PRO, letters to be sent to Medical Officers dismissed HM Service by order of Court Martial, draft, 28 August 1918. Letter from Chief Commissioner of Medical Services to Secretary of SMSEC, re alterations to the draft, 29 August 1918.

131 'Medical Demobilisation', BMJ, 1918 (II), Supplement, p. 77.

132 'The Dearth of Doctors', *The Times*, 15 July 1918, p. 8.

Chapter 4

Medical Students and Military Service

To ensure that adequate levels of civil and military health care were maintained it was essential that action be taken to protect the future supply of doctors. The extent to which the Government's recruitment policy responded to this need will now be examined.

There was a danger that unregulated voluntary enlistment would severely deplete the ranks of medical students, thus raising the prospect of a serious shortage of qualified practitioners. To guard against this medical students close to qualification were urged not to enlist, but to complete their studies. In December 1914 Keogh stated 'that the senior student is best fulfilling his duty to the country by getting his degree, and then joining the Army. The need for young qualified men will become great, and I should regret that the supply should be diminished.'[1] The President of the GMC issued a similar statement.[2]

It is evident that these appeals did have some effect; there were students who, impressed with the need to avoid a shortage, subordinated their desire to join the Army to the necessity of completing their courses.[3] The experience of Dr Reg Husbands suggests that from the beginning of the War recruiting officers had also been alerted to the importance of retaining medical students. Husbands was well into his final year when in August 1914 he tried to enlist as a despatch rider. At the recruiting office he was told that he would 'be more use to [the Army] as a doctor than a despatch rider' and advised to return to his studies.[4]

However, all recruiting officers could not be relied upon to be so vigilant and many medical students, eager to serve, were successful in proceeding to the front. A medical student at Manchester University recalled that in 1914 the most able male student 'went straight off, and he was killed, and everybody thought that was awful. He was such a brilliant student. And one or two others insisted on going, but the rest of them were all stopped and told they must qualify . . . as doctors were in such shortage.'[5] By January 1915 there were said to be 1,000 fewer students attending the various medical schools than at the same time the previous year. The reduction included 500 fourth and fifth years.[6] It was feared that if the leakage of medical students was not plugged, a 25 per cent reduction could be expected in the number of doctors annually added to the Medical Register.[7]

The War Office was not unaware of the problem. Already, in November 1914, it had circulated a letter that said, 'it has been decided that any students who have joined the medical units of the Territorial Forces and wish to immediately resume their studies, shall be released from service'.[8] The War Office advised medical students that it was their duty to return home and qualify as soon as possible.[9] This was followed in 1915 by a decision to recall medical students acting as dressers in the military hospitals.[10] Arrangements were also made for the release of medical students in their fourth and fifth years who had enlisted with combatant units,[11] although this did not apply to those holding commissions.[12] Under these arrangements, F.J. Escritt, who had enlisted with the Artists Rifles, reluctantly returned to complete his medical training at Guy's Hospital.[13]

Sir Donald MacAlister praised these efforts to safeguard the immediate supply of doctors. Instead of the expected decrease in the number of doctors added to the Register in 1915, the recall of senior students, and the establishment of reciprocity with Belgium and the Dominions, took the number of registrations to 1,526; 354 above the average for the previous five years.[14]

The sight of young men carrying on their pre-war studies led to accusations that medical students were shirkers. The BMJ, referring to accusations of this type, which had appeared in the Edinburgh press, pointed out 'that almost every one of the ninety-nine men, or thereabouts, who are up for their final professional examination in [Edinburgh] University is going into the service in one way or another'.[15] To protect returning students from accusations of shirking, they were allowed to wear uniform. At Guy's Hospital, however, complaints from officer casualties about the complicated treatment which students were required to carry out prompted the Dean to suggest that students discard their uniforms. As a result many of the students suffered the 'embarrassing and demoralising' experience of being presented with white feathers. Some felt so badly about the situation that they attempted, unsuccessfully, to re-enlist.[16]

It had been suggested that, rather than return to qualify, students who had passed their second MB examination should be granted the rank of sub lieutenant and act as medical assistants. The War Office rejected the idea, believing that fully qualified doctors would be of more value to the Army and that in the meantime the students would be able to assist in the civil hospitals.[17] It was suggested that medical students who were required to spend their final year in clinical work could meet this stipulation by offering themselves as house physicians and house surgeons, for which there was a desperate need.[18] And in a further effort to relieve the strain on the civil hospitals, it was decided that newly qualified doctors would not be called up until they had completed a three-month hospital appointment.[19]

Rendering assistance in the civil hospitals was not the only way that medical students could obtain the necessary level of clinical experience; authorization had been given for them to include assistance to the armed services as part of their clinical training:

> time spent as Assistant on active service in one of His Majesty's Ships or in a Naval or Military Hospital utilised by the Naval and Military authorities not exceeding six months [should] be allowed to count for the equivalent period of Medical and Surgical Hospital Practice and for three months each of the required period of Medical Clinical Clerkship and Surgical Dresserships, provided that a satisfactory certificate is produced from the Principal Medical Officer under whom the Assistant serves.[20]

Of the options open to medical students, F.K. Escritt felt that work on Hospital Ships offered the best opportunities: 'Plenty of medical work, time for study and good pay.'[21] He was attached to HMHS *Letitia*, bound for Gallipoli. On the way out there was no work to be done so the students studied and received instruction from the surgeons and physicians on board. Once at Gallipoli their work consisted mainly of dressing the wounded patients, although occasionally they were able to assist in the operating theatre.[22]

One student who had his studies almost completely halted by the War was Gordon Flint. He had gone to Germany on holiday in 1914, was caught up in the outbreak of hostilities and consequently found himself in prison. However, whilst a prisoner he was allowed to take (and pass) his anatomy examination under the supervision of a well-disposed German doctor.[23] Quite why Flint received this privilege is not explained but it would seem likely that his experience was uncommon. There is no mention of any other British students sitting the examination with him and no similar cases have come to light.

The Army's refusal to grant commissions to those not fully qualified was in tune with the profession's determination that standards be maintained. Universities and medical schools were keen to hasten the qualification of their students by modifying their regulations and shortening the academic year. The GMC was willing to authorize such changes as long as the requirements of the minimum curriculum were substantially fulfilled, and that the public could be guaranteed 'the present standard of knowledge and skill'.[24]

Standards satisfactory to the GMC were maintained, but it was a task made difficult by the depletion of teaching staffs. A student at Manchester University, up for the second MB, describes the difficulties that arose in the first months of the War:

> Our professor was Elliot Smith and he and nearly all the scientists had gone to Sydney for the British Association, including Rutherford. They couldn't get back because the Emden was about . . . they wouldn't allow them back because they were such valuable people. And so we had no professor. We had Mr Stopford, then only an anatomy demonstrator. He did everything he could for us and a senior student who wasn't even qualified . . . coached us what he could in physiology. That was the only coaching we had until our second MB exam at Christmas.[25]

With the standard of medical qualifications guaranteed, the profession increasingly focussed its attention upon the need to ensure that the number of students taking medical qualifications remained sufficiently high to prevent a shortage of doctors. Distinguished medical voices were expressing anxiety about the growing need for medical men[26] and confusion began to surround the duty of junior medical students. Replying to an inquiry in the House of Commons, the Under Secretary of State for War seemed to suggest that first- and second-year students should not be encouraged to enlist in the Army:

> Any expression . . . of official opinion which might seem to place on them the obligation of taking up immediate military duty would hardly be in the interests of the Army or of the Community as a whole.[27]

But just over a month later, the Secretary of State contradicted this statement; he informed Professor Halliburton of King's College that the War Office was unwilling to suggest that junior students be discouraged from taking combatant commissions.[28] The apparent prevarication on the part of the War Office could not be allowed to continue; a clear decision was needed as to whether the Army's need for combatant personnel or the nation's need for doctors should be the principal factor governing the duty of junior medical students.

Given that recruitment of medical students would only provide a few hundred recruits to the combatant ranks, it was argued that the exemption of students from military service would have little effect on the Army, whereas their withdrawal from medical study would have serious implications for medical manpower. Attention was drawn to the disruption caused by the unrestricted enlistment of industrial workers in the opening months of the War, and the fact that measures had since been taken to safeguard the levels of industrial and agricultural labour. The importance to both the military and civil services of a steady supply of qualified medical practitioners led to calls for similar or greater restrictions to be placed upon the medical profession.[29]

The War Office, which understandably was more concerned with the downturn in recruiting than it was with the supply of doctors, was not prepared to sanction a complete exemption for the medical profession. It made plain that winning the War would have to take precedence over concerns for post-war levels of medical manpower.[30] In October 1915 the CMWC was informed that whilst fourth- and fifth-year students should continue with their studies, the action of junior students was 'entirely a matter for their own personal consideration'.[31] On this basis Dr R.A. Duff, Director of Studies in Glasgow University, saw it as the duty of all junior medical students to join up as combatants:

with the exception of the fourth and fifth year medical students, no adequate reason seems to me to exist for the rest of our students pursuing their normal life while their comrades who sat on the same benches with them are giving up not only their careers, but health and limb and life, to make this possible.[32]

With the Derby scheme of attestation, the position of medical students was clarified further. Derby stated that it was the duty of all medical students, other than those in their fourth or fifth years, to enlist with the forces.[33] However, those within the profession who were alarmed by the depletion of student numbers pressed him to reconsider his position. As a result the War Office agreed to extend the scope of exemptions:

Students who at or before the close of the present winter session will be qualified for entry to one of the examinations for the third year students in medicine, and duly enter for the examination for which they are studying, will not be attested until after its conclusion; and if they are successful will be included in the class of fourth year men under Lord Derby's scheme.[34]

At Leeds University the Derby Scheme reflected the policy that was already in operation. At the outset of the War, it was decided that the 'Kitchener dictum' was 'the safest guide . . . and therefore students who had passed the second professional were deliberately discouraged from taking up combatant service and urged to qualify at the earliest possible moment'. Students in the first and second years were advised to obtain combatant commissions.[35]

Of course, those who felt that a complete exemption of medical students was necessary remained dissatisfied. But although uncertainty remained about the more distant future, the provisions of the Derby scheme, combined with the recall of fourth- and fifth-year students, were, for the time being, sufficient to reassure the GMC about the immediate supply of practitioners.[36]

The failure of the Derby scheme and the introduction of compulsory military service little altered the position of medical students. Those in their third, fourth and fifth years of study were required to attest, or else become liable to military service; if attested, fourth- and fifth-year students were not called up, nor were those third years who passed their next set of examinations. First, second and third years (who had failed their examinations) were liable for general service, but if unfit were allowed to continue their studies.

Students allowed to continue their studies were not, however, exempt from military training. Exempted medical students were as much a safeguard against wartime depletion of Army Medical Officers as they were a precaution against shortages in the post-war profession. It was felt desirable that instruction be given to medical students in drill, ambulance drill, military sanitation and the organization of the RAMC. Under the Derby scheme, medical students in their fourth and fifth years were therefore impressed with their obligation to join medical units of the OTC; and with the passing of compulsory service, membership of the OTC became incumbent upon all students proceeding with their courses.[37] The importance of preparing students for the duties of a military Medical Officer was recognized in the United States where, even before her declaration of war, steps were taken to introduce military training into the medical schools.[38]

In addition to membership of the OTC, it was also recommended that senior medical students be given the opportunity to work as dressers in military hospitals. The intention was to accustom them to the injuries and ailments commonly confronted at the front and in the military hospitals, and to educate them as regards the proper lines of treatment.[39]

By autumn 1917 there was growing concern about the reduction in the number of medical students due to qualify. The GMC's Committee on Medical Students and Schools had estimated, in 1916, that an annual addition of 1,100 new practitioners to the Register was required to meet the military and civil needs of the country;[40] yet the expected number of newly qualified male practitioners was only around 900 per year in 1917 and 1918, falling to less than 520 in 1919. The few hundred women students expected to qualify during this period were largely discounted from the equation because 'considered as medical practitioners, members of the two sexes are not yet generally interchangeable'.[41]

This argument underplayed the potential contribution of female practitioners. The opportunities open to women certainly remained limited, but the prejudices against their employment had begun to crack under the pressure of war. If the War had continued into 1919 and beyond it is probable that necessity would have forced a further widening of career opportunities for women doctors. Moreover, the standard and range of medical work being undertaken by female practitioners in both the civilian and medical spheres provided powerful evidence contrary to the view that they were not the equal of their male colleagues. The work of the independent women's medical units on various fronts indicated that women were eminently capable of performing military hospital duties, and could have been employed more widely to relieve male doctors for service with front-line units. As will be seen in the following chapter, it was persistent prejudice that prevented more effective utilization of women doctors. There is no suggestion that newly qualified female practitioners would have been sufficient in themselves to meet the demands of the war emergency. Given the continuing drain upon the profession and the uncertain duration of the conflict, there was every need to safeguard the future supply of male practitioners. But the ready dismissal of the potential contribution of female medical students demonstrated the extent to which the work of women doctors, in over three years of war, had failed to overcome deep-seated prejudice.

The shortsighted attitude towards the employment of women doctors ensured that attention continued to focus upon the need to ensure that sufficient numbers of male students were qualifying. A memorandum issued by the Committee of Reference in August 1917 and later endorsed by the GMC urged the necessity of taking the following steps:

97

a) That medical students now serving in the Army, whether as officers or privates, who have already passed the examination in anatomy and physiology for a medical qualification, should be demobilised and returned to their medical schools to complete their studies.

b) Medical students now serving in the Army, whether as officers or privates, who have not passed the examination in anatomy and physiology, should be seconded to their medical schools for a reasonable period, and if successful they should be demobilised to complete their studies.[42]

There were also calls in the medical press for an end to the calling up of bona fide medical students who had completed their first year; and for the return to study of all medical students who had served six months with the Navy as surgeon probationers.[43] Indeed, with regard to the latter point, there were those who felt that the practice of sending students to serve with the Navy was harmful and should be abolished: 'In the Navy . . . they learn very little, have as a matter of fact done very little, and in many instances have only acquired habits of idleness and other things even worse.'[44] By way of contrast, the six months clinical experience that students were allowed to undertake with the Army was said to allow them useful, supervised occupation. But whilst recognizing that naval service did not offer the surgical experience available in the military hospitals, such scathing criticism was unwarranted; the work of surgeon probationers as dressers was generally felt to be important.[45] Moreover, the Admiralty, recognizing the need to minimize the disruption of medical study, had already committed itself to a system of short service for surgeon probationers.[46]

In addition to safeguarding the future supply of doctors, it was hoped that the reassessment of medical students' military service would remove the injustice currently being suffered by those first, second and third years who had enlisted prior to the Military Service Acts. For whilst their fellow students who had not enlisted were allowed, under the terms of the Acts, to complete their studies, those who had volunteered would have to wait until the end of the War. It was now argued that the nation's need for medical practitioners should be met by rewarding the patriotism of these students, and allowing them to return to their studies. The memorandum by the Committee of Reference recommended such a course;[47] and numerous letters appeared in the correspondence pages of the BMJ demanding justice for these students. The following letter is typical of many that appeared in 1917:

My only son . . . accepted a commission in 1914 when in his second year. He has now been on foreign service for over two years, and . . . looks like serving . . . two more years. By that time he will be twenty-four years of age and will still have four more years before he can qualify, not to speak of the year or two of hospital work before he will be fit to succeed me. Meanwhile, those students in his year who, quite as fit as he, but endowed with less patriotic feelings and more concern for their own individual welfare, resisted their country's call, are now enjoying complete immunity from service, together with good hospital appointments as unqualified house-surgeons (at £90 a year) and are within a year of being able to take up practice. One wonders whether patriotism really pays. Still I do not envy them or wish my son had emulated them.[48]

By the end of 1917 growing concern about the reduction in the number of students in the third year (and the consequences this would have on the number qualifying in 1919) forced the War Office to take action. It accepted the recommendations outlined in the Committee of Reference's memorandum: under ACI 1751, 1917, all third-year students were to be allowed to return to their studies; and under the terms of this instruction, students who had completed two years of medical study, and who passed the examination in anatomy and physiology within six months of resuming their studies were to be classed as third years.[49] In 1918 the War Office went further, issuing ACI 153, which enabled all students who had been in attendance at a recognized medical school for six months prior to their enlistment, and had passed the whole of the first professional examination, to return to their studies.[50]

Alongside the War Office's policy of recalling increasing numbers of medical students to their studies, the Ministry of National Service took action to protect medical students already in civil life from being called up for military service. NSI 35 (March 1918) exempted from military service all medical students who, on 5 March 1918, were full time at a recognized medical school and had at that date passed their professional examinations in chemistry, physics and biology (or botany or zoology) for a medical degree or licence. The exemption, of course, was dependent upon the student continuing his medical studies, whilst other conditions were also attached: the student would be called up if he failed to pass his professional examination in anatomy and physiology within thirty-six months of beginning his professional studies; the student was required to enrol in an OTC, and to abide by the conditions of service; unsatisfactory behaviour, including the unnecessary delay of qualification, was to be reported to the DGNATS; and any student failing to enrol as a surgeon probationer within twenty-one days of being requested to

99

do so, by the Ministry of National Service, would forfeit his exemption.

Also protected by this scheme were any students who, on the date of its publication, were pursuing full-time medical studies and were able to provide their local Assistant Director of Recruiting with a certificate from the Dean of their school, to the effect that he should be capable of passing his professional examination by 31 July next. Those who succeeded were to be allowed to continue their studies, subject to the above conditions; unsuccessful candidates would be taken for military service. Finally, any medical student placed in the fitness categories B2, B3, C2, or C3, or in grade 3, who was, or became, engaged in full-time medical study received protection from military service, conditional upon his passing his first professional examination within a year of commencing study, and upon his fulfilment of all the aforementioned requirements.[51]

Sir A. Geddes was confident that these arrangements were sufficient to safeguard the future supply of male doctors. In July 1918 he assured the House of Commons that there were no longer any grounds for anxiety, pointing out that in 1917 there were 1,378 freshly registered medical students as opposed to 1,366 in 1914.[52]

However, not everyone was content with the situation as it emerged under ACI 153 and NSI 35, as the following extract demonstrates:

> The arrangement . . . penalises those first year medical students who volun-
> tarily rushed to arms at the call of their country. While, as may be judged
> from the matriculation lists our medical schools are to be used as funk-
> holes under the plea that the dearth of doctors makes the exemption
> necessary, first year students of 1915 and 1916 who did not wait to
> complete the whole of their first professional examination, but joined the
> colours as soon as they were 19, these after suffering two or three years of
> the hardships and hazards of war are to be passed over for younger lads
> who have done nothing for their country and cannot qualify any earlier.[53]

One can easily sympathize with the injustice felt by students in this position. However, it is not difficult to understand that the War Office, confident that the future supply of doctors had been secured, was reluctant to release men who were trained and experienced soldiers; especially when they would be unable to qualify much sooner than those about to embark on their studies.[54] Given that only a few hundred men were involved, it might appear that the War Office was being unnecessarily harsh. But with the growing manpower crisis by March 1918, and the imminent German offensive, one cannot expect individual cases of injustice to have weighed heavily in the decision. Recognizing the need to ensure a continuous supply of doctors to the military and to the civil population, the War Office had taken the necessary steps to release those medical students who had progressed furthest in their studies. With victory as its principal aim, however, the War Office could not afford to start discharging trained men whose release would bring no appreciable gain to either the civil or military war effort; the students concerned fell into this category. Of course their release would have helped secure the long-term supply of doctors, but this was just as easily done under the terms of NSI 35, and without further depriving the Army of experienced soldiers.

The other criticism contained in the above, that the protection of medical students from military service was turning the medical schools into funkholes, was not an isolated one; nor was it simply the cry of a malcontent. In December 1917 the Academic Sub Dean of Leeds University informed the Ministry of National Service that he felt any further protection for medical students was unnecessary. He believed that the effects of the shortage of second- and third-year medical students had been exaggerated; that the population had become accustomed to medical attendance only in emergency; and that the shortage of medical students would merely compensate for the overcrowding likely to occur in the profession on the return of thousands of doctors from the War.[55] A similar line was taken by the Dean of University College Hospital Medical School (University of London) who argued that, when considering the future supply of doctors, the pre-war rate of wastage should be ignored, since the ratio of doctors to population had been excessive.[56] Moreover, not only were further exemptions for medical students considered unnecessary, it was felt that they would encourage unscrupulous individuals to see in medical study a means of avoiding their duty to the nation. In his letter to the Ministry of National Service, the Academic Sub Dean at Leeds expressed the belief that the profession would become a haven for shirkers:

It is obvious that any further relief from service for the medical students would bring in a number of men who had previously no intentions of joining the profession. I have had numerous interviews with parents who were prepared to make every effort to qualify their sons for matriculation to enter the Medical School, and, in some cases, have gone so far as to suggest advantages to myself if I could stretch regulations to admit them with insufficient certificates.[57]

Undoubtedly, there were those who would attempt to abuse the regulations. But from the outset if is clear that the authorities were aware of the need to ensure that medical students were genuine and committed, and not merely taking advantage of the exemption. In May 1917, ACI 842 pointed out that the postponement of fourth- and fifth-year students' military service was to be subject to review every six months; any student deemed to be delaying his qualification unnecessarily was liable to be called up.[58] And as we have seen, the extension of the exemption to second- and third-year students was subject to the fulfilment of various conditions, whilst the provisions of NSI 35 (1918) only applied to students who had already embarked on their studies by the date of the instruction,[59] thus guarding against the influx of large numbers of students into the profession looking to evade conscription.

The argument that there was no need to exempt medical students because pre-war over-supply would compensate for any anticipated downturn in the number of newly qualified practitioners cannot be examined without detailed local studies of the distribution of doctors. The fact that there was no apparent shortage in the post-war years might be taken as evidence that there had been no need for alarm over the future supply of doctors; but it could just as easily have been due to the importance which, from the end of 1915, the Government attached to the maintenance of a steady supply of new practitioners. Certainly the post-war glut of doctors, predicted by many critics, did not materialize.

Moreover, within the context of increasingly total war, it would surely have been folly to disregard the possible shortage of doctors. The projected reduction in the number of practitioners being added to the Register in 1919 could have been damaging to Britain's morale and her war effort had the conflict continued for another year, especially given the great burden which the influenza epidemic placed upon an increasingly short-handed civil medical profession. The exemption of medical students not only protected the future supply of doctors for the civil and military services but also helped to relieve the strain on the profession's manpower. Returning students gave assistance in the hospitals by filling residents' posts. During the influenza epidemic they were able to offer their services to a tired and overworked civil profession, itself thinned by the disease.[60]

The arrangements regarding the release of medical students from military service can be criticized for relying on the voluntary ethic. A medical student, like A.W. Brown who was invalided out of the Army in 1915, should have been required to return to his medical studies. Instead, on completion of his convalescence, he first got a job training men to fight, and then a desk job with the Northern Command Staff; it was only boredom which persuaded him to return to his studies.[61] The reliance on voluntarism was severely criticized by another student writing in April 1917:

> I will not be a victim of the damned voluntary system again. If I am given my choice I shall stay in the Army, but if I am ordered to continue my studies I am willing to do so. I will not let the authorities shift their responsibilities onto my shoulders. They alone are capable of judging the situation and it ought not to be left to one's personal wishes.[62]

This student had lost his enthusiasm for the profession and only decided to return to his studies because of boredom with Army life. His application for release was approved in November 1917.

The problem with a system that relied on the students themselves applying for release from the colours was that it was open to confusion; there was evidence to suggest that Officers Commanding were not informing men of the nature of the instructions and that some officers were deliberately obstructing the return of medical students. The Ministry of National Service appealed to the War Office to make the position clearer,[63] and urged medical schools to inform those of their students affected by the new provisions that their return to study was in the national interest.[64]

Despite these defects the War Office deserves credit for recognizing the need to take some measures to safeguard the future supply of doctors, and for its co-operation with the Ministry of National Service. The increase in the number of male medical students from 4,947 in January 1917 to 5,380 in May 1918 is evidence of their success.[65] On the ending of the War, the return of students to their studies was rapid, the universities and medical schools being filled to capacity. In November 1919 the President of the GMC announced that there was 'no doubt that in a few years the professional ranks will be more than replenished'.[66]

Notes

1   'Senior Students and the War', BMJ, 1914 (II), p. 1087.
2   Minutes of the GMC, LI, 1914, President's Address 100 Session, 24 November 1914, p. 68.
3   Captain L. Gameson, IWM, Typescript memoirs, p. iii. Dr N. Bruce, LC., Tape recording 602.
4   Dr R. Husbands, LC., Tape recordings 696 & 697.
5   Dr R. Verney, LC., Tape recordings 476 & 480.
6   'Civil Medical Practice and the War', BMJ, 1915 (I), p. 24.
7   'Civil Practitioners and War Needs', BMJ, 1915 (I), pp. 29–30.
8   'Senior Students and the War', BMJ, 1914 (II) p. 1044.

9 'Dearth of Doctors', *The Times*, 7 January 1915, p. 7.

10 **Major F. Gamm**, LC., Tape recording 654.

11 'Medical Organisation for War Emergencies', BMJ, 1915 (I), p. 300.

12 *Hansard*, Parliamentary Debates, Commons, Fifth Series, LXXII, 1915, col. 246.

13 **Major General F.K. Escritt**, LC., Hand-written recollections, p. 1. Tape recording 554.

14 Minutes of the GMC, LIII, 1916, p. 57.

15 'Medical Students and the War', BMJ, 1915 (I), p. 977.

16 **F.K. Escritt**, LC., Recollections, p. 1. Tape recording 554.

17 *Hansard*, Parliamentary Debates, Commons, Fifth Series, LXXII, 1915, col. 1793.

18 'Students in their Final Year', BMJ, (I), p. 684. **Dr R. Verney**, LC., Tape recordings 476 & 480.

19 'The Civilian Sick – Difficulties of the Hospitals', *The Times*, 28 December 1915, p. 5. **Gameson**, *IWM*, Memoirs, p. iii. **Dr G.H. Rossdale**, LC., Recollections.

20 'Students in their Final Year', BMJ, 1915 (I), p. 684.

21 **F.K. Escritt**, LC., Recollections, p. 1. Tape recording 554.

22 **F.K. Escritt**, LC., Recollections, p. 2. Tape recording 554.

23 **Dr C. Seward**, LC., letter to Dr Peter Liddle (Keeper of the Liddle Collection), 6 April 1981, Research File.

24 Minutes of the GMC, LI, 1914, p. 68. 'Medical Students and the War', *Edinburgh Medical Journal* (EMJ), XIII, 1914 p. 363.

25 **R. Verney**, LC., Tape recording 476 & 480.

26 'The Dearth of Medical Students – A University Appeal', *The Times*, 4 December 1915, p. 5.

27 *Hansard*, Parliamentary Debates Commons, Fifth Series, 1915, LXXII, col. 931.

28 'Medical Students', letter from Philip Magnus, *The Times*, 27 August 1915, p. 7.

29 'Medical Students and Combatant Commissions', BMJ, 1915 (II), p. 388. 'Medical Students and Combatant Commissions', BMJ, 1915 (II), p. 421. 'Medical Students', letter from Philip Magnus, *The Times*, 27 August 1915, p. 7. 'The Supply of Doctors', letter from J. Herbert Parson (Dean of University College Hospital Medical School), *The Times*, 9 November 1915, p. 9.

30 *Hansard*, Parliamentary Debates, Commons, Fifth Series, LXXV, 1915, col. 445.

31 'Medical Students and the War', BMJ, 1915 (II), p. 648.

32 *Ibid.*

33 'Medical Students and Recruiting', BMJ, 1915 (II), p. 686. 'The Supply of Doctors', letter from J. Herbert Parsons *The Times*, 9 November 1915, p. 9.

34 'Lord Derby's Scheme and Medical Recruiting', BMJ, 1915 (II), p. 785.

35 **NATS 1/812**, PRO, Medical Students, letter from the Academic Sub Dean (University of Leeds) to the Ministry of National Service, 11 December 1917.

36 'Medical Registrations and Medical Students in 1915', BMJ, 1916 (I), p. 134. Minutes of the GMC, LIII, 1916, p. 5.

37 WO 293/3, PRO, War Office Instructions, July–December 1915: instruction 103, Military Training for Medical Students, 10 December 1915. 'Recruiting for the Naval and Military Medical Services – Medical Students and Military Training', BMJ, 1916 (I), Supplement, p. 5. *Hansard*, Parliamentary Debates, Commons, Fifth Series, LXXXVIII, 1916, col. 671.

38 'Medicine in the Army', BMJ, 1917 (I), p. 270.

39 WO 293/2, PRO, War Office Instructions, January–June 1915: instruction 3, Attendance of Medical Students at Military Hospitals, 1 April 1915.

40 NATS 1/814, PRO, Shortage Of Medical Students, GMC Committee on Medical Students And Schools, observations submitted to the Army Council.

41 'The Shortage of Medical Students', BMJ, 1917 (II), p. 428.

42 NATS 1/711, PRO, Medical Students – Shortage of, Memorandum on the Shortage of Medical Students (Adopted by the Committee of Reference), 30 August 1917. NATS 1/814, PRO, Shortage of Medical Students, GMC Committee on Medical Students and Schools, observations submitted to the Army Council.

43 'The Shortage of Medical Students', BMJ, 1917 (II), p. 429.

44 NATS 1/812, PRO, Medical Students, letter from the Dean of University College Hospital Medical School (University of London) to the Ministry of National Service, 11 December 1917.

45 'Naval Medicine in the Great War', BMJ, 1917 (I), p. 225.

46 'Surgeon Probationers, Royal Navy', Letter from Donald MacAlister, BMJ, 1915 (II), p. 488.

47 NATS 1/711, PRO, Medical Students – Shortage of, Memorandum on the Shortage of Medical Students (Adopted by the Committee of Reference), 30 August 1917.

48 'Medical Students in and out of the Ranks', letter from J.A.A., BMJ, 1917 (II), p.100. For similar letters see BMJ, 1917 (II), pp. 64–5; 135; 166; 274–5; 306.

49 'Medical Students in the Ranks', BMJ, 1917 (II), p. 769.

50 *Hansard*, Parliamentary Debates, Commons, Fifth Series, 105, 1918, col. 1680.

51 'Medical Students and Military Service', BMJ, 1918 (I), p. 320.

52 *Hansard*, Parliamentary Debates, Commons, Fifth Series, 108, 1918, col. 489.

53 'Medical Students and Military Service', GMJ, LXXXIX, 1918, p. 366. Similar discontent had been aroused by the exemption of third-year students at the end of 1917; see letter from *Aux Absents Les Os*, BMJ, 1917 (II), p. 812.

54 'Medical Students and Military Service', GMJ, LXXXIX, 1918, p. 368.

55 NATS 1/812, PRO, Medical Students, letter from the Academic Sub Dean (University of Leeds) to the Ministry of National Service, 11 December 1917.

56 NATS 1/812, PRO, Medical Students, letter from the Dean of University College Hospital Medical School (University of London) to the Ministry of National Service, 11 December 1917.

57 NATS 1/812, PRO, Medical Students, letter from the Academic Sub Dean (University of Leeds) to the Ministry Of National Service, 11 December 1917. *Medical Students and Military Service*, letter from Perplexed expresses similar fears, BMJ, 1918 (I), p. 524.

58 **WO 293/6**, PRO, Army Council Instructions, January–June 1917: ACI 842, Medical and other students – Cancellation of Exemption in certain cases, 24 May 1917.

59 'Medical Students and Military Service', GMJ, LXXXIX, 1918, pp. 366–7.

60 **Dr P. Hickey**, LC., Tape recordings 220 & 223. **Sir Clement Chesterman**, LC., Papers: Tropical Trail – Presidential Address to the Hunterian Society, 16 October 1967, p. 10. **Dr Soloman Wand**, LC., Papers: Medical Training in 1915, article in the Queen's Medical Magazine, Winter 1984, p. 19.

61 **Dr A.W. Brown**, LC., Tape recording 502.

62 **Dr F. Moor**, LC., Diary 1917: 12 April 1917, p. 7.

63 NATS 1/812, PRO, Medical Students, letter from Ministry of National Service to the War Office, 23 November 1917.

64 NATS 1/812, PRO, Medical Students, letter from Ministry of National Service to medical schools, 3 November 1917.

65 'Medical Students', BMJ, 1917 (I), Supplement, p. 42. 'The Number of Medical Students', BMJ, 1918 (II), pp. 67; 118.

66 Minutes of the GMC, LVI, 1919, p. 52.

Chapter 5

Medical Women and War Service

The withdrawal of male doctors from civil service in order to augment the RAMC created an increasing number of vacancies on hospital staffs, on administrative medical staffs and in general practices. It was soon realized that, given the RAMC's continued demand for doctors, women would have to be employed to fill these civil posts if a serious shortage was to be avoided. However, the War Office refused to countenance the idea of women doctors serving with the forces abroad; the role of women was to relieve male doctors in the home hospitals and to act as locum-tenentes. Dr Norman Walker, convenor of the SMSEC, summed up the predominant attitude to women doctors in the early months of the War: 'I cannot think that the front, or very near it, is the place for them.'[1] The War Office's rejection of women's services was followed by the BRCS which refused to accept female doctors for foreign service. In the face of this opposition medical women established their own voluntary organizations.

The first such organization to prove the value of medical women was the Women's Hospital Corps (WHC), backed by the Women's Social and Political Union. In September 1914 it established a hospital in the Hotel Claridge, Paris which quickly gained the admiration of the wounded and the military authorities; the RAMC came to treat the hospital as if it were a British auxiliary.[2] With the hospitals in Boulogne being overwhelmed with work the War Office was sufficiently impressed by the women to invite them to establish a hospital at Wimereux. This request was a triumph for the cause of medical women as it was the first time that the War Office had given them equal responsibility with their male colleagues.[3]

107

The largest of the women's voluntary organizations was the Scottish Women's Hospitals (SWH) which was established by the Scottish Federation of the National Union of Women's Suffrage Societies. The driving force behind the SWH was Dr Elsie Inglis; after the War Office refused her offer of a fully equipped hospital, staffed by women, the French, who lacked the reserves of medical manpower available in Britain, gladly accepted the women's assistance. The result was the establishment of a hospital at the Abbaye de Royaumont in December 1914. The following year the SWH sent units to Serbia, Salonika and Corsica; in 1916 they extended their work to Russia; and in 1917 an additional hospital was established in France at Villers Cotterets.

Thus it was amongst Britain's allies that British medical women found their earliest opportunities to serve. Certainly, necessity appears to have made other nations more willing to accept a front-line role for female doctors. In Russia all women medical students who had studied for a minimum of six semesters had been made liable for service in the hospitals at the front.[4]

The response of medical women to the SWH was enthusiastic. One of the volunteers, Dr Lydia Henry, recalls a feeling that was probably common to many energetic and experienced medical women:

As I watched my [male] colleagues enter military service I felt equally competent to deal with war injuries, given an opportunity.[5]

The confidence of medical women in their ability was justified by the skill and devotion to duty that they displayed, confounding those commentators who had argued that women would not be able to cope with the pressures of front-line work. Nowhere was this fortitude evinced more clearly than in Serbia where the women had to work long hours in terrible, insanitary conditions, treating not only the injured but those suffering from rampant diseases such as typhus and smallpox.[6]

In France the work of the SWH during the German advance on the Aisne in 1918 was its finest hour. The unit at Villers Cotterets provided relief for the wounded, with operations being carried on day and night in the face of German bombardment right up to the last minute. Dr Elisabeth Courtauld, one of the women working at Villers Cotterets, described the situation:

There came an order for the hospital to evacuate. . . . Then came an order that heaps of terribly wounded were expected, and we could stay on. We were glad. It seemed horrid to be told to go and leave things behind us. All the night we were hard at it and working under difficulties. Terrible cases came in. Between 10.30 and 3.30 or 4 a.m. we had to amputate six thighs and one leg, mostly by the light of bits of candle, held by the orderlies, and as for me giving the anaesthetic, I did it more or less in the dark at my end of the patient . . . air raids were over us nearly all night and sometimes we had to blow out the candles for a few minutes and stop when one heard the Boche right over. Next morning [30 May 1918] about 11 a.m. we were told the whole place must be evacuated, patients and all. . . . So during the day we did have a strenuous time. Patients had come in all through the night, some practically dying, all wanting urgently operating upon. But we had to stop operating, dress the patients' wounds and splint them up as best we could, and all day ambulances came up and we got patients away.[7]

By the end of the day the whole of the hospital had been evacuated on to the hospital at Royaumont. During the period of the Aisne fighting (31 May–13 July) this hospital proved a godsend, being the only one in the vicinity that was in full working order. This was to be the hospital's busiest time with three operating theatres working all day and two of them all night. The women of the unit achieved remarkable results under severe physical and mental strain, many of them having been out in France for two or three years.[8]

Professionally, the work undertaken by the women was of the highest calibre. Dr Weinberg, from the Pasteur Institute in Paris, was so impressed with the standards at Royaumont that he decided to use it as an experimental unit for the anti-gas gangrene serum that he was developing. Royaumont soon gained a reputation for its expertise in this field. It had a lower amputation rate and the lowest mortality rate; the military authorities were forced to concede this and began directing the most severe cases to Royaumont.[9] On other fronts the SWH was doing equally good work; in Salonika, they ran the only physiotherapy unit.[10]

Their reputation was equally high with the men in the trenches; wounded had been known to ask to be sent to Royaumont, and one young patient, on leaving the hospital, asked to be evacuated to 'another Royaumont'.[11] A Senegalese patient was so impressed by the women that he announced he would never beat his wives again. As for maintaining discipline, the women found no difficulty; the threat of the only punishment employed, evacuation to a regular hospital, was sufficient to keep order.[12]

At home the pressure on the medical profession had forced the military authorities to employ women as Civil Medical Practitioners in the military hospitals. The rate of pay was 20s a day, and the contract was terminable at one month's notice by either side. They were given no rank, or uniform, and were not entitled to ration or travel allowance. The work of CMPs was undertaken in their own locality and was therefore convenient for women with family responsibilities. A good deal of resentment was stirred up against their conditions of service, especially their lack of rank and uniform, but in this respect they were treated the same as male CMPs.[13]

Dr Helena Wright's pacifist principles ensured that her views on the wearing of uniform were untypical. However the unenthusiastic response that her request to serve in a military hospital elicited from the War Office indicates the level of opposition which women doctors faced from the military:

> [The Colonel in charge] was very surprised to have a woman doctor coming right [into his office]. I said, 'I want to find out if it is possible to be employed in any of the ordinary military hospitals to deal with soldiers wounded in the war, because I'm a pacifist, and I should like to do what I could to restore them. And I will not wear any uniform.' He looked very surprised. He said, 'It'll be a matter of great difficulty.' I said, 'I expect it will. That's why I'm here. That's what you do.' He tried to get rid of me and I wouldn't go. I said, 'Please just telephone now, I won't be any nuisance. I'll just sit quietly.' He rang up hospital after hospital. Response – woman doctor – not in the Army! I said, 'It's not quite hopeless, you haven't tried them all.'[14]

Her persistence was rewarded by an appointment at Bethnall Green Military Hospital, under the command of Colonel H. Fenwick. His was a wartime commission and he did not share the military's prevailing suspicion of women doctors:

> What should be recorded is the extreme generosity and open-mindedness of Harry Fenwick, because he knew no more well of me than anybody else did and here I was turning up in ordinary civilian clothes to be enrolled as a doctor among his thirteen ordinary R.A.M.C. medical officers. . . . I was treated in exactly the same way [as the men]. I was given a ward of my own, which was called Mersey Ward.[15]

Although an accepted part of the hospital staff, Wright was concerned to limit any upset that her presence might have caused to soldiers unaccustomed to women doctors:

> I felt very sympathetic for the soldiers. A woman doctor was very rare. So I made friends with the sister of my ward. By this time I'd had a good deal

of experience of ward sisters and I said, 'Look here! this is very hard on these men to have a young woman here. I want you to promise every time I have to operate you will ask privately that person, on the night before, if he wishes it or not.' She was rather surprised and said, 'Yes, that's quite fair.' She did – no one objected.[16]

The successful record of women such as Wright in the home hospitals, and the work of the volunteer units overseas, led the military authorities to reconsider their own objections to women doctors. Despite the achievements of the women's volunteer units, Sir Alfred Keogh held to the War Office view that the front was no place for female doctors.[17] But in the matter of their employment in the UK, the cause of medical women found Keogh a valuable ally. As the usefulness of the WHC hospital at Wimereux declined he was keen to employ its services in the UK where the pressure of work was great. He proposed that the Wimereux hospital be closed down and offered the women the large military hospital at Endell Street, London. The WHC accepted Keogh's offer and took control of the hospital on 22 March 1915. The Medical Officers were not given commissions but were graded as lieutenants, captains, majors or lieutenants colonel, drawing the pay and allowances of their respective rank. By refusing to grant the women even honorary rank the War Office did nothing to strengthen their hands with regard to the maintenance of discipline. Despite this handicap the women appear to have had little difficulty keeping order, and it was only in 1919, with the arrival of large numbers of men transferred from other hospitals, where discipline had been lax, that problems arose.[18]

Indeed, the manner in which the women ran the hospital silenced those critics who had questioned the wisdom of Keogh's faith in their ability. The medical and surgical work undertaken at the hospital was of the highest standard. Particularly noteworthy was the standard of pathological work, and in surgery, the adoption of Professor Rutherford Morrison's new method for treating septic wounds and fractures. Nor was it just at Endell Street that women were impressing the military authorities with their abilities; the standard of Dr Florence Stoney's X-ray work at the Fulham Military Hospital, where she was the only woman, gained her the respect of her male colleagues.[19]

The wartime work of medical women, especially in the SWH and the WHC, had proved that women were equal to the task of military work. Nevertheless, many in the RAMC remained uncomfortable with the idea of employing women with the forces. By 1916, however, the growing crisis in medical manpower left the War Office with no choice but to invite female doctors to volunteer for military service. There was a ready response and the women were employed with RAMC units in Egypt, India, Malta and Salonika, as well as with military hospitals at home. Unlike their male colleagues, the women were not given temporary commissions. The women were merely 'attached' to the RAMC, denied rank and, as regards 'equivalent' status, rarely rose above the rank and pay of captain.

The failure to grant rank and status to these women was far more damaging than it was to those working at Endell Street. Whereas the latter were working only with women, these new recruits were distributed throughout various hospitals and worked alongside male RAMC officers; without rank they were placed at a grave disadvantage professionally. Whatever their experience or skill, they would always be junior to even the most recently commissioned male officer. Without rank the women were placed in an awkward state of limbo, between being CMPs and Temporary Officers; they appeared to suffer all the disadvantages of both positions,[20] and none of the advantages:

> Two of my full-time women colleagues were instructed to examine women colleagues for the W.A.A.C.

> The pay for this to C.M.Ps. is £2 per diem (or 2s 6d per capita if less than 16 women be examined). The A.D.M.S. told my colleagues that they were not C.M.Ps., but Temporary Officers of the R.A.M.C. and therefore not entitled to be paid at the rate for C.M.Ps. They accepted this.

> A day or two ago, Dr. Patricia Dent, also a full-time colleague, applied for a half warrant for a railway journey as a Temporary Officer of the R.A.M.C. The same A.D.M.S. refused the warrant on the ground that she was considered by the War Office to be a C.M.P., though in any case, he added, it would not be granted because she was not in uniform.[21]

Whilst women medical officers were denied the half warrant for travelling, it was available to all their male colleagues and to all Army sisters, nurses and VADs in uniform. Thus a VAD was entitled to travel with the male medical officers in a first-class compartment; women medical officers had to travel third class with the NCOs and privates. This situation was hardly conducive to firm discipline. The women's lack of uniform also ensured that they did not receive the respect they deserved; compared to the uniformed VADs they appeared as slackers in their civilian attire.

Although some of these points might seem trivial, they were important as regards social standing in the Army, and helped to further undermine the authority of women medical officers. The Medical Women's Federation (MWF), which was formed in February 1917 with the aim of establishing an authoritative voice to speak in the interests of medical women, spent the remainder of the War campaigning to improve the conditions of women in the military medical service.

In co-operation with the BMA the MWF was eventually successful in persuading the Government to grant women relief under the service rate of income tax in the 1918–1919 budget; and this was backdated to 1915–1916.[22] Another grievance brought to the attention of the MWF and the BMA was the fact that the panel practices of women doctors on war service were not, unlike those of men, protected by regulation. The matter was raised at the Annual Representative Meeting of the BMA in August 1918 and it was announced that the Insurance Commissioners were prepared to alter the regulations to rectify the situation.[23] Given the financial sacrifices that many women had made (the position of women within the profession was one of limited opportunity, and so it was difficult for them to achieve economic security), these were important concessions, although in the latter case somewhat late in the day for those who had been serving since the early years of the War.

However, the issue at the top of the agenda for women serving with the Army was their lack of military status. Hopes had been raised by the formation of Queen Mary's Army Auxiliary Corps (QMAAC)[24] early in 1917, as its founder, Mrs Chalmers Watson, had extracted a promise that a section of the RAMC would soon be formed to encompass all medical women serving under the War Office. But the women's section did not materialize and those who served with the QMAAC were not granted commissioned rank. Their position was, however, more favourable than that of women contract practitioners; they had a uniform, uniform allowance and were entitled to wear the RAMC badge.[25] Also, because their duties were confined to the health of Corps members and did not bring them into contact with fighting troops or RAMC regulars, they did not face the prejudices that their 'contract' colleagues serving with RAMC units had to endure.

Complaints about the invidious position of women medical officers, due to their lack of commissioned rank and uniform, continued to reach the MWF. Discontent was aroused in Salonika by the fact that they were not entitled to the same treatment as other officers as regards the censorship of letters.[26] It was also pointed out that the women's lack of rank meant that their position was entirely dependent upon the attitude of their commanding officer (CO). A liberal CO might allow the women to wear badges of rank, but if his successor was hostile to the women's cause he would order them to be removed; such incidents discredited the women, making it harder for them to command respect and maintain discipline.[27] Women in charge of medical units also faced the humiliation of being supplanted by any male officer, no matter that he might be her junior in service and unable to match her experience and competence.[28] Meanwhile, without uniform it was difficult for women to establish themselves in military society and overcome prejudice. One male doctor, whilst conceding that there was no reason why women should not serve and recognizing the quality of their work, nevertheless admitted that the idea of women medical officers stuck in his gizzard. It was the idea of a mixed mess with women clad in 'white blouses and blue skirts, and floppy panama hats and parasols' instead of uniform which made him particularly uncomfortable.[29] But of even greater importance were the dangers attached to women having to serve in civilian clothes. Many of those captured in Serbia experienced a good deal of anxiety for their life and honour; their lack of uniform laid them open to accusations of spying and at the same time made it easy for a spy to pass as a woman doctor.[30]

Calls were made upon the MWF to take steps to help improve the iniquitous position of women on service with regard to their allowances, gratuity and travel warrants. But the principal demands were for commissioned rank and uniform. A letter from medical women serving in Egypt urged on the MWF the importance of pressing for the concession of these latter during the War.[31] The majority of their male COs sympathized with their position and supported their recommendation that no more women doctors should volunteer for service until uniform and commissioned rank were granted.

The President of the MWF, Jane Walker, wrote to General Goodwin,[32] informing him of the upsurge of discontent:

> We are constantly receiving letters of complaint describing the annoyance our women are suffering from because of their lack of rank and status. We fear there will be a general stampede of them if something is not done to ease the situation. Nothing will satisfy most of them except equal terms for equal work with men, and as they truly say men in the A.S.C. have rank and so have the Chaplains and if they have there is no earthly reason why women should not have it too.[33]

Following this letter the War Office received a deputation from the MWF and as a result of this meeting the Government agreed to allow women to wear uniform;[34] the uniform was to be the same as that of the

QMAAC with the RAMC badge. To the majority of women, however, uniform without commissioned rank was not worth having as it would bring no great improvement in their status;[35] without rank they lacked the necessary authority to carry out their duties and maintain discipline. The uniform itself also came in for criticism; the fact that women were to wear the same uniform as members of the QMAAC, rather than that of the RAMC, was seen as creating a needless distinction between them and their male colleagues, creating confusion and hindering them in their work.[36]

The War Office would have been able to make far greater use of the medical women in its employ if they had all been given commissioned rank within the RAMC, as Mrs Chalmers Watson had hoped. However the War Office refused to consider the idea and remained unmoveable on the matter of commissions, having been advised by the Crown Law Officers that legislation was required before women could be given commissions. The initial snub to medical women in 1914, when their offers of help were refused, is perhaps understandable in the context of the then widespread failure to appreciate the scale and likely duration of the conflict. But subsequent events indicate that a more likely explanation lies in the continued prejudice against the cause of female equality. Once the work of voluntary organizations like the SWH had proved women's ability and wartime necessity had forced the War Office to employ women, there was no excuse for continued discrimination against them. Men and women were professionally equal and this ought to have been reflected in equal military status.

The failure to grant commissions to women was a waste of a valuable commodity – qualified medical personnel. At a time when there was mounting concern about the Army's employment of Medical Officers everything possible needed to be done to ensure that the best use was being made of medical skill. There was a clear parallel between the women's experiences and the difficulties under which male Medical Officers had laboured, prior to the formation of the RAMC, and the passing of the Edwardian Army reforms. It ought to have been apparent to those in authority that the granting of rank was not a privilege or a reward, but essential for efficiency. Instead, similar arguments were used against bestowing commissions on women as had been used against male Medical Officers in the past. Winston Churchill[37] claimed that the women's lack of commissioned rank involved no disadvantage: 'The fact that they belong to the medical profession assures them the position to which they are entitled.'[38] Moreover, he said that it was impossible to give women equal status with men since there were duties which they were not capable of undertaking, including service in the trenches as RMOs; sanitary duties, which involved frequent visits to trenches and billets; and the carrying out of venereal inspections. He also pointed to the difficulties experienced in Egypt and Malta in finding employment for women, to suggest that there were substantial limitations to their military usefulness.[39] The only way around the problem would be to grant women special contracts for special duties, but this was dismissed as unworkable on the grounds that it would immobilize personnel and necessitate an increase in establishments.[40] Meanwhile others were worried that the granting of commissions for medical women would set a precedent for other branches of the service.

This latter argument was easily refuted, as the claim of medical women to a commission was based upon the fact that their qualifications were identical with those men who had commissions in the RAMC. Thus a precedent for other branches would only be set if a similar claim to equality could be established. As for the accepted fact that women Medical Officers would be restricted to certain types of work, this was no reason for saying that they were not entitled to commissions; just as it had been wrong in the past to claim that male Medical Officers should not be given commissions because they would not be competent to take military command. Women wanted rank not to extend the ambit of their duties, but simply to give them sufficient authority to carry out efficiently those that they already possessed. It was also the case that many men holding commissions were limited in the type of work they could undertake, either on grounds of age or physical fitness. Moreover, Churchill did the women an injustice by his claim that those serving in Malta and Egypt had been of little use. There was little work for them in these regions because the projected campaigns never materialized,[41] not because they were unsuitable.

The War Office's refusal to grant medical women commissions, despite the advocacy of Keogh and Goodwin, was a victory for the anti-feminists within the Army. Nevertheless, given the climate of the times, the very fact that equal rank for women entered serious debate represented a substantial advance. Moreover, had the War continued, it is likely that the increasing shortage of doctors and calls for further improvements in efficiency would have enabled women to demand a better deal. Once the War ended, however, it was difficult to bring pressure to bear and the issue fell from public prominence. On the eve of the Second World War it was still being maintained that medical women did not have a claim to rank equal with men,[42] and doubts were being expressed as to whether their services would be required. However, by

1942, when medical women were conscripted with their male colleagues, it had become clear that they had a vital role to play. Women were paid full military rates and there was no distinction from the men, other than the fact that they still did not hold the King's Commission. According to E.M. Bell this made little difference in practice as there was neither the time nor the inclination for quarrels about status; men accepted the women as medical colleagues and there was no friction.[43] After the War, of course, women were not prepared to continue with this unjustifiable distinction. With the support of the BMA, they succeeded in 1950 in persuading the War Office to grant them commissioned rank. Thus, it took another war and a further campaign of pressure on the War Office to gain for the women what the quality of their work and the logic of military efficiency should have won for them in the First World War.

The obstructionism that faced women doctors in the military did not appear to have its counterpart in civilian life. Female practitioners were urged to take on the civilian work of their male colleagues, thus setting the latter free for military service. This was seen as offering a great opportunity to women doctors to raise their status within the medical profession: 'No woman doctor who has the woman doctor's cause at heart has any business to remain idle just now.'[44] The war emergency certainly forced the lifting of some of the prejudices against the employment of women doctors. Dr Margaret Campbell, the first woman doctor to be employed by Doncaster Royal Infirmary, recalls that her appointment had 'created something of a furore'.[45] but the novelty rapidly wore off and she appears to have been accepted by both staff and patients. Dr Helena Wright and Dr Peggy Maitland caused a similar stir when they took up a double appointment at the outpatient department of the Hampstead General Hospital. Again, the novelty soon wore off, and they were perfectly treated, spending six happy months there. Indeed, so good an impression did they make that they were approached to become interns in the main hospital. Wright was appointed as house surgeon and Maitland as house physician. Initially everything went well and the patients 'were delighted to have women doctors to look after them'.[46] Unfortunately, things did eventually go sour, but this had nothing to do with the fact that they were women:

> The year 1915 grew into late spring, we gradually noticed that the atmosphere of the wards and hospital was changing and becoming vaguely uncomfortable. Nothing was said: we were puzzled. Our work was completely satisfactory and the ward patients were outspoken in their

117

surprise and pleasure in the novelty of women doctors to care for them. One morning I was handed an official letter from the chairman of the hospital board. It expressed satisfaction with my work and regret at what was happening. It had got about that my name was a German one [her maiden name was Lowenfeld] and uneasiness had been expressed about my national loyalty. He was extremely regretful but had no alternative to dismiss me from hospital service. I showed the letter to Peggy. We were sad that the hospital authorities had succumbed to rumour. She resigned her appointment in indignation at the behaviour of the hospital and we left the hospital together.[47]

The demand for doctors was such that Wright was able to find employment at another hospital, taking up the post of house surgeon at a children's hospital. As outlined above, it was only when she sought employment in a military hospital that she encountered difficulties on the grounds of her sex.[48]

Great Ormond Street Children's Hospital began employing women doctors for the first time during the War; although according to Dr G. Miall Smith, women were only employed by the hospital in preference to blacks.[49] Nevertheless, however grudgingly, it is clear from the number of advertisements in the medical and lay press offering posts to women doctors that barriers were being removed. One large hospital was so desperate for doctors that it requested the London School of Medicine for Women to 'send us <u>any</u> women at <u>any</u> salary'.[50]

The records of the Medical Women's Federation contain various letters requesting the assistance of medical women. One such letter contained a request from a Dr Raymond for 'a lady locum for my small practice at Griffiths Town, Mon., for country district practice, nice open place and not much work and a comfortable home. Want somebody who would be company for my wife.'[51] Another came from two doctors in practice over the age of fifty asking for recommendations regarding a good lady doctor to act as their assistant.[52] Letters also came from female practitioners indicating the range of work being undertaken by women, including appointments as house physicians and surgeons; gratuitous attendance on dependants of those serving with the forces; acting as locums; and working in asylums. The following letter from Dr C.E. Stewart of Leeds is representative:

At the commencement of the war my husband who is clinical pathologist to the General Infirmary had volunteered to help on the medical staff at the Infirmary as they were so short of qualified men and at the same time I offered to do the routine pathology of the hospital in his place (for some

Battle of Pilckem Ridge. Stretcher-bearers carrying a wounded man through the mud, which reaches their knees. Near Boesinghe, 1 August 1917. (*Imperial War Museum*, Q.5,935).

Battle of the Menin Road Ridge. A British doctor and RAMC orderly attending to wounded German prisoners at the dressing station at Potijze Chateau, 20 September 1917. (*Imperial War Museum*, Q.2,871).

3. Regimental Aid Post, near Guemappe, 29 April 1917 (*Imperial War Museum*, Q.5,277).

Foot inspection by the Medical Officer of the 12th East Yorkshires in a support trench. Near Reclincourt, 2 January 1918 (*Imperial War Museum*, Q.10,622).

Battle of the Menin Road Ridge. British doctor and padre attending to wounded British and Germans. Near Potijze, 20 September 1917 (*Imperial War Museum*, Q.2,857).

6. Doctor tending a man wounded in the shoulder at a captured German dump. Oostaverne, 25 August 1917. (*Imperial War Museum*, Q.5,916).

7. Battle of Amiens. Arranging blankets to shade from the sun wounded awaiting evacuation from a Field Dressing Station at Quesnel, 11 August 1918. (*Imperial War Museum*, Q.7,299).

8. Battle of the Ancre. British wounded at a Dressing Station. Aveluy Wood, 13 November 1916 (*Imperial War Museum*, Q.4,506).

9. A stretcher case being attended to by one of the Australian Advanced Dressing Stations near Ypres, 20 September 1917 (*Imperial War Museum*, E[Aus]. 714).

10. Attending to the wounded at an Advanced Dressing Station near Ypres, 20 September 1917 (*Imperial War Museum*, E[Aus]. 715).

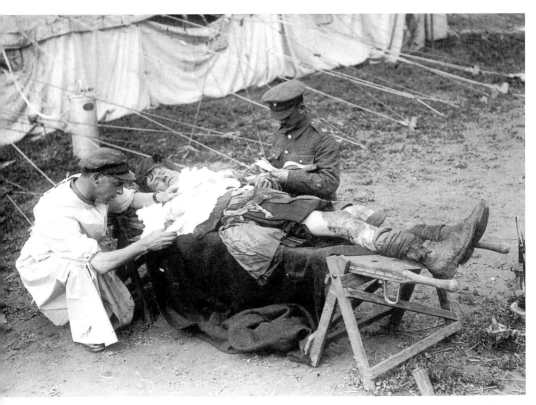

11. Battle of Estaires. A man of the Black Watch of the 51st Division having his wounds attended to at an Advanced Dressing Station, 11 April 1918. (*Imperial War Museum*, Q.11,577).

12. Second Battle of the Somme. Captured German doctors dressing the wounds of British wounded at an Advanced Dressing Station of the Royal Naval (63rd) Division at Grevillers, 25 August 1918 (*Imperial War Museum*, Q.11,265).

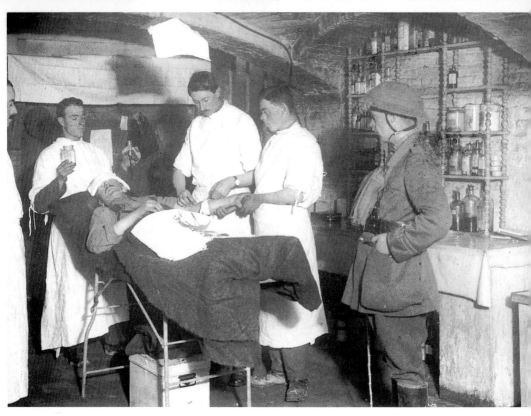

13. Interior of an Advanced Dressing Station. Operating theatre. (*Imperial War Museum*, Q.33,431).

14. An ambulance with ten horses coming across country after heavy rain. N.E. of Guillemont, October 1916. (*Imperial War Museum*, Q.4,421).

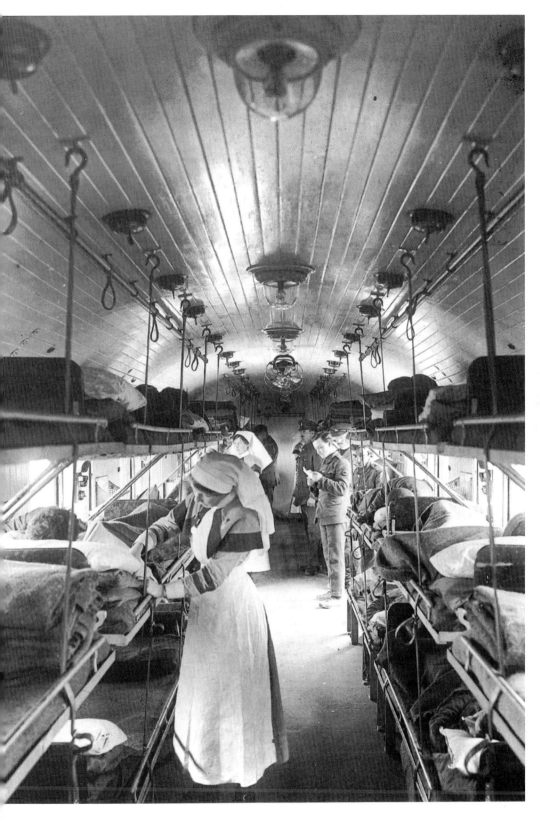

15. Interior of a ward on a British Ambulance Train. Near Doullens, 27 April 1918. (*Imperial War Museum*, Q.8,750).

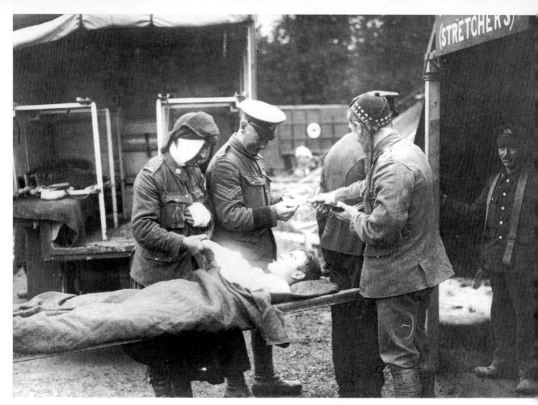

16. Wounded arriving at a Casualty Clearing Station from the front, October 1916. (*Imperial War Museum*, C.O. 911).

17. General view of huts at No. 10 Casualty Clearing Station, July 1916. (*Imperial War Museum*, C.O. 381).

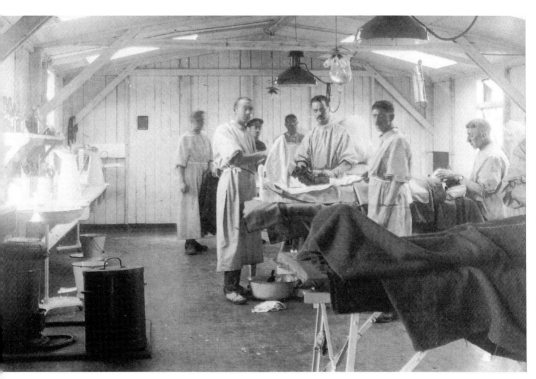

18. Operating Theatre of No. 3 Casualty Clearing Station, July 1916. (*Imperial War Museum*, C.O. 157).

19. Casualty Clearing Station – Canadian wounded about to leave for England on the 'Princess Christian' Hospital Train, October 1916. (*Imperial War Museum*, C.O. 916).

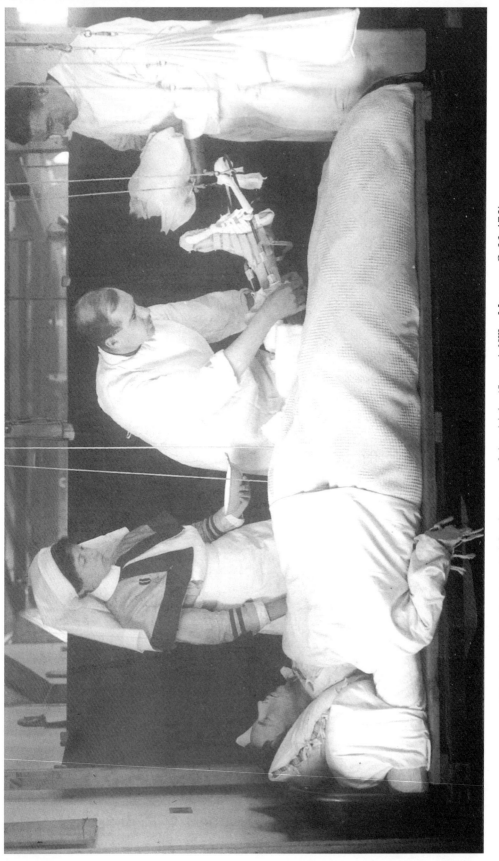

20. At work in the hospital for fractures of the thigh. (*Imperial War Museum*, Q.33,472).

weeks I have been locum assistant clinical pathologist). The Board accepted my services so that I am now doing a full time post at the Infirmary.

I know several women are also helping with the St. John's Ambulance lectures and one woman here is helping with the anaesthetics in place of a man who is in the R.A.M.C.[53]

As the War increased the demand for women doctors, so pressure grew to attract more women into the profession. Dr Mary Scharlieb, a prominent campaigner for more women in the profession,[54] made speeches at women's meetings and wrote letters to the press. At the annual prize giving at the Manchester High School for Girls in July 1915 she impressed upon her audience the great opportunities that were now appearing for medical women. Not only were employment prospects good, but the earning potential was high, and she urged the girls to opt for a medial career.[55] However, it was not only young women that she targeted. In a letter to the press she stressed that the older, educated woman, with her 'trained mind, experience of life, and savoir faire',[56] would be an asset to the profession. Later, in Wales, a committee was established for the promotion of the medical training of women; by July 1917 it felt that medical losses at the front, and the reduction in the number of medical students, had created an urgent need for more women to join the profession.[57] The success of efforts to encourage women to join the profession is clear from the figures: whereas in 1914 the 700 women medical students represented only 10 per cent of the total, by 1918 the number had reached 2,250, or 40 per cent of all medical students.[58]

These efforts to increase the number of women entering the medical profession were mirrored in Germany where it had been decided to recognize the diplomas of girls' schools as adequate entrance requirements for a medical course. The result was an increase in the number of women medical students enrolling in German schools from 874 in 1914 to 1,150 in 1915.[59]

The problem with increasing the number of women entering the profession was that there were not the facilities available to give them adequate clinical training. Given that the majority of medical women who served the nation's cause during the War had received their training in the schools of the enemy, pressure grew for improving women's access to a British medical education.

London experienced acute difficulties; most of the provincial schools were co-educational, but in London the schools remained barred to women, yet the London School of Medicine for Women was simply too small to cope with the growing number of female students. A sub-committee of the University of London's Academic Council arranged a conference of all the medical schools in the University to discuss the subject of admitting women students.[60] Little emerged from this conference, but circumstances forced the London Schools to accept women.[61] Similarly, Edinburgh University, which, whilst accepting women students since 1886, had refused them access to many of the classes held in the University, and many of the clinics in the Royal Infirmary,[62] was forced to change. In August 1916 the Court of the University of Edinburgh resolved to allow women to take the whole curriculum within the University.[63]

By 1917, a year after it had first admitted them, Dr Beatrice Pullinger felt that women had been pretty much accepted at St Mary's Hospital Medical School, but it is clear that prejudice remained:

> Anti-feminism was receding and at St. Mary's persisted only in the Inoculation department presided over by Sir Almroth Wright. Ida Mann recounted how she had to deliver a specimen there for examination and was warned to knock but not enter and wait until someone came to handover to. The consequence was that we learnt very little bacteriology and no immunology.[64]

There is little doubt that the War, as it did for their male colleagues, afforded women medical students with unprecedented opportunities to develop their skills:

> There was a shortage of people to act as locums for hospital house surgeons and physicians so that at the end of my third year I became casualty house surgeon for three months at the Birmingham General Hospital. This was a wonderful experience giving responsibility so early in my career even doing minor surgery.[65]

But the wartime extension of opportunity was not lasting. From the outset the London Schools that admitted women students during the War had made plain that this was only a temporary arrangement[66] and by 1929 women's right of access had largely been discontinued. Meanwhile, access at Oxford and Cambridge continued to be restricted. The exclusion of women from these schools was significant as two thirds of all English and Welsh doctors were trained in London or Oxbridge. It also tended to limit their advancement within the profession as graduates of these universities dominated its upper reaches.[67]

Some medical women did go on to enjoy successful peacetime practice.[68] Dr G. Miall-Smith, who qualified during the War and gained valuable experience both in the hospitals at home and with the Scottish Women's Hospital at Royaumont, successfully established herself in the profession.[69] Her success, however, did not come without a struggle. She had to fight a London Borough Council which argued that a married woman was not a proper person to take charge of the municipal maternity and infant welfare work.[70] That the War had failed to remove the prejudices against women doctors is evident from Miall-Smith's experience. Her career is also indicative of the War's failure to broaden the scope of medical work available to women. Prior to the War there had been a taboo against female doctors attending male patients. There had been few openings for women outside of gynaecology, obstetrics, public health, asylums, dispensaries and general practice.[71] The post-war pattern of employment suggests that these remained the areas where women were most likely to succeed. It was not impossible for women to move beyond these boundaries. Elston cites the example of Hazel Chodak Gregory. She was appointed acting Assistant Physician at the Royal Free Hospital in 1916, and was confirmed in the post in 1920 shortly after the birth of her son. But Gregory's experience was very much an exception to the norm. Few women who acted as substitutes during the War were actually confirmed in their posts on the return of peace.[72] Moreover, opportunities to continue war work were particularly limited in the more prestigious divisions of medicine, such as surgery.[73]

Amongst those women who qualified before and during the War, it is therefore possible to find evidence of individual careers that benefited greatly from wartime opportunities. For most, however, the War provided a brief chance to prove the range of their professional abilities; peacetime was to be a return to generally more restricted conditions. It was to be the large number of women who began their studies during the War, qualifying in the early 1920s, who were to suffer most in these circumstances. They were at a disadvantage because of the emphasis on giving appointments to male practitioners who were being released by the RAMC. The newly-qualified women lacked the experience to compete with the men, and faced a competitive market in the areas traditionally open to women doctors. As a consequence many of these women disappeared from the profession soon after qualifying.[74]

The First World War had many positive aspects for women doctors. They had successfully operated their own volunteer organizations, proving their ability to take on hospital administration, and forcing a reluctant War Office to take note of their abilities. In the civilian, the volunteer and the military hospitals women performed surgical work that was on a par with that of their male colleagues. They entered areas of medicine that were previously largely male preserves, and in doing so helped to lift the taboo on the treatment of male patients by female doctors. Yet in neither the civilian nor the military sphere did these demonstrations of ability lead to proper recognition for women doctors. Female practitioners faced a return to pre-war limitations on the posts generally open to them. There was no war-induced revolution in the medical profession. Instead, the inter-war period witnessed continuity with the experiences of women doctors prior to 1914: a gradual but slow advance on the whole, with one or two exceptional women able to obtain prestigious posts.

But if the War led to little lasting change it had at least helped to undermine the arguments of those opposed to women doctors. The latter's wartime work had shown, both in terms of quality and range, that they were able to match the work of male doctors. The First World War had strongly advanced the case for equality in the medical profession, but the case was by no means won.

Notes

1   'Civil Medical Practice and the War', BMJ, 1915 (I), p. 21.
2   Flora Murray, *Women as Army Surgeons*, Hodder and Stoughton, 1920, pp. 53–4.
3   Barbara McLaren, *Women of the War*, Hodder and Stoughton, 1917, p. 2.
4   'Russian Women Medical Students Called on for Professional Services in the Field Hospitals', JAMA, LXIV, 1915, p. 1926.
5   Dr L.M. Henry, LC, Papers: Reminiscences of Royaumont, 1914–1919, p. 5.
6   For a good account of the conditions faced by the women in Serbia see L.E. Fraser, 'Diary of a Dresser in the Serbian Unit of the Scottish Women's Hospital', *Blackwoods Magazine*, 197, 1915, pp. 776–97.
7   Dr E. Courtauld, LC, Letters 1918–1919: letter to father, 31 May 1918.
8   SKIA, 'A Hospital in France', *Blackwoods Magazine*, 204, 1918, pp. 613–40; see pp. 622–33.
9   Dr L.M. Henry, LC, Reminiscences, pp. 27–8.
10 Dr R. Verney, LC, Tape recordings 476 & 480.
11 SKIA 'A Hospital In France', *Blackwoods Magazine*, 204, 1918, p. 633. Dr L.M. Henry, LC, Reminiscences, p. 28.
12 Dr L.M. Henry, LC, Reminiscences, pp. 9–11.
13 Letitia Fairfield et al, 'Medical Women in the Forces', *Journal of the Medical Women's Federation.* (JMWF), 49, 1967, p. 99.
14 Dr Helena Wright, LC, Tape recording.
15 *Ibid.*
16 *Ibid.*

17 Leah Leneman, 'Medical Women at War', 1914–1918, *Medical History*, 38, 1994, p. 168.

18 Murray, 'Woman as Army Surgeons', pp. 156–7; 160.

19 McLaren, 'Women of The War', pp. 3; 42–3.

20 MWF, WIHM, Status of Medical Women under the War Office, SA/MWF/C159, letter from Margaret Riddell to the Secretary of the MWF, 3 June 1918.

21 MWF, WIHM, Status of Medical Women under the War Office, SA/MWF/C159, letter from H.M. Trevithick (MO Camel's Head Station, Fourth Southern General Hospital), 18 January 1918.

22 E. Moberly Bell, *Storming the Citadel*, Constable, 1953, pp. 181–2.

23 MWF WIHM, Status of Medical Women under the War Office, SA/MWF/C159, letter to Secretary of the MWF, 18 May 1918 (signatory unclear). 'Panel Practice of Women on Military Service' (Annual Representative Meeting of the BMA), BMJ, 1918 (II), Supplement, p. 28.

24 This was followed in November 1917 by the Women's Royal Naval Service, and in April 1918 by the Women's Royal Air Force.

25 Letitia Fairfield et al, 'Medical Women in the Forces', JMWF, 49, 1967, p. 100.

26 MWF, WIHM, Status of Medical Women under the War Office, SA/MWF/C159: Service Abroad, experience of Dr K. Waring in Malta and Salonika.

27 Murray, *Women as Army Surgeons*, p. 238.

28 MWF, WIHM, Status of Medical Women under the War Office, SA/MWF/C159: Birmingham and District Association of Medical Women, Resolution, passed at meeting on 2 February 1918. See also letter from H.K. Trevithick to the Secretary of the MWF, 18 January 1918.

29 J.M. McLachlan, LC, Letters: letter 915, 14 August 1917; letter 917, 15 August 1917.

30 MWF WIHM, Status of Medical Women under the War Office, SA/MWF/C159: Birmingham and District Association of Medical Women, Resolution, passed at meeting on 2 February 1918.

31 MWF, WIHM, Status of Medical Women under the War Office, SA/MWF/C159, letter from H.K. Trevithick to the President of the MWF, 20 January 1918.

32 Replaced Sir Alfred Keogh as DGAMS in March 1918.

33 MWF, WIHM, Status of Medical Women under the War Office, SA/MWF/C159, letter from the President of the MWF to General Goodwin, DGAMS, 11 March 1918.

34 MWF, WIHM, Status of Medical Women under the War Office, SA/MWF/C159, letter from General Goodwin to the President of the MWF, 14 March 1918.

35 MWF, WIHM, Status of Medical Women under the War Office, SA/MWF/C159, letter from H.K. Trevithick to the President of the MWF, 24 March 1918.

36 MWF, WIHM, Status of Medical Women under the War Office, SA/MWF/C159, letter from Madge S. Robertson (Area Medical Controller for the Southern Area of France) to the MWF, 22 May 1918.

37 Secretary of State for War in the post-war Government.
38 MWF, WIHM, Re Commissions in the Army 1917–1919, SA/MWF/C163, letter to the President of the MWF from Churchill, 2 May 1919, p. 2.
39 *Ibid*, pp. 2–3.
40 *Ibid*, p. 2. See Also MWF, WIHM, Re Commissions in the Army 1917–1919, SA/MWF/C163: Suggested Granting of Commissions to Medical Women Serving with the Forces, by E. Worthington.
41 Letitia Fairfield et al, 'Medical Women in the Forces', JMWF, 49, 1967, p. 99.
42 WO 32/4550, PRO, Grant of Commissions to Female Doctors, Minute 6, 22 March 1938; Minute 9, 5 May 1938.
43 Bell, *Storming the Citadel*, p. 187.
44 'Civil Medical Practice and The War', BMJ, 1915 (I), p. 21.
45 Dr M. Campbell, LC, Papers: The First World War – A House Surgeon Remembers, p. 4.
46 Dr Helena Wright, LC, Tape recording.
47 Dr Helena Wright, LC, Handwritten recollection.
48 Dr Helena Wright, LC, Tape recording.
49 Dr G. Miall-Smith, LC, Handwritten recollections, p. 1.
50 'Women Physicians and the War', *Journal of the American Medical Association (JAMA)*, LXV, 1915, p. 1823.
51 Papers of the Medical Women's Federation (MWF) WIHM. Association Of Registered Medical Women (ARMW), Subcommittee Re War Work, SA/MWF/C157, letter from J.A. Reaside to the Medical Agency, 31 August 1914.
52 MWF, WIHM, ARMW, Subcommittee Re War Work, SA/MWF/C157, letter from R. Hinqston, 15 September 1914.
53 MWF, WIHM, ARMW, Subcommittee Re War Work, SA/MWF/C157, letter from C.E. Stewart, 25 August 1914.
54 Dr Mary Scharlieb, 'The Medical Woman – her Training, her Difficulties, and her Sphere of Usefulness', *The Nineteenth Century and After*, 78.¹, 1915, pp. 1174–85. Dr Scharlieb was Consulting Gynaecologist, Royal Free Hospital; Consulting Surgeon, South London Hospital for Women; Governor of St Mary's College, Paddington.
55 'The Need for Women Doctors', BMJ, 1915 (II), p. 196.
56 'Medical Women for the Coming Shortage in the Medical Profession', *Lancet*, 1914 (II), p. 1427.
57 'The Medical Training of Women in Wales', BMJ, 1917 (II), p. 133.
58 M.A.C. Elston, 'Women Doctors in the British Health Services: A Sociological Study of their Careers and Opportunities', University of Leeds, Ph.D., 1986, p. 270.
59 'Women Physicians and the War', JAMA, LXV, 1915, p. 1823.
60 'Medical Education of Women in London', BMJ, 1916 (II), p. 776.
61 Bell, *Storming the Citadel*, p. 170.
62 'Medical Education of Women', letter from R. Mary Barclay, BMJ, 1915 (II), p. 488.
63 'Admission of Women Medical Students to University Classes in Edinburgh', BMJ, 1916 (II), p. 338.

64 Dr Beatrice Pullinger, LC, Handwritten recollections, p. 12.
65 Dr Olive Newton, LC, Handwritten recollection.
66 'Women Medical Students in War Time', BMJ, 1916 (II), p. 24.
67 Elston, 'Women Doctors in the British Health Services', University of Leeds, Ph.D., 1986, pp. 93–5.
68 *Ibid*, pp. 276–7.
69 Dr G. Miall-Smith, LC, Handwritten recollections, p. 3.
70 *Royaumont Newsletter* (Published by the Royaumont and Villers Cotterets Association of the Scottish Women's Hospitals), October 1927, p. 7. In the papers of Miss G. Miller, LC.
71 Leneman, 'Medical Women at War', *Medical History*, 38, 1994, p. 160.
72 Elston, *Women Doctors in the British Health Services*, pp.293–4.
73 Leneman, 'Medical Women at War', *Medical History*, 38, 1994, p. 160.
74 Elston, *Women Doctors in the British Health Services*, p. 277. See also Minutes of the GMC, LVII, 1920, p. 8.

Chapter 6

RAMC Administration
on the Western Front

The medical services which accompanied the BEF to France in August 1914 were under the command of the DMS, Surgeon General T.P. Woodhouse, who was responsible to the Adjutant General. Woodhouse's office was located at the Advanced Base. The RAMC was represented at GHQ by the Deputy Director of Medical Services (DDMS), Colonel T.J. O'Donnell, who was joined by Major S.L. Cummins, the Deputy Assistant Director of Medical Services (DADMS). For each division there was an Assistant Director of Medical Services (ADMS). There was an ADMS and a Sanitary Officer at the Advanced Base, and also at Rouen, Le Havre and Boulogne. The War Establishments had made no provision for administrative officers of the RAMC to be located at corps headquarters. However, by September 1914, it had become necessary to address this deficiency. A DDMS was appointed to I Corps, and later to III Corps, replicating a post that had already been established in II Corps. Further appointments included that of a DDMS at the headquarters of the lines of communication (L of C), and a DADMS at GHQ, responsible for sanitation.

The arrival in France, during late October, of Sir Arthur Sloggett[1] as DGMS presaged a more fundamental reorganization of RAMC administration. This was necessary to meet the requirements of an expanded British force which had been divided into two armies in late 1914. The DGMS established his office at St Omer which was the location of GHQ. His staff included a Deputy Director General of Medical Services (DDGMS) and an Assistant Director General of Medical Services

(ADGMS). There was also an ADMS, a DADMS, a medical inspector of drafts, a staff officer, an officer in charge of ambulance transport and a DADMS for railheads. Woodhouse, who was no longer DMS of the force, took up the appointment of DMS L of C. His office was combined with that of the DDMS, L of C. The appointment, to the L of C staff, of a DADMS (later an ADMS), responsible for ambulance transport, replaced the appointment of officer in charge of ambulance transport on the DGMS staff. The creation of two armies led to the appointment of DsMS to the headquarters of each army at the end of 1914 (similar appointments were made when the Third, Fourth and Fifth Armies were formed). With their appointment it was decided to abolish the post of DDMS to corps headquarters (with the exception of the Cavalry Corps), although this decision was reversed in April 1915. The DsMS had direct control over the medical units of their Army, such as the Casualty Clearing Stations. However, divisional ADsMS retained responsibility for the Field Ambulances.

In the spring of 1916 GHQ moved from St Omer in two echelons, to Montreuil and Hesdin. This change necessitated the division of the DGMS office. The DDGMS, a DADMS and the DADMS for railheads accompanied the Adjutant General to Montreuil, whilst the remainder joined Sloggett at Hesdin. According to the Official History much inefficiency resulted from this division, including difficulties of communication and duplication of function. The amount of work at Hesdin required the DGMS to make good the loss of officers to Montreuil, and so two additional DADsMS were appointed to his staff. Lieutenant Colonel Beveridge, the ADMS (Sanitation) and Colonel Sir W. Leishman, the Adviser in Pathology, were also attached to Sloggett's staff, although their offices were located with the DMS, L of C. Further additions to the staff of the latter included a DADMS (Sanitation), an Assistant to the Adviser in Pathology and a quartermaster.

A range of administrative officers were employed in the bases. The medical staff at Boulogne, Étaples and Rouen comprised a DDMS, a DADMS, an Embarkation Medical Officer and a Sanitary Officer. There was an ADMS, a DADMS, a Sanitary Officer and an Embarkation Medical Officer at each of the bases at Le Havre, Marseilles and Calais. Le Treport had an ADMS, a Sanitary Officer and an Embarkation Medical Officer, although this staff was expanded in 1917 when Le Treport became a hospital centre. At Paris there was an ADMS and a DADMS, whilst St Omer and Abbeville both had an ADMS and a Sanitary Officer.

Also on the administrative staffs, although not graded as administrative officers, were the various consultants. The first to arrive, in September 1914, had been Sir Anthony Bowlby and Sir George Makins. The latter was appointed Consulting Surgeon of the base hospitals, and the former was responsible for the forward areas. Later in the year they were joined by Colonel F.F. Burghard, who became Consulting Surgeon at Boulogne, and Colonel B. Moynihan, who was the Consultant Surgeon at Rouen. Three consulting physicians also arrived. These were Sir W. Herringham, Sir B. Dawson and Sir J. Rose Bradford who were appointed to GHQ (responsible for work at the front), Boulogne and Rouen respectively. The consultant body also included Leishman, the Adviser in Pathology, Sir A. Wright, who undertook bacteriological investigations into infected wounds, and Colonel W.T. Lister, who became the Consulting Ophthalmologist. Ultimately, consulting surgeons were attached to the staff of the DsMS of the various armies. By 1917 there was also a consultant surgeon at each of the following bases: Boulogne, Étaples, Le Havre, Le Treport, Rouen and St Omer. In 1916 consultant physicians were appointed to both the First and Second Armies, whilst the following year another consulting physician was given responsibility for the Fourth and Fifth Armies. Sir Wilmot Herringham at GHQ remained the Consultant Physician for the Third Army. Further appointments included a Consulting Psychologist, a Consulting Neurologist, a Consulting Radiographer and a Consulting Dermatologist. They were based in either Étaples or Boulogne, but their services were available to each of the armies, as required.[1]

The great test of this administrative system was its ability to deliver effective medical care. During the War the RAMC came under attack for failing to protect the interests of the sick and wounded. It was alleged that appropriate treatment came second place to an obsession with evacuation. The system was said to be riddled with cumbersome bureaucracy and neither interested in, nor capable of, promoting medical science. Civilian doctors who joined the RAMC complained that little regard was given to their expertise, and that opportunities for promotion were limited. The appointment of consultants had appeared to indicate a greater willingness to take advice from the civilian profession. However, the administrative structures were said to have placed unnecessary constraints on them. In order to test the validity of these accusations the remainder of this chapter will examine the record of the medical administration in France and Flanders.

Many Medical Officers felt that their duties entailed far too much administrative work, and complained that the whole medical service was bound up with red tape. According to Henry Gervis there was a mania for filling in forms. His memoirs give an impression of an RAMC administration riven with petty bureaucracy.[3] A.A. Martin was equally critical. He believed that the duties of Medical Officers should be confined to purely professional work and their administrative tasks taken on by the Army Service Corps (ASC).[4]

However, according to the committee of enquiry headed by Lord Charnwood, there was no evidence that medical treatment in France was being hampered by red tape.[5] Indeed, Charnwood countered that the clerical work undertaken by Medical Officers was essential if continuity of treatment was to be guaranteed and the progress of cases easily assessed. Medical history sheets, case sheets, special reports and index cards were not designed to obstruct medical work but to enable it to be carried out quickly and efficiently. Given their importance, Charnwood felt that the completion of such medical records could only properly be done by qualified medical men.[6] Martin's suggestion that clerical work be done by the ASC might well have released more Medical Officers for purely professional duties. But the advantages would have been outweighed by the disadvantages. The unified medical service, which successions of reformers had campaigned for from the time of the Crimea, would have been broken up, and the RAMC's independence forfeited. Stripped of their administrative responsibility and consequently the power of command, Medical Officers would, once more, have become second-class officers, and had their ability to promote medical science undermined. After the War the idea persisted that specialists employed in administrative posts were being wasted. Major M.B.H. Ritchie[7] feared that this belief revealed a dangerous 'disposition to leave the direction of medical affairs in the hands of less able medical men, or of lay administrators'.[8] It was important that specialists be more than just technical advisers; they needed to be able to participate in the general direction of medical affairs, if positive professional developments were to take place in the RAMC.

With the expansion of the RAMC, the increased number of staff posts were filled by regular officers who possessed the necessary knowledge of the RAMC machine. Medical work was largely undertaken by civilians.[9] Most of the Medical Officers with FAs and CCSs were civilians, and by the later years of the War usually only the CO would be a regular.[10] The manner in which the regulars carried out their administrative functions was praised by M. Whiting who 'was filled with admiration for the way in which the regular RAMC arranged the whole concern'.[11]

However, there were those who criticized the RAMC administration for being too distant and uninformed about the difficulties facing Medical Officers. Charles Symonds cited the case of his ADMS who had not been up the line to see the conditions of bearing wounded from the RAP to the ADS since taking up his post. Instead, he sent up his DADMS who, after a hasty inspection of the route on a day when there had been no rain for seventy-two hours, gave advice on the positioning of relay posts and the number of stretcher bearers at each. These recommendations took no account of the opinions of experienced Medical Officers at the units concerned; indeed they were in opposition to them.[12] Deeping, in *No Hero This*, condemned as 'absolutely damnable' a situation in which an ADMS could issue orders without extensive knowledge of the situation on the ground.[13]

This 'office wallah' method of administration was highlighted by James Barrett as the 'first and fundamental weakness' of the RAMC organization. He cites an occasion when he received a letter from 200 miles away instructing him in a matter covered by his own expertise, without any prior consultation. This was an extreme case and he admits that the temporary officers made up their minds to make the best of the RAMC machine. But after the War the majority believed that the system would require a rigorous overhaul, bringing it up to date 'with the scientific spirit of the time'. Barrett believed that this had to involve administrative officers having the opportunity to travel regularly throughout the command so that the Staff was constantly aware of developments.[14] There is an indication that in France the RAMC authorities did recognize that a problem existed. According to N.J.C. Rutherford, the 'staff of divisions marked down at home for coming to France are sent over to spend a week or ten days with the divisional headquarters of a division in the line. A very sound idea, because no human being has any idea of what a war is until he sees it going on and is in it himself.'[15] The tendency to isolation of the Staff, and of one unit from another, was never completely tackled, and Barrett correctly observed a need for better communication and greater flexibility.

Critics of the RAMC felt that more could have been done to keep the administration in touch with developments on the ground by employing civilian Medical Officers in administrative posts. However, aside from the consultants, little seems to have been done to involve civilians in the administrative side. The BMJ considered it a weakness that the AMS administration contained no Medical Officers who had experienced the process whereby a civil practitioner was converted into a temporary Medical Officer; especially given that, by the close of 1915, regulars already constituted less than a tenth of the total number of RAMC officers.[16] The Medical Establishment Committee considered it natural that regulars, with their intimate knowledge of the RAMC machine, should hold the majority of administrative posts, but felt it 'somewhat anomalous' that all the higher posts fell to them. Out of nearly 200 administrative posts in France, 140 were held by regulars, and sixteen by officers in the Special Reserve. Only twenty-two were held by Territorial Medical Officers, whilst fourteen were held by men on temporary commissions. Eight of the positions held by non-regulars were those of ADMS of Territorial Divisions; but with these exceptions, no one outside the Regular RAMC held a post higher than that of DADMS. The military authorities claimed that there were no non-regulars with sufficient administrative ability to fill these higher posts, but it was the opinion of the Committee 'that such men would be found'.[17] In a letter to the BMJ, a Territorial officer described the frustration which civilian Medical Officers experienced due to the refusal to recognize their abilities:

> even when Territorial Regimental Medical Officers had made themselves efficient in executive work and demonstrated their proficiency therein by passing examination D for promotion (from Major to Lieutenant Colonel), they were still 'held up' or rather 'turned down'.[18]

In the summer of 1917 an order was issued encouraging the promotion of civilian Medical Officers and their appointment to administrative posts. But continuing complaints and the observations of the Medical Establishment Committee suggest that no great change of policy took place. Clearly this was a waste of skilled manpower. An influx of civilian doctors, with their recent practical experience, would greatly have benefited the RAMC administration.

Even the eminent consultants lacked a clear position within the administrative organization.[19] However, in contrast to the position during the South African War, the consultants were awarded military rank. They were given temporary rank, junior only to that of a DMS. When the DsMS of the various armies were promoted to the rank of Surgeon General the senior consultants, such as Sir George Makins and Sir Anthony Bowlby, were also raised to this rank. Makins, who had along with Bowlby been one of those that served as a consultant in South Africa, considered that in 1914 the consultants 'arrived in France with a suitable rank, with no fully defined duties, but considerable freedom of action'.[20]

The consultants performed valuable work promoting the dissemination of the latest medical knowledge and techniques. However, their ability to undertake this task was limited by a system of deployment that some considered to be illogical. This was a concentric system whereby the consultant only had jurisdiction over a given area: the consultant at a CCS was not able to supervise the work being done at units in advance of or behind the zone where he was situated.[21] As the Commission on Medical Establishments observed, some means was required of enabling consultants to appreciate the situations confronted at the various medical units:

> [The] Committee were struck with the reluctance of those who are working at the base to discuss matters concerning the front, and vice versa. It seemed to the Committee that, from every point of view, it would be better if there were a freer interchange of thought between all the Consultants, and they strongly support the suggestion . . . that if the Consultants were periodically to change places with one another it would lead to more sympathy between the medical officers in the different areas.[22]

This method of deployment, known as the radial system, was actually employed during the Gallipoli campaign. The consultants worked to a rota, with each serving in turn at the Dardanelles, on the Lines of Communication, and at the Base. The advantage of the radial system was that it enabled consultants to observe the medical arrangements right down the line, see the effects of various treatments and make any necessary improvements. At the same time he was able to advise Medical Officers – advice that was infinitely more valuable when founded upon a wider understanding of the RAMC organization. The radial system, established under General Sir William Babtie,[23] was not, however, retained under his successors in the Mediterranean and Egyptian Expeditionary Forces. They introduced the concentric system that was in operation in other theatres. The concentric system was not entirely without merit as it gave the consultant the opportunity to become well acquainted with his Medical Officers and to assess their capabilities. But Makins, who had experienced the radial system in South Africa and observed its operation in the French medical service, considered that the concentric system was much the inferior of the two. Unlike their British counterparts the French consultants were able to monitor the progress of cases right down the chain of evacuation. Some improvement in the British system was effected when the two senior consulting surgeons, Makins and Bowlby, were assigned to a liaison role. Even so they worked on a concentric rather than a radial model. Makins believed that had they been deployed differently it would have been possible to have two types of consultant, thus combining the advantages of both systems. Instead, the consultants were constrained by the compartmentalism evident in other parts of the RAMC administration.[24]

The failure to recognize that civilian Medical Officers had an important administrative role to perform played into the hands of those who accused the RAMC organization of being inflexible and wasteful in its employment of doctors. But even worse was its failure to give adequate attention to the particular medical skills of civilian practitioners. The RAMC tended to regard Medical Officers as interchangeable units, without reference to their individual experience and abilities. According to a memorandum prepared by four eminent civilian practitioners there had been 'many complaints of Medical Officers being allocated to duty for which they are not so well qualified as for other work'.[25]

In a war situation it has to be recognized that Medical Officers were always likely to find themselves doing general medical work, rather than simply being confined to their own specialism. Without this flexibility the RAMC would have faced immense difficulties coping with its workload. At CCSs during busy times, specialists such as opthalmologists assisted with the general surgery. Nevertheless more ought to have been done to ensure that whenever possible Medical Officers were given work that suited their age and capabilities. It was wasteful to employ younger Medical Officers in units where the character of the work was light and routine (as in venereal hospitals), when there was a shortage of doctors for front-line service.

The problem, as revealed by the Medical Establishment Committee, was that there was little careful selection of Medical Officers in the initial stages of their service. During the course of their recruitment work the central professional committees had compiled elaborate records on virtually every practitioner in the country. From this mass of knowledge they were able to sift valuable information about the special skills of particular doctors and pass this on to the War Office. The result was a detailed card index from which it should have been possible to trace Medical Officers suited for particular duties and types of service. However the Committee were uncertain that this information ever reached the Headquarters in France, let alone was put to use.[26] Indeed, the allocation of Medical Officers to posts appeared to be based on an arbitrary set of principles. On arriving in France, if the Medical Officers were not immediately required by GHQ, instructions were issued regarding their temporary disposal. This usually involved them being attached to a base hospital where they assisted with the work until they were needed elsewhere. When Medical Officers were needed at the front, the DMS L of

C requested that the hospitals with the most doctors send up a certain number. Only on rare occasions would he specify anyone by name. In general the selection was left to the discretion of the hospital's CO; if he wished to keep a particular man, no matter how suitable he might be for service at the front, he was able to do so.[27]

The Committee urged that a Distributing Board be instituted for the selection of Medical Officers and the supervision of their subsequent careers. Since its work would mainly be concerned with temporary officers, the recommendation was that the organization be run by men drawn from the civil profession. Medical Officers, on arriving in France, would be inspected by the Board and classified according to their physical condition. Their professional qualities would then be recorded and a preliminary division made into two classes (either general practitioners; or those who practiced medicine, surgery, or a specialism). The Medical Officers would then be attached for three weeks to selected hospitals which were to act as schools of instruction. At the close of this training period a revised classification of their physical and professional capabilities would be made. On the basis of this information Medical Officers would be assigned to posts for which their qualifications and abilities most suited them. It would also be the duty of the Distributing Board to superintend the subsequent careers of Medical Officers. This would involve reliance on the reports of COs and consultants. However, in large hospitals sub-committees could be set up to report to the Board on the progress of officers.[28]

Card index systems listing the relevant qualifications, age and capacities of doctors were already in use in other organizations. The Joint War Committee of the BRCS and the Order of St John made initial classifications of all its personnel so that when requests for officers were received from abroad the cards could be consulted and the most suitable individuals appointed.[29] In France, in late 1915, the assistant secretary of the military medical service ordered a report to be drawn up for each officer and each civilian practitioner employed in a military establishment. The information listed included university titles (professor, anatomic assistant, head of a laboratory), hospital positions (physician or surgeon of a hospital, head of a clinic, surgical assistant, hospital intern) and any specialities (such as directing a surgical clinic, a bacteriologic or roentgenographic laboratory).[30]

It would be unfair to suggest that the RAMC took no account of individual expertise. The problem for the RAMC was that specialists had been given little consideration in its pre-war plans and organization. A small professional army, composed of fit, healthy men had no need for specialists such as opthalmologists or aurists, and on the outbreak of war there was no scheme of duties in place for specialists entering the RAMC. And in the early months of the War, as Professor A.D. Gardner discovered, the War Office had difficulty appreciating the contribution which specialists would be able to make:

> Arriving at the War Office [in August 1914], I was shown into a room where an unimpressive Major of the Royal Army Medical Corps sat at a desk. He sat me down and questioned me about my qualifications and experience, but when I said I was a Pathologist he looked down his nose and made it quite clear that the Army in war-time had no uses whatever for such persons. After a little reflection he said quite kindly that all the regular medical vacancies were now filled, and that he could only offer me a job to train stretcher-bearers in the Highlands of Scotland. Somewhat deflated, I regretfully declined his offer. Not only did I not myself know how to bear stretchers but I felt, perhaps conceitedly, that someone with less expensive qualifications than mine could do that job better than I could. So I returned for a while to my pathological work at St. Thomas's.[31]

In contrast, the large conscript armies of continental powers required, even in peacetime, the services of specialist Medical Officers; their position within foreign medical services was therefore much more clearly defined. The British military authorities were slow to recognize the important role to be placed by specialists, such as dentists, in remedying minor defects in recruits and in keeping the men fit. However more efficient use of specialists was secured by the formation of special front-line hospitals. The group of cases treated at such hospitals included opthalmic cases; those suffering from nerves or mental collapse; skin disorder; and venereal disease. These hospitals ensured better use was made of Medical Officers' expertise but also guarded against unnecessary wastage.

Consultants had an important part to play in ensuring that specialists' skills were put to good use. Unlike the regular Staff, the consultants knew from the positions held by doctors in civil life what their special experience had been, and were able to advise on their allocation to appropriate posts. Men with long surgical experience were consequently transferred from units where their abilities were of no avail to those where they would be an asset.[32] However, whilst in France the advice of consultants was sought on these matters, elsewhere this was not the case. In Egypt 'the consultants were not, either collectively or individually'[33] asked to give such assistance. The fact that consultants were not an integral part of the administration evidently meant that there were limitations to the supervisory role they could perform. Thus, as the

Commission on Medical Establishments recommended, there was a need for a more systematic approach to assessing the skills of Medical Officers which ensured that they were given work of an appropriate nature.

Calls were made in Parliament for the reconstitution of the Army Medical Advisory Board to scrutinize the employment of civilian medical men. The Board, established in 1901, had been in abeyance since the outbreak of war, but in the spring of 1918 the Government responded and appointed a new Board.[34] One of the first acts of the Board was to extend the card index of RAMC officers. It arranged for Medical Officers to complete a form, giving particulars as to age; medical school; qualifications; hospital appointments previously held; other appointments, such as MOH; any special training they may have undergone; research work conducted; and work published. They were also asked to detail their employment during the War, listing the units to which they had been attached; the expeditionary force or home command in which they served; and the nature of the duties performed. The resulting card index was kept at the office of the DGAMS in London. When an officer was posted to an expeditionary force or a command, a duplicate of his card would be forwarded to the headquarters of the force where it would be incorporated into a local card index. In cases of sudden transfer, Medical Officers were likely to arrive at their destinations before their files. However this problem was solved by arranging for information as to special experience, corresponding to that in the card index, to be inserted into Medical Officers' identity books.[35]

After being used to compile the card index, the Medical Officers' forms were passed on, following a primary classification according to their special experience and achievements, to a series of specialist committees appointed by the DGAMS. It was the duty of these committees to grade Medical Officers with special knowledge, taking into account the extent and nature of their experience. In the field of bacteriology an officer who had held an independent position and shown himself capable of completing independent research would be placed in grade one. From grade one men would be selected for higher appointments, such as director of a military laboratory. Grade two consisted of less experienced officers who had shown themselves capable of carrying out research under the general supervision of the director of a laboratory. They were eligible for employment in military laboratories, doing comparable work. Those who had completed their training in bacteriology, but had not yet undertaken any research, were classified as grade three. Officers in this category were employed as assistants in military laboratories and given the opportunity to undertake supervised investigations.[36] Similar classifications took place in other specialities. Thus these committees, in combination with the card index, ensured that during the final year of the War much greater care was taken, wherever possible, to employ doctors in posts appropriate to their skills and experience.

However, whilst greater attention was paid to the utilization of specialist knowledge, it remained a serious source of grievance amongst Medical Officers that professional ability was not recognized as grounds for promotion. This had a detrimental impact on both the efficiency of the medical service and on the level of morale within the Corps. Promotion was based upon administrative ability. Thus, as Medical Officers moved up the ranks of the RAMC they grew increasingly out of touch with medical work, or even completely uninterested in the professional side of things. In an organization like the RAMC, promotion was bound to be based primarily on administrative ability:

> [T]he vast majority of men when they attain the rank of Major and over, if they are any good at all get command of a unit – FA, CCS, General Hospital – what not, or a job in Divisional Corps or Army Headquarters: as ADMS, DMS, or DADMS, or whatever it may be. At any rate, having attained one of these eminences he thereupon ceases to do any actual medical work at all – because an OC with all the OCing [sic] involved or a pure administrator necessarily proceeds to become progressively more and more out of touch with and forgetful of medicine and surgery, both clinical and theoretical, except in so far as he deals with sundry diseases and injuries.[37]

But although recognizing that the emphasis on administration was unavoidable, Captain H.W. Kaye nevertheless felt that this tended to lead to an obsession with 'trifling points' and 'recognised precedent'.[38] There was a need for greater flexibility and men in the upper reaches of the RAMC who retained a close involvement in practical medicine. W.F. Tyndale noted a tendency to assume that administrative and scientific ability were necessarily divorced. This view was common amongst officers with no ambitions within the scientific sphere, and whose hopes for promotion rested solely upon administrative ability. In reality Tyndale found that scientific men, as well as making a valuable contribution in their specialist field, generally made effective administrators. Indeed he believed that 'in certain areas of fighting where arrangements were not so successful, there was a dearth of scientific officers, at any rate in responsible positions, and that where this was remedied matters improved'.[39]

The BMJ, in April 1918, criticized the scheme of promotion in the

RAMC for being obsessed 'by the idea that seniority in the service meant competence, and that without seniority there could not be competence'.[40] Insufficient recognition was given to the scientific and clinical skills of Medical Officers. As the War progressed there was growing frustration, particularly amongst the civilian intake, that work of a purely professional nature went unrewarded. The following exemplifies the discontent:

> In every other branch of the Army promotion is going on except on the surgical side of the RAMC work. I do not believe that it would be wise to promote every surgical specialist, but I believe that every surgical specialist of say two years' standing should be given his Majority. I am not particularly interested in the question of pay, but there again, there is a grievance. An officer in charge of surgical or medical divisions gets 10/- and 7/- per day charge pay, at a general or stationary hospital, but if he goes to a CCS, where he does much more work, he forfeits that.[41]

The sense of grievance was exacerbated by the knowledge that in the Dominion medical services promotion was given for professional ability. Often the situation arose whereby Australian or Canadian surgeons, ranking as Major or Lieutenant Colonel, were despatched with surgical teams to CCSs to find that the 'surgical specialist' directing their work was of no higher rank than Captain. No instance of this situation leading to friction has come to light, but it was certainly an indefensible anomaly that ought to have been tackled. However what was more trying for surgeons who had been working at the front for the duration of the War was the arrival from the UK of Medical Officers holding a rank which was denied to them; especially when this rank was awarded purely for administrative ability.

A situation in which medical or surgical ability was overlooked, taking second place in all decisions on promotion, did nothing but harm to the reputation of the RAMC. Few civilians were likely to wish to make their career in a service where the only prospect of advancement lay in administration. The RAMC's inability to recruit the Medical Officers it required in the immediate post-war years amounted to the profession's rejection of a service in which clerical ability appeared to take precedence over all else. Letters appeared in the medical press from former temporary Medical Officers in which its obsession with administration was cited as a major factor in their decision not to remain in the service. There were those who felt that some critics went too far in decrying administration,[42] which was essential to the RAMC's ability to carry out its work. Nevertheless, whatever the undoubted importance of administration, greater recognition needed to be given to professional skill.

The need for more specialist advisers in the upper ranks of the RAMC was highlighted by Sir Wilmot Herringham. He did not doubt that 'the administrative function is rightly in the superior position', but considered the divorce from practical work, necessitated by administrative posts, to be a source of weakness.[43] During the War the employment of eminent civilians had helped to bridge the gap between the administrative and executive branches. But on the return to peace the RAMC faced a shortage of specialist Medical Officers. In 1919, when the Consulting Physicians were returning to civil life, there were no regular officers suitable for these posts. This was not because regulars were inferior to civilians, but because they lacked the opportunity to specialize. The breakthroughs made by RAMC officers in tropical medicine demonstrated what could be achieved when such opportunities were available.

The advantages of broadening professional opportunities were recognized by the War Office. A promotion course was established at the Royal Army Medical College which aimed to prepare RAMC officers for membership of the Royal College of Physicians and Fellowship of the Royal College of Surgeons.[44] Despite these improvements the view persisted amongst medical students 'that the life the services offer is an idle one, that the amount of professional work available is slight, that its average quality is poor and its scope limited . . . [and] that no young medical man with any pretensions to professional keenness should enter the Services'.[45] The influence of such opinions is evident from the RAMC's failure to attract sufficient Medical Officers during the post-war decade.[46]

These, however, were problems for the future. Of more immediate concern to the RAMC were accusations that its entire organization was flawed and consequently was not satisfying the needs of the sick and wounded. The whole RAMC system was accused of militating against effective medical treatment. J.H. Dible likened army hospitals to processing plants, in which the treatment of the wounded came low down the list of priorities:

Army hospitals, as one soon finds to one's sorrow, do not exist for the purpose of curing sick men, but for that of indexing them, supplying a name to their disease, ascertaining their religion, and 'booting them out' elsewhere, with as much celerity as possible.[47]

Dible's grim observations on the army hospitals were made in 1915, but two years later they were made with still greater force by Sir Almroth

Wright. In a memorandum based on his experience as a consultant with the BEF in France he fulminated against the RAMC administration, for contenting itself with claiming credit for evacuating record numbers of wounded to the bases and home hospitals when 'it ought to lay emphasis on good service done in saving lives and healing the wounded'. Whereas a system based entirely on concern over the speed with which huge numbers of men were passed down the line was clearly convenient, from an administrative point of view he claimed that it operated 'as a damper upon all good and as an encouragement to all unconscientious professional work'.[48] He argued that this system was only kept from collapse because there existed 'in the ordinary medical officer an ineradicable standard of kindness and moral rectitude'. A similar conclusion was drawn by James Barrett, based on his experiences in Egypt. Whilst regarding the AMS's organization to be defective, he felt that the service showed much individual excellence.[49]

Wright believed that the system of evacuation employed by the RAMC interfered with the basic principles of wound treatment: that operation should take place at the earliest possible opportunity; that every wound should be closed up by surgical operation, as soon as bacterial infection has been overcome; and that compound fractures, especially those of the leg, should be retained in hospital until union has taken place. The emphasis on rapid evacuation meant that treatment was delayed, and that fracture cases were moved whilst still in a delicate state. Wright saw the consequences in large numbers of unnecessary amputations, with accompanying danger to life, performed on men who had been moved too early.[50] He felt that more could have been done to facilitate rapid front-line surgical treatment, and he deplored the policy of passing wounded from one unit to another. The Field Ambulance came in for particular criticism for standing in the way of early treatment.[51]

Wright also accused the RAMC administration of inadequately meeting its obligation to promote research into the medical problems which had arisen during the War. He proposed that a Medical Intelligence and Investigation Department be formed, to which all the staff of scientific committees working for the War Office, and all the Advisers in Hygiene and Pathology, would be affiliated. The new department would also include all the Medical Officers employed in bacteriological work so that all research would be concentrated within one organization. Its most important function would be to assess the possible effects of administrative orders upon professional matters. He believed that valuable help in establishing such a department could be obtained from the Medical

Research Committee which had already placed nearly all its resources at the disposal of the War Office.[52]

Sir Arthur Sloggett was stung by what he regarded as a bitter and disloyal attack upon the RAMC in France. In collaboration with his staff of consultants and scientific advisers, he mounted a vigorous rebuttal of Wright's criticisms. Sloggett pointed out that if evacuation to the UK were to be significantly reduced there would need to be a proportionate increase in the number of beds available in France. However scope for further expansion was extremely limited. He also refuted the suggestion that evacuation to the UK was unnecessary, pointing out the severe strain which the wounded from the recent Somme campaign had placed upon hospital accommodation in France. If suitable cases had not been evacuated, the whole system would have become clogged up, thus endangering the lives of those requiring urgent treatment. Meanwhile, during periods of relative quiet it was important to keep a reserve of beds free, in case of sudden emergencies.[53] Furthermore, he took issue with Wright's claim that the scheme of evacuation, and the Field Ambulance in particular, caused an avoidable and potentially fatal delay in the treatment of serious cases. Sloggett dismissed the idea that the FA prolonged active surgery for twelve hours and explained that serious cases were passed direct from the FAs to the CCSs, without stopping for intermediate medical attention. He admitted that some cases did face delays of many hours, if not days, but stressed that this was due to the immense difficulties involved in removing cases from the front line and not to any fault in the RAMC administration.[54]

Sir Berkeley Moynihan declared that it was 'a travesty of the truth' to suggest that the RAMC administration cared for nothing other than the rapid evacuation of the wounded. Moreover, he felt that 'in the vast majority of instances the rapid transit, the rapid evacuation of the wounded soldier, is perhaps the best means of saving his life and limb'.[55] Writing in 1919, Sir Wilmot Herringham argued that those who had criticized the RAMC for not retaining patients longer and treating them more fully before sending them down the line had been short-sighted. Such a policy would have required large front-line hospitals. Quite apart from the difficulties of supplying such hospitals, there was the danger that in case of retreat they would be impossible to evacuate and move. Evacuation was consequently forced upon the RAMC as 'a necessary evil', just as it was upon the French and German medical services.[56]

Wright's attack upon the evacuation arrangements was ill-conceived. However, this is not to imply that the system did not have its drawbacks from the medical point of view. There was a problem of compartmentalization, concerning which the RAMC administration may be criticized for reacting too slowly. More could have been done in the early years of the War to promote the free flow of information. At the end of 1917, however, arrangements were made for the interchange of surgeons between CCSs and general hospitals, allowing those with the forward units to follow up cases.[57] Valuable assistance in promoting the exchange of information between Medical Officers was afforded by the Medical Research Committee. Its work in this direction was facilitated by the appointment of Lieutenant Colonel T.R. Elliot to represent the Committee in France. The Committee highlighted the need for more complete clinical records and for a system which allowed 'for the forward transference of brief clinical notes with each patient as he moved from unit to unit, and also for sending information on his progress back to any Medical Officer who might wish to learn the result of the treatment that he had just used for any particular patient'.[58] During the course of 1917 the Army introduced a card index to replace the case sheet for all hospitals in France, and altered the Army Field Medical Card to form a continuous diary of each casualty's clinical history while overseas. Since June of that year, this card accompanied the patient to the UK for the information of any Medical Officer receiving him there. Of course the greater exchange of information between hospitals was no substitute for a patient being treated by one set of doctors in one hospital. Evacuation made this impossible; and unfortunately evacuation was an unavoidable necessity. Nevertheless, it was a necessity out of which the RAMC created a praiseworthy system, providing rapid and good quality treatment to the wounded, and making good use of the skills of its surgeons and physicians.

As with the criticisms of the evacuation procedures, support for Wright's position on the lack of priority given to research can be found in the diary of Captain J.H. Dible. As Commander of Number 7 Mobile Bacteriological Laboratory he encountered much hostility to his research work, and found the medical administration, at best, indifferent to scientific investigation. From early in the War, however, Keogh and Sloggett had been alive to the need to promote research. Dible himself acknowledges the co-operation which developed between the MRC and the Army, and the role played by the consultants in fostering medical research.[59] Indeed, the formation of the first mobile bacteriological and hygiene laboratories in October and November 1914 demonstrates an early recognition by the RAMC of the necessity for front-line investigation. Altogether, thirty-nine such laboratories saw service on the Western

Front during the War, four of which were transferred to Italy during 1917.[60]

It was unfair of Wright to suggest that the RAMC had been unwilling to accept the assistance of eminent medical men or had failed to promote the cause of research. From the beginning of the War the MRC devoted the majority of its activities to assisting the RAMC,[61] and in this it received not only the co-operation of Sir Arthur Sloggett, but his active encouragement. Referring to its work on cerebro-spinal fever, the MRC's annual report for 1916–17 gave an indication of the RAMC's readiness to facilitate the participation of its officers in scientific work:

> The Committee have again continued to give large assistance to the central organisation for the scientific study and control of cerebro-spinal fever among the military forces. The work is directed by Lieutenant-Colonel Mervyn Gordon, CMG, RAMC, assisted by Major Hine, RAMC, both receiving whole-time salaries from the Committee and holding honorary commissions. They have been assisted by other members of the Corps for varying periods, and during the first half of the year under notice they had the cooperation of Dr. Martin Flack (Hon. Captain RAMC), a member of the Committee's permanent staff, who had charge of the cerebro-spinal fever work for the London district.[62]

Indeed, much of the work undertaken by the MRC was at the direct request of the DGAMS. This included a special enquiry into a group of cases of acute nephritis (1915); the setting apart of a military hospital for the study and treatment of cardiac cases, with a view to reducing wastage from disorders of the soldiers' heart (1916); the appointment of a Dysentery Committee to advise the DGAMS on scientific and administrative matters relating to the subject, so that greater co-ordination could be achieved between the research work of the MRC, and the needs of the Army (1918); and the appointment of a Special Investigation Committee for the study of shock.[63]

The work of the MRC on shock illustrates the valuable results that emerged from its co-operation with the Army. The Special Investigation Committee 'had a very strong membership' and was chaired first by Professor E.H. Starling, and then by Professor W.M. Bayliss. Amongst its members was Professor W.B. Cannon of Harvard who was able to liaise with a corresponding committee in the United States.[64] Under the umbrella of the Special Committee work took place in the front line to ascertain the time and manner of the onset of shock. Captain Cowell[65] spent six weeks living in the aid posts which evacuated to Number 33 CCS, observing the conditions of soldiers both before and after wounding. As a result he was able to suggest the best means of over-coming shock and diminishing its incidence. At Number 33 CCS, Cowell worked alongside Captain Emrys-Roberts[66] and Professor W.B. Cannon, doing a series of tests on the alkalinity of blood, which established a defi-nite acidosis in cases of shock.[67] Initially it was thought that this depletion of the alkali reserve of the blood plasma was the cause of wound shock. However the Committee's further investigations concluded that a circu-latory deficiency was the chief factor in the development of shock, and that acidosis was a consequence and not the cause of this defective circu-lation. As a result of these investigations attention was focussed upon the treatment of shock by the replacement of lost blood with an artificial substitute.[68] The MRC gave equally valuable assistance in other areas, including: the diagnosis of typhoid and paratyphoid; dysentery and its occurrence in the eastern theatres of war; and the effects of chemical warfare.[69]

The MRC commended Keogh and Sloggett for the manner in which they had 'freely sought and accepted both initiative and criticism' from the consultants. Decisions regarding methods of treatment were largely in the hands of the latter. Consequently the Committee felt that blame for any inadequacies should fall upon the shoulders of the consultant body of which Wright was a member.[70] Indeed, Wright accepted this in his memorandum. He wrote to Sloggett emphasizing his belief that 'the Medical Military Organisation as such is extraordinarily efficient'. For him, it was the system of having consultants as an advisory body that was 'radically faulty'.[71] The MRC, however, made a point of distancing itself from the conclusions contained in Wright's memorandum, which it regarded as 'faulty both in tone and perspective'. It considered that the RAMC in France already possessed an effective advisory system, high-lighting in particular the appointment of Leishman as Adviser in Pathology.[72]

For the MRC the problem lay in the fact that the efficiency of the system in France was not replicated in the UK, or in the other theatres. In January 1917, Sir Walter Fletcher wrote to Bowlby explaining that 'you who work in France do not know as we do the conditions in the Mediterranean and in the UK, and its deficiencies in these two areas (deficiencies which are largely due to the inevitable concentration of the best talent in France) which we have been chiefly concerned with helping to remedy or diminish. Irritation which may be felt in the RAMC in France will, I think, be less felt at home and in the East, and inside the War Office itself.'[73] The MRC felt that the Army Medical Department (AMD) had not kept pace with other branches of the War Office in expanding to meet the requirements of a large Army. It highlighted the paucity of scientific advice at the centre which had directly contributed to failures of preventive medicine both in the eastern theatres and amongst the troops in the UK. To meet this deficiency the MRC proposed that the Army's chief Adviser in Pathology be based, not in France, but at the War Office. This change was to be underpinned by the formation of two new departments, one responsible for Pathological Investigation and Epidemiology, and the other responsible for Army Sanitation. The MRC also expressed dissatisfaction with the continued exclusion of the DGAMS from the Army Council. It argued that 'no progressive military system out[side] of England' made the DGAMS subordinate to the Adjutant General 'as if questions of personnel were his only main concern'. [74] This case was made forcibly in *The Times* by Lord Esher, one of the architects of the prevailing system:

> How much of the suffering undergone by our soldiers since the war began has been due to the shortsightedness of my committee, and notably of myself, will never be known. Certainly, the control of the adjutant-general's branch over the Royal Army Medical Corps was and is responsible not only for the early failure to grip the medical factors of the war, but they hampered conditions under which the surgeon-general has worked. His triumphs and those of the Royal Army Medical Corps have been achieved in spite of obstacles that the subordination of science to ignorance and of elasticity to military discipline explains but can not justify. [75]

Underlying all of the MRC's observations was a concern to ensure that medical science was placed at the heart of the AMS. It agreed with those who questioned a system of promotion that was so biased towards administrative ability, stressing that 'it is of fundamental importance that there should be no general cleavage between scientific officers on the one hand and executive officers as such, on the other'. [76] The experience of war certainly seems to have brought the importance of science to the attention of the AMD, as is evident from the positive tone of the MRC's report for 1918–1919:

> It has been increasingly realised during the war, if not in its earliest stages, that only a true knowledge of nature can guide physical activities rightly, and that research work is a vital necessity for success in warfare, which is a contest of activities. This truth has been brought home in a thousand lessons, and as its realization has gained ground during the war, so men fitted for the work of enquiry have been increasingly permitted to perform it . . . Before the end of the war it may be said that most of the men best

fitted for original inquiry were given opportunity for it, and given pay for it from public funds, whether by way of commissions in the Navy or Army or Air Force or of research grants from the Committee out of the Medical Research Fund, and that in the main this national system of medical research was welded into a coherent intellectual service by appropriate arrangements made between the different disbursing authorities.[77]

The year 1919 saw the establishment within the AMD of a Directorate of Hygiene and a Directorate of Pathology. This step clearly reflected the influence of the MRC's proposals. The two new Directorates were intended to bring greater co-ordination to preventive medicine and to raise the status of the Medical Officers involved. The organization was designed to promote co-operation between those working in the preventive field, both within and outside the Army, and to place the RAMC in a position whereby its officers had the opportunity to contribute to the advancement of knowledge. Included in the scheme was provision for establishing schools of hygiene in each command where RMOs could receive instruction in practical methods of sanitation and those aspiring to posts in the directorate be given special training. Medical Officers were given the opportunity to sit for diplomas in public health, hygiene and tropical medicine.[78] The BMJ welcomed these developments as 'the Magna Carta of science in the Army Medical Service' and considered that they constituted 'the most important medical reform that has taken place since the creation of the RAMC'.[79]

There is no doubt that in certain respects the War found the RAMC administration wanting. At the outset of the conflict it lacked an adequate system for assessing doctors' skills and allocating them to appropriate positions. During the War, the need for such a system soon became clear, but it was 1918 before the War Office made an adequate response. As in so many other aspects of Britain's war effort the problem was one of lack of preparation. Prior to the War no consideration had been given to the mechanics of expanding the RAMC by recruiting large numbers of civilian doctors; let alone to the skills they might possess, and their role within a wartime medical service. It is also evident that no substantial plans for the medical treatment of a large conscript army had been made, hence the failure to appreciate the need for medical specialisms not previously required. The failure of the War Office and the RAMC to anticipate these difficulties, and more importantly their delay in making the necessary improvements, are deserving of criticism.

However the severest contemporary criticisms of the RAMC do not accurately reflect the situation on the Western Front. Wright's vilification of the medical organization in France proved to be an isolated view amongst the consultants. Meanwhile other critics, such as James Barrett, were drawing, for their evidence, on experiences outside of France. There was no denying that the medical services in the eastern theatres had often been woefully inadequate. But as the MRC commented, this was, at least in part, a consequence of the commitment of the best medical personnel and equipment to the principal theatre of operations. The conduct of the RAMC administration in France and Flanders demonstrated that many of the lessons of the South African War had been learnt. Medical Officers possessed sufficient authority to carry out their duties and, on the whole, medical science was unrestricted in its campaign to protect the health of the troops. There were, of course, administrative difficulties such as the tendency to compartmentalism. However, as the following chapter will demonstrate, improvements in the system for training and updating Medical Officers went some way to rectify this. Altogether the RAMC proved remarkably successful at utilizing doctors' skills, and in providing for the needs of the sick and wounded. Sir Anthony Bowlby, reviewing over four and a half years service as a senior consultant, felt that he had 'been able to develop and control the surgery of the war to the help of the army and to the saving of lives and limb'.[80]

Notes

1   Sloggett served until June 1918 when he was succeeded by Lieutenant General C. Burtchaell.
2   This is only a brief summary of the development of the administration. A more detailed account is available in MacPherson, *General History*, II, pp. 1–14.
3   Gervis, *Arms and the Doctor*, pp. 19–20.
4   Martin, *Surgeon in Khaki*, pp. 130–2.
5   'Report of Lord Charnwood on Criticisms of the Medical Service of the British Expeditionary Forces in France', JAMA, LXIX, 1917, p. 739.
6   *Ibid.* p. 738.
7   Served in France from January 1915 as DADMS III Corps.
8   Major M.B.H. Ritchie, 'The Training of RAMC Officers for War', JRAMC, XLII, 1924, p. 270.
9   Captain W.H. Kaye, WIHM, RAMC 739, Diary: 12 February 1916.
10 Herringham, *Physician in France*, pp. 50–1.
11 M. Whiting, LC, Papers: Rough draft of an article for the Middlesex Hospital Journal, p. 2.
12 Second Lieutenant Charles Symonds, LC, Letters: letter 21 November 1917.
13 Deeping, *No Hero This*, p. 258.
14 Barrett, *Vision of the Possible*, pp. 163–4.
15 Rutherford, *Soldiering with a Stethoscope*, p. 165.
16 'Medical Lessons of the War', BMJ, 1915 (II), p. 901.

17 Commission on Medical Establishments, WIHM, RAMC 1165, p. 94.
18 'Reconstruction of the Territorial Medical Service', BMJ, 1919 (II), p. 87.
19 'The Army Medical Service Today', BMJ, 1918 (I), p. 155.
20 Sir George Makins, 'The Part of the Consulting Surgeon in War', BMJ, 1919 (I), p. 789.
21 George W. Crile, 'Standardization of the Practice of Military Surgery – The Clinical Surgeon in Military Service', JAMA, LXIX, 1917, p. 291.
22 Report of the Commission on Medical Establishments, WIHM, RAMC 1165, p. 44.
23 Principal Director of Medical Services, Mediterranean, during operations in Gallipoli, Egypt and Salonika, 1915–1916.
24 Sir George Makins, 'Introductory', British Journal of Surgery, BJS, VI, 1918–1919, p. 11.
25 Burtchaell papers, WIHM, RAMC 446/9: Memorandum Containing Severe Criticism of the Medical Services by Sir Alfred Fripp, Sir Alexander Ogston, Sir E. Cooper Perry and Dr T.J. Horder, point number two. Sir Alfred Fripp was Surgeon to Guy's Hospital; Professor Sir Alexander Ogston was President of the BMA; Sir E. Cooper Perry was superintendent of Guy's Hospital (and, with Ogston and Fripp, a member of the Committee which reformed the RAMC and established the Advisory Board after the South African War); Dr T.J. Horder was Physician at St Bartholomew's Hospital, and had seen service in France.
26 Commission on Medical Establishments, WIHM, RAMC 1165, p. 112.
27 Commission on Medical Establishments, WIHM, RAMC 1165, pp. 99–100.
28 Commission on Medical Establishments, WIHM, RAMC 1165, pp. 104-8.
29 'Reports by the Joint War Committee and the Joint War Finance Committee of the British Red Cross Society and the Order of St. John of Jerusalem in England', HMSO, 1921, p. 75.
30 'Measures for the Better Utilisation of Medical Ability [France]', JAMA, LXV, 1915, p. 1929.
31 Professor A.D. Gardner, LC, Typescript recollections, p. 96.
32 Herringham, Physician in France, pp. 52–3.
33 Tubby, Consulting Surgeon in the Near East, p. 253.
34 The membership of the Board consisted of the DGAMS, Lieutenant General T.H.J.C. Goodwin; Major General Sir Bertrand Dawson (physician to the London Hospital, and a consulting physician with the BEF in France); Major General Sir Berkeley Moynihan (surgeon to the Leeds Infirmary and consulting surgeon to Northern Command); Colonel W.H. Horrocks (sanitary expert); Colonel Sir Robert Jones (Inspector of Military Orthopaedics); and Lieutenant Colonel Sir Harold J. Stiles (Assistant Inspector of Military Orthopaedics for Scotland, and a member of the Commission of Inquiry on Medical Establishments in France).
35 'Work of the Army Medical Advisory Board', BMJ, 1918 (I), pp. 568–9.
36 'Work of the Army Medical Advisory Board', BMJ, 1918 (I), p. 569.
37 Kaye, WIHM, RAMC 739, Diary, Vol. II, 27 January 1916.
38 Ibid.
39 W.F. Tyndale, 'An Assistant Director of Medical Services in War Time', JRAMC, XXXVI, 1921, p. 408.

40 'If Good Why Not Better?', BMJ, 1918 (I), p. 486.
41 Bowlby, WIHM, RAMC 365, Papers: Memorandum, 24 October 1917, p. 1.
42 'The RAMC as a Career', BMJ, 1919 (II), pp. 511; 546; 615; 691.
43 Herringham, *Physician in France*, pp. 47–8.
44 Sir Robert Drew, *Medical Officers in the British Army 1660–1960, Vol II 1898–1960*, The Wellcome Historical Medical Library, 1968, p. xv.
45 Report of the Committee on the Medical Branches of the Defence Services, cmd. 4394, 1932–33, XI, p. 7. (Henceforth the Warren Fisher Committee.)
46 The General Annual Reports on the British Army: 1922, cmd. 2114, 1924, IV, p. 637; 1923 cmd. 2272, 1924, XIV, p. 777; 1924, cmd. 2342, 1924-25, XVII, p. 891; 1925 cmd. 2582, 1926, XVIII, p. 905; 1926, cmd. 2806, 1927, XIV, p. 905; 1927, cmd. 3030, 1928, XIV, p. 911; 1928, cmd. 3265, 1928-29, XI, p. 913; 1929, cmd. 3498, 1929-30, XIX, p. 895; 1930, cmd. 3800, 1930-31, XIX, p. 879.
47 J.H. Dible, IWM, Diary, 9 August 1915, p. 133.
48 Bowlby, WIHM, RAMC 365, Papers: Memorandum on the Necessity of Creating at the War Office a Medical Intelligence and Investigation Department to get the best possible Treatment for the Wounded, diminish Invaliding and return the men to the Ranks in the shortest time, by Colonel Sir A. Wright (henceforth the Wright Memorandum), pp. 1–2.
49 Bowlby, WIHM, RAMC 365, Papers: Wright Memorandum, p. 2. Barrett, *A Vision*, p. 174.
50 Bowlby, WIHM, RAMC 365, Papers; Wright Memorandum, p. 3.
51 Bowlby, WIHM, RAMC 365, Papers; Wright Memorandum, p. 4. The role of the Field Ambulance, and the question of whether employment there was a waste of a Medical Officer's abilities, will be assessed in the next chapter.
52 Bowlby, WIHM, RAMC 365, Papers: Wright Memorandum, pp. 6–8
53 Bowlby, WIHM, RAMC 365, Papers: Letter from Sir A. Sloggett to Bowlby, 15 January 1917, pp. 9–10.
54 Sir Arthur Sloggett, WIHM, RAMC 365/4, Papers: Response to Sir Almroth Wright's Memorandum, 15 January 1917, p. 12.
55 Bowlby, WIHM, RAMC 365, Papers. Report of the Meeting held in the Medical Board Room on 15 January 1917, p. 10.
56 Herringham, *Physician in France*, pp. 100–1.
57 MacPherson, *Surgery of the War*, I, p. 226.
58 Third Annual Report of the Medical Research Committee 1916–1917, cmd. 8825, 1917–18, XVII, p. 708.
59 J.H. Dible, *IWM*, Diary 1916, pp. 148-52.
60 MacPherson, *General History*, II, p. 308. MacPherson, *Hygiene of the War*, I, p. 12. MacPherson, *General History*, III, pp. 508–9.
61 Interim Report of the Work in Connection with the War at Present Undertaken by the Medical Research Committee, cmd. 7922, 1914-1916, XXXI, pp. 533–8. A. Landsborough Thompson, *Half a Century of Medical Research, Volume Two*, HMSO, 1975, p. 273.
62 Third Annual Report of the Medical Research Committee, 1916–1917, cmd. 8825, 1917-18, XVII, p. 733.
63 First Annual Report of the Medical Research Committee, 1914–15, cmd. 8101,

1914-1916, XXXI, p. 584. Second Annual Report of the Medical Research Committee, cmd. 8399, 1916, XIV, p. 260. Fourth Annual Report of the Medical Research Committee, 1917-18, cmd. 8981, 1918, XII, p. 481. Third Annual Report of the Medical Research Committee, 1916-1917, cmd. 8825, 1917–18, XVII, p. 746.

64 Thompson, *Half a Century of Medical Research, Volume Two*, p. 282. Fourth Annual Report of the Medical Research Committee, 1917–18, cmd. 8981, 1918, XII, p. 494.

65 E.M. Cowell: Surgical Specialist, BEF, 1915–18; OC Number One CCS, BEF, 1918–19; Commandant First Army School of Instruction, RAMC.

66 Edward Emrys-Roberts: Professor of Pathology and Bacteriology, University of Wales; OC Welsh Mobile Bacteriological Laboratory, BEF, France, 1915–18.

67 WO 95/197, PRO, DMS First Army, Diary, 1917: October, Appendix XLI: Colonel Cuthbert Wallace, Consulting Surgeon, First Army, to DMS First Army, re. Research Work conducted in the First Army, 24 October 1917, p. 1.

68 Thompson, *Half a Century of Medical Research, Volume Two*, pp. 282-3. Fourth Annual Report of the Medical Research Committee, 1917–18, cmd. 8981, 1918, XII, p. 495.

69 For an overview of the MRC's wartime work, see Thompson, *Half a Century of Medical Research, Volume Two*, pp. 273-91.

70 FD 5/27, PRO, Observations of the Medical Research Committee made at the request of the Prime Minister upon a Memorandum by Sir Almroth Wright, 30 January 1917, pp. 2–5.

71 Sloggett, RAMC 365/4, WIHM, letter from Wright to Sloggett, 17 January 1917.

72 FD 5/27, PRO, Observations of the Medical Research Committee made at the request of the Prime Minister upon a Memorandum by Sir Almroth Wright, 30 January 1917, pp. 1917, pp. 1–2. Bowlby, WIHM RAMC 365, Papers: Letter to Bowlby from the MRC, 13 January 1917.

73 Sloggett, RAMC 365/4, WIHM, letter from Fletcher to Bowlby, 13 January 1917.

74 FD 5/27, PRO, Observations of the Medical Research Committee made at the request of the Prime Minister upon a Memorandum by Sir Almroth Wright, 30 January 1917, pp. 6–18.

75 Lord Esher, *The Times*, 3 February 1917, p. 7.

76 FD 5/27, PRO, Observations of the Medical Research Committee made at the request of the Prime Minister upon a Memorandum by Sir Almroth Wright, 30 January 1917, p. 21.

77 Fifth Annual Report of the Medical Research Committee, 1918–1919, cmd. 412, 1919, XXVI, pp. 196–7.

78 Major General J.G. Gill, IWM, Papers: Biographical details. Major General P.H. Henderson, IWM, Papers: Biographical details.

79 'The Scientific Future of the RAMC', BMJ, 1919 (I), p. 554.

80 Sir Anthony Bowlby, Royal College of Surgeons of England (RCS), Papers, diary, 3 April 1919.

Chapter 7

Doctors and Military Medicine: The Training of Medical Officers

At the outset of the War there was a tendency to assume that placing a doctor in uniform transformed him into a military Medical Officer.[1] This chapter questions the extent to which pre-war medical training and experience of civilian practice was adequate preparation for the work of an army doctor. It will highlight the degree to which the priorities of military medicine differed from those of its civilian counterpart. However, it will also demonstrate that even doctors with a military background found themselves facing unfamiliar situations. In 1914 there was little inkling of the problems that were to confront medicine on the Western Front. Thus there was a need to give civilian MOs a foundation in military procedures, and to ensure that they understood the full extent of a Medical Officer's duties. But there was also a need to keep all MOs informed of the latest treatments and medical techniques and to establish some uniformity of approach. The chapter will evaluate the RAMC's response to this imperative requirement for an on-going programme of military medical instruction.

Throughout the War certainty was expressed concerning doctors' ability to adapt their knowledge in order to meet the challenges of military medicine. Colonel T.H. Goodwin, writing in July 1917, believed that pre-war medical training had provided sufficient preparation for the duties of an army doctor, 'as it teaches self reliance and confidence in personal ability, quickness of judgement, and power to apply theory to practice in a case of emergency'.[2] His faith in the determination of doctors to apply their knowledge to war conditions, and to do their utmost for the men, generally proved well-founded. Nevertheless, to perform proficiently, doctors required a breadth of knowledge that was not supplied by traditional medical training. They needed to appreciate the differences between civil and military medicine and to understand the procedures of the military medical organization. Most doctors lacked military experience;[3] others had received some training in OTC units or the Reserve Forces; but only a small proportion had seen active service. British doctors were not alone in their ignorance of military medical organization. In Germany, pre-war conscription ensured that doctors had some military experience, but this was not necessarily in a medical context. Colonel H.N. Thompson, who assisted in a German hospital whilst a prisoner, praised the surgical skill of the six doctors with whom he worked. However, he found them to be largely uninformed about administration, sanitation and feeding arrangements. Their pre-war service had not been in the Medical Corps, but in cavalry, artillery or infantry units.[4]

The experience of J.M. McLachlan suggests that new Medical Officers were simply left to muddle through by the military authorities. In April 1915, shortly after becoming the MO of the 17th (Service) Battalion, Northumberland Fusiliers, he complained of being in 'a slightly fogged condition as to how much I'm supposed actually to do'.[5] His responsibilities included leading his men in stretcher drill, about which he confessed to knowing 'jolly little'. To his embarrassment, he found that his sanitation and water orderlies were more knowledgeable concerning sanitary matters than he was himself.[6] When, in May 1915, he was stationed at No. 9 Stationary Hospital, Le Havre, in charge of venereal cases, he again admitted to being 'a trifle foggy' as to his duties.[7] Another doctor, L.W. Batten, had similar experiences. He recalled that his civilian training had done 'very little to fit me for service as a Field Ambulance or Regimental Medical Officer which is what I was to become'.[8]

The limitations of doctors' pre-war experience were commented upon by the Official History. It pointed out that the majority of general practitioners had been unable to keep up with the latest surgical developments.[9] Sir Geoffrey Keynes, however, recalled that even those, like himself, who had recently qualified, found that they were completely unprepared for the surgical work that confronted them in France.[10] There was rarely sufficient time for thorough training. Thus, Medical Officers were forced to develop their expertise as they carried out their duties, adapting their medical skills to meet military requirements. Noel Chavasse[11] read books on military hygiene and typhoid fever, virtually teaching himself in the field.[12] Warwick Deeping, the novelist, had been out of the profession for some time. He sought to ready himself for service by taking a refresher course at the Middlesex Hospital prior to enlisting.[13] Even doctors with knowledge of military medicine were inadequately prepared for the medical challenges that arose on the Western Front. Lieutenant Colonel G.W. Hughes, a Regular Officer in the RAMC from 1903 to 1926, remembered nothing in his military training that prepared him for trench warfare. Trench conditions gave rise to difficulties in the evacuation of wounded not previously considered, and diseases and sanitary problems not met with before.[14] In September 1914, Lord Esher informed Kitchener:

> Keogh, who organised the RAMC, admitted to me that such a war as this was never thought of. Just as *you* were called upon to fight through with an army raised to 'reinforce India'; so the RAMC were organised to meet casualties on the South African basis![15]

The RAMC faced a problem not encountered by combatant units. Cavalry, infantry and artillery were organized in peace along the same lines as they were in war. Their daily training concentrated upon their duties in war and they had no peacetime role to play. However, the RAMC's function in war differed widely from that in peace. Its wartime organization only sprang into being on mobilization, and with onerous peacetime responsibilities for dealing with the sick, there was little opportunity to study the changing demands that active service would impose. In the post-war years, this difficulty remained. RAMC training was still failing to consider future problems of war organization: personnel, equipment and transport. A course in medical administration at the Royal Army Medical College would have corrected the situation, but financial stringency worked against this. It was therefore suggested that the Journal of the RAMC be used more readily as a forum for discussing developments, such as the impact that the tank, the aeroplane and the motor lorry were likely to have on the medical service.[16]

The RAMC's approach to surgery in 1914 was rooted in its Boer War experience, where wounds had frequently recovered without immediate surgical intervention. General Sir Neil Cantlie[17] remembered the unfortunate consequences of this early faith in the expectant approach:

> I had an artillery officer hit in the abdomen by a stray bullet – evacuation was only possible by night then and I remembered the South African experiences when some of those wounded in the stomach and had been left out on the veldt survived, the others who were moved died. So little did I know, I had only been qualified a few weeks, I deliberately stopped evacuation

for the officer and he died in my RAP. You will be horrified at my action, but I truly believed I was giving him the best treatment.[18]

The conditions that pertained in South Africa were different to those on the Western Front. In contrast to the Boer campaign where the fighting had been over the clean veldt, the battles in France and Flanders were fought over land that was highly cultivated. Wounds were unavoidably contaminated with this rich soil and quickly became septic.[19] Seasoned military doctors had to recognize that the surgical experiences of the Boer campaign had no relevance to the conditions in France and Flanders. Subsequently, early operation came to be regarded as offering the wounded their best chance of survival. In the civil branch of the profession, many retained a negative opinion of the surgical skills of their military brethren. According to A.A. Martin there were few able surgeons in the RAMC.[20] Sir Alfred Keogh, however, rejected such notions and felt that, apart from the consultants, 'RAMC officers are as good as anything that the civil profession can produce in France'.[21] Moreover, civilian surgeons were no better prepared than were their military colleagues for the surgical work of the Western Front. Severe gunshot wounds differed from even the most critical wounds which doctors were likely to have encountered in civil life, both in terms of the quality and quantity of the damage inflicted. Civilian surgeons were also forced to recognize that current treatments for sepsis, which were efficacious in civilian cases, were not adequate to tackle the severe infections that characterized the war wounds.

Thus it is evident that the regulars, and their civilian colleagues, had much to learn. In no area of medicine was pre-war knowledge sufficient preparation for the problems that arose between 1914 and 1918. Even a consultant of the stature of Sir Wilmot Herringham, admitted that he learnt more medicine in his five years with the RAMC than in any previous five years of his life.[22] Some degree of further professional training and guidance was therefore essential for all Medical Officers.

The obvious advantage that regulars had over the civilian intake was their experience of military procedures. The accounts of temporary commissioned officers demonstrate that they were largely ignorant of the RAMC's ways. Those with Territorial records were better placed, but prior to the War concern had been expressed about the effectiveness of Territorial training. In 1913, Major Josiah Oldfield recorded that 'my experience leads me to say that in practice it works out that [the RMO] has very little training in the duties that will be required of him on mobilisation'.[23] To effectively utilize civilian doctors some instruction in military procedures was necessary. An Australian Medical Officer who joined No. 12 CCS in May 1915 noted the important role that regulars played in this regard:

> The presence of two regular officers was of the greatest value, for while they frankly confessed to great ignorance of the science and art of the profession, yet they understood the necessity and the machinery of military organisation and the importance of carefully kept records. It is not easy for a civilian at first to appreciate the necessity of the detailed care of maintaining the admission, discharge, and other books of a military medical unit . . . I think I may fairly say that units raised in the Dominions and staffed by men entirely from civil practice at the outset, failed in this respect.[24]

Doctors needed to be aware of the differences between military and civilian medicine. Accustomed to clean, well-lit hospitals, with up-to-the-minute facilities and an ample supply of trained assistants, accomplished surgeons had to adjust to working in often cramped, cold and dirty conditions, with only the most basic equipment.[25] Medical Officers also needed to understand that the application of surgical principles varied, depending upon the type of unit to which they were attached. They had to appreciate the differing requirements of work at a Field Ambulance, a Casualty Clearing Station and at the base and home hospitals. This included being able to discern which cases demanded immediate operative treatment, and which ought to be evacuated to units further in the rear. Even the most able surgeons could not give of their best without an understanding of these differences.[26] Prior to the War, Oldfield had criticized Territorial training for failing to give Medical Officers a standard training that would prepare them for work in all types of medical unit.[27]

Military requirements imposed a new set of priorities on doctors. Whereas in civil life the doctor's first duty was to the individual, in the RAMC the needs of the State were paramount. Excessive sympathy and concern ran the risk of 'desoldierising' the men,[28] and wasteful sentimentality was discouraged.[29] The Medical Inspector of Drafts with the BEF noted that many inexperienced young doctors were far too ready to find men unfit for service. Administrative Medical Officers had to impress on them the importance of avoiding leniency.[30] Medical Officers needed to develop a suspicious attitude towards their patients:

> The attitude of regarding almost every man who goes sick as a scrimshanker and strafing ad nauseam isn't acquired in a single day exactly. I think I must be pretty horrible sometimes to the men.[31]

The function of the Army doctor to maintain the mental and physical well-being of the men so that they might be fit to face death or injury was bound to give rise to moral dilemmas.[32] Some doctors were clearly uncomfortable with the ethical implications of subordinating the concerns of the individual in what appeared to be a departure from the Hippocratic tradition. Harold Dearden found difficulty marrying his former understanding of his calling with his military duties, and decided that the best way to cope was not to undertake searching self-examination,[33] but to adopt a detached approach. In times of heavy casualties it was difficult to maintain such an attitude. Medical Officers had to discriminate between cases to an unaccustomed extent, often completely ignoring those individuals whose lives could not be saved:

> Stretchers were brought down on which were the mangled remains of manhood. The doctor sees him at once, he says, put him round the corner, he's beyond all assistance and in three minutes he will be no more. Time could not be wasted on such as those for no earthly power could restore them.[34]

Dr Brent, Warwick Deeping's fictional Medical Officer, faces a similar situation. He is forced to realize 'that I can do nothing [for a man with a bullet through his head], and the space is needed. He is breathing in snoring gasps, and it seems heartless to put him outside to die, but I have no alternative'.[35] T.D. Cumberland recorded a case in which he did not bother to splint the leg of a wounded man, knowing that he was going to die.[36] Sir Geoffrey Keynes spoke of his distress at seeing men left to die in the moribund ward of a CCS.[37] These were the harsh realities of war, and no amount of training or experience made it any easier for Medical Officers to accept these limitations on their sense of duty to the sick, wounded and dying. Medical Officers had to put these doubts to the back of their minds and make the best of the situation, as Captain J.H. Dible discovered:

> The wounded were too numerous to be coped with and in consequence many of them received half-measures of attention which did them no good, and only wasted the time and energy of those working on them. The thing was done with open eyes and an entire inability to do anything else; we struggled against it as a man might struggle to lift a ton weight.[38]

The problem was not simply one of having to discriminate between those who might live and the hopeless cases, but of whether to give enemy wounded equal consideration with Allied soldiers. In June 1915, at the opening session of the American Surgical Association, Dr George Armstrong stated that the spirit of antagonism should be far removed from the work of the Army Medical Service.[39] The duty of the doctor in war, as in civil life, was to treat all those who came to him in need. It would appear that most doctors recognized that their duty as Medical Officers was to all the wounded, regardless of nationality. During the 1916 Somme campaign Captain G.D. Fairley treated and evacuated some grateful German wounded;[40] Henry Harris gives an instance of a German officer receiving the same treatment as his British counterpart could expect;[41] Captain E.B. Lathbury recorded that he treated three German prisoners who seemed appreciative of kind treatment;[42] and A.A. Martin described the even-handed treatment which the wounded received:

> There is no nationality amongst the men in a hospital, and English, French and German all had a little bit of floor space and a bit of straw in our schoolhouse that night.[43]

The Germans appear to have been equally fair to enemy wounded. In 1914, reports from the front indicated that the wounded were being treated well by the enemy.[44] Colonel H.N. Thompson, who was captured by the Germans, found them 'most particular' to treat all the wounded alike.[45] Philip Gosse's account confirms this picture,[46] whilst Charles Symonds, referring to the treatment of some Argyll men, felt that 'they had been treated with great care: their wounds had been dressed and they had been given food, and been laid on bunks in the dugout. I think they had been treated as well if not better than we should have treated Hun wounded.'[47]

It would thus appear that, on both sides, whatever Medical Officers felt about the enemy cause, they did not allow this to interfere with their treatment of the wounded. Most seem to have treated enemy soldiers ungrudgingly, and even those who were less sympathetic did not refuse treatment.[48] Medical training had clearly inculcated in doctors a sense of a higher duty that patriotism, and even the experience of war, with the loss of comrades to enemy fire, failed to undermine. Charles Symonds summed up the dominant attitude:

> [The] Prussian ideals I hate and am in favour of continuing the war till we have made sure of crushing them. But individually I don't believe the Hun is really any worse a man than ours is.[49]

157

In some respects, then, Colonel Goodwin's faith in the sufficiency of medical training was justified. It nurtured in doctors a strong devotion to duty, and a calm, dispassionate approach to their work which proved of great value in the difficult conditions at the front. But there were clearly areas in which the doctors required further instruction in order to become efficient Medical Officers. J.W. Barrett felt that throughout the War not enough had been done to train new Medical Officers. He found that they continued to arrive unsure of the functions of the various units, ignorant of the organization of the medical service, and consequently resentful of much of the work which they had to undertake, because they did not understand its importance:

> [Newly] joined medical officers were thrown now into this and then into that position without preparation or adequate training of the kind, and the result . . . was a great deal of what is known popularly as 'grouse'.[50]

This state of affairs reflects the urgent demands for Medical Officers coming from the various fronts, which limited the time available for training, especially during the early months of the War. The benefits of further training were, however, recognized and steps taken to facilitate this. Prior to the War there was only one depot for the training of RAMC personnel. Situated in Aldershot, it comprised three depot companies, a training establishment and had accommodation for 800. In August and September 1914, seven additional companies were added and the accommodation expanded. The new depot companies became training centres in September and October 1914, being transferred to Crookham and Llandridrod Wells. Later, further training centres were established at Limerick, Sheffield, Eastbourne, Tidworth Park, Prestatyn, Ripon, Codford and Birr. Medical units of the Territorial Force were trained separately at their own depots.[51]

Lieutenant R.W. Murphy, who served with the 41st FA, did his initial training at Tidworth Camp, Salisbury Plain, and was impressed with the preparation which it gave him:

> The first month [October 1914?] was chiefly taken up with drill, stretcher drill and discipline generally, officers taking their place in the ranks with the men. Later on Field Ambulances were formed and Officers allotted to them, so that friendly rivalry built up, each unit struggling to be the best. The result was outstanding – officers and men trained hard and became rapidly more efficient. The seeds of an esprit de corps were sown, friendships sprang up between individuals of all ranks and a link of comradeship was formed that went far to lessen the hardships that were to follow.[52]

In April 1915, he was attached to the 13th Division for training. To enable it to participate in divisional training the FA was now fully equipped. the training included practice in treating the wounded with troops advancing, retiring and stationary, and the collection of casualties from a variety of difficult situations.[53]

It was, however, often difficult to assemble Field Ambulances before embarkation, with sufficient time to allow for training. Major E.S.B. Hamilton arrived in France on 15 July 1915 with the 45th FA, 15th Division. He recorded that 'we naturally felt at a great disadvantage from not having any previous training in England *fully equipped* as a Field Ambulance'.[54] His ADMS acted to rectify this deficiency by ordering Hamilton, along with three fellow officers and twenty men, to join the 3rd FA on 22 July for four days training.[55] Later in the year the RAMC changed the mobilization procedure for Field Ambulances to give more time, prior to embarkation, for training. From September the whole of the horse transport, including vehicles, harness and transport equipment were mobilized separately under the officer commanding the divisional train, and was trained under him as a complete unit from a transport point of view.[56]

The training of Territorial medical units, although carried out separately, followed the same lines as that for the remainder of the RAMC. Immediately before the outbreak of war, Major A.W. French was embarked upon his annual training with the 1st SW Mounted Brigade Field Ambulance. This consisted of routine infantry, stretcher and wagon drill, combined with lectures and instructional courses in map reading, logistics and army field organization.[57] H.J.B. Fry, who arrived in France on 25 January 1917 with the 2nd/3rd Home Counties Field Ambulance, underwent similar training. He also describes his involvement in divisional manoeuvres, which gave him experience of a Regimental Medical Officer's duties. This included the establishment of a medical inspection room; supervising the construction of latrines; taking sick parade; checking the condition of billets; liaising with the Field Ambulance; moving forward with an attack; establishing a site for a camp; securing a water supply; and making sanitary arrangements.[58] In addition, Fry was able to attend lectures: he went to a lecture by Major Montgomerie Smith describing the medical organization on the Western Front; and heard Surgeon General Sir A. Bowlby's Bradshaw lecture at the Royal College of Surgeons.[59]

Medical Officers also received instruction in the military hospitals of the Home Commands. Douglas McAlpine arrived at the Cambridge Military Hospital, Aldershot, on 19 August 1914. He remained there until the end of the month, doing light work (mostly inoculations), prior to embarking for France.[60] Colonel A.H. Habgood, a Special Reserve Officer who served in France was able to put his experience to good use, after being returned to the UK due to illness. He was sent to Colchester, at that time the headquarters of the 18th Division, [61] where he undertook the training of newly enlisted doctors:

> Part of my duties was to instruct the Temporary Medical Officers, general practitioners of all ages and shapes in elementary drill and army routine of which they knew nothing. This was amusing to me, if not to the MOs.[62]

Complaints from Medical Officers about the amount of drill involved in their training were not unusual. Many felt that the time would have been better spent preparing them for the medical challenges of war. Such complaints, however, resulted from a failure to appreciate that Medical Officers' duties did not confine them to purely medical work. They needed to be able to maintain discipline and give effective leadership to the men under their command; skills that drill enabled them to develop. J.M. McLachlan, when made OC of a draft of troops from Blackpool and later of troops on board a ship, wished that he had been taught more, not less, about how to handle men.[63] In November 1917, MacPherson made it clear to Parliament that there was no question of removing drill from a Medical Officer's training.[64]

Time spent in camp with a regiment awaiting embarkation could also be an important component of a Medical Officer's training. Whilst in camp he could begin to familiarize himself with the procedures for obtaining supplies, and to acquaint himself with the methods of RAMC administration. It gave him the opportunity to learn how to handle men, to get to know them as individuals and to gain experience of preventive medicine.

At the end of 1916 the entire system for training Medical Officers in the UK was altered when the various depots[65] were transferred to Blackpool and concentrated under an administrative headquarters. Initially, each of the old institutions retained its individuality, but in July 1917 a single large training centre, with a separate depot, was formed. The change resulted from a need to economize on personnel by reducing the multiplicity of instruction, and from a desire to achieve greater uniformity in training.[66] The centre at Blackpool was placed under the command of Surgeon General A.A. Sutton and to begin with was entirely staffed by RAMC officers and men:

The RAMC prided themselves on the fact that they could administer and organise a centre for 30,000 men all on their own without any assistance from their fighting brethren. And very well they did it. But it seemed odd to see a doctor walking about as a Provost Marshal, keeping strict discipline and checking doctors for not saluting properly or for being improperly dressed![67]

By August 1917, however, the increasing shortage of Medical Officers meant that this policy could no longer be continued. Gradually, infantry officers unfit for overseas service replaced RAMC officers in command of the depot companies, for company duties, and for instructing in anti-gas measures.[68]

The centre at Blackpool instructed newly enlisted RAMC officers in both medical and military matters. Captain M.D. MacKenzie discovered that he had 'much to learn and I find all day occupied'. The course included drill, tropical diseases, equitation and bacteriology.[69] Particular emphasis was placed upon preventive medicine. The RAMC School of Hygiene was formed at Blackpool to meet the urgent need for Medical Officers with a specialized training in preventive work. They were taught the general principles and practice of hygiene, including practical bacteriology and the analysis of food and water. There were also demonstrations of all sorts of sanitary appliances.[70]

The impossibility of adequately preparing every doctor, prior to his embarkation, meant that further training once in the theatres of war was essential. In spring 1915, Sir Arthur Sloggett issued an order informing all commanding officers of medical units that their duties involved taking every opportunity to instruct the Medical Officers under their command. Instruction needed to cover not just the organization and function of their current unit, but also that of other units to which they might be transferred.[71] Regular officers were detailed to give guidance to their temporary commissioned colleagues. Amongst them were retired officers who had returned to the service for the duration. They were commonly referred to as dug-outs. Captain J.H. Dible had one such dug-out as his SMO and found him completely unhelpful:

I was new to the game, and wholly ignorant of the routine of the RAMC. The one man in the district who knew about these things was the SMO. He knew also of my ignorance and it seems to me that if he had cared for efficiency; that if he had had any interest in his country's need; that even if he had desired to conscientiously earn his large salary, he should have made it his business to help the youngster who was trying to help the RAMC. He could have. Did he? No.[72]

According to Dible, it was common knowledge that the majority of regulars were characterized by a similar attitude. Henry Gervis, however, did not share his opinion, finding the regular officers under whom he served courteous and considerate, and ready to do everything to promote the efficiency of the units under their command.[73] M. Whiting refers to a regular 'who was able from his long experience to give the temporaries much useful advice and assistance'.[74] And, A.G.B. Duncan, who served as a Field Ambulance Officer and as an RMO, was also full of praise for the regulars:

> If one felt worried at first or later, when faced by new troubles with little or no apparent means of overcoming them, then the officers of the Regular RAMC always proved invaluable. These officers had to face the situation at the beginning of the war and make the first sanitary arrangements. Later, when one found them mostly in command of medical units or in administrative posts, their knowledge of military sanitation, gathered in various stations and in previous campaigns, was ever imparted willingly to us less instructed ones.[75]

Sir Charles Burtchaell did not believe that there was any ground for saying that RAMC officers dealt unreasonably with civilian doctors, and referred to investigations that had revealed such allegations to be nothing more than 'pernicious mendacity'. Moreover, a case had come to his attention of one temporary officer accusing another of carrying out certain orders because he was a regular; showing that those temporary officers who did not like complying with orders always assumed that anything distasteful to them originated from the regular RAMC.[76] The problem was that many Medical Officers were unaccustomed to administrative procedures. They failed to recognize that, when dealing with a large group of men who were passing through the hands of a number of different Medical Officers, adherence to administrative procedures was essential.

Medical Officers at the front needed to be made aware of the importance of preventive medicine in keeping an army fit. Neglect of hygiene and sanitation posed a threat to the maintenance of military effectiveness through increased wastage and depressed morale. The South African War had demonstrated to the military authorities the consequences of an inadequate sanitary organization. Progress had been made, prior to 1914, in improving arrangements and teaching RAMC officers the importance of preserving firm sanitary discipline. An article in the BMJ expressed confidence that Medical Officers were now well drilled in the necessary measures for disease prevention, and pointed out the need to ensure that those civilian doctors entering the service received comparable training.[77] Even civilian doctors with a background in preventive medicine needed to learn about military procedures. But this was not always recognized during the War, and there were instances of civilian MOsH, ignorant of sanitary administration in the Army, being placed in authority over men who were well-versed in military hygiene.[78]

In the UK routine training in sanitation was provided by three establishments: the London sanitary companies; the School of Army Sanitation, Leeds; and the Royal Army Medical Corps School of Hygiene, Blackpool. Supplementary training was given in many of the home commands through lectures and demonstrations of sanitary appliances. However, in France, the Commission on Medical Establishments complained of a continued lack of systematic instruction for Medical Officers.

With the formation of sanitary schools on the Western Front steps had been taken to promote understanding throughout the Army of the necessity for strict sanitary discipline. An example was the 13th Corps School of Sanitation where lectures were given to officers and NCOs on the medical organization and field sanitation. The intention was to create a better understanding between the combatant and medical branches, and resulted in an improvement of the sanitary situation in the Corps.[79] Such schools helped to ensure that information on the various health risks was widely disseminated throughout all ranks and branches of the Army.[80] By 1917 they were widespread on the Western Front,[81] showing that the Army was making a concerted effort to press home the need for careful attention to hygiene. The Medical Establishments Commission recommended that MOs be admitted to the courses run by these schools, so that they could keep abreast of developments in preventive medicine and be made aware of particular health hazards in the local area.[82] It would appear that some action was taken as a consequence of this recommendation. In January 1918, Lieutenant A.L.P. Gould wrote that he had just 'been switched off to a five days' sanitary course'.[83]

Sir Almroth Wright was critical of the guidance given to Medical Officers.[84] He claimed that the AMS had not taken sufficient action to direct them in matters of treatment, accusing the medical service of being content to leave decisions over 'these professional matters to the arbitrament of the individual Medical Officer, who may sometimes be quite untaught and inexperienced'. The RAMC, in his view, needed to lay down a broad outline of treatment to be adopted.[85] However, other consultants serving with the RAMC did not share his opinions. Professor

James Swain[86] refuted the idea that matters of treatment were left to the individual Medical Officers, pointing out that various instructions had been issued. At the same time he felt it inadvisable to lay down too strict a set of recommendations because 'progress is not made from uniformity'.[87] Sir Berkeley Moynihan[88] firmly agreed with the latter point:

> [No] one ever decided upon the right way of treating wounds. The whole of the progress of surgery has depended upon the different interpretations that different men have given to the different methods of solving the same problem . . . It is true of surgery there are many ways of treating the same problem and every one of them is right.[89]

Contrary to Wright's assertion, there is ample evidence of official guidance having been supplied to MOs. One means of disseminating information was the publication of memoranda: 1915 saw the publication of a Memorandum on the Treatment of Injuries in War, which summarized the experience amassed in military hospitals in France during the previous ten months, with a view 'to attaining some uniformity in method of treatment based upon definite observation'.[90] Sir Arthur Sloggett felt that this memorandum met Wright's demand that the RAMC set out a broad outline of methods to be adopted.[91] The Official History noted that 'the memorandum was of great assistance in establishing definite methods and it enabled general instructions to be easily circulated over the front'. It was the duty of DDsMS, ADsMS and commanders of medical units to ensure that all Medical Officers serving under them possessed a copy of the Memorandum, and that the treatments advocated therein were carried out as closely as possible.[92] A similar publication, issued in 1918, was the Manual of Injuries and Diseases of War.[93] This set out the role of the various medical units along the line of evacuation and the recommended treatments to be carried out at each.

Another memorandum was published as a result of work done by the War Office Committee for the study of tetanus; it dealt with the diagnosis and treatment of tetanus, and was constantly updated. In addition, forty Medical Officers with the necessary experience were appointed as local inspectors of tetanus, to supervise and advise regarding a disease with which most doctors were unfamiliar.[94] Publications were also issued detailing the results of the research undertaken by the various war committees of the Medical Research Committee. These included reports arising from the MRC's work on typhoid, bilharzia, cerebro spinal fever, acute nephritis and frostbite.[95]

Various forms of guidance and further instruction were given to assist doctors with war surgery. The formation of surgical teams, at the beginning of 1915, was seen by Sir Berkeley Moynihan as a means of preventing junior and inexperienced Medical Officers undertaking serious operations on their own responsibility.[96] Inexperience had also led to occasions when Medical Officers evacuated, to the base or home hospitals, patients who could have been treated nearer the front and consequently returned to duty more rapidly. Supervision of the less experienced was needed to minimize instances of undue evacuation. Medical Officers were also kept informed of the latest developments in surgical practice. One of the most significant was the Carrel-Dakin method for the surgical toilet of wounds, which involved the constant flushing of a deep wound with hypochlorite solution. During 1917 opportunities were given for doctors to observe this method being practised in the CCSs.[97]

The medical journals were a valuable source of information, the majority of their pages being devoted to war subjects. Dr G. Moore, describing his employment of hypochlorite solution to irrigate a wound, referred to having read a BMJ article about it which his father had sent to him.[98] Articles in the medical press, relevant to the treatment of wounds or diseases at the front, were also officially distributed.

Lectures were another means employed by the RAMC to keep its officers informed of the latest developments, or to guide them on matters likely to be new to them. These lectures covered such subjects as gas poisoning; tropical diseases; sanitation; head injuries; medical aid in trench warfare; the role of the RMO; and RAMC administration.[99] Possibly the most important surgical development to occur during the War was the adoption of blood transfusion. Lectures were one way of teaching doctors the techniques involved. Dr W. Sharrard attended a lecture on blood transfusion, ably delivered by an American physiologist;[100] and H.J.B. Fry heard a talk on blood groupings and the methods of transfusion which he found interesting, followed by an 'even more interesting discussion'.[101]

By 1917 blood transfusion was firmly established in the Casualty Clearing Stations as a routine measure in the prevention of shock. MOs had been trained to lead special resuscitation teams and to take charge of the pre-operative wards where severe cases of wound shock were dealt with.[102] However, it was felt that not enough had been done to educate front-line Medical Officers in the method. The difficulty of performing transfusions in RAPs and dressing stations was recognized, but there were parts of the line where it was possible, thus saving the lives of men likely to die on the journey back down the line. Consequently it was decided to form a training centre, attached to a group of CCSs in the Third Army area, where Field Ambulance and Regimental Medical Officers could obtain instruction in the technique.[103]

In addition to issuing guidance on medical treatment the DGMS acted to ensure that all instructions were vetted with a view to securing a high level of uniformity of method and procedure throughout the medical services.[104] At the same time, however, he was anxious not to hamper initiative and the rigid prescription of medical treatments was avoided. Certain general procedures regarding the recording of symptoms, the treatments adopted and the evacuation of cases obviously had to be abided by. But on professional matters the instructions were intended as guides, leaving Medical Officers some room for manoeuvre.

Such guidance was essential since doctors were unfamiliar with many of the medical conditions (trench fever, trench foot, gas gangrene, gas poisoning) that they encountered. It was, however, not always impossible for the RAMC administration to lay down strict rules regarding prevention and treatment. In many instances it was equally uncertain about the exact nature and causation of the cases. For instance, it was not until 1918 that a link was established between trench fever and the louse,[105] as a result of the work done by the Committee for the Study of Trench Fever, chaired by Major General Sir David Bruce.[106] Only with this discovery could valuable advice be issued to Medical Officers. This included information on the constructing of delousing pits in which clothes could be hung and exposed to high temperatures, killing the lice.[107] Gas gangrene, which had never emerged on such a scale in previous campaigns, provides a further example. It was late 1918 before a breakthrough was made in its prevention.[108]

The heavy rains during the winter of 1914–1915 led to terrible conditions in the trenches and a high incidence of frostbite and trench foot. During November and December 1914 there were 6,378 cases of frostbite amongst British soldiers in France and Belgium; and weekly returns of trench foot cases in the First Army showed an incidence of 3,013 between 27 December 1914 and 28 February 1915.[109] There was, however, no clear idea of how to tackle the problem:

> The pain of this frostbite seems intense, and no one seems to have any remedy for it. Sir Berkeley Moynihan told me that the best thing was to keep the feet cool, but in every hospital I have seen they swathe the feet in cotton-wool and flannel. No one seems to know how long it will take before these frost-bites can be cured.[110]

As Colonel Arthur Lee noted, there was no effective system of treatment approved by the central authorities. Instead, Medical Officers were left to experiment with various remedies. These included putting rum in boots, which proved useless; and the placing of braziers of burning charcoal in the trenches, but these did more harm than good. Moreover, the practice of wrapping feet in cotton wool was found to aggravate the condition. However this process of experimentation did enable a recommended programme of treatment to emerge. On 16 January 1915, Army Routine Order 554 was issued. It recommended that before going into the trenches boots be wiped inside and outside with whale oil. Feet were to be washed regularly in cold water, dried, and fresh, dry socks put on.[111] When feet had become chilled, massage and gentle rubbing with oil were the best means of relief. On no account were they to be held near a fire. The recommended lines of treatment did reduce the incidence of trench foot (never again did it emerge in France on the scale that it had done in 1914–1915) and helped not only Medical Officers, but all ranks, to better understand the condition.

The use of poison gas was another unexpected development which called for guidance to be given to Medical Officers. The initial difficulties of protecting the men, however, meant that there was a need for individual initiative and experimentation. Sir John Boyd, who was at Ypres during the first gas attack, was appointed anti-gas officer, 80th Brigade, in April 1915. He was given a modicum of instruction but really knew nothing about the treatment of gas other than what he termed 'common sense methods'. These included the use of mild cough mixtures to try and relieve the congestion, but which proved of little use. He was also involved in the development of the first primitive respirators. These consisted of pads of surgical gauze, sewn by local French women into long strips of bandage. The pads were soaked in a strong solution of hypochlorate of soda and left to dry. Prior to a gas attack these pads were soaked with water, or if this was unavailable with urine, and the bandage tied around the head and neck so that the pad covered the mouth and nostrils. The chlorine gas combined with the hypo solution in the pad, making the air safe for the men to breathe. Boyd was dubious about the effectiveness of these early masks and relieved that they never had to be used in his brigade.[112] They were soon replaced with gas helmets which covered the whole head, offering far better protection.

His job also included an educational role. With very little training himself he had to go around lecturing to units on the precautions to be taken in a gas attack.[113] The RAMC authorities quickly recognized the need to give instruction on gas and the DGAMS issued various memoranda on the subject.[114] Chemical advisers were appointed to the First and Second Armies, and lectures on gas were arranged.[115] In October 1915, arrangements were made for an MO from each division to meet the Director of the Central Laboratory and his assistants in order to be instructed in the theoretical background to the anti-gas appliances. It was suggested that this officer should be an ADMS or a DADMS. It would then be his responsibility to instruct MOs serving with regiments and in the FAs.[116] Subsequently, gas courses, usually lasting for about five days, were set up, giving Medical Officers instruction 'in how to deal with Boche vapours and stink pots'.[117]

Dysentery had been a common scourge of armies in the past and occurred in all the major theatres of operations during the War. It was a disease about which most doctors possessed a sound theoretical knowledge but many had no practical experience. Instructions were issued drawing the attention of Medical Officers to the importance of isolating suspected cases; and to the need for strict sanitary vigilance to limit its incidence and prevent relapses.

Understanding about the psychological impact of war was limited. In the early years of the War it was felt that mental breakdown due to the effects of battle was a new phenomenon; an impression reinforced by the invention of 'shell shock' as a descriptive term. Its employment as a blanket term had the advantage of drawing together under a single heading the various mental disorders of wartime. Medically speaking, however, the term was inaccurate and extremely damaging as it suggested a casual connection between the effects of a shell explosion and the development of neurotic symptoms which, in the majority of cases, did not exist:

> The term shell shock has hindered the acceptance of a purely psychological explanation of the war psychoneuroses, and the gradual disuse signifies a growth of a belief that the continuation of symptoms is not, save in a small proportion of cases, due to the physical effects of concussion or burial.[118]

Less than 10 per cent of the psychiatric casualties were consequences of the physical effects of explosions, the rest were emotional in origin.[119] In fact, there was no need for a new term because the symptoms that emerged under the emotional stress of war were virtually identical to those already known in civil life. Once this became apparent, doctors with previous experience of treating psychiatric cases were able to correctly classify the various disorders that comprised emotional shell shock.

Unfortunately few doctors possessed sufficiently in-depth knowledge of psychiatric medicine to make such a definite diagnosis of mental and nervous symptoms. Pre-war, no attempt had been made to give such grounding to Medical Officers; the course at the Royal Army Medical College had given no consideration to the trauma that war could cause. In an attempt to rectify this deficiency a training programme was established at Maghull Hospital which turned out sixty-five Medical Officers versed in modern psychiatric principles during the last two years of the War.

The remainder of the Army's psychiatric service was recruited from neurological hospitals, mental hospitals and from a group of insufficiently trained volunteers. Amongst these sources of psychiatric personnel, even those with training did not necessarily have experience of dealing with psychosomatic disorders. This inexperience led to the misdiagnosis of many hysterical disorders.[120]

Most doctors lacked the confidence to make firm diagnoses in cases of mental collapse. Reluctant to commit themselves and wishing to avoid the stigma to the patient of describing his condition as 'mental', the majority of Medical Officers preferred to send cases of this kind down the line, labelled as 'shell shock (wound)'. This led to the unnecessary evacuation to the base of patients suffering from fatigue, early hysterical dissociations and simple conversion hysterias, who could have been more effectively treated in a forward hospital. The consequent delay in treatment led to a worsening of these conditions.[121] Responding to this problem, the RAMC eventually established separate sorting centres for shell shock. RMOs were discouraged from making an immediate diagnosis. All suspected cases were to be sent to the special centres where an expert assessment would be given. However, these efforts to discourage Medical Officers from making a wrongful diagnosis were not matched by any attempt to broaden their knowledge of the various mental and emotional disorders. Indeed, steps were taken to limit the availability of information on shell shock. Even after the Somme experience, the DGMS felt it inadvisable for articles on the subject to be published in the BMJ and the Journal of the RAMC.[122]

The insufficiency of the instructions on shell shock is evident from the difficulties that Medical Officers faced when trying to determine the mental state of men on trial for cowardice or self-inflicted wounding. Without any experience of psychiatry, ordinary Medical Officers were called upon to determine the mental responsibility of men on trial for their lives.[123] In their ignorance, some allowed their distaste for nervous cases to colour their judgement:

> There's a fellow here ran away from the trenches. They are going to shoot him and they want me to say if he's responsible. I shan't be long.[124]

Others, however, found inexperience in these matters undermining their ability to make confident assertions about an individual's state of mind especially since, away from the front, it was difficult to assess the strain under which he had been labouring:

> [It] was almost impossible for the medical officer to make a decisive state-ment that the man had been responsible for his actions when he ran away. In fact, after my first two or three courts martial I found I was practically in every case giving evidence in favour of the man. The reason was that I felt his state of mind in the line, where he was under heavy shell fire, was not the same as when he was at the Base or somewhere between the Base and the line.[125]

Extensive training in psychiatry would have been impracticable in wartime, except for a few specially selected individuals. Further guidance could, however, have been given to Medical Officers to supplement their paltry knowledge of mental conditions. That it was not is partly the fault of the military authorities. They reacted slowly to the whole problem of shell shock. But it was also a reflection of the widespread suspicion and scepticism with which the relatively new science of psychiatry was viewed within the profession. Indeed, Medical Officers generally tended to be more dismissive of psychiatry than many of their combatant colleagues, a fact discernible from the evidence to the War Office's enquiry into shell shock.

Venereal disease was another controversial medical issue on which Medical Officers received insufficient guidance. Some instructions were issued regarding the content of lectures on VD and the procedures for the disposal of cases.[126] However, as late as 1918, War Office guidelines were criticized for 'not really conveying to our doctors any definite instruc-tions of any sort as to what they should do under given circumstances'.[127]

The formation of military medical societies provided opportunities for MOs to discuss the medical aspects of the War. Occasional meetings of Medical Officers began to take place towards the end of 1914 out of recognition of the need for greater interchange of information between hospitals and other medical units. The RAMC authorities actively encouraged the organization of these front-line medical societies, and various forms of meeting began to take place. Some resembled the usual format of medical societies at home, with the reading of a paper followed by a discussion. At others there was no formal paper; instead there was an interchange of views regarding a development that was unfamiliar to all. Whatever form their meetings took these societies provided a useful addition to the available stock of military-medical information, supplementing the knowledge gained from official instructions and publications. They were also an important means of promoting contact between MOs working in different units, and so combating the problem of compartmentalism by facilitating exchanges of information on the latest medical techniques and on the efficacy of particular treatments.

One of the best known was the 3rd Corps Medical Society, formed in November 1915, which largely consisted of RMOs or members of Field Ambulances. The subjects discussed included the sanitary arrangements of front-line units; gas attacks and smoke helmets; the treatment of abdominal wounds; trench feet; and arrangements for preventing lice and skin diseases. Another example was the Rouen Medical Society, formed at Number 11 Stationary Hospital in January 1915, for the reading of discussion papers. Papers read during the course of the year included the following topics: frostbite; bacteriology and the treatment of wounds; sanitation in war; and gunshot wounds of blood vessels. The benefit of such papers was not confined to those who were actually able to attend the meetings. Encouragement was given by the DGMS for their publication in the medical press.[128]

The exchange of information, which medical societies facilitated, played a part in addressing the problem of compartmentalism that characterized the RAMC organization. It was particularly important that MOs with forward units be given information on the subsequent progress of cases so that they might assess the effectiveness of various treatments and appreciate the value of their work. Officers commanding medical units were charged with ensuring that the doctors under their command were familiar with the correct lines of treatment. H.W. Kaye, who served with the 43rd Field Ambulance in France, found his OC helpful in this regard as he had spent over nine months at a CCS. He was therefore able to impart information about CCS work and the observations made there upon the work of the Field Ambulance, which included a suggestion that they had 'erred on the side of doing too much surgically'.[129] Later, when attached to Number 8 CCS, in an attempt to overcome the problem of compartmentalism, Kaye devised a scheme for getting systematic notes on a fixed plan for head injuries so that there could be greater continuity of treatment. He hoped to be able 'to stimulate the men at the base to continue it, and so get complete histories for the information of all', making it easier to follow up the results of treatment.[130]

However, insufficient communication between medical units remained a difficulty throughout the War. In 1917 the Report of the Commission on Medical Establishments noted that Medical Officers on the Lines of Communication seemed to know little of the medical arrangements at the front, and vice versa.[131] The need for better understanding between Medical Officers was an important lesson of the War and was not lost on the post-war committee that looked into the reorganization of the RAMC:

> In order to achieve the best results in the treatment of wounds, the principle of the periodic exchange of Medical Officers (of suitable age, physique and qualifications) between General Hospitals and Advanced Field Medical Units should be borne in mind.[132]

The employment, as consultants, of eminent civilian surgeons and physicians did help to improve the free-flow of information during the War. Part of a consultant's role was to act as a liaison officer, taking news of recent medical developments from area to area.[133] As seen in the previous chapter, there was a problem in that the consultants themselves were subject to compartmentalism. Despite the inadequacies of the system, however, the consultants were able to make a valuable contribution to the diffusion of knowledge and the regularizing of procedures within their areas. Increasingly, consultants were drawn into the decision-making process. From the time of the Somme, the consultants were brought into counsel and informed of the situation before a battle.[134] The DGMS regularly summoned the consultants for advice and issued orders in accordance with their recommendations on such subjects as trench feet, cerebro spinal fever, gas poisoning, tetanus and wounds of the chest.[135] Similar meetings took place between consultants and the DsMS of the various armies.[136] Thus, consultants were able to provide advice on the most efficacious forms of treatment and promote knowledge of developments in disease prevention.[137] The distribution of such information throughout the RAMC helped to ensure that high professional standards were maintained:

> [The] most important duty of all was to stimulate an interest in medicine among the officers in charge of medical cases, and to prevent the tendency to careless methods which the circumstances of military work and the deficiency of scientific equipment in the Clearing Stations are apt to produce.[138]

The fact that Medical Officers could not easily follow up the results of their cases made this task particularly difficult.[139] The consultants were, however, able to stimulate interest by organizing conferences, giving lectures and promoting the establishment of medical societies.[140]

It is clear from the various methods discussed above that the RAMC did recognize the need for an on-going process of training. However, all of these arrangements were the result of ad hoc responses to the challenges of war. In 1917 the Medical Establishments Commission recognized the necessity for a more systematic programme of instruction. It recommended that Medical Officers destined for France be sent there immediately upon receiving their commissions. They would then be trained in special front-line schools and spared the course at Blackpool, which would be reserved for those proceeding to tropical or sub-tropical districts. Such a scheme had a weakness in that officers initially sent to France might later be despatched to the East without the benefit of instruction in tropical medicine. However, the Commission felt that this was outweighed by the advantage of having Medical Officers in France completely conversant with their duties and the procedures of the RAMC.[141]

In the French Army the benefits to be gained from some form of front-line education had already been appreciated. Throughout 1915 and 1916, centres of study and instruction were established and a general scheme adopted whereby groups of between twenty and forty Medical Officers could be sent for a brief course of instruction, mainly concentrating on the treatment of war wounds.[142]

Shortly after the Commission on Medical Establishments concluded its work, an RAMC School of Instruction was formed in the First Army which provided the level of comprehensive training that had been recommended. In addition to instruction for Medical Officers, there were courses for other ranks of the RAMC; officers and men of the combatant branch; and officers and men of the American and Portuguese armies. Altogether, the school had accommodation for forty RAMC officers and sixty other ranks; and for ten combatant officers and 130 other ranks.[143] The courses for Medical Officers covered such subjects as the treatment of wound shock; the pathology of gas gangrene; the duties of RMOs; medical clerking and records; indents and how to prepare them; military law; the prevention of sick wastage; and the prevention of trench foot.[144] In addition, all Medical Officers were given riding lessons as mobility was important, especially for RMOs (for further details on the syllabus of the school, refer to Appendix E). The value of such a school was soon recognized by Britain's other armies in France which began steps to establish similar centres in their areas. However, these preparations were brought to an abrupt end by the German advance of March 1918.

The War had exposed the deficiencies of traditional medical training as preparation for the demands of modern warfare. Doctors could not simply rely on their pre-war medical experience. This proved to be as much the case for regulars as it was for the civilians. However, the latter also had to accustom themselves to the different priorities of military medicine. There was a need to understand that the oft-derided RAMC bureaucracy was an essential means of dealing with large numbers of men, of ensuring continuity in treatment, and of delivering men back to their units as quickly as possible. The work of an MO also involved attention to issues such as sanitation, which many doctors had regarded as a non-medical concern. They had to learn that, whilst treating the sick and wounded was an obvious part of their duties, the most important aspect of RAMC work was disease prevention. Addressing these differences from civilian medicine, and the need to educate MOs about the developing techniques of war medicine, posed difficulties for the RAMC. The demand for doctors limited the time available for training, whilst in the early months of the conflict there was an assumption that military medicine involved no great departure from civilian practice. Added to this, of course, there was the problem that the evolution of medical knowledge during the War necessitated an on-going programme of training. Contrary to the allegations of its detractors, however, the RAMC did not ignore these issues. A system of continuous training emerged, employing a variety of means for disseminating information alongside greater access to short, formal courses. However, there was still no guarantee that an MO would attend such courses; whilst the provision of information pertaining to diseases such as VD and shell shock remained deficient. Not until 1918, with the development of schools of instruction like that in the First Army, did a more systematic response emerge.

Notes

1   This is a revised, shortened version of a chapter that will be appearing in R. Cooter & M. Harrison (eds), *Medicine and the Management of Modern Warfare*, Rodopi Press, 1999. I am grateful to the editors for permission to include it here.
2   T.H. Goodwin, 'The Army Medical Service', *New York Medical Journal* (NYMJ), CVI, 1917, p. 1. Goodwin was at this time the British liaison officer to the United States Medical Service in Washington, working to obtain American assistance as regards medical and nursing personnel. See MacPherson, *General History*, I, p. 147.
3   N. King-Wilson, LC, Jottings of an MO (typescript), p. 1.

4 Colonel H.N. Thompson, 'An Account of my Capture and my Experiences in Germany', *Journal of the Royal Army Medical Corps* (JRAMC), XXIV, 1915, p. 123.

5 J.M. McLachlan, LC, Letters: letter 321, 3 April 1915.

6 J.M. McLachlan, LC, Letters: letter 341, 27 April 1915.

7 J.M. McLachlan, LC, Letters: letter 359, 18 May 1915.

8 Dr L.W. Batten LC, letter to son, 18 March 1970, p. 1.

9 W.G. MacPherson, *Official History of the War – Medical Services, Surgery of the War*, I, HMSO, p. 338.

10 Sir Geoffrey Keynes, LC, Tape recordings 556 & 557.

11 Noel Chavasse, MO with the Liverpool Scottish, twice awarded the VC.

12 Ann Clayton, *Chavasse – Double VC*, Leo Cooper, 1992, pp. 60; 174.

13 Captain M. Whiting, LC, Papers: Rough draft of an article for the Middlesex Hospital Journal, p. 3.

14 Lieutenant Colonel G.W. Hughes, IWM, Autobiographical sketch, p. 11.

15 PRO 30/57/59, PRO, Kitchener Papers, Letters from Lord Esher to Kitchener: letter 30 September 1914, pp. 3–4.

16 Major M.B.H. Ritchie, 'The Training of RAMC Officers for War', JRAMC, XLII, 1924, pp. 267 & 273.

17 General Sir Neil Cantlie entered the RAMC in July 1914; was appointed to the rank of Captain in 1915; served throughout the War in France and Flanders. He went on to become DGAMS (1948–1952).

18 General Sir Neil Cantlie, WIHM, RAMC 465, Papers: Speech on retirement, March 1952.

19 Herringham, *Physician in France*, pp. 78–9. Redmond McLaughlin, *The Royal Army Medical Corps*, Leo Cooper, 1972, p. 35. Owen Richards, *The Development of Casualty Clearing Stations*, Guy's Hospital Reports, LXX, 1922, p. 116.

20 Martin, *Surgeon in Khaki*, p. 133.

21 Sir Anthony Bowlby, WIHM, RAMC 365, Papers: letter from Sir Alfred Keogh to Bowlby, 26 February 1915.

22 Herringham, *Physician in France*, p. 44.

23 Major Josiah Oldfield, 'Regimental and Field Ambulance Training in the Territorial Force', *Journal of the Royal Army Medical Corps* (JRAMC), XX, 1913, p. 440.

24 'Experiences in a British Military Hospital', MJA, 1917 (I), p. 479.

25 H.M.W. Gray, 'Surgical Treatment of Wounded Men at Advanced Units', *New York Medical Journal* (NYMJ), CVI, 1917, p. 1013. Herringham, *Physician in France*, p. 53.

26 H.M.W. Gray, 'Surgical Treatment of Wounded Men at Advanced Units', NYMJ, CVI, 1917, pp. 1013–14.

27 Major J. Oldfield, 'The Scope of the Field Ambulance as a Training School', JRAMC, XXII, 1914, p. 687.

28 James W. Barrett, *A Vision of the Possible: What the RAMC Might Become*, H.K. Lewis & Co Ltd., 1919, pp. 155–6.

29 L. Gameson, IWM, Typescript, p. 56.

30 W.O. 95/52, PRO, Medical Inspector of Drafts, Diary, April 1915 – March 1916: 14 October 1915; 17 November 1915; 20 November 1915. Lord Northcliffe wrote that without special training ordinary civilian doctors could not undertake the medical examination of recruits. See **Lord Northcliffe**, 'The Medical Corps of the Army', *Journal of the American Medical Association* (JAMA), LXVIII, 1917, p. 1331.

31 **McLachlan**, LC, Letters: letter 689, 26 July 1916.

32 **G.E. Berrios & H.L. Freeman**, *150 Years of British Psychiatry, 1841–1991*, Gaskell & Royal College of Physicians, 1991, p. 246.

33 Dearden, *Time and Chance*, pp. 3–4.

34 **Private E. Auger**, LC, 'This is my life', hand-written recollection, pp. 13–14.

35 **Deeping**, *No Hero This*, p. 244.

36 **T.D. Cumberland**, LC, Diary 1918: 19 September 1918.

37 **G. Keynes**, LC, Tape recordings 556 & 557.

38 **Captain J.H. Dible**, IWM, Diary 1918: 30 October 1918, p. 285.

39 **George E. Armstrong**, 'Surgery and War', *Annals Of Surgery*, LXII, 1915, p. 137.

40 **G.D. Fairley**, LC, Diary: 1 July 1916, p. 171.

41 **Henry Harris**, WIHM, RAMC 493, Miscellaneous account of 87th FA (TA), 29th Division, Gallipoli 1915–1916, pp. 46–7.

42 **Captain E.B. Lathbury**, LC, Diary 1914, 22 August 1914.

43 **Martin**, *Surgeon in Khaki*, p. 177.

44 'The Way Home of the Wounded (by One Who Has Travelled It)', BMJ, 1914 (II), p. 850.

45 **Colonel H.N. Thompson**, 'An Account of my Capture and my Experiences in Germany', JRAMC, XXIV, 1915, p. 123.

46 **Gosse**, *Memoirs of a Camp Follower*, p. 97.

47 **Second Lieutenant Charles Symonds**, LC, Letters: extract from letter dated 26 April 1917.

48 It is possible that instances of Medical Officers going out of their way not to treat the enemy did occur, but none have come to light in the course of my research.

49 **Charles Symonds**, LC, Letters: extract from letter, 26 April 1917.

50 **Barrett**, *A Vision of the Possible*, pp. 154–5.

51 **MacPherson**, *General History*, I, pp. 154–5. **Lovegrove**, *The Crusade*, p. 38.

52 **Lieutenant R.W. Murphy**, IWM, 'Some Experiences of a Field Ambulance', pp. 1–2.

53 *Ibid*, p. 4.

54 **Major E.S.B. Hamilton**, IWM, Diary, 10–15 July 1915.

55 **Major E.S.B. Hamilton**, IWM, Diary, 22 July 1915.

56 **MacPherson**, *General History*, I, p. 155.

57 **Major A.W. French**, LC, Introduction to diary, p. 1.

58 **H.J.B. Fry**, LC, Diary 1916: 2–4 November 1916.

59 **H.J.B. Fry**, LC, Diary 1916: 6 December 1916; 20 December 1916.

60 **Douglas McAlpine**, LC, Recollections, p. 11.

61 The 18th Division was in Colchester for training, awaiting despatch abroad. It was sent to France on 24 July 1915. See **Brigadier Sir James E. Edwards**, *History*

of the Great War based on Official Documents, Military Operations, France and Belgium, 1915, II, MacMillan, 1928, p. 86.

62 Lieutenant Colonel A.H. Habgood, IWM, Recollections, p. 85.
63 J.M. McLachlan, LC, Letters: letter 1032, 25 June 1918.
64 Under Secretary of State for War.
65 See above, p. 187.
66 MacPherson, *General History*, I, p. 156.
67 Colonel N.J.C. Rutherford, *Soldiering with a Stethoscope*, Stanley Paul & Co. Ltd., 1937, p. 194.
68 MacPherson, *General History*, I, p. 157.
69 M.D. MacKenzie, IWM, Letters: 16 June 1917; 20 June 1917; 24 June 1917.
70 An Army School of Sanitation had been established in Leeds, primarily for training American Medical Officers serving with the British Army in the details of British field sanitation; it was also used as a demonstration centre for specialist sanitary officers and others. It was, however, a temporary wartime measure, and Blackpool met the need for a more permanent and complete establishment. See MacPherson, *Official History of the War – Medical Services Hygiene of the War*, I, pp. 35–61.
71 'Army Medical Procedure', BMJ, 1915 (II), p. 451.
72 J.H. Dible, IWM, Diary, p. 56.
73 Gervis, *Arms and the Doctor*, p. 81.
74 M. Whiting, LC, Papers: Rough draft of an article for the Middlesex Hospital Journal, p. 3.
75 A.G.B. Duncan, LC [Health, Fitness, Cleanliness and Disease. Item 12], Sanitary Methods and Preventative Medicine adopted by Units in the Field in France, M.D. thesis, account of sanitary work as a Field Ambulance Officer and an RMO, summer 1915 to March 1918, p. 1.
76 Sir Charles Burtchaell, WIHM, RAMC 446/24, Complaints about Treatment and Antipathy between Regulars, Temporary Officers and VADs etc., 27 July 1917.
77 Christopher Childs, 'Prevention of Typhoid in our Home Camps', BMJ, 1914 (II), p. 1087.
78 MacPherson, *Hygiene of the War*, I, p. 63.
79 W.O. 95/903, PRO, DDMS XIII Corps. Diary: 30 June 1917; 3 August 1917.
80 MacPherson, *Hygiene of the War*, I, pp. 63–4.
81 Gosse, *Memoirs of a Camp Follower*, pp. 137–8.
82 'Report of the Commission on Medical Establishments', WIHM, RAMC 1165, p. 63.
83 Lieutenant A.L.P. Gould, LC, Letters: letter 28 January 1918.
84 Wright served with the B.E.F. as a Consulting Physician.
85 Sir A. Bowlby, WIHM, RAMC 365, Papers: Memorandum on the Necessity of Creating at the War Office a Medical Intelligence and Investigation Department to get the best possible Treatment for the Wounded, diminish Invaliding, and return the men to the ranks in the shortest possible time, by Colonel Sir A. Wright, p. 1.
86 Professor James Swain, Consultant Surgeon to the troops serving in the Southern Command, 1914–1919.

87 Bowlby, WIHM, RAMC 365, Papers: Report of the meeting between the DGAMS and Consultants to the Forces held in the Medical Board Room on 15 January 1917, p. 5.

88 Sir Berkeley Moynihan, Consultant Surgeon to the troops·serving in the Northern Command, 1914–1918.

89 Bowlby, WIHM, RAMC 365, Papers: Report of Meeting between DGAMS and consultants, pp. 11–12.

90 *Memorandum on the Treatment of Injuries in War*, HMSO, 1915, p. 1.

91 Bowlby, WIHM, RAMC 365, Papers: letter to Bowlby from Sloggett, 15 January 1917, p. 3.

92 W.G. MacPherson, *Official History of the War – Medical Services, Surgery of the War*, I, HMSO, 1922, pp. 213–14. W.O. 95/44, PRO, DGMS Diary 1915: 1 September 1915.

93 *Manual of Injuries and Diseases of War*, HMSO, 1918.

94 MacPherson, *Surgery of the War*, I, pp. 151–2.

95 *First Annual Report of the Medical Research Committee 1914–15*, cmd. 8101, 1914–1916, XXXI: see pp. 577, 580, 584 & 587.

96 W.O. 95/44, PRO, DGAMS, Diary 1915: 27 January 1915. MacPherson, *General History*, I, p. 45.

97 See Captain H. Upcott, WIHM, RAMC 1101, Diary: 11 January 1917; Dible, IWM, Diary: 12 February 1917.

98 Dr G. Moore, LC, Letters: Letter 15 March 1916.

99 Some references to the organization of, or attendance at, lectures can be found in the following: J.M. McLachlan, LC, Letters, letter 609 (6 April 1916) and 941 (16 September 1917); Dr W. Sharrard, LC, Diary 1917, 17 February 1917: W.O. 95/197, PRO, DMS First Army, Diary 1917, 24 February 1917; W.O. 95/903, PRO, DDMS XIII Corps, Diary 1917, 2 December 1917 and 12 December 1917, W.O. 95/5300, PRO, DDMS East African Expeditionary Force, Diary, 26 February 1918; H.J.B. Fry, LC, Diary, 19 January 1917.

100 Dr W. Sharrard, LC, Letters: 19 October 1917.

101 H.J.B. Fry, LC, Diary, 16 April 1918.

102 MacPherson, *Surgery of the War*, I, p. 109.

103 *Ibid*, p. 126.

104 W.O. 95/44, PRO, DGMS Diary 1915: 16 June 1915.

105 'Transmission of Trench Fever by the Louse', BMJ, 1918 (I), p. 354. 'The Etiology of Trench Fever', BMJ, 1918 (II), p. 120. 'Interim Report of the War Office Committee for the Study of Trench Fever', JRAMC, XXX, 1918, pp. 352–3.

106 Commandant of the Royal Army Medical College, 1914–1918.

107 W.O. 95/47, PRO, DGMS Diary 1918: 12 May 1918.

108 MacPherson, *Surgery of the War*, I, pp. 134–49. McLaughlin, *The RAMC*, p. 37.

109 MacPherson, *Surgery of the War*, I, p. 173.

110 W.O. 159/17, PRO, Letters from Sir Walter Lawrence to Lord Kitchener on the medical arrangements in France: letter 31 December 1914, p. 4.

111 W.O. 95/44, PRO, DGMS Diary 1915, 19 January 1915.

112 Boyd, LC, recollections, pp. 3–4. Tape recording 463.

113 **Boyd,** LC, recollections, p. 8.
114 **MacPherson,** *General History*, II, p. 364.
115 **Fairley,** LC, Diary: 9 November 1915.
116 **WO 95/50,** PRO, DDGMS diary, 25 October 1915; Appendix 28, 27 October 1915.
117 **Dr G. Moore,** LC, Letters: letter 4 June 1916.
118 'The Treatment of War Psychoneuroses', BMJ, 1918 (II), p. 634.
119 'Shell Shock', BMJ, 1922 (II) p. 392.
120 **E. Miller,** *The Neuroses In War,* London, Macmillan, 1940, p. 175.
121 **W.A. Turner,** 'The Bradshaw Lecture on Neuroses and Psychoses of War', JRAMC, XXXI, 1918, p. 411. **E. Miller,** *The Neuroses in War,* p. 140. **N. Fenton,** *Shell Shock and its Aftermath,* St. Louis, Mosby, 1926, p. 23. **A.F. Hurst,** *Medical Diseases of War,* Arnold, 1943, p. 163.
122 **W.O. 95/45,** PRO, DGAMS, Diary: 25 November 1916.
123 **Gameson,** IWM, Memoirs, p. 163.
124 **Anthony Babington,** *For the Sake of Example,* Cooper, 1983, p. 143.
125 **W. Brown,** late Neurologist Fourth and Fifth Armies, France; Wilde Reader in Psychology, University of Oxford. Cited in the *Report of the War Office Committee of Enquiry into Shell Shock,* HMSO, 1922, p. 44.
126 **W.O. 293/1,** PRO, War Office Instructions, August–December 1914: Instruction 80, Lectures on Venereal Disease, 6 November 1914. **W.O. 293/2,** PRO, War Office Instructions, January–June: Instruction 127, Venereal Disease, 12 June 1915.
127 **W.O. 32/11404,** PRO, Conference re VD and its Treatment in the Armed Forces, May 1918, p. 11.
128 'A Military Medical Society', BMJ, 1915 (II), pp. 905–6; 'Medical Arrangements of the British Expeditionary Force', BMJ, 1916 (I), p. 701; 'Royal Army Medical Corps, Rouen Medical Society', JRAMC, XXIV, 1915, pp. 45–8, 262, 353–8; 'Royal Army Medical Corps, Third Corps Medical Society', JRAMC, XXVI, 1916, p. 93; 'Publication of Scientific Papers', BMJ, 1916 (I), p. 27.
129 *Ibid.*
130 **H.W. Kaye,** WIHM, RAMC 739, Diary, Volume II, 8 November 1915.
131 'Report of the Commission on Medical Establishments', WIHM, RAMC 1165, p. 44.
132 **W.O. 32/11395,** PRO, 'Report of the Babtie Committee on the Reorganisation of the Army Medical Service, 1921–1923', p. 22.
133 'Consultants with the Armies Abroad', BMJ, 1919 (I), p. 804.
134 **Herringham,** *Physician in France,* p. 77.
135 **Bowlby,** WIHM, RAMC 365, Papers: letter to Bowlby from Sir A. Sloggett, 15 January 1917, p. 3.
136 **Tubby,** *A Consulting Surgeon in the Near East,* p. 249.
137 'Consultants with the Armies Abroad', BMJ, 1919 (I), p. 804.
138 **Herringham,** *Physician in France,* p. 43. See also **Tubby,** *A Consulting Surgeon in the Near East,* p. 248.
139 **Herringham,** *Physician in France,* pp. 54–5.
140 'Consultants with the Armies Abroad', BMJ, 1919 (I), p. 804. **Stephen Paget,** *Sir Victor Horsley,* Constable, 1919, p. 302.

141 'Report of the Commission on Medical Establishments', WIHM, RAMC 1165, p. 79.
142 'French War Surgery', BMJ, 1919 (I), p. 745.
143 'Recent Developments in RAMC Front Line Education', BMJ, 1918 (II), pp. 141–2.
144 Stephen, 'Recent Developments in Royal Army Medical Corps Front Line Education', JRAMC, XXXI, 1918, pp. 158–9.

Chapter 8

The Way of the Wounded:
The Medical Officer's Work
from Front to Base

The focus of public interest in the RAMC was on its ability to administer rapid and effective treatment to the wounded. It was this area that the Army's utilization of doctors was most likely to be judged. This chapter will examine the development of arrangements for evacuating the wounded with a view to establishing the nature of the army doctor's work. It will consider the validity of wartime claims that the system militated against good medical practice, and that it consequently wasted the talents of medical men.

The initial treatment of the wounded was undertaken by the regimental medical personnel. This consisted of a staff of sixteen stretcher bearers,[1] who were responsible for retrieving the wounded from the battlefield. The stretcher bearers were under the command of the RMO who trained them in first aid, paying particular attention to the question of arresting haemorrhage, so that some immediate treatment could be given to the wounded even before they arrived at the Aid Post.[2] The RMO was responsible for receiving and treating the wounded, and then evacuating them on to the Field Ambulances. The duty of an RMO was to establish an Aid Post in whatever shelter he could find, and as near to the firing line as was deemed safe. He was to remain there, awaiting the arrival of the sick, and wounded. By 1917 the typical Aid Post consisted of a '[cross-shaped] heavily propped and timbered series of wide passages', with a central compartment wide enough to allow two stretchers to pass each other. Along the walls were tiers of bunks for the wounded, whilst separate compartments were generally provided to accommodate the MO and his staff.[3]

In certain circumstances, it was possible for an MO to develop more sophisticated facilities. Lawrence Gameson was with the 71st Brigade RFA at Arras in 1917. It was 'now a quiet sector', and he obtained approval from his ADMS to establish a small hospital 'for retaining mild, tractable cases'. Construction work began in September. He was given the component parts of a Nissen hut, and made his own beds from trench boards with 'wire netting, not too taut, for spring mattresses, insulating layers of newspaper next, and finally a couple of blankets'. He had an ablution section with an iron boiler from a forgotten French wash-house serving as a bath. This ablution section enabled him to treat cases of scabies within the unit, removing the need to send the men away for the three-day treatment. The men praised this 'comfortable' little hospital, but its life was short as Gameson's Brigade received orders to move in November. This showed the impossibility of having a regular in-patient section at an RAP, and Gameson admitted 'it had been largely a hobby'.[4]

Once the wounded man arrived at the Aid Post, the RMO would check that the wound was clean; carry out any emergency amputations that were required; oversee the splinting of fractures, using the Thomas splint; and ensure that everything possible was done to prevent the onset of shock. More extensive operative treatment was discouraged, the prime concern being to evacuate the wounded to hospitals in safer locations where the settled environment would contribute to their chances of survival.[5] It was the job of the regimental medical personnel to fit the wounded for their journey down the line. Thus the quality of the treatment received at the Aid Post was vital to the patients' later recovery, and it was essential that a qualified medical practitioner be there to supervise it. This was certainly the view of those who subsequently handled the wounded at the CCSs,[6] and it remained an unfortunate consequence of the evacuation system that the RMOs themselves were rarely able to observe the successful results of their endeavours.

Yet, despite the critical importance of the work undertaken by RMOs, the Army's employment of doctors in this role was a source of some considerable controversy throughout the War.[7] There were constant claims that the nature of the work did not demand the skills of a qualified medical practitioner, and that RMOs were often idle. The duties of an RMO were also seen to expose doctors to too great a danger. There was a high casualty rate with over 1,000 RMOs being killed. In the context of a growing strain on Britain's medical manpower, critics suggested that in the winter, when there was little military activity, RMOs should be sent home from France to assist their hard-pressed civilian colleagues.[8] Others advocated the complete removal of doctors from regimental duties, arguing that NCOs, trained in first aid, were capable of undertaking the work.

However, the RAMC remained unmoved in its conviction that RMOs were indispensable. By 1918 there was agreement that doctors would be spared from the FAs, by giving the post of bearer officer to non-medical men, as the responsibilities were largely those of leading and directing the men. In contrast, the work of the RMO was considered, for the following reasons, to require the services of qualified doctors:

a) The actual diagnosis of illness and prescription of drugs must be done by a qualified medical man.

b) The RMO represents the medical profession and our own Royal Corps, now as always, on the actual battle field, and looms large as such in the eyes of the combatant officer and man. It seems to be essential that he remain as at present. It is impossible to withdraw him.[9]

The removal of RMOs would have been detrimental to the interests of the wounded. It was essential that a trained doctor be present to supervise and conduct the vital work undertaken at an RAP. Part of the problem was the sporadic nature of the work; in quiet times there were naturally fewer casualties, and it seemed to many Medical Officers that their skills were not in sufficient demand to justify their constant presence in the front line. But it was essential that the medical services remained at all times prepared to deal with the consequences of unexpected enemy action. Idleness in quiet times had to be balanced against the potential costs of having no doctor with a battalion in battle. Moreover those who advocated the removal of RMOs failed to appreciate the full range of duties that the latter had to carry out. As will be seen in the next chapter, the most important functions of the RMO related to preventative medicine. Maintaining the health and fighting fitness of the men in their charge was a full-time job, which ought to have demanded the constant attention of any RMO. According to Sir Wilmot Herringham, an RMO claiming to have only half an hour's work a day was simply not doing his duty.[10] The Medical Establishment Commission was in agreement.[11] It concluded that abolishing RMOs would inflict great harm on battalions. The failure of some RMOs to appreciate this, particularly in the early years of the War, reflected a failure to understand that their duties extended beyond the treatment of wounds. There was a need for doctors to recognize that medical work in the Army differed from that undertaken by the majority of practitioners in their civilian careers. Many doctors were unacquainted with preventative work in civilian life and were unaware of its importance in military medicine. Improvements in RAMC training, however, enabled most RMOs to comprehend the full range of their duties.

The nature of regimental medical work inevitably exposed doctors to danger. By 1917 the death rate amongst RMOs and regimental orderlies was reportedly as high as 40 per 1,000 per month.[12] However, particularly in the early years of the War, confusion surrounding the exact duties of an RMO meant that many doctors were unclear as to exactly how much risk they were expected to run. Many RMOs were leaving the comparative safety of their Aid Posts and going forward with their bearers to treat the wounded. According to Lieutenant Colonel F.S. Brereton, such action was frequently 'a matter of urgency', and the risk involved was not remarkably greater than if the RMOs remained in their Aid Posts.[13] Undoubtedly, it was sometimes essential for them to tend men in the trenches since there were cases that could not be moved until they had received expert medical attention. But many RMOs were going into the trenches as a matter of course. One such was Captain Hugh Llewelyn Glyn-Hughes, RMO to the 1st Battalion Wiltshire Regiment, whom Private G.H. Swindell called 'the most courageous doctor I served under in our war'.[14] During a 1959 edition of *This Is Your Life*, an officer of the Wiltshire Regiment described Glyn-Hughes's approach to his duties:

> Doc here was always in the thick of it. By rights he should have been back in the Regimental Aid Post waiting for casualties to be brought back. But not him, he was up there in the attack, going over the top with the men, attending to them as they got wounded. That's when I remember the occasion when he amputated some fellow's foot with a pocket knife and saved his life.[15]

In a later attack, when all the other officers had been killed, he ended up taking command of two companies.[16] It was not unique for a Medical Officer to take military command. Probably the most famous example is that of Captain J.C. Dunn, author of *The War the Infantry Knew*, and RMO of the 2nd Battalion Royal Welch Fusiliers.[17] Nevertheless, instances of Medical Officers commanding combatant units in active operations appear to have been rare. For the vast majority of RMOs their

184

experience of front-line service did not take them beyond the confines of their medical work.

However, a great many shared Glyn-Hughes's approach to his duties, choosing to go into the trenches rather than remain at their Aid Posts. From some quarters, this definition of an RMO's duties received encouragement. An article appeared in *The Great War*, in 1915, heaping praise on doctors who advanced under fire. It declared that there were 'few more splendid records than those of the eager young medicos who put regulations on one side and went where danger was greatest'.[18] Despite having reservations about the advisability of employing Medical Officers so close to the front, Captain E.C. Deane was among those who ran such risks. His disregard for personal safety won him the MC, but only ten days later he lost his life when trying to bring wounded in under fire.[19] Hugh Shields was another who insisted upon attending to casualties under fire. He recognized that having the MO close to hand could have a tremendous moral effect upon the men during a push, and he was determined to make his presence felt:

> I make a point of entirely disregarding fire when it comes to the point of seeing to a wounded man and pay no attention. I don't believe precautions beyond the ordinary ones of not exposing oneself more than one can help do any good. After all, I always think if one is killed doing one's duty, one can't help it and it is the best way of coming to an end.[20]

Only a month later, he was to meet his death in just the manner he described: shot through the neck whilst tending to a wounded man in the open. Officers in the Irish Guards, with whom he served as an RMO, admired his bravery and devotion, but frequently advised him against taking risks far beyond the bounds of duty.[21]

There were many RMOs with records equally as distinguished as those of Deane and Shields; their countless acts of courage receiving recognition in the form of the large number of gallantry medals awarded to RAMC officers.[22] But whilst their bravery won them deserved praise, there was concern that their enthusiasm and devotion to duty was leading them to be too reckless with their own lives.

It is not difficult to ascertain why RMOs were not content simply to remain in their Aid Posts. Young doctors who volunteered to serve as MOs were equally as motivated by a sense of patriotic duty as those men who became combatant officers. It is understandable that conscious of their non-combatant status, and close to the thick of the fighting, they wished to prove their mettle and show that they were just as willing to risk their lives for their country as others in the regiment. G.D. Fairley felt that it was his duty as a young medical man to be in the front line,[23] whilst Captain Lawrence Gameson recorded his satisfaction at having been attached to a combatant unit.[24] Much more challenging medical work (professionally speaking) was available at the Base, but many found the atmosphere there dull and uncongenial.[25] There was a sense that their war service, however commendable it might seem to others, was somehow incomplete unless they experienced close physical contact with the fighting.

Once at the front, in close proximity to the fighting, many RMOs became uncomfortable with their non-combatant status. Some reacted by taking great risks in pursuit of their medical duties. Others, however, continued to find their position frustrating. With friends dying around them, it was difficult for doctors to resist the urge to hit back. H.S. Souttar remembered how a desire for vengeance consumed him:

> my eyes were fixed on the mitrailleuse standing on the garden path under the trees. My fingers itched to pull the lever and to scatter withering death among them [the Germans]. It slowly came into my mind how good it would be to kill these defilers.[26]

In his diary, F.C. Fenwick describes an occasion when an MO gave way to this desire to retaliate:

> Snipers are damnable . . . One medic shot one at 400 yards this week and was not reprimanded.[27]

Such an action contravened the Geneva convention and, like the instances of Medical Officers assuming military command, does not appear to have been a regular occurrence. However, the emotions which this action expressed were widely shared. And although few doctors fired in active operations, many let off steam by practising with revolvers or bomb-throwing.[28] Charles McKerrow enjoyed bomb-throwing practice, but did not 'expect ever to require to use such knowledge'.[29]

Others, however, not only considered such skills to be useless to Medical Officers but felt that, as non-combatants, they ought to have nothing to do with weapons. D. McAlpine was convinced that he should not be carrying a revolver and gave his to a combatant officer.[30] A.A. Martin took a similar view, seeing the possession of arms as completely at odds with the role of a Medical Officer. He refused to obtain a revolver and found doctors who did so highly ridiculous:

I have seen mild-looking young surgeons arrive at the front armed to the teeth, with swords, revolvers and ammunition, clanking spurs, map cases, field glasses and compasses strung all around them, and on their left arm the brassard with the Red Cross. We called them Christmas Trees.[31]

The War Office's justification for issuing arms to Medical Officers was that they might need them to defend the wounded. However such a situation was unlikely to arise, and the military authorities were keen to avoid medics becoming embroiled in the fighting, as is evident from the following instructions, which were issued in 1914:

A Medical Officer serves the force best by remaining unwounded and efficient. A battle ground can only be effectively cleared of wounded after the battle is over. The enemy is a signatory of the Geneva Convention and any captured wounded should be safe in his hands.[32]

Colonel Arthur Lee informed Lord Kitchener that in France 'Medical Officers are inclined to expose themselves too recklessly and that in consequence of gallant but fatal attempts to succour one wounded man a whole unit may be deprived of medical assistance for the remainder of a day's fighting.' He felt that this situation needed to be remedied by the issuing of clear orders restraining Medical Officers from these 'acts of mistaken gallantry'.[33]

In September 1916, the DADMS 6th Division recorded the promulgation of an order 'forbidding MOs to hop over the parapet at once'; a restriction which commanded his wholehearted support:

They must remain behind, no good purpose will be served advancing too quickly. Fourteen MOs were lost . . . in this last attack [Delville Wood] and MOs can't be replaced like this.[34]

Charles McKerrow sought to allay his wife's fears for his safety by stressing, in his letters home, the strictness of such orders:

A doctor is not allowed to advance in the first line of his regiment, so, of course, he is not in danger much.
. . . you know that I am only a doctor and can hide amongst the baggage. The orders about doctors exposing themselves are most stringent.[35]

An article in the BMJ expressed the confident belief that Medical Officers' sense of duty would prevent them from taking unnecessary risks.[36] But by 1917, with a growing shortage of doctors, there was serious concern that despite being 'severely warned'[37] against dangerous exploits, many were still failing to exercise sufficient caution. The Medical Establishment Committee argued the importance of battalion commanders impressing upon the RMOs that the proper place for them was either at their Aid Post, or with their COs, and that they should resist the temptation to go over the top. It also felt that the RMOs should be given better instruction with regard to this matter.[38] The Committee was critical of the lack of systematic training for RMOs.

Articles in the medical press continued to emphasize the fact that it was no longer considered the duty of the RMO to hunt for wounded under fire.[39] A similar lesson had been learnt by the German Army, which, early in the War, had lost great numbers of Medical Officers due to a policy of sending them out to attend to a single casualty. These losses led to a more cautious and sensible approach, in which the dangers to the Medical Officer were balanced against the good he might achieve.'[40]

British Medical Officers were reminded of the need to maintain this balance, which meant that they had to recognize that they owed it to the men not to be heroic, or unnecessarily risk their lives.[41] It was the RMO's duty to keep himself safe so that the men could rely upon him being there should they need him. A Medical Officer who served at the front pointed out the dangers of doing otherwise:

> If the MO is placed hors de combat while attempting to collect a few men who are already hors de combat it is sure to mean the weakening of the battalion.[42]

F.J. Blackley recognized the importance of avoiding unnecessary risks and operated a policy of remaining in his Aid Post rather than 'heroically leading a stretcher party', because he thought it essential that the RMO be at a central position to which the stretcher bearers could bring the wounded. He feared that this would make him look 'funky', but was determined to continue with this approach regardless. In fact, from their letters home, it became clear that the men, far from thinking him 'funky', were appreciative of his methods.[43]

There were times when there was advantage in the RMO leaving his Aid Post. For instance, occasional visits to the firing trench were beneficial from the point of view of troop morale, as they reminded the men that skilled medical attention was always near at hand. Also, with serious cases such as severe fractures, when it was difficult to move the patients, RMOs could go forward to administer aid and oversee the arrangements, as long as this did not take them too near to the thick of the fighting.[44] Only in such circumstances did Blackley leave his Aid Post. On one occasion, when it became difficult to carry men from the firing trench, he went up to administer morphia and cheer the men up. Another time he led a stretcher party to collect a severely wounded artilleryman.[45] They came under heavy shelling but, whilst displaying great courage and composure, he was careful to minimize the risk to himself and his men by moving slowly and taking all available cover.

The unavoidable risks attaching to their work inevitably placed a great strain on RMOs, contributing to a high incidence of nervous disorders.[46]. It was also undeniable that their work, whilst vital to the progress of the wounded, had a tendency to become somewhat routine and lacking in professional stimulation. After a year in the front line, spent mostly as RMO to the 23rd Brigade RFA, Geoffrey Keynes 'was spiritually and physically exhausted and felt that I had earned at least a spell of more creative work'. He successfully transferred to a CCS where the work was much more varied, and he was able to progress with his surgical career.[47] Charles McKerrow experienced similar feelings, although eventually he decided to remain because he felt he could do more for the men. He was very conscious of the importance of the work and felt that every young Medical Officer should do at least six months' work as an RMO.[48] In a case like McKerrow's, where he had become a widely respected member of the battalion, himself having developed strong loyalty to the unit, there was much to be said for his remaining. But in general it was felt advisable to limit a doctor's spell as an RMO to a maximum of twelve months.[49]

The medical unit lying next behind an RAP was a Field Ambulance. Each infantry division had three FAs, whilst a cavalry division had one for each of its brigades. Their principal function was to relieve the RAPs of sick and wounded; to assist the regimental medical staff (at nightfall and during pauses in the fighting) with the removal of wounded from the battlefield; and to treat cases until they could be sent down the line for more extensive treatment at hospitals away from the fighting. Each FA usually served around three or four battalions at once; and in order to fulfil its duties properly, it was divisible into three sections (A, B and C) capable of independent action. These sections were of similar composition, except that Section A (the headquarters section) had four motor ambulance cars (or horsedrawn wagons), whilst B and C had only three. Each of these sections, A, B, and C, was, in turn, subdivided into a stretcher-bearer section (for collecting the wounded) and a tent section (for treatment of the wounded). During a battle the general organization was as follows: the stretcher bearers brought wounded down from the RAPs, via an Advanced Dressing Station, to a Main Dressing Station, formed by the tent division. The organization of the FA, with its divisions and subdivisions, was intended to allow sections to be detached for duty with small bodies of troops, operating at a distance from the main body, such as units fighting in hill regions.[50]

On most fronts this was essentially the system that operated. However, in the principal theatre of operations, the Western Front, changes were required; the FA was designed for mobile warfare, not for the static conditions that generally prevailed. During the opening months of the War, when the BEF was engaged in mobile warfare, most of the surgical work fell upon the FAs.[51] But, their functions were curtailed when it became possible for the CCSs to form large, settled hospitals. Given their proximity to the firing line, extensive operative treatment at the FAs was considered inadvisable; the priority became the rapid evacuation of the wounded to the CCSs, where the proper conditions for surgery existed.[52] The primary role of the FAs thus became to ensure that the wounded were fit for their journey down the line. At the ADS, dressings and splints were inspected and adjusted; and any essential early treatment, such as the splinting of fractures that had not been possible at the RAP, was undertaken here. On arrival at the MDS, the cases were classified, ready for distribution to other units. But immediate evacuation was not always possible, and it might have to retain the wounded for some time. For this reason the MDSs were generally situated sufficiently far behind the lines to be beyond the range of all but the heaviest artillery fire. If the wounded were retained, some treatment might be given; whilst whatever the circumstances arrangements were always made to rest, dry, warm and feed the patients, and to ensure that they had received antitetanus serum. However, on a settled front, with a manageable number of casualties, it was often possible for a seriously wounded man to by-pass the MDS altogether.[53] The efficient evacuation of the wounded was facilitated by the formation of motor ambulance convoys which consisted of up to fifty vehicles, each having accommodation for eight sitting patients or four stretcher cases.[54]

Some critics came to regard the FA as a unit sandwiched uncomfortably between the RAP and the CCS, with no real function to justify its continued existence. It appeared to be nothing more than an unnecessary drain upon the nation's medical manpower. Meanwhile, some Medical Officers employed with FAs complained that the work was little in quantity, lacking in interest and undemanding of medical skill. H.W. Kaye thought that it was 'very difficult to see what advantage the FA brings to the casualties and why they should not be taken direct from the aid post to the CCS'.[55] He wrote that 'half the officers in each FA are employed on non-medical work – administration, transport, and supplies – which is not a doctor's work and does not require a medical education and experience . . . a curious contrast to the official urgent cry for more doctors for the Army'.[56] N. King-Wilson, who served in Gallipoli, recorded the dull routine of separating dysentery from diarrhoea cases: 'a most melancholy procedure, and, at the end of my first day I felt that I was neither soldier nor physician, and that the Corporal . . . could have done quite as much'.[57] He was frustrated by the lack of opportunity for carrying out treatment available at an FA, and complained that 'one soon got the feeling that the Medical Officer in charge of a dressing station was little more than a traffic manager at a wayside railway station, sorting and labelling goods for their ultimate destination and arranging for their shipment'.[58] Indeed, FA work appeared to amount to nothing more than 'merely scratching the surface'.[59]

At the beginning of 1917, Sir Almroth Wright launched a three-pronged attack on the FAs. First, being equipped for only the most basic treatment, he argued that they stood 'in the way of that immediate surgical treatment which is, in the opinion of all, a point of fundamental importance'. Secondly, he complained that 'its numerous staff of doctors is from the nature of the case principally occupied in non-professional duties connected with the keeping up of the efficiency of the mobile unit'. Thirdly, he argued that the practice of having at least one FA in reserve, with a division that was resting, for every FA in service with a division in the line, was extremely wasteful.[60]

Wright's attack encapsulated the numerous criticisms that had been levelled against FAs. As the Committee on Medical Establishments acknowledged, 'from an early period of the War the staffing of the FA has been subjected to more criticisms than that of any other unit'.[61] The RAMC did respond to this criticism, by reducing the number of MOs with an infantry FA from nine to eight.[62] However, the Committee felt that since the functions of the FA were unlikely to increase further reductions could be made. Thus, the number of MOs with an infantry FA was lowered from eight to seven, and with cavalry FAs from six to five. The MOs released were to be those with responsibility for the supervision of transport. Their work was to be undertaken by a non-Medical Officer. There were proposals before the Committee for more radical reorganization of FAs, but in the end it was decided that the present system be retained.[63]

This decision was highly commendable because those who called for more fundamental change, or even the effective abolition of FAs, were not only exaggerating the problem, but also failing to recognize the crucial importance of these units. Whilst it was quite correct to make sensible economies in medical manpower, given the reduced role of FAs, it was necessary to remain prepared for a time when trench warfare might come to an end. Thus it would have been folly to make radical alterations, or greatly denude them of skilled manpower. The importance of FAs in a war of movement was demonstrated during the great retreats and advances of 1914 and 1918. In these conditions, evacuation to CCSs was gravely disrupted, and MDSs took on an important surgical role.[64] The experience was similar on other fronts, such as Palestine and Mesopotamia.[65]

Even in trench warfare, however, FAs had a crucial part to play, which many critics failed to appreciate. According to Deputy Surgeon General A. Gascoigne Wildey, the thoroughness of the early care at an FA was a significant factor in a patient's subsequent progress.[66] This care involved not only the proper cleansing of wounds, but also the provision of rest, warmth, dry clothing and hot drinks; all of which contributed to the prevention of shock.[67]

It was equally wrong to belittle the role of the MDS as a sorting centre for the wounded. It was here that a careful MO could perform a vital medico-military role: to ensure that patients received appropriate treatment as quickly as possible; and to minimize the loss of men to units in the divisional area. One of the FAs in a division would form a Rest Station, which acted as a convalescent hospital for patients requiring nursing, but not considered ill enough to justify further evacuation down the line. Men could remain here for up to a fortnight; if after that time they were still unfit for duty, then they were passed on to a CCS.[68] Thus, by sending men suffering from minor ailments to a Rest Station, an MO could minimize the losses to his division without hindering the patient's progress. The post-war Babtie Committee on the Reorganization of the Army Medical Service attached great importance to the FA's role in 'holding men on the strength of their units as long as there is a reasonable prospect of their speedy return to duty'.[69]

It was true that during quiet times there was often very little for MOs to do. However, in no sense did this provide justification for the abolition or further downgrading of FAs; for in major battles they were extremely busy, playing a crucial part in the treatment and evacuation of the sick and wounded.[70] At Ypres, in 1915, H.W. Kaye recorded that there was 'a great press of surgical work every night'.[71] Similarly, on the

Somme in 1916, the FAs were heavily congested,[72] and did much vital work. E.S.B. Hamilton, who served with the 45th FA, described the pressure of work:

The dugout [of the ADS] is awfully overcrowded both night and day and it is impossible to get it cleaned or aired. [There were] something like 800 people through here in about thirty hours the day before yesterday. This is far too much work for the personnel [of] three officers and about 115 men. Result [is] a lot of the men are done up and the officers seedy and depressed.[73]

There is no evidence to support Wright's contention that the FA stood in the way of proper treatment. On the contrary, it is clear that whenever possible every effort was made to ensure that patients requiring urgent treatment were evacuated as rapidly as possible from the ADS to the CCS, often completely by-passing the MDS. However, during major advances or retreats this was simply impossible. The sheer number of casualties and the disruption unavoidably caused to the evacuation process meant that both the ADS and MDS had a vital role to play in handling the wounded, tending to their injuries and carrying out measures for the avoidance of shock. In 1918 the Fifth Army's decision to eliminate MDSs led to great problems and much anxiety during the German offensive.[74] Clearly, FAs were indispensable when the lines of evacuation became extended. Moreover, their work was not just confined to affording shelter, administering first aid and overseeing evacuation. On the Somme in 1916 they established Advanced Operating Centres, providing emergency treatment for serious cases such as those hit in the abdomen. Ordinarily these cases would have been treated at a CCS, but due to the extension of the line, evacuation to a CCS would have involved a potentially fatal delay in treatment.[75] Thus, in times of great upheaval FAs appear not as obstacles 'in the way of . . . immediate surgical treatment', but as providers of the same.

FAs were involved in a great variety of work, depending upon their location and the conditions of warfare which they faced. Important though it all was, some of this work, in its nature, can only be described as boring; a fact that explains the complaints referred to earlier. Therefore, as in the case of RMOs, such complaints cannot be taken as evidence that FA work was wasteful of medical skill. Indeed, in this chapter we have already seen that H.W. Kaye, who at one point questioned the need for FAs, later spoke of the great surgical work carried out by them. According to G. Moore there was 'plenty of interesting work', and he told his sister:

> I'm having the time of my life [running an ADS]. I am responsible for the collection of wounded from two of our brigades who are spread out over a good many miles of country. I have got a small hospital in a wrecked village here with two Medical Officers and about 100 men under me. We do all emergency work as there is no properly fitted hospital within fifteen miles.[76]

As well as interesting work for those MOs who wanted a sense of active participation in the campaign (and who loathed the 'quiet life' at a Base Hospital) service with an FA promised an 'adventurous life'.[77] The FA accompanied its division at all times, shared its fortunes and witnessed the fighting at close quarters. Captain M.S. Esler, an RMO temporarily attached to an FA, found his time there anything but dull:

> I should have been very happy to have remained with them for the rest of the War, for there is always plenty of excitement in an FA, with very much less risk to life and limb than with a regiment.[78]

Generally speaking, Esler was correct in his assessment that there was less risk at an FA than there was as an RMO. There does not appear to have been as great a debate about the dangers to precious skilled lives as there was in the case of RMOs. FAs were, however, only relatively safe and the risk was still considerable. ADSs, in particular, were sufficiently close to the front line to be in range of shell fire; whilst during an advance the MOs and their bearers would move forward to establish new dressing stations, and often tended to the wounded under fire. Boyd Cable describes one highly respected MO whose bravery in the trenches led to a wound that cost him his sight.[79] As many references can be found to the courage of MOs serving with the FAs as to their regimental colleagues.[80]

Nevertheless, no matter how interesting the medical work could sometimes be, or how exciting the life, it is clear that not all MOs shared Esler's desire to remain with an FA for the duration. Those who complained about the work being boring had substance to their arguments, especially if their service included long periods when the unit was not involved in active operations. Upon first joining the 36th FA, J.M. McLachlan was enthusiastic and thought that he 'should get some quite good surgery here of the rapid, rough and ready kind'. But after six months he was feeling frustrated by the limitations of this surgery and by the first aid type work of a dressing station:

I'm debating a lot within myself whether I should put in for a transfer to a Casualty Clearing Station. I should like very much to know about the running of these places and the work is, I think, more strictly surgical and medical, and less of the pitch and toss game that this is.[81]

Clearly, as in the case of RMOs, there was a strong argument for limiting the length of an MO's service with an FA. After a spell with an FA, MOs were often moved on to work with a regiment. Of course, the medical work here could be even more basic, but there would at least be the challenge of new responsibilities. Moreover, experience at an FA, including the initial treatment of wounds and its work as regards hygiene, was great preparation for duties with a battalion. On the other hand the surgical work undertaken and the understanding gained of the early treatment of wounds was an asset to Medical Officers when they moved on to CCSs and Base Hospitals. Thus, quite apart from its essential role within the medical organization, the FA performed a useful service as a training centre. Given the limited time and facilities available for the formal training of MOs, the importance of this 'on the job' training at an FA is not to be underestimated.

The notion that FAs were superfluous and that employment there was wasteful of Medical Officers grew out of the particular conditions of warfare that emerged on the Western Front. On other fronts their usefulness could be more immediately appreciated. However, even in the trenches of France, they had an important part to play. The work was often far from glamorous but their care for the wounded could be the difference between success and failure when surgery was undertaken further down the line; and in emergencies they themselves carried out vital operative treatment. Of course, some adaptation to the changed conditions was necessary and there were slight reductions in the number of MOs with an FA. But wholesale changes were both unnecessary and inadvisable, as was proved by the vital role they performed in 1918. Moreover, after the War the centrality of FAs to the RAMC's treatment and evacuation of the sick and wounded was reaffirmed.[82]

The diminution in the role of the FAs during the War was a consequence of the evolution of the Clearing Hospitals. The Clearing Hospital was originally designed as a mobile unit, serving as a link between the Field Ambulance and the base hospitals. Its functions were threefold:[83]

1. To receive and treat until fit for further transport those sick and wounded who were seriously ill.
2. To expedite the immediate evacuation to the bases of those fit to travel.

3. To retain for early return to duty cases of wounds and sickness likely to recover within a few days.

In the early stages of the War the Clearing Hospitals proved to be inadequately prepared to fulfil these tasks. Having only been created a short time prior to 1914, they had never actually operated in war conditions. Their equipment was small, sufficient only to deal with 200 cases who had to lie on stretchers. The surgical equipment was, in Sir Arthur Sloggett's words, 'very limited in every way'.[84] Indeed, due to difficulties of transportation during the fighting at Mons and Le Cateau most of the Clearing Hospitals remained to be unloaded from their trains. It was not until early 1915 that they really became effective units.[85] At this point they were officially designated as Casualty Clearing Stations. The change in the name was intended to emphasize that their primary function was to facilitate the rapid evacuation of the sick and wounded. The inclusion of 'hospital' in the title was deemed likely to encourage, amongst both the wounded and the public at home, expectations of much more comprehensive treatment than these units were capable of providing.[86] The CCSs were simply intended to act as sorting centres. They were to provide for patients to be rested, fed and prepared for their further journey. The injured were to have their wounds inspected and redressed. It was never intended that anything more than the most urgent operative procedures should be performed, and the CCS was organized as a light, mobile unit, capable of removal by eight or nine three-ton lorries.[87]

However, this scale of organization rapidly proved itself inadequate for handling the volume of casualties on the Western Front. At the same time the high incidence of gas gangrene brought home to the medical authorities the importance of early operation.[88] Surgeons who dealt with the wounded from the First Battle of Ypres were convinced that facilities were required to enable surgery to take place nearer the front and so prevent a potentially fatal delay in the treatment of infected wounds.[89] The FAs could not provide such facilities. Their positions were never sufficiently settled to allow the recuperation time that was necessary for surgical cases. But the onset of trench warfare meant that the railheads and their associated units, which included the CCSs, became static. In these conditions the organization of the CCSs was gradually modified. Despite their change of title the CCSs now effectively became hospitals to which the bulk of the operative work on the Western Front was gradually transferred.

The principal architect of these developments was Sir Anthony Bowlby. He had, since 1914, been the consultant surgeon responsible for surgery in the forward areas. In early 1916 he became 'Advising Consulting Surgeon, British Armies in France'. This post involved the co-ordination of the surgical work of the Western Front. From the earliest days of the War he took a keen interest in the CCSs, recognizing their potential to provide the immediate surgery that was so desperately needed. Throughout 1915 he pressed the case for more CCSs to be deployed in the field, for them to be placed nearer the fighting line and for an increase in the staff of Medical Officers. During the fighting of that year he argued that the First Army medical arrangements had failed to capitalize on the potential of the CCSs, using the example of abdominal operations to prove his point.

All the evidence indicated that the success rate for abdominals was much higher at the CCSs than it was at the FAs. He therefore recommended that responsibility for abdominal surgery be centred on the CCSs, advising the FAs to evacuate abdominal cases as quickly as possible. But W.G. MacPherson, the DMS First Army, had failed to push his CCSs sufficiently forward. In the Loos campaign they had been held back at Aire and Lillers. As a consequence there had been a huge accumulation of wounded at Chocques and Noeux-les-Mines. After some delay an FA was expanded to deal with the emergency. It was specially equipped to deal with abdominal cases, but was swamped with work as all abdominal and head cases were sent there. Bowlby believed that the positioning of two CCSs at this point would have prevented the difficulties. Instead, thanks to a disorganized train service, the wounded faced a delay of up to three days before reaching a CCS. This was evidently an unsatisfactory situation. Bowlby reminded Sir Arthur Sloggett 'that public and professional opinion were united in urging that cases should be treated [as] thoroughly as possible at the front'. CCSs had to be placed as near to the front as conditions permitted.[90]

However, in March 1916 he continued to regard as unsatisfactory the arrangements in the First Army. Wounded were having to travel a distance of up to twenty miles to reach CCSs at Lapruznoy and Lillers. To remedy the situation, the DMS proposed the establishment of a CCS at Bruay to deal with wounded from IV Corps. To supplement this an 'Abdominal Hospital' was opened at Estée Couchée. Bowlby was unimpressed with these arrangements. He considered it 'a farce' to keep CCSs so far from the action. The CCS at Bruay was a move in the right direction, but on its own it was incapable of meeting the needs of a corps of three divisions. He had no faith in the separate 'Abdominal Hospital' which he dismissed as a measure to save the face of the DMS. Bowlby, with the support of Cuthbert Wallace (consulting surgeon with the First

Army), informed the DGMS that 'a sufficient number of CCSs should be within 10,000 yards of the front'. He felt that the RAMC authorities had failed to appreciate that 'we have really created "advanced general Hospitals" and that these are demanded by the public. The recent attacks on the AMS in parliament proved that this was the case and the failure to send CCSs forward for the Loos fight resulted in a genuine cause for complaint.'

Sloggett accepted Bowlby's case, which was enthusiastically endorsed by the DDGMS, Surgeon General O'Donnell. He 'constantly backed up the pushing forwards of the CCSs', and Bowlby credited him with doing more than anyone to prepare them for the fighting of 1916.[91] Following the Somme campaign, Bowlby reported that the advancement of CCSs had significantly reduced the evacuation times from the FAs.[92] The importance of the CCS as a forward hospital was now being recognized. Indeed, during the Third Battle of Ypres in 1917, problems arose with CCSs being placed too far forward and consequently finding themselves under enemy attack.[93] Clearly a balance had to be struck between the need for immediate surgery and the importance of providing a safe, stable environment for the recovery of patients.

From the beginning of 1915, when the DGMS approved the increase in their surgical work, extra surgical equipment was supplied. This included the 'Bowlby box' which contained items such as a high pressure steriliser, drainage tubing, eye instruments, rubber gloves, scalpels and scissors.[94] There also began a steady expansion in the capacity of the CCSs. Initially, they were asked to increase their intake to 500 patients, for whom proper bedsteads now began to be provided. By the Third Battle of Ypres the average accommodation was between 800 to 1,200 patients.[95] The total number of CCSs was also increased to keep pace with the expansion of the British Army. In June 1917, the DGMS agreed that they should be deployed in proportion to the number of divisions involved in active operations. By September 1917 there were fifty-nine CCSs serving on the Western Front.[96]

The early CCSs were established in buildings. However, from the Battle of Loos, it became standard practice to erect them on open ground, using tents to accommodate the wounded. Operating theatres and wards for acute cases were housed in Hospital Nissen huts. Portable generators provided the operating theatres with electric lighting. The CCSs were now functioning as hospitals but they continued to fulfil a variety of additional responsibilities. It should be recalled that they were originally intended as mobile units. Their expansion meant they could no longer fill this role. This problem was overcome by the formation of Advanced

Operating Centres formed from light sections, capable of keeping pace with the advance or retirement of the troops.

The CCSs also had to be ready, at a moment's notice, to handle large numbers of wounded. These had to be accommodated and redressed, or classified for further evacuation. In accordance with this role the CCSs had to take account of the need for good communications with both the FAs and the base hospitals. This meant ready access for the motor ambulance convoys and close proximity to a railway. The organization of the CCSs had to anticipate this full range of duties. Hence, a standard system for the distribution and treatment of the wounded evolved, according to which the CCSs were arranged as follows:[97]

1. A general admission tent or hut in which the necessary particulars were entered as each patient arrived.

2. A tent for the dressing of walking patients.

3. A tent for the dressing of lying down patients.

4. A pre-operation tent.

5. A resuscitation tent.

6. Tents where patients might be kept for treatment.

7. Tents where patients for evacuation were placed.

The increase in surgical work placed a heavy load upon the personnel of the CCSs. The establishment of six MOs, including one surgical specialist, remained unchanged, although its composition was altered early in the War to include a second surgeon. There was also an addition of seven nursing sisters although this complement was never a fixed part of the war establishment. In quiet times, Bowlby believed that this nominal staff was capable of dealing with the routine admissions of wounded.[98] However, in times of heavy fighting, additional surgical staffs were essential. Prior to the Battle of Loos, reinforcements were provided from the base. Thereafter it became the practice for additional MOs to be supplied by CCSs, or FAs, which were not engaged in active operations.

Greater operative work was also facilitated by the formation of surgical teams. Each team comprised a surgeon, an anaesthetist,[99] a sister and a couple of theatre orderlies.[100] These teams were developed on the initiative of Bowlby in preparation for the Somme offensive. He believed that the reinforcement of CCSs, actively engaged, by teams from elsewhere, had 'been a huge success and [had] saved the situation'.[101] In the campaigns of 1917 the employment of surgical teams became standard practice. For the Battle of Arras three surgical teams reinforced each of the ten CCSs involved, with an additional four MOs supplied from amongst the FAs. The twelve CCSs engaged during the Messines offensive received three additional surgical teams, and between three and six MOs from FAs and other CCSs. As 1917 progressed, however, the reliance for reinforcements on other CCSs became problematic, as the prospects of three armies being involved in operations reduced the pool of available MOs. The problem was highlighted when, two days before the commencement of Third Ypres, Second Army requested the return of all the MOs that it had loaned to Fifth Army. Recognizing this difficulty, Bowlby fought to ensure that this was the first battle for which teams were also supplied from the base hospitals. By 31 July, the ten CCSs engaged had been reinforced by three surgical teams from the bases, a further three from other CCSs and by six additional MOs. Each CCS therefore possessed a staff of twenty-four MOs.[101] The teams from the bases gave the CCSs a truly international flavour. In addition to nine British teams there were eleven from the USA, six from Canada, three from Australia, one from New Zealand and one from South Africa.

The employment of teams facilitated further significant increases in the operative work of the CCSs. Three teams, working eight-hour shifts (eight hours on and four hours sleep) could keep two operating tables running continually for as long as a week. A report on the use of the 'twin table' at the 23rd CCS gave a favourable verdict:

During the pressure of work in April and again in August of this year [1917] the 'Twin Table' system has been thoroughly tested and proved most satisfactory. By this method the surgical team can perform the maximum amount of operative work in the minimal time.[103]

During April three teams are recorded as working sixteen hours on and eight hours off. In August the stretches were reduced to twelve hours, which proved more satisfactory, sixteen hours having been too great a strain. Understandably it was found that the longer the team had been working without rest, the less work per hour it did. Working teams in this way enabled each CCS to maintain a minimum of four and a maximum of eight operating tables in continual use. Thus the team system demonstrated the RAMC's recognition of the need to take full advantage of the available surgical skill. It also helped to relieve some of the strain on the surgeons, as did the policy of grouping CCSs. Two or more CCSs were sited adjacently, carrying on their work independently.

The wounded were brought to them in rotation, each taking not more than 150 lying cases before the incoming wounded were switched to the next CCS in the group. This rotation scheme allowed more careful and thorough surgery to be done.[104]

The statistics bear witness to the results of the massive expansion of the CCSs. In 1915, they operated on 15 per cent of cases in quiet times and 5 per cent in periods of heavy fighting. The following year the figure for quiet times had risen to 25 per cent. During the Battle of the Somme, 10 per cent of the 300,000 cases admitted were operated upon. Over half of all admissions were operated on in the quiet periods of 1917, whilst Third Ypres recorded an operation rate of over 30 per cent. The CCSs were now performing more operations than the stationary and general hospitals. Reports from the base hospitals detailing the subsequent good progress of the patients testified to the importance of this immediate surgery.[105] After the Battles of Arras and Messines, Bowlby toured the base hospitals and found the following positive results from the policy that he had so vigorously advocated:

1. Out of 5,271 patients only 58 had died.
2. Out of 5,271 [patients] only 22 serious cases of gas gangrene.
3. Hardly any amputations or secondary haemorrhage.
4. General opinion of base surgeons that early operation was responsible for excellent condition of wounded.[106]

These results encouraged Bowlby to seek the further improvements in the surgical work of the CCSs. In January 1918 he drew attention to the unsatisfactory position of anaesthetists. Often these were MOs with no special skill and, as they had no security of tenure, were liable to be moved to other units before establishing themselves in the post. Bowlby issued instructions that each CCS should possess at least one expert anaesthetist, capable of overseeing the conduct of anaesthesia in the unit, training anaesthetists, checking the supply of suitable anaesthetics and maintaining the apparatus. His concern reflected the importance of anaesthesia in the prevention of wound shock, and the need to have anaesthetists capable of administering gas and oxygen anaesthesia which had now been introduced on a wide scale.[107]

The number of MOs available to the CCSs continued to exercise Bowlby's mind. He was anxious that the supplementing of CCS staffs should no longer be confined to preparing them for Allied attacks. They also needed additional MOs in anticipation of the large numbers of wounded likely to result from unexpected enemy action. He concluded that 'several hundred more surgeons' were needed, but faced the problem of where these were to be found. He was informed that none were available from the UK, whilst the Passchendaele offensive had revealed an increasing tension between the needs of the CCSs and those of the base hospitals. Clearly manpower issues were threatening the further expansion of surgery at the front. In January 1918 a solution appeared to offer itself in the reduction in strength of the FAs, coincident with the reduction in the number of battalions per division. Bowlby suggested that the MOs thus released be transferred to the CCSs, bringing their total of MOs up to nine each. To further facilitate immediate surgery he suggested that in future the practice, which had developed during 1917, of directly evacuating cases from the ADSs to the CCSs, and so missing out the tent sections of the FAs, should be adopted as routine.

However these matters soon became academic, as the circumstances of 1918 thwarted Bowlby's ambitions for the further expansion of the CCSs. The German offensive of March 1918 placed the CCSs in some danger and necessitated their frequent movement. Those in the Third and Fifth Armies proved the most vulnerable and were forced to withdraw rapidly. No patients were lost as a consequence but some equipment had to be abandoned. Numbers 50 and 53 CCSs lost all of their tent sections. Bowlby believed that this situation was due to the DMS Fifth Army, Surgeon General Skinner, having 'made a hash of things'. He had left the commanding officers of these units without orders or any information on the general situation for over forty-eight hours.[108] Had he acted sooner, the equipment of these units might well have been saved. In these circumstances the operative work of the CCSs came to a halt. They virtually returned to their intended role, clearing the FAs, and the bulk of the operative work fell to the base hospitals.

By June 1918 the CCSs were much reduced in size. Most were no longer located on railways and were some distance from the fighting. However, the line had stabilized and Bowlby began, once again, to press for the CCSs to be sited as far forward as possible. He was also having to explain to Surgeon General Burtchaell, the new DGMS, the importance of providing for large numbers of operations to be undertaken at the front.[109] In preparation for the British offensive in August, Bowlby arranged for the Fourth Army to receive an additional forty-eight surgical teams.[110] The CCSs had now recovered their material losses of March and, with all but the theatres and x-ray apparatus housed in tents, they were sufficiently mobile to keep pace with the advance. Bowlby expressed himself satisfied that '[we] have kept pace with the surgical situation and have had plenty of trains for [the] wounded. Evacuation has been rapid.'

He was particularly pleased with the establishment of two CCSs in the Asylum, at Dury, which 'had saved the long journey, so bad for severely wounded men'. In the first four days of the August offensive, the CCSs treated over 19,000 cases, approximately 15 per cent of whom were operated on.[111] Only in October were serious difficulties encountered. The destruction of roads and railways hampered the further advance of the CCSs. In his diary for 22 October 1918 Bowlby noted that:

> There is great difficulty in moving anything across the old Ypres salient because of the mud, so two advanced 'op centres' have been started, one near Daddizele, and the other in a chateau near Roubaix. All transport is very short, because all hospitals are moving up, and all old bases are being dismantled. Lorries are very difficult to get and CCSs are therefore difficult to move.[112]

A reduction in the number of seriously wounded in the latter days of October helped to ease the surgical situation. Even during the period of difficulty, the subsequent progress of the patients, with low rates of mortality and little incidence of wound infections or amputations, confirmed the success of the CCSs.[113] Thus, with their development, it is possible to see the steady progress of surgery on the Western Front, as the AMS adapted to changed circumstances and learnt from mistakes. Moreover, in its readiness to heed the advice of Sir Anthony Bowlby, the AMS had recognized the importance of maximizing its utilization of available surgical skill. This was the view of the Commission on Medical Establishments which praised the benefits of early surgery.[114]

Yet, as mentioned earlier, the Commission had been a response to mounting accusations, by 1917, that the system of evacuation did not serve the interests of good surgery. The CCSs were criticized for being too far in the rear, and for being too concerned with evacuation at the expense of treatment. Surgeons were alleged to lack advice on the best treatment of wounds and had no information on the subsequent progress of cases. The merits of these accusations have been dealt with already. Certainly, the RAMC did suffer from compartmentalism, although it is clear that efforts were being made to tackle this problem. In general, however, the attacks revealed only ignorance of RAMC practice. This is evident from an examination of claims that the surgical results from the British CCSs were much inferior to those achieved by the French system, which provided immediate surgery in advanced ambulances sited in dugouts and shell-proof shelters. Bowlby admitted that wounded often arrived more quickly at these French surgical units than they did at the

CCSs. However this was not always so and, in any event, the average journey to a CCS was no longer than half an hour. Thus, for the price of a relatively short delay, the British wounded received treatment in comparatively stable conditions where, in addition to expert surgery, they enjoyed the warmth and comforts that were vital to recovery. Meanwhile, all the indications were that the French ambulances were often incapable of dealing with the pressure of operative work, and that shortage of space meant that serious post-operative cases had to be moved to the Hopitals d'Evacuation. These were much further away from the front than were the CCSs. Bowlby also argued that the French system was less effective at utilizing medical manpower since at all times their ambulances had to be staffed by four MOs, including at least two surgeons:

> These surgical staffs would be to a great extent wanted when no heavy fighting was in progress, yet they could not be released from duty, as emergencies may arise at any moment. The result would be that many of our best surgeons would be locked up, while plenty of the ordinary work was being done at the Cas[ualty] Clearing Stations by less skilled men. It is difficult enough as it is to find enough skilled surgeons for all the Cas[ualty] Clearing Stations and it would be still more difficult if some 50 additional operating centres were at work.[115]

The greatest defence of the British system was to be found in its operative results. There was general acceptance that the British arrangements had been instrumental in saving the lives of hundreds of men. The CCSs proved particularly decisive in improving the prospects of abdominal cases, with survival rates of 40 per cent being recorded.[116] This contrasted with the poor record of French abdominal operations which was so bad that, according to Major Chevasson, a consulting surgeon with the French forces, some surgeons actually refused to carry them out.[117] The British results were seen to be as much a consequence of an effective evacuation system as they were of excellent surgery.[118]

The sheer pressure of work ensured that the standard of surgery was often below that which surgeons would have been accustomed to in civil life. This led some surgeons to question the value of their work. They were particularly concerned with what they regarded as the disturbingly high death rates.[119] But comparisons with civil life did not reflect the realities of dealing with large numbers of battle casualties. Some deterioration in the standard of surgery was unavoidable, given the number of operations involved and the long shifts that the surgeons worked. It was far more important, both for the surgeons' morale and for the prospects of the wounded, to consider the benefits of immediate surgery. The work at the CCSs, rough and ready though it often necessarily had to be, played a key part in saving the lives and limbs of many men.

Principal amongst the surgical challenges of the War was the need to manage infected wounds. There was also recognition of the importance of preventing and treating shock. The CCSs played a vital role in both of these areas.

The condition of the wounds that appeared on the Western Front took the medical profession completely by surprise. The expectation had been that the aseptic system of civilian practice could be relied upon, with the possible addition of some minor antiseptics.[120] At the beginning of the War there was little understanding about the nature of modern gunshot wounds. Surgeons had been led to expect that wounds inflicted by rifle and machine-gun bullets would be sterile.[121] This led to an assumption that extensive operating would be unnecessary – an assumption that was encouraged by recollection of the South African War during which wounds had healed with minimal surgical intervention. Cuthbert Wallace lamented that recollections of this campaign proved to be 'something of a handicap'.[122] The highly fertile ground over which the battles of the Western Front were fought ensured that dirt was easily transmitted into wounds, with the result that every wound became grossly infected. Tetanus and gas gangrene took a heavy toll. As Makins pointed out, the War quickly forced the profession to draw upon much older teachings than those of the South African campaign:

[W]e allowed it to be necessary to rediscover for ourselves what our grand-fathers and greatgrandfathers could have taught us: the terrible nature of injuries produced by fragments of shells and bombs – characterised at the present day by a still greater degree of destruction of tissue as a result of the introduction of high explosives . . . [W]e appreciated neither the number of shell wounds we should have to deal with, nor their gravity and extent.[123]

Those such as H.S. Souttar, who dealt with the wounded from the opening battles of 1914, found themselves in unfamiliar surgical territory:

With surgery on rather bold lines it was extraordinary how much could be done, especially in the way of saving limbs . . . We were dealing with healthy and vigorous men, and once they had got over the shock of injury they had wonderful powers of recovery. We very soon found that we were dealing with cases to which the ordinary rules of surgery did not apply. The fundamental principles of the art must always be the same, but here the conditions of their application were essentially different from those of civil practice. Two of these conditions were of general interest: the great destruction of the tissues in most wounds, and the infection of the wounds which was almost universal.[124]

It was with the dawning of these realities that surgeons generally came to appreciate the need for immediate surgery, and the necessity of having hospitals located as near to the front as possible. The results of post-mortems revealed that very many abdominal cases had died of haemorrhaging, which might easily have been arrested by early surgery. These revelations encouraged a final break with the expectant treatment of the South African War. In the middle of 1915, instructions were issued that all abdominal cases be evacuated to the CCSs. This also became standard practice for head injuries, compound fractures and penetrating wounds of the limbs.[125]

For the remainder of the War it was the issue of wound infection that galvanized the attention of the medical profession. The problem of tetanus had been addressed by the routine administration of anti-tetanic serum immediately after wounding. Infection by the gas bacillus, however, proved to be a more taxing question. The initial response to the infected wounds of war had been to drain them and to return to the use of the older antiseptics such as carbolic and hydrogen peroxide. But the results were poor, and these early failures necessitated amputation in cases of malignant gas infection of wounds of the limbs.[126] Sir Almroth Wright attacked the use of antiseptics, arguing that they were incapable of sterilizing wounds. Instead his research focussed upon the treatment of wounds by the application of an hypertonic salt solution. In 1915 this treatment was adopted as standard practice on the Western Front and the results showed a marked improvement on the use of antiseptics. However the salt solutions did not sterilize the wounds. There followed an often bitter debate between Wright and those such as Sir William Watson Cheyne, who continued to advocate the merits of antiseptics.[127]

In fact, the more important development in 1915 was the final recognition that the complete excision of wounds, at the earliest opportunity, was the critical factor in the subsequent performance of cases. It was in this respect that the development of the CCSs proved decisive in providing the immediate surgical preparation of wounds. Sir Anthony Bowlby stressed this in his evidence to the Committee on Medical Establishments:

[It is] absolutely essential for success that this excision should be done as soon as possible after the infliction of an extensive wound because in such cases gas gangrene may become widely spread within 24 hours. It is therefore necessary to operate on such cases before the patient is sent by train to the base, as he will seldom be surgically treated there until more than 24 hours has elapsed since the time at which he was wounded. This method of treatment has entirely supplanted the application of strong antiseptics to a recent wound, or the use of continual saline infusions. It is a method whose value is agreed upon by the surgeons of all the Allies, and has recently been unanimously approved by the Meeting of the Surgeons of the Allied Armies in Paris.

It was Alexis Carrel and Henry Dakin who developed the most widely adopted method for treating wounds following their initial surgical preparation. The Carrel-Dakin method involved the cleansing of wounds by a solution of sodium hypochlorite administered by a system of tubes. The method was widely adopted in 1917, although it did not always prove practical in the CCSs. The installation of tubes in the wound took too much time. Also, the method called for continuous supervision which the CCS surgeons were unable to provide. For this reason alternative antiseptic treatments such as BIPP were employed in the CCSs.[128] However, there was general agreement amongst the Allied consultants that, where practicable, the Carrel-Dakin method was the best. It appears that Wright was alone amongst the British consultants in opposing the Carrel-Dakin treatment, remaining unconvinced about the efficacy of antiseptics.[129] Bowlby, however, reported that both BIPP and Carrel cases performed well, and that these treatments had apparently been responsible for significant reductions in the incidence of gas gangrene. At number 47 CCS, he noted that out of 235 cases admitted, on 18 June 1917, there had been no cases of gas gangrene.[130] Bowlby had little patience with Wright. He believed that Wright's opposition to Carrel, and his attacks on the RAMC administration, were motivated by resentment at the dropping of his saline treatment. He informed Lord Derby that in his view 'Wright was a self seeker, quite ignorant of surgery, the self styled inventor of the saline treatment of wounds, which was now "as dead as Queen Anne", and the obstructer of all other forms of treatment.' Wright was justified in his opposition to antiseptics in that they did not sterilise wounds. Nevertheless, in an age before penicillin, the Carrel treatment does appear to have produced good results, including a marked diminution in the incidence of amputations.[131] Certainly, surgeons were sufficiently impressed that, particularly in the United States, it was widely adopted in civil practice. However the most important factor in the effectiveness of any of the wound treatments was the provision of immediate surgical care; if wounds were not excised soon after infliction the antiseptics could not prevent infection.[132] Thus it appears that it was the provision of expert surgery at the CCSs that was the critical factor in the battle against gas gangrene.

Shock was recognized as a serious threat to the survival of all seriously wounded men. As we have seen, much emphasis was placed on the role of forward medical units in preventing the onset of shock prior to the arrival of patients at the CCSs. In periods of heavy fighting, however, the necessary precautions were not always possible. It was therefore essential that the CCSs be prepared to treat existing cases of shock. This meant putting the cases to bed immediately upon arrival, keeping them warm and providing hot drinks for those capable of keeping them down. Otherwise the loss of fluids was to be made good by administering saline. These steps alone certainly helped to save lives. However it was recognized that if the blood pressure remained low, blood transfusion was the best solution.[133] The popularizing of blood transfusion was one of the most important surgical results of the War. By 1917 transfusions had become widespread in the CCSs, with excellent results, especially in efforts to prevent operative shock.[134] The War promoted greater understanding of the latter. It was accepted that, unless the condition of the patient demanded otherwise, operation should be delayed until adequate measures had been taken to raise the blood pressure. Steps were taken to keep the patient warm throughout the operation and to ensure that he was kept in theatre for as little as possible. A critical factor in the development of shock was the type of anaesthesia employed. In the early years of the War there had been problems associated with the use of both chloroform and ether. It was found that much better results were achieved with the use of gas and oxygen anaesthesia. The moves made in 1918 to promote its use must, therefore, be seen as evidence of the RAMC's ongoing determination to ensure that the wounded received the best possible standards of care, at the earliest possible opportunity.

From the CCSs the wounded were evacuated to the base hospitals, mostly by ambulance trains, but also by motor ambulance convoys or, occasionally, in areas with an adequate canal system, by ambulance barges. The average load for an ambulance train was around 400 cases. Working backwards from the engine, a typical train came to be organized with '[a] carriage used as an isolation ward; a coach with its compartments arranged as sleeping quarters for the medical and nursing staff; a kitchen coach; four or five ward carriages; an administrative carriage, providing an office, a room for the performance of operations, and a dispensary; four or five coaches for sitting-up patients; a carriage for general cooking purposes; a coach to serve as sleeping quarters for the subordinate personnel; a van for stores; and a guard's van'.[135] Ambulance barges were a slower means of transport, but offered a smooth journey for delicate cases such as wounds of the chest and the abdomen. In addition to accommodation for the staff and the kitchen facilities, the barges had room for thirty hospital beds and space where operations could be conducted. Thus, for vulnerable cases, the barges were able to provide facilities akin to those of a small, mobile CCS.[136]

There were two classes of hospital at the bases, namely stationary hospitals and general hospitals. Stationary hospitals had not been intended for work at the base. They were originally organized as light hospitals, equipped with sufficient folding bedsteads to accommodate 200 cases. Their purpose was to act as intermediaries between the medical units of the front and those at the base. However this function became largely defunct, thanks to the transformation of the CCSs and the improved evacuation facilities provided by the motor ambulance convoys and the ambulance trains. In these circumstances the stationary hospitals became almost indistinguishable from general hospitals. Instead of being located in the evacuation zone they were increasingly to be found in the same areas as general hospitals, and were expected to undertake similar work. To cope with this change their accommodation was increased to 500 and arrangements were made for augmenting the regulation staff of seven Medical Officers.[137]

The general hospitals had to be capable of dealing with all the types of wounds and sickness that were likely to afflict an army. To meet this requirement they were generally divided into two sections, a medical division and a surgical division. The records of Number 26 General Hospital provide an insight into the typical organization of a general hospital. This opened at Étaples in June 1915 with accommodation of 1,040 cases. It consisted of thirty-five wooden huts, each with room for twenty-seven beds. There were also four wards for accommodating serious surgical cases which were housed in a galvanized-iron building. The latter also contained two operating theatres and an x-ray room. In readiness for the pressure of emergency work the potential capacity of the hospital was raised to 2,010 by erecting tents. Additional galvanized buildings housed the kitchen, laboratory, dispensary, baths and latrines.[138]

The official establishment of the hospital allowed for a staff of thirty-four officers, including two Quartermasters. This was found to be 'a very generous scale' and was not maintained. In May 1916 the hospital possessed a staff of twenty-one MOs. It was a staff that was constantly in flux, owing to the need to reinforce the medical units at the front. During its first year of operation, the hospital saw eighty-three doctors go through its doors.[139]

For many doctors, life in the base hospitals lacked the excitement associated with medical work in the forward areas. L.W. Batten found his service at a base hospital to be 'very dull', recalling the doctors there to have been a 'mouldy lot', seemingly determined to hang on to their jobs for the duration of the War.[140] G. Moore agreed, commenting thus on his experience of Number 5 General Hospital, Rouen:

> Dreadful life! rather [sic] uncongenial society, not much risk of my becoming a 'base wallah'.[141]

Others had a less disparaging view of base work and of those who undertook it, but nevertheless felt drawn towards the front. H.B. Owens treated 'some very interesting cases', whilst at Number 13 General Hospital, Boulogne, but recorded that '[although the] front isn't always very pleasant when you are there . . . after you have been at the base for 3 months you begin to feel "rather out of it"'.[142] Harold Dearden, too, recalled a busy time doing interesting work but 'after a few months spent in this backwater, half military, half civilian, and wholly oppressive and enervating, [he was glad] to escape to the more robust and colourful environment of a Field Ambulance'.[143]

Such views, however, do not accurately reflect the importance, or variety, of the work carried out in the base hospitals. It is also the case that the emphasis on the establishment of immediate surgery in the CCSs tended to overshadow the work being undertaken at the bases. It was in the general hospitals that the techniques which were introduced into the forward units were first attempted and developed. Herringham agreed that the work was less exciting than that available elsewhere, but that this was more than compensated for by its professional interest. Doctors at the base were able to follow the progress of their cases to an extent that was seldom possible in the advanced hospitals, and had greater opportunities for specialization.[144] The custom in the base hospitals was to segregate different classes of wounds. Thus there would be separate wards for amputees; for chest cases; for wounds of the head and spine; for abdominals; for compound fractures; and for wounds of the joints. This practice, and the assignment of MOs to particular wards, enabled doctors to develop expertise in the relevant treatments.[145]

The priorities of wound treatment at the base were exactly those of the CCSs: complete excision followed by sterilization using the Carrel-Dakin method. Increasingly, as the War progressed, it was a matter of continuing treatment already commenced in the forward units. This involved an inspection of the wound and the replacement of the drainage tubes. The treatment was kept up until such time as the wound became sterile, at which point secondary suture was carried out. In cases where it had been impossible to begin treatment at the CCSs excision and drainage were undertaken immediately. In these cases the prospects of success diminished and the limbs frequently required amputation.[146] However, as a general rule, the condition of the wounded on arrival at the base steadily improved. By May 1916 the records of Number 26 General Hospital show that most abdominal and head admissions had already been operated on prior to their arrival.[147]

The German offensive of March 1918 halted the transfer of surgical work to the CCSs. The consequence was a busy time for the base hospitals. Between 25 and 29 March thirteen base hospitals at Étaples admitted a total of 19,292 wounded and conducted 3,698 operations. This represented an operation rate of 19 per cent which Bowlby regarded as 'very praiseworthy' in the circumstances, and as proof 'that the work was mastered'.[148]

During the War the RAMC's procedures for evacuating and treating casualties on the Western Front generally met with a favourable press. This good reputation appears to have been well deserved. The evidence does not support the claims of contemporary critics that the system worked against the interests of the patients, or that it failed to make sensible use of doctors' skills. On the contrary, every effort was made to bring the wounded rapidly into care, and to ensure that they received the best available treatment in the most appropriate environment. The system protected the vital interests of the casualties, whilst at the same time serving the military purpose of returning men to active duty in the quickest time possible. Of course there were faults and imperfections. But throughout the conflict the RAMC endeavoured to improve the standard of medical care. Above all, it possessed the flexibility to adapt its pre-war organization to the unexpected conditions and challenges posed by trench warfare.

Notes

1   In periods of heavy fighting this number could be increased to thirty-two.
2   Sometimes, as when a Division held a narrow front, RMOs might combine to form a Joint Aid Post. See **Cantlie**, WIHM, RAMC 465, Papers: War Diary when DADMS 6th Division; 24 September 1916. Also **A.L.P. Gould**, LC, Diary: 25 March 1918, p. 60.

3   S.W. McLellan, RCS, printed diary (no publication details), Book 5, 1917, p. 22.
4   Gameson, IWM, memoirs, pp. 190–1.
5   *Manual of Injuries and Diseases of War*, London, HMSO, 1918, p. 2.
6   H.S. Banks & B. Hughes, *War Surgery from Firing Line to Base*, Baltimore Wood, 1919, p. 262.
7   A more concise consideration of these issues can be found in I.R. Whitehead 'Not a Doctor's Work? The Role of the British Regimental Medical Officer in the Field', in H. Cecil and P.H. Liddle, *Facing Armageddon*, Leo Cooper, 1996, pp. 466–74.
8   As late as June 1918, such a proposal was being made by the Council of the Edinburgh Branch of the BMA; see 'The Medical Profession and the Military Service Act', BMJ, 1918 (I), p. 658. Writing after the War, Sir Wilmot Herringham condemned the short-sightedness of such proposals; see Herringham, *Physician in France*, p. 99.
9   WO 95.198, PRO, DMS First Army, Diary, April 1918, Appendix 10.
10 Herringham, *Physician in France*, p. 97.
11 Commission On Medical Establishments, WIHM, RAMC 1165, pp. 63 & 66.
12 Sir Henry Burdett, Bodleian Library, MS Eng. d. 2871, letter 748, Burdett to Sir A. Keogh, 29 September 1917.
13 F.S. Brereton, *The Great War and the RAMC*, Constable, 1919, pp. 225–6.
14 Captain Hugh Llewelyn Glyn-Hughes, WIHM, RAMC 1218, Papers: letter written by G.H. Swindell, 21 May 1961 (RAMC 1218/1/11).
15 Captain Hugh Llewelyn Glyn-Hughes, WIHM, RAMC 1218, Papers: transcript of *This Is Your Life* television programme, 9 March 1959, p. 10.
16 Captain Hugh Llewelyn Glyn-Hughes, WIHM, RAMC 1218, Papers: transcript of *This Is Your Life* television programme, 9 March 1959, p. 10.
17 Keith Simpson, introduction to J.C. Dunn, *The War the Infantry Knew*, Jane's, 1986, p. xxiv.
18 H.W. Wilson & J.A. Hammerton, *The Great War*, Volume 4, The Amalgamated Press, 1915, p. 124.
19 E.C. Deane, LC, Diary: 21 September 1915–24 September 1915, pp. 67–9.
20 Hugh Shields, WIHM, RAMC 383, Diary: 25 September 1914, p. 27.
21 Hugh Shields, WIHM, RAMC 383, Papers: letters to family after his death, pp. 42–4.
22 R. McLaughlin, *The RAMC*, pp. 56–60.
23 Fairley, LC, Tape recording.
24 Gameson, IWM, Memoirs, p. 58.
25 Among those who refer to the dull routine of Base life are: L.W. Batten, LC, who remembered his time at the Base as being dull, and referred to the doctors there as 'a mouldy lot' (see letter to son, 18 March 1970, pp. 2 & 18); Dr G. Moore, LC, Letters: letter 31 August 1917.
26 H.S. Souttar, *Surgeon in Belgium*, p. 59.
27 Fenwick, LC, Diary: 5 May 1915, p. 8.
28 G.D. Fairley, LC, Diary: 31 December 1915, p. 31; he wrote 'Along with the Officers I practised some shooting with revolvers.' On 31 May 1917, the entry

reads: 'I performed some bomb-throwing using unloaded Mills and German hand bombs.'

29 C. McKerrow, LC, Letters: letter 12 March 1916, p. 133.
30 D. McAlpine, LC, Recollections, p. 11.
31 Martin, *Surgeon in Khaki*, pp. 9–10.
32 N.S. Deane, LC, Papers: Rules for the Guidance of Medical Officers.
33 Sir C. Burtchaell, WIHM, RAMC 446/7: Papers: letters of Lee to Kitchener, 12 October 1914.
34 Sir Neil Cantlie, WIHM, RAMC 465, Papers: War Diary when DADMS 6th Division [September and October 1916, Battle of the Somme], 24 September 1916.
35 C. McKerrow, LC, Letters: 28 September 1915, p. 14; 2 October 1915, p. 16.
36 'The Medical Service on the Somme', BMJ, 1916 (II), pp. 397–8.
37 N.J.C. Rutherford, *Memories of an Army Surgeon*, Stanley Paul & Co Ltd, 1939, p. 29.
38 'Commission on Medical Establishments', WIHM, RAMC 1165, p. 65.
39 'Medicine in the Spring Offensive', BMJ, 1917 (II), pp. 94–5.
40 'Changes in the German Army Medical Service', BMJ, 1917 (I), p. 437.
41 Anon, 'Six Weeks Active Service as MO to an Infantry Battalion', WIHM, RAMC 1192, pp. 29–30.
42 *Ibid*, pp. 29–30.
43 F.J. Blackley, LC, Diary: 22 September 1915.
44 'The Royal Army Medical Corps and its Work', BMJ, 1917 (II), p. 218.
45 F.J. Blackley, LC, Diary: 22 September 1915; 24 September 1915.
46 C. McKerrow, LC, letter, 29 July 1916.
47 Sir G. Keynes, LC, recollections, pp. 196–7.
48 C. McKerrow, LC, Diary: 31 May 1916, pp. 174–5.
49 'The Army Medical Service by Medical Officer in Charge of an Infantry Battalion', BMJ, 1916 (II), p. 528' 'The French Army Medical Service: Recruitment, Organisation and Work', BMJ, 1917 (I), p. 628. Commission On Medical Establishments, WIHM, RAMC 1165, p. 64.
50 'The Royal Army Medical Corps and its Work', BMJ, 1917 (II), pp. 220–3. MacPherson, *General History*, II, pp. 22–4.
51 F.S. Brereton, *Great War and the RAMC*, pp. 16–17; 140; 275.
52 MacPherson, *Official History of the War – Medical Services, Surgery of the War*, I, pp. 186–7.
53 *Manual of Injuries and Diseases of War*, HMSO, 1918, pp. 3–6 'The Royal Army Medical Corps and its Work', BMJ, 1917 (II), pp. 221–2.
54 'The RAMC and its Work', BMJ, 1917 (II), pp. 222–3.
55 H.W. Kaye, WIHM, RAMC 739, Diary, Volume I: 17 June 1915, p. 36.
56 H.W. Kaye, WIHM, RAMC 739, Diary, Volume I: 21 June 1915, p. 45.
57 N. King-Wilson, LC, recollections, p. 17. J.M. McLachlan agreed that much of the work of an FA MO could have been done 'with ease' by 'any orderly'. See McLachlan, LC, Letters: letter 586, 9 March 1916.
58 N. King-Wilson, LC, recollections, p. 19.
59 Gameson, IWM, memoirs, p. 53.

60 Bowlby, WIHM, RAMC 365, Papers: Wright Memorandum, pp. 4–5. See Bayly, *Triple Challenge*, p. 151, for a similar attack upon the 'harmful . . . waste of time' and 'unnecessary movement' caused by FAs.

61 Commission on Medical Establishments, WIHM, RAMC 1165, p. 57.

62 'The Royal Army Medical Corps and its Work', BMJ, 1917 (II), p. 220.

63 Commission on Medical Establishments, WIHM, RAMC 1165, pp. 58–61; 120–1; 126–33.

64 Brereton, *Great War and the RAMC*, pp. 16–17; 140; 275. WO 95/48, PRO, D.G.M.S. Diary, 1918; Report by Australian Corps Resuscitation Teams Committee, dated 14 October 1918. A.M. Boyd, LC, memoirs, pp. 160–1.

65 MacPherson, *General History*, III, p. 476. WO 95/4975, PRO, DMS Mesopotamia, Diary: 2 June 1916.

66 Deputy Surgeon General A. Gascoigne Wildey, 'The Medical Officer and the Fighting Man', *The Medical Annual*, 1916, p. 655. General T.H. Goodwin made the same point a year later. See T.H. Goodwin, 'Medical Service in the British Area on the Western Front', JAMA, LXIX, 1917, p. 120.

67 MacPherson, *Surgery of the War*, I, p. 188. WO 95/197, PRO, DMS First Army, Diary: Appendix – The Initiation of Wound Shock with Suggestions for its Early Treatment.

68 Herringham, *Physician in France*, pp. 62–3.

69 WO 32/11395, PRO, Report of The Babtie Committee on the Reorganisation of the Army Medical Service, 1921–23, p. 8.

70 C. Huxtable, LC, Tape recording.

71 H.W. Kaye, WIHM, RAMC 739, Diary, Volume I: 1 July 1915, p. 62.

72 MacPherson, *General History*, III, p. 50.

73 E.S.B. Hamilton, IWM, Diary: 19 August 1916, p. 31.

74 MacPherson, *General History*, III, pp. 229–30.

75 MacPherson, *General History*, III, pp. 20–1. It became the practice to place these Advanced Operating Centres under the command of a CCS, and in times of heavy fighting they would be reinforced by MOs from the CCSs. It also became the practice for advanced units from the CCSs themselves to establish similar centres.

76 G. Moore, LC, Letters: 2 March 1916 (to sister); 15 March 1916 (to father); 12 April 1916 (to sister); 12 March 1917 (to father); 8 April 1917 (to sister).

77 Herringham, *Physician in France*, p. 66.

78 M.S. Esler, IWM, recollections, p. 67.

79 Boyd Cable, *Between the Lines*, Smith, Elder & Co., 1916, pp. 218–26.

80 Some examples include: G. Moore, LC, recollections, p. 12. 'Distinguished Service Order – Captain J.S. Dunne', BMJ, 1914 (II), p. 995. 'Honours', *BMJ*, 1915 (II), p. 733. Brereton, *Great War and the RAMC*, pp. 43–5, 62–8, 224–5.

81 J.M. McLachlan, LC, Letters: letter 473, 4 October 1915; letter 586, 9 March 1916.

82 WO 32/11395, PRO, Report of the Babtie Committee on the Reorganisation of the Army Medical Service, p. 8.

83 MacPherson, *General History*, II, p. 42.

84 Sloggett, WIHM, RAMC 365/1, Papers, Evidence presented to the Committee of Enquiry, 7 September 1917, p. 1.

85   MacPherson, *Surgery of the War*, p. 209.
86   'The Royal Army Medical Corps and its Work', BMJ, 1917 (II), p. 254.
87   C.S. Wallace and J. Fraser, *Surgery at a Casualty Clearing Station*, New York, Macmillan, 1919, p. 2.
88   Sloggett, WIHM, RAMC 365/1, Papers, The incidence of Gas Gangrene and the numbers of Operations necessitated by it in France and other seats of war, 17 January 1917.
89   MacPherson, *Surgery of the War*, p. 210.
90   Bowlby, RCS, Papers, diary, 18 September 1915; 22 September 1915; 26 September 1915; 27 September 1915; 28 September 1915; 6 October 1915.
91   Bowlby, RCS, Papers, diary, 22 March 1916; 21 April 1916.
92   Sloggett, WIHM, RAMC 365/1, Papers, Notes on the Surgery of the Fourth and Reserve Armies during the Months of August and September 1916, p. 1.
93   I.R. Whitehead, 'Third Ypres – Casualties and British Medical Services: an Evaluation', in P.H. Liddle, *Passchendaele in Perspective*, Leo Cooper, 1997, pp. 185–7.
94   'Experiences in a British Military Hospital', MJA, 1917, I, p. 480.
95   Sloggett, WIHM, RAMC 365/1, Papers, Evidence presented to the Committee of Enquiry, 7 September 1917, p. 1.
96   Bowlby, RCS, Papers, diary, 15 June 1917, Sloggett, WIHM, RAMC 365/1, Papers, Evidence presented to the Committee of Enquiry, 7 September 1917, pp. 7–10.
97   MacPherson, *Surgery of the War*, I, pp. 211–16. MacPherson, *General History*, II, pp. 42–3. C.S. Wallace, *War Surgery of the Abdomen*, Blakiston, 1918, pp. 45–7.
98   MacPherson, *General History*, II, pp. 44–6. Sloggett, WIHM, RAMC 365/1, Papers, Evidence presented to the Committee of Enquiry, 7 September 1917, p. 3.
99   As male Medical Officers grew scarce, women were trained to fill the anaesthetist posts.
100 Owen Richards, 'The Development of Casualty Clearing Stations', *Guy's Hospital Reports*, LXX, 1922, p. 117.
101 Bowlby, RCS, Papers, diary, 4 July 1916.
102 Sloggett, WIHM, RAMC 365/1, Papers, Evidence presented to the Committee of Enquiry, 7 September 1917, p. 4. Bowlby, RCS. Papers, diary, 22 July 1917; 29 July 1917.
103 Major General Sir Ernest Cowell, WIHM, RAMC 466, Papers: Report on the 'Twin Table' System in use in the Operating Theatre of Number Twenty-three CCS., April–August 1917, p. 1.
104 Sloggett, WIHM, RAMC 365/1, Papers, Evidence presented to the Committee of Enquiry, 7 September 1917, p. 5. MacPherson, *General History*, II, p. 468; MacPherson, *General History*, III, p. 29.
105 Sloggett, WIHM, RAMC 365/1, Papers, The incidence of Gas Gangrene and the numbers of Operations necessitated by it in France and other seats of war, 17 January 1917; Evidence presented to the Committee of Enquiry, 7 September 1917, pp. 5–6.
106 Bowlby, RCS, Papers, diary, 22 June 1917.

107 Sloggett, WIHM, RAMC 365/1, Papers, The Appointment of Anaesthetists at Casualty Clearing Stations, 17 January 1918.

108 Bowlby, RCS, Papers, diary, 31 March 1918.

109 Bowlby, RCS, Papers, diary, 11 August 1918.

110 MacPherson, *General History*, III, p. 299.

111 MacPherson, *Surgery of the War* I, pp. 228–9. Bowlby, RCS, Papers, diary, 9 August 1918.

112 Bowlby, RCS, Papers, diary, 22 October 1918.

113 MacPherson, *Surgery of the War*, I, p. 231.

114 Commission on Medical Establishments, WIHM, RAMC 1165, p. 48.

115 Sloggett, WIHM, RAMC 365/1, Papers, letter from Bowlby, 17 July 1917.

116 Sloggett, WIHM, RAMC 365/1, Papers, Wounds of the Abdomen, p. 7.

117 Bowlby, RCS, Papers, diary, 5 May 1918.

118 Sloggett, WIHM, RAMC 365/1, Papers, Wounds of the Abdomen, p. 8.

119 Banks & Hughes, *War Surgery from Firing Line to Base*, p. 303.

120 Makins, 'Introductory', BJS, VI, 1918–1919, p. 4.

121 Banks & Hughes, *War Surgery from Firing Line to Base*, p. 269.

122 Wallace, *War Surgery of the Abdomen*, p. 2.

123 Makins, 'Introductory', BJS, VI, 1918–19, p. 4.

124 Souttar, *A Surgeon in Belgium*, pp. 24–5.

125 Sloggett, WIHM, RAMC 365/1, Papers, Wounds of the Abdomen, p. 7. Wallace, *War Surgery of the Abdomen*, p. 10. Banks & Hughes, *War Surgery from Firing Line to Base*, p. 268.

126 Banks & Hughes, *War Surgery from Firing Line to Base*, p. 268. J.S. Haller, 'The Great War: Its impact on the British and American medical communities', *New York State Journal of Medicine* (NYSJM), 1991, vol. 91, pt. 1, p. 23.

127 J.S. Haller, 'Treatment of Infected wounds during the Great War, 1914 to 1918', *Southern Medical Journal* (SMJ), 1992, vol. 85, no.3, pp. 310–11. Banks & Hughes, *War Surgery from Firing Line to Base*, p. 270.

128 Whitehead, 'Third Ypres – Casualties and British Medical Services: an Evaluation', in Liddle, *Passchendaele in Perspective*, p. 192.

129 Later, however, it appears that Wright praised the work of Carrel. See Sloggett, WIHM, RAMC 365/4, papers, joint reply of Sloggett and Advisory Board to Wright's Memorandum, 15 January 1917, p. 8.

130 Bowlby, RCS, Papers, diary, 14 June 1917; 18 June 1917.

131 A. Carrel & G. Debelly, *The Treatment of Infected Wounds*, University of London Press, 1917, pp. 215–17.

132 Haller, 'Treatment of Infected Wounds during the Great War, 1914 to 1918', SMJ, 1992, vol 85, no. 3.

133 Wallace & Fraser, *Surgery at a Casualty Clearing Station*, pp. 18–19. Banks & Hughes, *War Surgery from Firing Line to Base*, p. 280.

134 Sloggett, WIHM, RAMC 365/1, Papers, A Memorandum on the Surgical Work of the Casualty Clearing Stations of the Second and Fifth Armies between 31 July and 16 November 1917, p. 1.

135 'The RAMC And Its Work', BMJ, 1917 (II), pp. 256–7.

136 *Ibid*, p. 257.

137 **WO 32/11395**, PRO, Report of the Babtie Committee, paragraphs 177–180, p. 21. 'The RAMC And Its Works', BMJ, 1917 (II), pp. 257–8.

138 War Diary of 26 General Hospital, WIHM, RAMC 728/2/1, Summary of situation, July 1915–May 1916, pp. 2–8. War Diary of 26 General Hospital, WIHM, RAMC 728/2/3, Medical History of No. 26 General Hospital, p. 1.

139 War Diary of 26 General Hospital, WIHM, RAMC 728/2/1, Summary of situation, July 1915–May 1916, pp. 18–20.

140 **L.W. Batten**, LC, letter to son, 18 March 1970, pp. 2 & 18.

141 **G. Moore**, LC, letter to sister, 13 August 1917.

142 **H.B. Owens**, IWM, diary, 29 April 1917.

143 **Dearden**, *Time and Chance*, p. 17.

144 **Herringham**, *Physician in France*, p. 89

145 **Banks & Hughes**, *War Surgery from Firing Line to Base*, p. 304.

146 *Ibid.*, p. 322.

147 War Diary of 26 General Hospital, WIHM, RAMC 728/2/1, Summary of situation, July 1915–May 1916, pp. 22–5.

148 **Bowlby**, RCS, Papers, diary, 13 April 1918.

Chapter 9

The Fight against Disease

Undoubtedly, the most important function performed by a Medical Officer was disease prevention. To make effective use of its doctors the Army needed to promote firm sanitary discipline, and ensure them the authority required to enforce this discipline. These were the lessons of the South African War and from the outset it is clear that the authorities on the Western Front were at pains to implement them. The sanitary organization of the BEF was highly efficient and merely needed expanding to meet the needs of a growing force. The guiding principle of the sanitary organization was that responsibility for the sanitary conditions of the quarters or localities of units and formations lay with the officer in command who took all measures necessary for preserving the health of his men. The DMS was the Commander-in-Chief's adviser on all medical and sanitary matters, and his representatives were similarly the advisers of the commanders to whose headquarters they were attached.

Each unit had regimental personnel for sanitary duties which consisted of one NCO and between two and eight men, depending upon the strength of the unit. Also, one corporal with two to four trained RAMC men was attached for water duties.[1] A sanitary section was attached to every base, and sanitary squads to each railhead and the advanced base. Sanitary squads were also allotted to each permanent post on the lines of communication. It was possible to subdivide sanitary sections into squads, or increase their size by the addition of further sanitary squads. The personnel of a sanitary section consisted of one officer of captain's or subaltern's rank,[2] two staff-sergeants or sergeants, and twenty-three rank and file, while that of a sanitary squad was one sergeant and five rank and file. A sanitary committee comprising two or three selected medical experts (military or civil), with a senior combatant officer as President, was formed to assist general officers and the medical service in their efforts to maintain the health of the Army.[3]

On arrival in France the BEF found the standard of sanitation in towns such as Amiens and Rouen extremely poor. There were no adequate municipal arrangements for the removal of refuse and excreta, and enteric was endemic. However the arrival of sanitary squads and sanitary sections during August 1914 led to an immediate improvement in the sanitary conditions of these towns. According to Lieutenant Colonel W. Beveridge[4] the towns were in a filthy state when the British first arrived, and the sanitary personnel deserved 'great credit for the prompt manner in which they tackled a difficult problem'. Their success led to the deployment of sanitary sections with the field army, a scheme for the formation of divisional sanitary sections being drawn up in October 1914. These sanitary sections followed the division to which they were attached and were responsible for cleaning up recently occupied ground, incinerating rubbish, filling in latrines, disposing of manure, disinfecting clothes and supervising the sanitary arrangements of towns in the divisional area.[5] Particular attention was paid to purifying water and ensuring that men only drank from safe sources. There was also careful supervision of the arrangements for the disposal of waste. The method of burying waste in shallow trenches, as advocated in the Manual of Military Hygiene, proved inadequate and incineration became the recommended means of disposal.[6]

The work of these squads ensured that sanitary standards in the BEF were high, in contrast with the much less rigorous arrangements currently enforced in the French Army. Many Medical Officers recorded their dissatisfaction with the standards of hygiene in areas recently occupied by the French. On 26 August 1915, Dr F.J. Blackley was amongst the first British troops to arrive at Mondicourt where the French had recently been billeted. He described the terrible filth and stench left behind by them, and took a lead in the operation to clean up the tremendous amounts of litter and dirt, to put the sanitary and water supply arrangements in order.[7] It was not until November 1916 that sanitary squads were established in the French Army.[8]

Thus the BEF took the lead in recognizing that an efficient sanitary organization was essential if Medical Officers were to have the correct environment for carrying out preventive work. Moreover improvements continued to be made. During the 1916 Somme campaign the constant movement of divisions meant that sanitary sections were unable to settle down to their work, with the consequence that sanitary measures were neglected and there was an outbreak of dysentery among the troops.[9] According to Dr L.W. Batten, 'The Somme was easily the messiest, untidiest and most insanitary (though not the muddiest) battleground of the war and, though fully inoculated', he went down with typhoid. A memorandum to the DGMS, dated 19 November 1916, stated that the 'duties of a sanitary section can only be carried out successfully if the section is well acquainted with the sanitary circumstances and requirements of the area in which it is working. Sanitary Sections therefore should be allotted a definite area,' so that they could maintain constant supervision of its sanitary arrangements. The following April the DGMS acted upon this recommendation, introducing a scheme which made sanitary sections extra-divisional troops.[10]

A major threat to the health of the troops was posed by the enormous rat population which thrived in the trenches. Rats carried epidemic diseases such as infective jaundice, and spoilt food supplies. In the Second Army it was decided to organize specific measures to control the rat population, and Captain Philip Gosse, RAMC, was appointed Rat Officer. Gosse was chosen because of his reputation as a keen naturalist; whilst in the trenches he collected specimens of many small mammals which he sent back to the British Museum. Thus his appointment demonstrates not only the high profile given to preventive measures by the Army in France, but also its ability to appoint an individual to a position where his experience could be of most use. There were those who considered the appointment of a doctor to such a post to be wasteful, and others looked down upon the work. However, the maintenance of sound hygiene was an important part of a Medical Officer's duties, and Gosse's work soon began to attract the appreciation that it deserved. Gosse drew up schemes for the catching and destruction of rats, travelled the Army area making recommendations on improving anti-rat measures, and delivered lectures to audiences of RMOs and young combatant officers. Gosse's work won praise from the DMS Second Army who commended his work to the ADMS (Sanitation). Gosse wrote a memorandum on the destruction of rats throughout the whole front which was received and acted upon by headquarters. Schools of Sanitation ran classes on rats and there were rat lectures at the First Army RAMC School of Instruction.[11]

The attention given to sanitation in France demonstrated an awareness on the part of the military authorities of the importance of preventive measures, and also of the need to ensure that Medical Officers had the authority to impose the most effective precautions against infection.

However, the commitment to sanitation was not, on its own, a guarantee against the threat of disease. Despite improvements in French town sanitation rapidly carried out under the supervision of British sanitary sections, the arrangements were not entirely reliable. Meanwhile, even with the best will in the world, the sanitary conditions in the trenches were bound to deteriorate during the course of a battle. Consequently, anti-typhoid inoculation was the surest means of diminishing the likelihood of infection.

Prior to the War the work of Wright and Leishman had established the effectiveness of anti-typhoid inoculation. But whilst recognizing the benefits of inoculation the British Army declined to enforce vaccination. This position was attacked by senior figures at Oxford University who felt that it was 'high time that the Army Medical Department should be empowered to insist upon compulsory inoculation. That they should in time of war be required to proceed by "persuading officers and men" is well-nigh incomprehensible.'[12] Certainly it was wasteful of medical manpower for doctors to have to spend time cajoling men into agreeing to inoculation. With its effectiveness in preventing disease Medical Officers had strong justification for demanding compulsory inoculation. The voluntary system made their job harder and was equally unsatisfactory from a military point of view, since it led to unnecessary loss of manpower. These facts had been recognized in other national armies. Both the Australian and United States armies made inoculation compulsory, and in Germany all prisoners of war were inoculated.[13]

In Britain, an active campaign was mounted by the British Union for the Abolition of Vivisection (BUAV) which opposed inoculation. On 13 January 1915 it placed notices in *Punch*, the *Evening Standard* and *St James' Gazette*, suggesting that inoculation was a dangerous procedure. These publications were roundly criticized for taking the BUAV's advertisement, and all reacted by making statements in favour of inoculation. *Punch* published the following disclaimer:

> The advertisement which appeared in our last week's issue, opposing the principle of the inoculation of soldiers against typhoid, came in very late, and unfortunately its contents were not submitted to the Secretary, who was merely told of the source from which it came – namely, the Anti-Vivisection Society. *Mr Punch* is himself absolutely in favour of inoculation against typhoid.[14]

The BMJ considered the BUAV's activities highly irresponsible, and found it 'difficult to conceive of a more unpatriotic movement'.[15] Indeed, as the figures below[16] illustrate, anti-typhoid inoculation was nothing but an advantage:

	CASES	DEATHS	DEATH RATE %
British troops: not inoculated within 2 yrs	305	34	11.11
British troops: inoculated – 1 dose within 2 yrs	83	1	1.20
British troops: inoculated – 2 doses within 2 yrs	33	0	0.00
Indian troops: not inoculated	23	3	13.04

In November 1914, Lieutenant Colonel Beveridge sent out information on the incidence of enteric in units of the 1st, 2nd, and 5th Divisions. In the 2nd Division there were forty cases, none of which had been inoculated. Altogether, across the three divisions, he reported seventy-one cases, only two of them having been inoculated.[17] With such clear evidence of its effectiveness it is not surprising that Medical Officers felt frustrated by the Army's decision to allow conscientious objection to inoculation. A.A. Martin believed that the effectiveness of inoculation against disease made the case for compulsion indisputable:

> Soldiers should not be allowed liberty of conscience in these matters. They should be made immune against typhoid and smallpox at 'the word of command' in spite of the screeching of fanatics suffering from distorted cerebration.[18]

All Medical Officers seemed to share this view[19] and did their utmost to inoculate as many men as possible. In these efforts they received the full cooperation of the military authorities,[20] but lacking the full force of military law they had to spend valuable time persuading objectors to agree to inoculation. Charles McKerrow had no patience with the arguments of anti-vivisectionists, and told objectors that he was only interested in making them aware of the dangers of diseases like typhoid.[21] In his experience most men soon realized the importance of the protection afforded by inoculation:

> I am inoculating the men again, and did about 300 today. It is rather a nuisance but is very necessary. The men who went through the Somme make no objection, having seen the dirt of a battlefield, but some of the new men would like to evade the needle. They have a stern MO fortunately.[22]

The DGMS in France was anxious that every possible effort be made to counteract the propaganda of the anti-vivisectionists, and to promote the benefits of inoculation. He recommended that care be taken to inoculate as many men as possible in the UK prior to despatch abroad.[23] The failure to adopt compulsory inoculation undermined the effectiveness of a valuable weapon in the Medical Officer's fight against disease. Nevertheless the vast majority of men were inoculated and the incidence of disease was dramatically lower than in previous conflicts. The incidence of enteric was only 2 per cent of that during the Boer War. The Army learnt the lessons of these figures. During the Second World War, Medical Officers were able to strictly enforce inoculation.[24]

Critical to the maintenance of health in an army was the work of the RMO. His primary duty was to maintain the fighting strength of his unit. He kept a close eye on the health of the men at daily sick parades. In judging the fitness of a man, the RMO's main concern had to be the efficiency of the Army; he could not afford to indulge the individual. Early in the War young, inexperienced Medical Officers were being far too lenient with the men, sending them back down the line as unfit, when they should have been retained at the front. The need for greater strictness was impressed upon RMOs by the RAMC authorities.[25] J. Hartsilver recalled the attitude of a Medical Officer with a garrison battalion who had clearly heeded this advice:

> The Medical Officer here was a most brutal sort of fellow and made things as uncomfortable as he possibly could for everyone going sick, unless they were nearly dying.[26]

For Charles Huxtable, this need to be hard-hearted was the worst part of the job. He recalled having to insist on a man with sore legs participating in an attack. Although this made him feel rotten, he knew the consequences of doing otherwise: 'if you relax and give favours to one man you may get a flood of others'.[27]

RMOs had to be alert to the possibility of malingering. Hartsilver, referring to the same MO as above, believed that 'no doubt there were a good many men trying to avoid going up the line by going sick and the doctor had his work cut out to find out who really was ill'.[28] S.W. McLellan cautioned that '[a] regimental sick parade is very different from ordinary doctoring, and all too frequently degenerates into a mere trial of wits – "patient versus the doctor"'.[29] Meanwhile, A.L.P. Gould records that on first joining the 2nd Royal Marine Light Infantry some of the old hands came along to test him out: 'I had to harden my heart and keep the sick list down.'[30] Others have recorded similar experiences upon first joining a unit, among them M.S. Esler who was 'taken for a sucker', by men of the 9th Border Regiment:

> The first morning that I took sick parade the complaints varied and about six or eight complained of lumbago pains. I had had lumbago pains in the

past, which I had found painful. I excused them all duties. The glad news must have got around, for the next morning about fifteen turned up with lumbago, and the following morning when there was a route march on with full equipment to be carried, about thirty men presented themselves with lumbago, and were excused duty. After seeing the sick list that morning the Colonel sent for me and said as follows: 'I thought, last week, that I was commanding a regiment of fit and virile men. I find now that I am in charge of a regiment of crocks. I have no doubt that, tomorrow morning, I shall find fifty men off duty with lumbago. I fear, doctor, that they are taking you for a ride. Tomorrow, I want to see all those men complaining of lumbago sent back on duty unless they are unable to stand, or are sent in on a stretcher.' He was quite right, of course, and the following morning I sent all but two back on full duty, with a warning from the corporal that they would get a little extra physical labour as movement was good for lumbago! Strange to say, the epidemic disappeared like magic![31]

That incident occurred while the regiment was in the UK. Later, in France, he encountered no such difficulties and the men's early attempt to dupe him actually helped to bind him to them and maintain morale: 'when we might be having a tough time in the trenches, I would turn to a group of men and say "any of you feel lumbago coming on?" That always got a good laugh, for they remembered my first few days with them.'[32]

There undoubtedly were 'professional skrimshankers', described by H.W. Kaye as members 'of Infantry Battalions who manage to get left with their Transport while the Battalion is in the trenches, and then come down here [to the FA] hoping to delude the MO who does not know them to send them on down the Line of Command'.[33] In extreme cases force was necessary to deter malingerers. H.J.B. Fry recorded how a man in a platoon moving up the line for an attack 'tried to fall out and pretended to be sick and had to be threatened with a revolver'.[34] And T.D. Cumberland describes how, during an attack, a number of men passed him by, apparently panic-stricken. He and the Adjutant stopped them and, upon finding that most of them were wounded, sent them on their way. But amongst them Cumberland found 'one of the Battalion malingerers and, when he could not show me a wound, I cursed him and told him to rejoin a unit or I would inform on him and he would be court-martialled and shot after the battle was over'.[35]

On the whole, however, a consensus appears to emerge from Medical Officers' papers to the effect that serious cases of malingering were rare. Charles McKerrow noted that whilst some men would 'try it on' out of the line, men very rarely went sick in the trenches.[36] The differing attitude that prevailed in the line was described by W. Brown who recorded that men about to go on a stunt would not report sick for fear of missing the action.[37] T.D. Cumberland shared this assessment. Moreover, on one occasion when out of the line, he actually found himself in sympathy with a group of malingerers:

> I was surprised when I saw the large sick parade at the 8th SWB aid post. So I asked the orderly what was the matter and was informed that there was a parade church service and, since the men disliked the Padre, they all appeared on sick parade. By Jove, when I heard that the Padre was Thomas [for whom Cumberland had an equal dislike] I sympathised with them and let them off easy.[38]

Thus, malingering was 'remarkably rare',[39] and in any case easily detectable. Its incidence in a unit was a measure of the quality of the RMO: 'the moral effect of a weak medical officer is very bad for any battalion'.[40] Lawrence Gameson recognized that poor discipline was also a contributory factor, but agreed that malingering 'was largely influenced and conditioned by the MO's own approach'.[41] A Medical Officer who judged the men fairly and firmly would win their respect.[42] One who showed weakness would produce a large sickness rate, consequently undermining the strength and morale of the unit. At the same time, however, it was essential that the RMO's need to be firm did not cause him to be unnecessarily harsh. Some Medical Officers went too far and tended to treat every man attending sick parade as a malingerer.[43] J.H. Dible thought that it was a 'debasing idea' to regard the majority of sick soldiers as 'skrimshankers', and was convinced that such an approach could only lead to inadequate treatment and avoidable suffering. He cites examples to prove his point:

> [my SMO] has already punished one man of mine for having synovitis of the knee. The man, a fortnight later, had a knee the size of a football and I have since persuaded the SMO that he is unfit for the service and he has been discharged. Also, a second has been punished for having a cerebral tumour which has since killed him and which my late chief assures me is a very nice specimen of a glioma and not a gumma as the MO from the hospital who attended the post mortem (which I did) suggested. This shows the inate suspicion of poor Tommy which pervades the RAMC; alive he was called a malingerer; dead he is accused of being a syphilitic. Well, Thomas, I have proved you not guilty on both counts, though you had to die to get the verdict.[44]

Dible's suggestion that this approach pervaded the RAMC is something of an exaggeration. Nevertheless it is clear that there were some Medical Officers who failed to appreciate the point at which firmness became harshness. Malcolm Brown refers to a doctor who returned to the firing line a man suffering from varicose veins, and one whose finger had been shot off.[45] In *Subaltern on the Somme*, Max Plowman describes the 'callous brutality' which a Medical Officer in France displayed towards a Gallipoli veteran who had suffered from fever.[46] Such an approach did nothing for the reputation of the RAMC; and even now it is surprising how the activities of a minority of bad RMOs have helped to perpetuate an image of doctors in the trenches as lazy and callous. In the vast majority of cases nothing could have been further from the truth as the instances of bravery and devotion to duty cited above have already testified. But an even more damaging consequence of a harsh doctor was his effect upon the morale of his unit. An unsympathetic RMO could be at least as damaging as one who was too soft with the men.

A good RMO would maintain the strength of his unit by adopting a firm yet fair attitude towards men going sick; an attitude which in turn had a good moral effect, and so further strengthened the unit. Indeed the Medical Officer had an important role to play in sustaining a regiment's morale. Frequent inspections of the trenches by the RMO made an important contribution to the morale of a unit.[47] It was good for the men to be able to see that skilled medical assistance was at hand. These inspections, along with the sick parades, were also important in allowing the RMOs to get to know the men in the battalion. It was essential that the Medical Officer be acquainted with all the officers and men in his unit so that he could detect the earliest signs of fatigue, mental breakdown or the recurrence of previous illnesses. Charles McKerrow took just such a close interest in his men and after his death the Battalion Commander paid him this tribute:

> no man in the Battalion was more loved, admired and respected. I believe he had the Medical History of every man in the Battalion, who had passed through his hands, written down in his private diary.[48]

By taking a keen interest in the health of his men, and making himself well known and approachable, the RMO could avert the loss of valuable fighting material:

> [the men] sometimes come to see me [F.J. Blackley], chilly, nervy and eyes dropping out for want of sleep so although not ill I generally pack them

into my dugout for wounded and let them have hot drinks and three hours' sleep before sending them back.[49]

When the unit was on the march, it was the RMO's job to keep up morale, enforce strict water discipline and prevent serious cases of exhaustion. He had to be firm with men dropping out, but also ready to give assistance to those in genuine difficulties. M.S. Esler saw his role as being a 'sort of wet nurse' to the unit on the move:

in France, when we had long distances to cover, I could often spot the limping man or the exhausted man and get them a lift in one of the wagons at the rear.[50]

Such care for the physical well-being of the men also had implications for their mental health. The BMJ emphasized that RMOs had a responsibility to deal with the mind of the soldier as well as his body. The prevention of fatigue, the provision of adequate food, care to ensure that the men were warm and comfortable, and action to avoid boredom – these were all factors critical to the maintenance of morale and the avoidance of mental breakdown. Doctors were reminded that, whilst a professional army was likely to bear up under the strains of war, the morale of a citizen army was more vulnerable. Men capable of maintaining level composure in the ordinary course of their lives might lose their self-control at the front, to an extent that was likely to surprise the MO. The BMJ admitted that this display of weakness might well offend the doctor, but counselled that it was his role to minister to the mind of the man. It opined that the greatest danger of a collapse in morale was in the winter, expressing particular concern that by October 1918 many officers and men were facing their fifth year in the trenches. The RMO's responsibility was to prevent this collapse and he could best achieve this, according to the BMJ, by 'reverting to the Hippocratic tradition and making the case of each soldier peculiarly his own'.[51]

This advice appears to have been contradictory to the view that in military medicine the first duty of the physician was to attend to the needs of the mass, rather than to those of the individual. In 1917 P.S. Lelean reminded doctors that the War offered limited opportunities for their humanitarian instincts, and that military effectiveness and defeat of the enemy were the principal considerations. He likened these military responsibilities to a treatment for the disease of war:

[T]he first aim of the practitioner is not to remove pain but to remove the cause of the pain. As the cause of suffering in war is the state of war itself, victory is the one remedy for both the disease and the suffering it occasions. No individual considerations – whether of suffering or death – can be permitted to retard the prosecution and progress of the national cure.[52]

Yet Lelean accepted that the psychological impact of modern warfare might require the doctor to give expression to humanitarian concerns, which ought usually to have been suppressed.[53] In fact, care for an individual's morale might well be a factor in maintaining the strength of an army. The BMJ believed that an RMO ought to be the confidant of all the officers and men of the battalion, and needed to keep a close watch for signs of weakness in an individual's morale. In cases of shaky morale it was considered important that the doctor be free to prescribe rest and recreation on medical grounds, when military circumstances permitted.[54] The RMO also shored up morale by his very presence which symbolized the medical care that would be immediately available to the men in their time of need. The positive impact of RMOs on troop morale is evident from the many tributes which were paid to them by men of their regiments.[55]

High amongst the means by which an RMO helped to sustain the strength of his unit was the enforcement of strict measures for the avoidance of preventable diseases. This also had obvious benefits as regards morale; a unit in which disease was at a minimum was bound to have a more positive outlook. Thus the sanitary work of RMOs, so often underestimated by wartime critics of the RAMC, was of great value.

Frequent inspections of the trenches were essential to ensure that adequate standards of sanitation were being maintained. Out of the line, too, it was important that the RMO retain his sanitary vigilance, checking that the conditions in billets did not pose a health risk.[56] This role as guardian of the unit's health involved a variety of tasks, and required constant attention. Claims that there was insufficient work for RMOs were dismissed by the BMJ, which argued that those who gave only two hours a day to routine duties were 'lamentably lacking in the understanding of what [was] expected from [them]'.[57] The majority of RMOs' accounts agree with this assessment, and provide an indication of the range of activities that their work encompassed: supervising the siting of camps; establishing and maintaining a safe water supply; getting latrines erected and checking them daily; checking food supplies; ensuring that basic rules of hygiene were being followed in kitchens; taking measures to prevent fly infestation; inspecting the men for scabies and lice; and doing their best to keep the men's clothing and

228

bodies clean, including, whenever possible, the provision of bathing facilities.[58] The RMO also had to be on the alert for outbreaks of contagious diseases and had a crucial part to play in schemes for their prevention.[59]

Prevention of disease necessitated checking the health of the local civilian population with which the troops were likely to come into contact. Cases of contagious disease were isolated, and treatments administered. RMOs also co-ordinated with local civil authorities to ensure that adequate standards of sanitation were maintained. However their contact with foreign civilians often went beyond the bounds necessary to the protection of the men's health, becoming more a form of humanitarian aid to Britain's allies. Given the increasing shortage of doctors at home, it must have been galling to some to hear reports of British Medical Officers tending to foreign civilians. However, with reference to the situation in France, the Medical Establishment Committee made a strong defence of continued British medical assistance:

> In estimating the amount of work that devolved on the RAMC in France, it must not be forgotten that a very large number of French doctors have been called away, and that both in the Lines of Communication and at the Front, much of the care of the civilian population has been left to the British Army. Though this may not, at first sight, commend itself to the overworked doctors or the civilian population at home, the duty is clearly one which the British nation is in honour bound to undertake, when it is remembered that we are not only defending France against the Germans, but defending our own country at the same time, with the advantage of fighting our battles upon French soil.[60]

Many RMOs came to establish what amounted to small panel practices amongst the local population: they attended confinements; treated sick children and the elderly; dealt with cases such as pneumonia or influenza; and treated minor complaints.[61]

No matter how vigilant a Medical Officer was with regard to sanitary matters, or how much care he took over the health of his men and the local population, some disease was always going to break out. This was especially the case during heavy fighting when the difficulties of maintaining adequate sanitary standards were immense. In these conditions the best defence against the spread of diseases, such as typhoid, was inoculation. However, as mentioned above, inoculation was not compulsory in the British Army. RMOs consequently had an important role to play in persuading their men to agree. Lawrence Gameson was able to persuade men in his unit by first inoculating himself:

I've no record of the number of times I 'inoculated' myself. I did it often in front of the paraded men. It encouraged the troops to see me stick a needle into myself. Usually, of course, I used sterile water.[62]

Charles McKerrow used a combination of gentle persuasion and warnings about the consequences of refusing inoculation. These warnings included the distribution of pamphlets highlighting the danger of typhoid infection. However his trump card was his familiarity with the men: 'knowing [them] as I do gives me a good deal of influence'.[63]

The BMJ agreed that 'their [RMO's] personal influence' was the principal factor in the success of measures to keep men fit, and that those who put their backs into their work could accomplish a great deal as regards inoculation. In one unit, it suggested that the hard work and influence of the RMO had led to 100 per cent of the men being inoculated.[64]

McKerrow's use of pamphlets to push his message home highlights another role of the RMO: that of health education officer to the unit. H.W. Bayly attached great importance to this role:

I realised that if an MO was to be of any use to his unit it would not be through what he could do in the line but what he could teach in rest. Every man . . . must be taught first aid and everyone . . . must be taught the elements of hygiene and sanitation.[65]

The ADMS (Sanitation) in France agreed, seeing education as the principal means of avoiding 'insanitary practices in the forward areas'. He proposed that particular attention be paid by RMOs to platoon officers and section NCOs who could then be enlisted in the campaign to educate the men.[66] Thus, officers and NCOs were lectured on such subjects as the care of feet, hygiene and the avoidance of gas poisoning. Combatant officers were also instructed by the RMO in their duties regarding the health and well-being of the men, duties which may well have been neglected had a trained medical man not been present.

This is evident when looking at the issue of trench foot. As mentioned in an earlier chapter, a variety of therapeutic and preventative measures were experimented with in the early months of the war, which helped to diminish the incidence of this affliction. However, the most important factor in its prevention was for MOs to recognize that it did not represent a new disease of war, and to ensure that all ranks were made aware of this. In December 1915 the DMS First Army noted that '[the] term Trench feet [sic] is to be discontinued and "chilled feet" substituted, it seems to me that the terms "Trench" feet, "Trench" fever etc are likely to centre too much attention on the trench inconveniences in the soldiers mind and he is too much on the look out for diseases caused or said to be caused by being in the trenches'.[67] Of course, flooded trenches undoubtedly provided conditions that were conducive to the onset of chilled feet. Measures were introduced to limit the time that soldiers spent in such conditions to a maximum of thirty-six hours. But it was important to recognize that it was neglect of the feet, whether in the trenches or not, which was the root cause. Feet had to be washed regularly and benefited from the application of dry foot powder. Boots and socks had to be removed regularly, and clean socks supplied each day. The importance of maintaining comfortable, warm, waterproof boots was stressed, whilst in wet sectors the wearing of gum boots became widespread. In cold damp conditions attention was focussed upon the need to prevent wet socks and puttees from constricting the circulation. Adherence to these precautions came to be seen as an important disciplinary matter and, consequently, responsibility for enforcing them was placed on company and platoon commanders.[68] Thus the incidence of foot disorders provided a measure for gauging the levels of discipline and morale within a unit.

It was the MO's job to keep a regular check of the men's feet, and to ensure that combatant officers remained attentive to this important matter bearing upon the fighting efficiency of their men. The following intervention by T.D. Cumberland shows that the presence of an MO could be critical to maintaining awareness of this issue, and thus in preserving the health and morale of a unit:

> I held a foot inspection [after the march] and raised a row about the men's socks [many of the men's feet were in a poor condition]. By Jove, the CO backed me up and the Company Commanders were ticked off for not looking after their men.[69]

Those who called for the abolition of RMOs failed to recognize the vital role that qualified practitioners had to play in maintaining the strength and efficiency of their units. It was the RMO's duty to provide expert medical advice to the Commanding Officer on all questions bearing upon the health of the men; and it was his vigilance that ensured his advice was acted upon. By being attentive to the individual needs of the officers and men under his care he also proved critical to the maintenance of morale. The BMJ was concerned that the work of the RMO should not be dismissed lightly, and that it should not be allowed to drift into the appearance of being a dull routine. Far from seeing the role as one undemanding of the highest calibre of doctor, it argued that RMOs needed to be men of the Hippocratic spirit 'who have proved in civil life that they have the real qualities of the physician'.[70]

The work of the regimental doctors was reinforced by the Field Ambulance MOs. On a march the FAs were able to mop up men who had become detached from their units and subsequently to give treatment that prevented minor ailments from developing into more serious conditions:

> We had about 20 patients, all of them British soldiers with sore feet – men who had fallen out of their regiments on the march and had waited by the roadside for the ambulance waggons. We always ordered these poor devils to jump into the waggons and take off their boots and socks. This gave instant relief. The sores on the heels and across the instep were painted with iodine. In a few days the men were generally well and fit to rejoin their regiments.[71]

One of the greatest dangers to the health of the Army was that of louse borne disease. Lice were implicated in the spread of relapsing fever and typhus. The latter had for centuries been the scourge of armies in the field, since a soldier's tendency to neglect civilian standards of personal hygiene, and his close proximity to his comrades, provided the ideal conditions for lice to breed, infest clothing and to carry disease from man to man.[72] Knowledge of this link meant that during the First World War MOs were charged with maintaining close vigilance over standards of personal hygiene amongst the men, and overseeing necessary measures for the eradication of lice. It was felt that the latter task was best achieved on a divisional level and so this was largely undertaken by the FAs. They established divisional bathing facilities and arranged for the distribution of clean clothing. The men's dirty clothing underwent steam disinfection and was then sent to be washed in an adjacent laundry.

In 1918 a link was finally established between lice and trench fever. Up until this point there had been some uncertainty surrounding the etiology of the disease, with suspicion falling upon a variety of possible culprits, including flies, mosquitoes, fleas, rats and mice.[73] The confirmation that lice were responsible focussed attention upon improving the procedures for delousing. In May 1918 delousing pits were introduced on the Western Front, following a design developed in Rumania and Russia which enabled men, wherever they were billeted, to delouse their own clothing:

> [this consisted of] a dugout in which clothes would be hung or placed on racks, and brick stoves kept lighted in the interior. A simple pit constructed

in this way showed that the temperature inside could be raised to 80° or 90° Centigrade, and that this temperature – and indeed a very much lower temperature – killed lice effectually.[74]

The FAs played a far more important role, both militarily and medically, than the RAMC's critics were prepared to grant. By operating rest stations FAs were able to provide early treatment for minor illness, preventing the loss of men from the divisional area. Separate wards were organized for a variety of conditions including slight cases of gas poisoning, trench foot, measles, diarrhoea and scabies.[75] Men would be kept here for about ten days before being returned to their units fit for duty.[76] Only more serious cases were passed on to the CCSs. Early in the War, however, large numbers of men continued to be lost to the Army, due to unnecessary evacuation to the base hospitals and, from there, to the UK. This was recognized as not being 'conducive to the upkeep of either individual or national morale'.[77] Particular concern was exercised by the tendency of treatment in UK hospitals to retard recovery, with patients acquiring the habit of reflecting on the horrors of war that they had left behind. In response to this problem arrangements were made to increase the capacity in France for the care of recoverable sickness, and 1915 witnessed the formation of convalescent companies in the divisional and corps areas, which functioned to take the strain off the CCSs by providing accommodation for cases likely to make a quick recovery.[78] The following year there was an increase in the number of convalescent depots at the bases. The capacity of the depots was also expanded so that each could now accommodate 5,000 recovering patients.[79] Convalescent depots worked in close collaboration with the General Hospitals and, according to the Babtie Committee, they proved to be one of the important products of the War in the area of medical organization. Testifying to their significance is the fact that, during the period of March to November 1918, over 16,000 officers and 474,000 men were returned to fighting fitness.[80] All of the arrangements at rest stations, convalescent companies and convalescent depots applied equally to men recovering from wounds as they did to those recuperating after sickness.

In addition to dealing with previously unencountered diseases like trench fever, the RAMC had to cope with the impact of other unanticipated aspects of modern warfare. The medical service was involved in the introduction of steel helmets which were designed to reduce the incidence of serious head wounds from trench mortar and shrapnel fire. The RAMC also took an interest in experiments to develop protective clothing and shields against the German flamethrowers.[81] Most importantly, the AMS was involved in the development of anti-gas protection. Collaboration between chemists and physiologists at the Army's Central Laboratory in France, and at the laboratories of the Royal Army Medical College, Millbank, produced a swift response to each of the different gases employed by the enemy. Beginning with the primitive pad respirators, introduced in May 1915, a series of increasingly sophisticated masks were developed, culminating in the small box respirator. The latter became the standard issue of the British Army, offering protection against most gases.[82] So effective were the masks in preventing gas injuries, the DGMS was confident by 1917 that '[if] men are gassed now it is because they are unexpectedly, as while asleep, caught without their helmets on'.[83]

Venereal diseases were amongst the more predictable foes to face the medical profession, and ought to have been easily preventable. However, the ability of doctors to deal with this problem was constrained by non-medical considerations and VD emerged as a significant threat to military efficiency, even before the troops left the UK. According to the Official History, venereal diseases accounted for 'the greatest amount of constant inefficiency in the home commands', their incidence being especially high amongst Dominion troops.[84] Yet the War Office made little effort to control the situation. This inactivity was severely criticized by the Dominions, which were naturally perplexed, given the British Government's calls for assistance, that it was prepared to tolerate such a massive drain on manpower: among some imperial troops the annual wastage due to venereal disease was as high as 287 per 1,000.[85] At the Imperial Conference in 1917 the Dominion Governments pointed out that the failure to take adequate steps to deal with venereal disease was hindering recruitment.[86] In New Zealand the sense of outrage was such that influential figures began to suggest 'that no more New Zealand troops be quartered in England till England is rendered hygienically safe, so far as VD is concerned'.[87]

This pressure from the Dominions forced the British Government to act with the addition of regulation 40 D to the Defence of the Realm Act (DORA). Under this regulation it became an offence to solicit, invite or perform sexual intercourse with any member of the Armed Forces.[88] However the Dominions remained dissatisfied with the situation. At a meeting of the Imperial War Conference the Canadian representative stated 'that they had been unable to see that any very adequate steps had been taken to carry out the resolution'.[89] In particular, it was argued that not enough had been done to curb diseased women or to establish clinics in Britain where servicemen could obtain treatment immediately after exposure to venereal disease. The War Office disregarded the calls for early treatment centres but undertook to encourage the Home Office to obtain more convictions of women under 40 D.[90]

Among certain sections of the British public there was growing opposition to 40 D which was considered to be discriminatory against women. The Government feared a backlash from the six million newly enfranchised women and decided to appoint a royal commission to consider whether any arrangements should be made.[91] The Deputy Secretary of State for War defended 40 D against those who claimed that it was one-sided:

> It penalises the woman who is the source of the infection if she communicates it to a member of H.M.'s Forces . . . it does not refer at all to the civilian male population . . . [but] it is not true to suggest, as is done, that a soldier gets off scot free. If he contracts this disease and conceals the fact he is court martialled, and the penalty upon proof that he has done so is imprisonment with hard labour for two years. If he does not conceal it, but reports it in the ordinary way, he goes to hospital and loses all his pay and emoluments, and his wife loses her separation allowance during the time that he is there.[92]

Yet the War Office made no attempt to explain the situation to the public, and worse, failed to give adequate support to the Home Office in the implementation of the DORA regulation. This inactivity represented a serious abrogation of duty for which there can be no excuse. Venereal disease was costing the nation dearly, both in terms of manpower and financially, and the War Office should have taken responsibility for dealing with the problem.

At the front the precautions against venereal disease were equally inadequate. The British attitude to prevention was based upon an approach which had been outlined by Kitchener in a memorandum of 1905. This emphasized the virtues of 'self restraint' and participation 'in all healthy outdoor sports and games'. It also invoked regimental pride, pointing out that a regiment's good name 'necessarily suffers if the men become inefficient through venereal'. Those who did contract the disease were duty-bound to report to the Medical Officer as soon as possible, and faced punishment in the form of loss of pay, gratuities and privileges, such as indulgence passes.[93] During the War punitive measures of this type were adopted, as the Deputy Secretary of State for War explained in the above quotation. However these measures proved ineffective in reducing the incidence of the disease.[94] Captain Lawrence Gameson felt that instead of looking on venereal disease as a crime, more attention ought to have been focussed upon ensuring the availability of rapid and effective forms of treatment:

> an officer . . . just back from leave asked urgently to see me. I found that he had gonorrhoea . . . Had I sent him away the results would have been unpleasant; venereal disease (quite idiotically) was then classed as a 'crime' with punishments designed to fit it. I knew the answers to gonorrhoea having worked for Frank Kidd, the leading expert in those days. I decided to keep him with his battery and to treat him myself; which, by the way, was a 'crime' too.[95]

He sent to London for the equipment necessary for the treatment, and, despite the difficulties involved in keeping the matter secret, the patient made a full recovery. More should have been done to enable Medical Officers to give immediate treatment in this manner without having to worry that they were concealing a crime.

But of even greater importance than treatment, was the question of a Medical Officer's ability to keep the incidence of the disease to a minimum, the maintenance of the Army's strength being the RAMC's principal duty. However the British military authorities were reluctant to sanction the issuing of prophylactics, and paid too much attention to those who opposed prophylaxis on moral and religious grounds. The National Council for Combating Venereal Disease (NCCVD) took the lead in promoting these moral arguments: it was against the introduction of the 'packet system' of prophylaxis, favouring early treatment after infection.[96] Lieutenant Colonel W. Beveridge felt that there should have been no question of 'social polity and conventional morality' dictating the policy on venereal disease. However it is quite clear that moral considerations were allowed to prevent a purely medical solution to the problem, as Sir George Riddell pointed out:

> an Order was issued some time ago stating that no steps were to be taken which would countenance or tend to lead to immorality. I am further told that as a result most of the Army doctors are afraid to recommend prophylaxis. Some, however, in the face of the prohibition have secured wonderful results. We,[97] however, want to go a step further, and are anxious that facilities should be provided.[98]

As a result of this order, many Medical Officers felt that 'they are held back from performing what they feel should be regarded as their medical duty'.[99] Medical Officers in the New Zealand Army Medical Corps faced no such difficulty. Whilst the New Zealand military authorities did everything possible to encourage men to abstain from sexual intercourse (including a purity campaign by the chaplains; lectures by Medical Officers pointing out the evils; and talks by Regimental Officers persuading them of the risks), it was recognized that some men were always likely to transgress, and that consequently it was wise to issue them with means of protection against the disease. According to General Richardson,[100] from the moment that prophylactics were issued to the New Zealand troops the incidence of venereal disease dropped dramatically.[101] Despite evidence of the efficacy of prophylactics the NCCVD continued to resist their introduction, claiming that they would encourage immorality. However the experience on other fronts did not bear out this claim. Information from Port Said, where prophylactics had been issued, suggested that a knowledge of prophylaxis did not promote promiscuity.[102]

To its credit the RAMC resisted those in the War Office who had been prepared to placate the moral lobby, and eventually succeeded in winning approval for a medical solution to the problem. A system of prophylaxis and early treatment was introduced by the Army, which was the first time that self-administered disinfectants became available in Britain.[103] Obviously this represented a tremendous victory for the RAMC in its campaign to establish venereal disease as a primarily medical matter; but it was a battle that it should never have had to fight. There was always going to be strong vocal opposition to the use of prophylactics but it was verging on the criminal for the War Office not to sanction their adoption when they could so easily have prevented the invaliding of a great deal of men.[104] The War Office's inactivity, as well as being wasteful of manpower in general, was specifically wasteful of the skills of Medical Officers. The failure to issue prophylactics meant that their time was taken up dealing with large numbers of easily avoided cases whilst they were denied adequate means of treatment. It was grossly unsatisfactory that they should have to wait until the middle of 1918 for medicine to have a free hand in dealing with venereal disease. Even then, the arrangements were inferior to those in other armies, especially that of Germany (see Appendix G).

One of the final medical challenges to confront the RAMC was the influenza pandemic. The first outbreak in the spring of 1918 was followed by further waves in the autumn and in the winter of 1918–1919. Initially, there was some confusion in the British Army as to whether the disease was influenza. Prior to this fact being established, troops who succumbed were marked PUO (Pyrexia of Unknown Origin).[105] However, once the disease was recognized, the British approach to influenza, both civilian and military, was characterized by a faith in the prospects for prevention and cure. This was a faith encouraged by the medical profession which was confident of its ability to find a vaccine that would defeat the disease. The MRC co-ordinated research that led to the development of vaccines which were administered on a prophylactic and therapeutic basis. Research into the etiology of the disease was undertaken by laboratories attached to the military hospitals in France. H.J.B. Fry was in the laboratory of Number 8 General Hospital, Rouen, where he was working on bacilli isolated from cases that had died from influenza. He was initially enthused by the results of his experiments. But his diary entry for Armistice Day includes an admission that 'my experiments had almost certainly failed to be of any value'.[106] In fact, none of the experiments conducted during the War proved conclusive. It was not until 1933 that the influenza A virus was identified. Until such time effective vaccination against influenza was impossible. British troops were vaccinated during the War, but the Adviser in Pathology with the British Armies in France remained sceptical about the results.[107]

The medical profession in Britain has been criticized for encouraging an official response to the pandemic that emphasized futile preventative measures to the detriment of providing adequate practical and palliative measures.[108] Certainly the RAMC was faced with the problem of dealing with large numbers of cases. The FAs and CCSs were swamped by the epidemic. In June, W.J. Webster recorded that the 72nd FA was full, having admitted over 250 influenza cases.[109] To relieve the pressure on the forward units during the spring and autumn outbreaks, General Hospitals at the base had to be set aside for influenza. Altogether a total of 226,615 cases were reported by the Army from the spring outbreak, with a further 93,670 incapacitated, and 5,555 deaths during November and December.[110] Thus, for the Medical Services of the British Army, the influenza epidemic ensured that the Armistice brought no respite. The War Diary of the 26th General Hospital records that '[the Armistice] has made very little difference to the work of the hospital. Heavy admissions of influenza went on all the month and the bronchopneumonia proved very fatal.' The situation was made worse by the fact that many of the staff themselves succumbed to the disease.[111] As well as tending to the needs of stricken British soldiers the RAMC was also called upon to treat French civilians. Number 6 CCS, which had become an infectious diseases hospital, had to be divided into male and female wards due to the level of civilian admissions.[112]

Whenever an outbreak of sickness occurred the principal concern of the medical services was accurate diagnosis. From a medical viewpoint this was critical to determining both the type of treatment necessary and the most appropriate location for this to be given. However, it was also vital from a military perspective that the fighting strength of an army should not be depleted by the evacuation of patients further down the line than their recovery required. It was therefore essential that the medical services had the facilities to enable them to reach accurate, early diagnoses; and that the expertise of MOs in this field was effectively utilized.

Bacteriologists played a bigger part in the Great War than in any previous conflict. This reflected the growing reputation of bacteriology. The contributions of such individuals as Leishman, Wright and Fleming had helped to establish it as an essential branch of medical science. Civilian medicine had become characterized by a close co-operation between the clinician and the pathologist. The BMJ, therefore, felt that bacteriology's prominence at the front represented proof of an understanding by the military of the role of medicine in warfare, and a recognition that 'all wars are doctors' wars'.[113] The first Mobile Bacteriological Laboratory arrived on the Western Front in 1914, just prior to the Aisne battle. It quickly made its mark in the campaign against diseases such as enteric and cerebro-spinal fever. All men who came in contact with cases of the latter spent at least three weeks in isolation, during which time they were observed and swabs were taken to test for meningococcal infection. This testing of contacts placed 'a good deal of work on the various laboratories'.[114] More laboratories followed, becoming standard units of the field medical organization. In addition to their work in the laboratories, the bacteriologists were also on call to deal with cases of infectious disease appearing in the FAs and CCSs of their sector.[115]

The role of laboratory work in developing anti-gas measures in isolating the cause of trench fever, and in the research concerning the influenza bacillus, has already been mentioned. Other medical conditions that benefited from such investigation were trench feet, dysentery and epidemic jaundice. An outbreak of the latter in the Second Army was dealt with by Captain A. Stokes, the local bacteriologist, who found the spirochete responsible in the brown rats that inhabited the trenches. His discovery was the prelude to a vigorous anti-rat campaign on the orders of the DMS.[116] Such successes for army pathology ran counter to the claims by contemporary critics that the RAMC had failed to appreciate the importance of research.

Good standards of hygiene ensured that dysentery had been reduced to isolated outbreaks prior to 1916. However, in that year it became a larger problem, partly due to the arrival in France of troops from Gallipoli where the disease had been widespread.[117] It also occurred in greater numbers amongst the troops in France. This resulted from a deterioration of sanitary standards during the Somme campaign, combined with a spell of warm weather that created ideal conditions for the disease to spread. MOs had to be on the lookout for any outbreaks of diarrhoea which had to be reported at once to the mobile laboratories. It was the responsibility of the FAs to arrive at a diagnosis, and for all severe diarrhoea and suspected dysentery cases to be evacuated to the CCSs where thorough bacteriological examination would be made.[118] To facilitate this work, instructions were issued that diarrhoea cases were to be attended by a special officer in each FA.[119] It was important that the men be carefully observed so that cases of mild diarrhoea were not unnecessarily evacuated down the line.

All cases evacuated from the FAs had to be accompanied by a preliminary diagnosis. This practice was essential to ensuring that patients were retained as near to the front as their condition permitted, and also avoided confusion and mistaken diagnoses at units in the rear. Particular difficulties arose with suspected mental cases. As discussed in an earlier chapter the majority of MOs lacked the expertise to accurately diagnose many of these cases. The term shell shock directed MOs towards an assumption that these cases were organic in origin, consequent upon the physical effect of shell explosions. In fact the majority of cases were functional nervous disorders brought on by the stresses of the battlefield. There was also the problem that the condition was becoming contagious. More and more men were appearing at aid posts claiming to have symptoms of shell shock, and were being evacuated to the CCSs and base hospitals. Inability to accurately diagnose these cases was therefore undermining morale and fighting strength. In January 1916, the DMS First Army took steps to address these problems. He issued instructions to FAs that in any case of shell shock where a certain diagnosis could not be reached the 'mental expert' was to be sent for.[120] If there was no doubt, then the cases were to be evacuated to the CCSs, where alterations to the initial diagnosis were discouraged:

> [O]nly under very exceptional circumstances is a diagnosis made by a Field Ambulance to be so altered in the Casualty Clearing Station that the case becomes a battle casualty. This refers particularly to cases being diagnosed 'shell shock' in which Regimental and Field Ambulance Officers are far better placed for obtaining a true diagnosis than [a CCS].[121]

Lieutenant Colonel C.S. Myers, Consultant Psychologist in France, was pressing for a more thorough reorganization of the arrangements for dealing with shell shock. He wished to see a change to the diagnostic terminology, preferring to see cases classed as 'nervous shock'. In his view men were less likely to boast of having such a condition whilst the new term more accurately described cases that were not attributable to shelling. He was also convinced that many of the cases, such as hysterical disorders, currently being evacuated to the base hospitals, could be treated more successfully in army areas. However he made little headway with his suggestions until a significant increase in shell shock, during the 1916 Somme campaign, prompted the military medical authorities to reassess the entire system for dealing with these cases. MOs with forward units were instructed to avoid a diagnosis of shell shock. Instead, they were to be evacuated to advanced psychiatric centres bearing the label, NYDN (Not Yet Diagnosed Nervous). These centres were to be located at the rear of army areas under the charge of a specialist officer. This had the advantage of providing immediate care so that patients did not leave behind the atmosphere and military discipline of the front. Yet at the same time they offered locations that were sufficiently quiet to be conducive to recovery. At these centres the few malingerers could be weeded out, thus helping to remove the stigma that had attached to genuine cases. The latter could then be separated into those who required evacuation to the base and home hospitals, and those likely to benefit from immediate treatment in the advanced centres. By the time of the Passchendaele campaign, a separate line of evacuation for shell shock cases had been established, with specific CCSs being designated as the NYDN centres. Specialist receiving centres now operated at the bases and separate mental wards were set aside in the general hospitals. Myers wished to develop this organization further, with the establishment of sorting centres at the front of army areas where specialists would be able to treat cases deemed likely to recover within two to three days in an atmosphere of strict military discipline. Centres along these lines were experimented with in early 1917 but did not become a permanent feature of RAMC organization, much to Myers's disappointment. Nevertheless, under his guidance more accurate diagnosis had been introduced, with terms such as hysteria and neurasthenia coming to displace shell shock. He also oversaw a reduction in the number of these cases leaving France, so that patients received more immediate and appropriate treatment that avoided the fixation of symptoms associated with long evacuation and the 'soft' atmosphere of civilian hospitals. Thus significant wastage of manpower was avoided.[122]

Equal concern was aroused with relation to the diagnosis and treatment of gas cases. The DDGMS noted in late 1915 that too many men in the First Army had used the presence of gas 'as an excuse for malingering, either by feigning or exaggerating the symptoms of gas poisoning'.[123] To prevent dubious characters from slipping through the net and to aid accurate diagnosis, it became the practice for all suspected gas cases to be sent to Not Yet Diagnosed Gas Centres, which were established in each army area. The more serious cases were evacuated to designated CCSs for specialist treatment. However the Passchendaele campaign demonstrated that the pressure of casualties did not always facilitate the separation of gas cases from the other sick and wounded.[124] Thus, it became standard practice for each CCS to have a gas specialist attached. Meanwhile, the establishment of forward centres facilitated immediate specialist treatment for less serious cases. For example, in October 1917 the FA of the 47th Division was designed as the Corps Gas Centre. Five Nissen huts and a marquee were supplied, providing facilities for the treatment of mild gas poisoning and accommodation where dubious cases could be assessed, thus minimizing wastage.[125]

The benefits of immediate treatment were also evident in other areas. In August 1917 the DMS First Army noted that too many men were needlessly being referred to eye specialists at the base. Most of the conditions were easily treatable in an FA. Guidelines were issued to the effect that only the following classes of patient required specialist treatment:

a) Errors of refraction likely to be improved by suitable glasses.
b) A few presbyopic cases.
c) Severe cases of disease or injury requiring the services of a specialist possessed of skill and experience superior to that of the ordinary Medical Officer.[126]

Central to the reduction of wastage were measures to prevent unfit men from entering the Army. The recruitment of men unfit to fight placed an additional burden on the medical services and helped to undermine military discipline. During the early rush of recruitment the RAMC had been unprepared for the pressure of numbers. Its arrangements for the medical examination of recruits were swamped, and many unfit men were passed for service by civilian doctors keen to rush through as many men as possible. The introduction of standing medical boards and travelling medical boards in 1915 went some way to remedying the situation. Further improvements followed the introduction of the Military Service Acts.

Equally important was the need to ensure that minor ailments did not prevent otherwise fit men from joining up, or require them to be invalided out of the service at a later date. In certain areas, however, the British Army was slow to develop the specialist care that would help to avoid such unnecessary wastage. One of the most neglected areas was that of the soldiers' teeth. The teeth of most recruits were in an appalling condition, but dentists did not believe that men with bad teeth should be rejected. At the same time it was considered unjustifiable that men be sent to face the strains of war with the additional pain and misery of decaying teeth.[127] Soldiers needed expert dental treatment. The British Dental Association responded to the situation by offering free treatment to recruits otherwise fit for active service who faced rejection on the grounds of neglected teeth.[128] The War Office, however, remained utterly indifferent to the matter of dental health, and failed to recognize the important contribution which dentists could make to maintaining the strength of the Army. Not a single dentist accompanied the BEF in 1914 and dentists as a class were not excused from combatant service. In May 1915 the Medical Inspector of Drafts noted the desperate need for more dentists,[129] but by the end of the year there were still only 179 Dental Officers, and these were working under the supervision of junior Medical Officers who possessed no expert knowledge in dentistry.[130] Few in numbers, and lacking sufficient power and authority, the dentists had difficulty coping with the large numbers of men requiring treatment.

Treatment was not commenced until the troops neared the end of their training, and consequently many men left for the front either untreated or requiring further attention. This led to an unnecessary wastage of manpower as men were rapidly incapacitated, and congestion grew at the bases where the small number of dentists were deluged with work.[131] According to the DDMS XIII Corps there were too many cases coming to see the dentist each day, and the amount of dental treatment required by troops in the line had been underestimated.[132] This was not the case in other armies which gave a much higher priority to dentists. The dispositions in the Australian Army Medical Corps (AAMC) were largely based on those of the RAMC, but in the area of dentistry they were much more advanced. Each Field Ambulance had a small dental unit, commanded by a dentist with the rank of lieutenant.[133] The other Dominion armies also had well organized dental services, as did that of the United States.[134] The following figures[135] demonstrate the extent to which the British Army lagged behind the American and Dominion Forces:

Canadian Army	1 dentist per	1,000 men
New Zealand Army	" " "	2,500 "
Australian Army	" " "	2,600 "
United States Army	" " "	1,000 "
British Army	" " "	10,000 "

The Medical Establishment Committee recommended more extensive use of dentists as a means of reducing the workload of Medical Officers. It should also be noted that many Medical Officers simply were not capable of carrying out dental work. Captain E.C. Rycroft, who was qualified in dentistry, recorded that 'the M.O. had had a "go" at a molar the day before, unsuccessfully. Thank goodness he had stopped before doing too much damage.'[136] The War Office had been short-sighted in not recognizing that dentistry was a specialized skill and not one which all Medical Officers possessed. The Establishment Committee's recommendation for increasing the number of dentists was echoed by a Parliamentary Committee chaired by Mr D.F. Pennefather.[137] It recommended the immediate withdrawal of dentists serving with combatant or non-dental units and measures to ensure that all dentists were detailed to dental work.[138] Both committees criticized the general lack of organization in the dental service, and proposed that a Dental Adviser be appointed to oversee the organization.[139]

During the course of 1918 the Government did begin to make substantial improvements in the military dental service. Responding to calls to place the service under a single officer, an Advisory Dental Officer, with the rank of lieutenant colonel, was appointed in March 1918 to the staff of the DGAMS at the War Office. This appointment led to a marked improvement in dental organization.[140] Meanwhile, to ensure efficient distribution of dentists both at home and with the forces a tribunal system was established. The Dental Service Committee[141] was enlarged, at the request of the Ministry of National service, to form the Dental Tribunal. It was the duty of this body to designate dentists who it considered suitable for service with the forces, in addition to acting as a committee of reference to the Ministry in regard to dental students. A separate tribunal was established by the Scottish Office to cover the profession north of the border.[142] The upshot of these improvements was that in October 1918 the Army Council issued an instruction which promised that dental officers would be appointed as the necessity arose.[143] As with so many other developments it took almost the full course of the War for the Army to develop a system for the efficient utilization of dentists.

Similar results were achieved when heart specialists were employed. Under the direction of Thomas Lewis, working with the Medical Research Committee, a system of graded drills was introduced to test the capacity of men's hearts. In the early years of the War inadequate testing had led to many men with defective hearts being accepted for military service. The introduction of searching physical tests helped to prevent the acceptance of recruits unlikely to be able to stand the strains of military service. These tests were also used in the hospitals on the various fronts and in the UK to gauge whether patients suspected of heart afflictions were capable of continued service.[144]

By the outbreak of the War the military authorities had learnt that the fight against disease was a critical part of the fight against the enemy. The commitment to maintaining the health of the men was evident on the Western Front in the evolution of an effective sanitary system. Medical Officers also possessed greater authority than ever before to impose strict standards of hygiene. Despite such positive developments, however, obstacles continued to be placed in the path of military medicine, as is evident from the deficiencies regarding inoculation and venereal disease. These deficiencies were largely the responsibility of the Government. In the case of inoculation it was overly concerned with those who claimed a conscientious objection; whilst, as regards venereal disease, it gave too much weight to those who opposed a medical solution to the problem. Creditably, the RAMC recognized that the work of its officers was being handicapped and fought to remove these obstacles from their path. On the other hand, the RAMC can be criticized for its somewhat tardy recognition of the role to be played by specialists in the prevention and treatment of disease. Some mitigation is to be found in that the RAMC organization was designed to deal with the medical needs of a small professional army. The needs of a citizen force were less appreciated by the British than they were by her continental neighbours. This lack of preparation was compounded by the unexpected challenges of trench warfare. These circumstances, however, are not sufficient to justify the British Army's poor dental arrangements, or its comparatively slow response to the shell shock question.

Nevertheless, by 1918 the RAMC had in place effective measures for disease prevention and facilities for immediate treatment that helped to minimize wastage. Within this organization it is evident that MOs in the forward zones had vital medical and military roles to perform. Above all arrangements had gradually evolved that enabled specialists to oversee preventative measures, and to regulate the diagnosis and treatment of disease at various points along the line of evacuation, enabling expert care to be delivered at the most appropriate location. This served both the needs of the individual and the needs of the Army, thus combining the humanitarian instincts of the doctor with the military responsibilities of the MO.

Notes

1   As the War progressed, and the available manpower became limited, the RAMC personnel were replaced by men of the unit, specially trained in water duties.

2   Initially, when choosing officers, preference was always given to MOsH., holders of the Diploma of Public Health or bacteriologists. As the War progressed and Medical Officers became scarce, sanitary sections were increasingly placed under the command of non-medical men, who nevertheless had expertise in sanitary engineering, or some related field.

3   MacPherson, *Hygiene of the War*, I, pp. 4–5. See also 'The Duties of a Sanitary Section in the Field', BMJ, 1916 (I), p. 215.

4   ADMS (Sanitation).

5   MacPherson, *General History*, II, p. 61.

6   MacPherson, *Hygiene of the War*, I, Chapters III to XI. MacPherson, *General History*, II, p. 356.

7   F.J. Blackley, LC, Diary: 26 August 1915; 4 September 1915.

8   'French Sanitary Squads', BMJ, 1916 (II), p. 665.

9   MacPherson, *General History*, II, p. 62.

10   MacPherson, *General History*, II, p. 62.

11   Gosse, *Memoirs of a Camp Follower*, pp. 124–36. W. Beveridge, WIHM, RAMC 543, War Diary, Volume 30: Memorandum on the Destruction of Rats.

12   Letter from the Professor and Lecturer in Pathology in the University of Oxford, BMJ, 1914 (II), p. 408.

13   Bean, *Official History of Australia in the War of 1914–18*, III, p. 167. 'Anti-typhoid Inoculation', BMJ, 1915 (I), p. 171.

14   *Punch*, CXLVIII, p. 42.

15   'Anti-typhoid Inoculation', BMJ, 1915 (I), p. 171.

16   'Leishman's Figures: Incidence and Mortality from Typhoid Fever in the Expeditionary Force since the Commencement of Operations', BMJ, 1915 (I), p. 264.

17   Lieutenant Colonel W. Beveridge, WIHM, RAMC 543, War Diary, Volume IV: 7 November 1914. The results of tests on British troops in India had shown that the incidence of enteric amongst the uninoculated was six times that amongst the inoculated, and that when an inoculated soldier was attacked by enteric his chances of recovery were twice as great as they would have been had he not been inoculated. See W.J. Simpson, 'War and Disease', *The Nation*, XV, p. 861.

18   Martin, *Surgeon in Khaki*, pp. 10–11.

19   W. Beveridge, WIHM, RAMC 543, War Diary, Volume III: 31 October 1914.

20   As mentioned in the Introduction, Kitchener promoted the cause of inoculation. See p. 28.

21   Charles McKerrow, LC, Diary: 4 March 1916, p. 50.

22   Charles McKerrow, LC, Letters: letter, 12 November 1916, p. 263.

23 WO 95/44, PRO, DGMS Diary: 22 January 1915.
24 McLaughlin, *The RAMC*, p. 37. Humphrey Humphreys, 'Some Medical Memories of Two World Wars', JRAMC, 101, 1955, p. 238.
25 WO 95/52, PRO, Medical Inspector of Drafts, Diary, April 1915–March 1916: 14 October 1915; 17 November 1915: 20 November 1915.
26 Dr J. Hartsilver, LC, memoirs, pp. 298–9.
27 Charles Huxtable, LC, Tape recording.
28 Dr J. Hartsilver, LC, Memoirs, pp. 298–9.
29 S.W. McLellan, RCS, printed diary (no publication details), Book 5, 1917, p. 7.
30 A.L.P. Gould, LC, Letters: letter 1 March 1918.
31 M.S. Esler, IWM, recollections, p. 49.
32 M.S. Esler, IWM, recollections, p. 49.
33 H.W. Kaye, WIHM, RAMC 793, diary; Volume 1: 8 October 1915, p. 216.
34 H.J.B. Fry, LC, Diary: 18 September 1917.
35 T.D. Cumberland, LC, Diary: 19 September 1918.
36 C. McKerrow, LC, Letters: letter 25 October 1915.
37 Captain W. Brown, LC, Diary: 20 February 1917.
38 T.D. Cumberland, LC, Diary: 25 August 1918.
39 Gameson, IWM, memoirs, p. 85.
40 Dolbey, *Regimental Surgeon*, pp. 39–40.
41 Gameson, IWM, memoirs, p. 85.
42 N. Chavasse, LC, Papers: newspaper tribute (extract).
43 Malcolm Brown, *Tommy Goes to War*, J.M. Dent & Sons, 1978, p. 218.
44 J.H. Dible, IWM, Diary, p. 48.
45 Malcolm Brown, *Tommy Goes to War*, p. 218.
46 Max Plowman [Mark VII], *A Subaltern on the Somme in 1916*, J.M. Dent & Sons, 1927, pp. 55–6.
47 C. McKerrow, LC, Letters: extract from letter to his family describing his practice of visiting the trenches every day. This was the height of devotion and 'the men loved him for it'; p. 308.
48 C. McKerrow, LC, Letters: letter from Robert Manners, Lieutenant Colonel Commanding 10th Battalion Northumberland Fusiliers, to McKerrow's mother, 27 December 1916, p. 291.
49 F.J. Blackley, LC, Diary: 29 September 1915.
50 M.S. Esler, IWM, recollections, p. 51. On a march, H.J.B. Fry would often carry the rifles or packs of exhausted men. See Fry, LC, Diary: 1 April 1917; 2 April 1917.
51 'The Western Front', BMJ, 1918, (II), pp. 414–15.
52 P.S. Lelean, *Sanitation in War*, Churchill, 1917, p. 166.
53 *Ibid.* p. 167.
54 'The Western Front', BMJ, 1918, (II), p. 415.
55 E.C. Deane, LC, Papers: Copy of letter from H. Gordon, Lt. Col. 2nd Leicestershire Regiment to Deane's father, 28 September 1915; copy of letter from R.D. Nimis, Senior Chaplain Meerut Division, to Deane's father, 30 September 1915; copy of letter from J. Fallen, Colonel Army Medical Service, to Deane's father. S.S. Greaves, IWM, Papers: biography, p. 11. G.D. Fairley, LC, Papers: letters from the parents of two deceased soldiers, Keith MacDonald

and Sergeant Perry, which indicate the high esteem in which he was held by the men concerned. 'The Work of the RAMC at Ypres', BMJ, 1915 (II), p. 112. Malcolm Brown, *Tommy Goes to War*, pp. 218–19.

56 'The Medical Needs of the Army', BMJ, 1915 (I), p. 511.

57 *Ibid.*

58 Deputy Surgeon General A. Gascoigne Wildey, 'The Medical Officer and the Fighting Man', *Medical Annual*, 1916, pp. 652–5. Gameson, IWM, Memoirs, pp. 190–2, 202. A.L.P. Gould, LC, Papers: letter to father, 1 March 1918. H.J.B. Fry, LC, Diary: 7 January 1916; 12 January 1917; 20 August 1917. T.D. Cumberland, LC, Diary: 9 May 1918; 11 May 1918; 16 May 1918; 8 August 1918; 16 August 1918. Captain N. Chavasse, LC, Letter, 4 August 1915. Charles McKerrow, LC, Letters, 17 November 1915; 3 February 1916; 28 May 1916. Dolbey, *Regimental Surgeon in War and Prison*, pp. 12–13. Deeping, *No Hero This*, pp. 100–2. C. Teichman, *Diary of a Yeomanry MO, Egypt, Gallipoli, Palestine and Italy*, Fisher Unwin, 1921, pp. 88 & 108.

59 Cumberland, LC, Diary: 16 June 1918; 17 June 1918; 23 June 1918; 24 June 1918.

60 'Commission on Medical Establishments', WIHM, RAMC 1165, p. 37.

61 References to the treatment of civilians on the Western Front can be found in the following: G.D. Fairley, LC, Diary: 29 October 1915, p. 19; 15 February 1917, p. 213; 18 February 1917, p. 214. F.J. Blackley, LC, Diary: 8 December 1915. H.J.B. Fry, LC, Diary: 1 April 1917; & August 1917; 17–20 August 1917; 7–15 October 1917. G. Moore, LC, Letters: letter 513, 27 November 915. C.K. McKerrow, LC, Papers: diary, 29 August 1915, p. 5; letter, 4 March 1916, p. 128. W. Sharrard, LC, Diary: 21–22 February 1917. Rutherford, *Soldiering with a Stethoscope*, p. 152. Deeping, *No Hero This*, pp. 428–9. Gosse, *Memoirs of a Camp Follower*, pp. 56–8.

62 Lawrence Gameson, IWM, memoirs, p. 202.

63 C. McKerrow, LC, Letters: letter 21 April 1916. Another reference to the use of persuasion can be found in N. King-Wilson, LC, memoirs, p. 9.

64 'The Medical Needs of the Army', BMJ, 1915 (I), p. 511.

65 H.W. Bayly, *Triple Challenge: War, Whirligigs and Windmills*, Hutchinson, 1933, pp. 101–2.

66 Beveridge, WIHM, RAMC 543, Diary: Vol XXIX, Appendix 2, 5 December 1916.

67 WO 95/195, PRO, DMS First Army, diary, 4 December 1915.

68 J.S. Haller, 'Trench Foot – A Study in Military-Medical Responsiveness in the Great War', 1914–1918, *The Western Journal of Medicine*, June 1990. 152, 6, pp. 732–3.

69 Cumberland, LC, Diary: 13 October 1918.

70 'The Western Front', BMJ, 1918, (II), p. 415.

71 Martin, *Surgeon in Khaki*, p. 72.

72 L.L. Lloyd, *Lice and their Menace to Man*, Hodder & Stoughton, 1919, pp. 100–19.

73 *Report of the Commission of the Medical Research Committee and the American Red Cross on Trench Fever*, OUP, 1918, pp. 40–1.

74 WO 95/47, PRO, DGMS, diary, 12 May 1918.

75 At the time of the Somme campaign, in 1916, FAs had also begun to institute scabies centres for men suffering from this complaint. See **MacPherson**, *General History*, III, p. 50.

76 **G.B. McTavish**, IWM, Letters, letter dated 18 January 1918, p. 61.

77 **WO 32/11395**, PRO, Report of the Babtie Committee, paragraphs 226–34, pp. 25–6.

78 **MacPherson**, *General History*, II, p. 443.

79 **MacPherson**, *General History*, III, p. 49.

80 **WO 32/11395**, PRO, Report of the Babtie Committee, paragraph 231, p. 26.

81 **WO 95/50**, PRO, DDGMS, diary, 8 September 1915; 16 September 1915.

82 **WO 95/50**, PRO, DDGMS, diary, 13 May 1915; 23 May 1915; 25 June 1915; 8 August 1915; 9 August 1915; 17 August 1915; 8 September 1915; 4 October 1915; 14 October 1915; 5 December 1915; 12 December 1915; 16 December 1915; 20 December 1915; 23 December 1915; 29 December 1915; 7 January 1916; 10 January 1916; 14 January 1916; & February 1916. See also L.F. **Haber**, *The Poisonous Cloud: Chemical Warfare in the First World War*, Oxford, Clarendon Press, 1986; and **J.S. Haller**, 'Gas Warfare: Military-medical responsiveness of the Allies in the Great War, 1914–1918', *New York State Journal of Medicine*, Vol. 90, No. 10, 1990, pp. 499–510.

83 **Sloggett**, WIHM, RAMC 365/4, papers, joint reply of Sloggett and Advisory Board to Wright's Memorandum, 15 January 1917, p. 6.

84 **MacPherson**, *General History*, I, pp. 201–2.

85 **Suzann Buckley**, 'The Failure to Resolve the Problem of Venereal Disease among the Troops in Britain during World War I', in **Brian Bond and Ian Roy** (eds), *War and Society*, Croom Helm, 1977, p. 71.

86 *Ibid.*

87 **WO 32/5597**, PRO, Venereal Disease: Letter from the Honorary Secretary of the New Zealand Soldier's Medical Club, Hornchurch, Essex, to Sir Bryan Donkin, M.D.

88 **Suzann Buckley**, 'The failure to Resolve the Problem of Venereal Disease among the Troops in Britain during World War I', p. 76.

89 **WO 32/4745**, PRO, Checking of Venereal Disease – DORA 40 D. Discussion of Venereal Disease at the Imperial War Conference, 1917–18: 20 August 1918.

90 **Suzann Buckley**, 'The Failure to Resolve the Problem of Venereal Disease among the Troops in Britain during World War I', p. 78.

91 *Ibid*, pp. 79–80. Because of the speed with which the Government desired to deal with the problem, it was decided to appoint a committee of inquiry rather than a royal commission. The Committee adjourned when the Armistice removed the need for a continuation of 40 D.

92 **WO 32/4745**, PRO, Checking of Venereal Disease – DORA 40 D – Memorandum by the Deputy Secretary of State of War, 26 August 1918.

93 **Lord Kitchener**, Memorandum on Venereal Disease – 1905, pp. 1–3, LC, [Health, Fitness, Cleanliness – Item 5].

94 **Peter Simkins** 'Soldiers and Civilians', in **I. Beckett & K. Simpson** (eds), *A Nation in Arms*, Manchester, Manchester University Press, 1985, pp. 185–6.

95 **Gameson**, IWM, recollections, p. 366.

96 W.O. 32/5597. PRO, Venereal Disease, Letter to Lord Derby (Secretary of State for War) from Lord Sydenham, President of the NCCVD.
97 Riddell was chairman of a small committee, established with the aim of encouraging the military authorities to adopt prophylaxis as a preventive of venereal disease. The committee included Sir W. Osler, Sir Bryan Donkin, Colonel Mott, Dr Sequeira and Dr Otto May.
98 WO 32/5597, PRO, Venereal Disease: Sir George Riddell to Lord Derby, 25 January 1918.
99 'Venereal Infection', letter from Bryan Donkin, *The Times*, 4 January 1918, p. 5.
100 General Richardson, Officer Commanding New Zealand Forces.
101 WO 32/11404, PRO, Prevention of Venereal Disease, Conference Re Venereal Disease and its Treatment in the Armed Forces, May 1918: statement by General Richardson, pp. 38–9.
102 WO 32/5597, PRO, Venereal Disease, Sir George Riddell to Lord Derby, 1 February 1918. .
103 Bridget A. Towers, 'Health Education Policy, 1916–1926: Venereal Disease and the Prophylaxis Dilemma', *Medical History*, 24, 1980, p. 77.
104 In 1916, venereal disease accounted for 19.24 per cent of all admissions to hospital among British and Dominion troops in France. See Simkins, *Soldiers and Civilians*, p. 185.
105 J. McIntosh, *Studies in the Aetiology of Epidemic Influenza*, HMSO, 1922, p. 6.
106 H.J.B., Fry, LC, Diary, 27 October 1918 – 25 November 1918.
107 FD1/529, PRO, Adviser in Pathology to Director General of Medical Services, 21 December 1918.
108 See S.M. Tomkins, 'The Failure of Expertise: Public Health Policy in Britain during the 1918–1919 Influenza Epidemic', *Social History of Medicine*, vol 5, no 3, 1992, pp. 435–54.
109 W.J. Webster, RAMC 384, WIHM, Diary, 23 June 1918.
110 McIntosh, *Studies of Influenza*, p. 7.
111 War Diary of 26 General Hospital, RAMC 728/2, WIHM, November 1918.
112 Number 6 CCS, RAMC 1667, WIHM, History of Number 6 CCS, p. 23.
113 'Bacteriologists', BMJ, 1915 (I), p. 223.
114 'Cerebro-Spinal Meningitis', BMJ, 1915, (I), p. 484.
115 MacPherson, *General History*, II, pp. 307–8; Herringham, *Physician in France*, pp. 115–16.
116 Sloggett, WIHM, RAMC 365/4, papers, joint reply of Sloggett and Advisory Board to Wright's Memorandum, 15 January 1917, pp. 6–7.
117 Whitehead, *Medical Officers and the British Army during the First World War*, p. 295.
118 WO 95/196, PRO, DMS First Army, diary, May 1916, Appendix 6 – DMS First Army, Circular Memorandum No. 14, 3 May 1916.
119 WO 95/903, PRO, DDMS, XIII Corps, diary, 9 January 1917.
120 WO 95/196, PRO, DMS First Army, diary, January 1916, Appendix 20 – DMS No. 995/1, 23 January 1916.
121 WO 95/196, PRO, DMS First Army, diary, February 1916, Appendix 26 – DMS No. 1257, 14 February 1916.

122 C.S. Myers, *Shell Shock in France, 1914–1918*, Cambridge, CUP, 1940, pp. 76–110. **Miller**, *The Neuroses in War*, p. 164. **Whitehead**, 'Third Ypres – Casualties and British Medical Services: an Evaluation', in **P.H. Liddle**, *Passchendaele in Perspective*, pp. 194–5.

123 WO 95/50, PRO, DDGMS, diary, 4 October 1915.

124 **Whitehead**, 'Third Ypres – Casualties and British Medical Services: an Evaluation', in **P.H. Liddle**, *Passchendaele in Perspective*, p. 195.

125 WO 95/903, PRO, DDMS, XIII Corps, diary, 11 October 1917.

126 WO 95/196, PRO, DMS First Army, diary, 1917, Appendix 14, 10 August 1917.

127 'The Teeth of Recruits', BMJ, 1914 (II), p. 929.

128 'Dental Treatment for Soldiers', BMJ, 1914 (II), p. 378. 'British Dental Association and The War', BMJ, 1915 (I), p. 143. **Montagu F. Hopson**, 'Dental Surgery and The War', *Guy's Hospital Reports*, LXX, 1922, p. 200.

129 WO 95/52, PRO, Medical Inspector of Drafts, Diary: 4 May 1915.

130 Hopson, 'Dental Surgery and the War', *Guy's Hospital Reports*, LXX, 1922, p. 200.

131 Hopson, 'Dental Surgery and the War', *Guy's Hospital Reports*, LXX, 1922, p. 201.

132 WO 95/903, PRO, DDMS, XIII Corps, Diary: 20 July 1917.

133 **C.E.W. Bean**, *The Official History of Australia in the War of 1914–18*, Vol. III, St. Lucia, University of Queensland Press, 1982, p. 43.

134 Hopson, 'Dental Surgery and the War', *Guy's Hospital Reports*, LXX, 1922, pp. 200–1.

135 Source: Commission on Medical Establishments, WIHM, RAMC 1165, p. 85; Hopson, 'Dental Surgery and the War', *Guy's Hospital Reports*, LXX, 1922, p. 201.

136 **Captain E.C. Rycroft**, LC, Diary: 2 December 1917, p. 4.

137 Conservative MP for the Kirkdale Division of Liverpool, since 1915.

138 Hopson, 'Dental Surgery and the War', *Guy's Hospital Reports*, LXX, 1922, p. 202.

139 Commission on Medical Establishments, WIHM, RAMC 1165, p. 89; Hopson, 'Dental Surgery and the War', *Guy's Hospital Reports*, LXX, 1922, p. 202.

140 Hopson, 'Dental Surgery and the War', *Guy's Hospital Reports*, LXX, 1922, p. 203.

141 Set up in July 1917 to deal with the cases of dentists who had obtained exemption, conditional on their placing their services at the disposal of the Committee for work in districts in urgent need of dentists.

142 'Army Dental Service', BMJ, 1918 (II), p. 244.

143 Hopson, 'Dental Surgery and the War', *Guy's Hospital Reports*, LXX, 1922, p. 203.

144 **Thomas Lewis**, *The Soldier's Heart and the Effort Syndrome*, London, Shaw & Sons, 1918, pp. vii, 104–13.

Conclusion

> British medicine can look back with pride on the part it has taken in the
> war and the share it has had in the winning of it. By an appeal to results
> it is justified before the nations. The old diseases of the armies have
> been stopped, the new have been held in check; to the wounded has been
> brought instant and sustained relief.[1]

Thus the BMJ welcomed the Armistice with fulsome praise for the record
of the RAMC. These comments stand in stark contrast to the recrimina-
tions that followed the medical catastrophes of the South African
campaign. Indeed that medicine was given an adequate voice between
1914 and 1918 was in no small part due to the lessons of that earlier war.
In particular, the Army entered the First World War with a clear appreciation of the contribution to victory that preventative medicine could
provide.

Nevertheless, the transition from war to peace was not an easy one,
either for the RAMC or the civilian medical profession. The RAMC, like
the rest of the British Army, was unprepared for the scale of the Great
War. Its organization had to be expanded and its personnel augmented.
This involved a massive increase in its staff of Medical Officers which
had to be achieved by the recruitment of civilian doctors, few of whom
possessed any military experience. It was a process that required careful
assessment of military and civilian needs, and which, to be successful,
had to retain the confidence of the bodies representing professional
opinion. On the whole a successful balance was struck between the military and civilian demands on the nation's doctors. Certainly the role
given to the profession in regulating the mobilization of medical prac-

titioners was important in maintaining public confidence in the measures for safeguarding the supply of doctors. The separate arrangements for enlisting doctors were also testimony to the vigorous manner in which an increasingly confident and respected profession sought to protect its interests.

However, although successful, the system for dealing with doctors was not perfect. The Government and the military authorities acted slowly and with excessive caution over the need to establish a co-ordinated system for mobilizing the medical profession. In 1917 this deficiency began to threaten the Army's generally good relations with the medical profession. The reluctance to introduce compulsory mobilization, despite the willingness of the profession to co-operate, meant that murmurings about the Army's allegedly extravagant demands for doctors were never entirely silenced. In fact, numerous investigations revealed that on the Western Front the RAMC's employment of doctors had generally not been wasteful.

Justifiable criticism can be made of the RAMC's neglect of female practitioners and also of its slow recognition of the contribution to be made by specialists. Particularly in the early years of the War there was a tendency to view all MOs as interchangeable, with little or no consideration given to individual expertise. This stood in the way of doctors being able to institute effective measures for the prevention and treatment of certain conditions. It also affected the morale of MOs, some of whom came to regard military work as a dull routine, offering no outlet for their talents. Such opinions often resulted from ignorance of military medicine. In 1914 it had been too readily assumed that standard medical training would be an adequate preparation for the work of an army doctor. Military medicine, however, imposed a set of priorities that few doctors were accustomed to. Information was required about the inter-relationship of the various medical units; about the methods of treatment to be followed; and about the military responsibilities of the medical branch. The RAMC was slow to establish a systematic training programme which met these requirements.

Yet criticism of the RAMC administration has to be tempered by recognition of the distance that had been travelled since the Boer campaign. The RAMC demonstrated a far greater willingness to utilize the skills of civilian doctors and, in particular, to be guided by the advice of a body of distinguished consultants. The BMJ regarded this as a tribute to the leadership shown by Sir Arthur Sloggett who possessed 'a mind open to suggestions, not only as to the best conduct of medical and surgical measures and laboratory investigations, but also as to their organization, on the sound principle of choosing the best man irrespective of his army status'.[1] Moreover, although the pace of change was rather slow in some areas, such as the arrangements for dealing with shell shock, the RAMC nevertheless responded with flexibility to the emergence of trench warfare. The sanitary arrangements were modified and a system of evacuation developed that provided immediate treatment for the sick and wounded. Particularly significant was the provision of constantly improving surgical facilities ever nearer to the front; the creation of specialist treatment units; and the efforts to ensure that as many men as possible received appropriate care in France, thus maintaining the strength of the Army. The combatant branch contributed to these achievements by adopting a generally sympathetic attitude towards the work of the RAMC.

The latter proved to be a critical factor as was evident from the disastrous lack of consideration given to medicine on other fronts, such as Gallipoli, Mesopotamia and East Africa. The events in these theatres demonstrated that it could not yet be taken for granted that the medical service would be consulted when drawing up the plans for a campaign. Thus basic issues relating to evacuation of the wounded and measures for disease prevention were neglected. It also became clear that the enlightened attitudes directing the RAMC in France were not replicated elsewhere. Civilian doctors came up against a brick wall of prejudice and found that insufficient recognition was given to their professional capabilities and potential. Despite the favourable record on the Western Front the War revealed that the process of reform within the AMS had not yet reached its conclusion.

The work of the doctor on the Western Front presented surprises for both the Regular officers and those on temporary commissions. All were unprepared for the septic nature of the wounds, and MOs with experience of the Boer War were forced to reassess their surgical procedures. Meanwhile nothing in civilian practice was likely to have prepared doctors for the extent of the injuries inflicted by modern weaponry. They also had to cope with unexpected developments such as the effects of gas poisoning, and previously unencountered diseases such as trench fever. The record of the profession in developing treatments and prophylactic measures to deal with these medical challenges was one of considerable success.

Civilian doctors also had to come to terms with the differences between civilian and military medicine. In the Army the relationship was not that of doctor and patient but that of officer and soldier. The doctor had important military functions to perform, maintaining the fighting fitness of the men and sustaining morale. He could not afford to show undue sympathy to the needs of an individual whilst priority in treatment had to be given to those men most likely to return to the front. The MOs responsibility was to the wider interests of the Army and to helping defeat the enemy. This emphasis on the mass appeared to involve a departure from the Hippocratic tradition and was undoubtedly a cause of concern for some doctors. On the other hand the common roots of the civilian and military doctor should not be ignored. The War demonstrated that the medical and military duties of the MO were difficult to disentangle. The provision of immediate treatment, whilst undoubtedly reducing military wastage, was also to the benefit of the individual. Certain doctors had difficulty with the fact that they were restoring men to health, only to send them off to face danger once more. However they could, at least, take comfort from the fact that maintaining the health of the Army might help to bring the War to a quicker conclusion. Moreover, it is evident that the psychological strains of modern warfare on a non-professional army required a balance to be struck between the needs of the man and the needs of the military. The whole consisted of a collection of individuals. Thus, as long as the constraints of military discipline were not relaxed, attention to an individual's general well-being was an important element in the maintenance of morale and the avoidance of emotional disorders.

The work of RMOs and of doctors attached to the FAs proved particularly vital in preserving both the physical and mental fitness of the Army. Attacks on the employment of doctors in these roles were not justified. Their work involved the application of medical knowledge to a military task and encompassed a wide range of issues impacting upon the health of the men. Many issues pertaining to sanitation and personal hygiene actually came under the remit of military discipline, rather than being solely medical questions. The MOs with forward units played an important part in advising combatant officers on the care of their men and helped to ensure the enforcement of measures to prevent wastage.

Military experience undoubtedly opened up new professional horizons for some doctors. L.W. Batten recalls that 'Plenty besides myself got a new and permanent insight into preventive medicine,'[3] and many doctors were drawn into public health work as a result of their military experience. Prior to the War, general practitioners tended to regard public health work with disdain, seeing it as little more than an 'affair of stinks and drains'.[4] The War helped to alter this situation, improving their understanding of the field of preventive medicine.

For others the War offered an 'unrivalled' opportunity to develop their surgical skills.[5] Sir George Makins[6] noted that military service had opened up the field of surgery:

> The great outstanding features of military service lie in the possibilities which are provided by the casualties of battle for the rapid accumulation of facts and experience in a special field, and in the wide distribution of this work amongst a large number of medical men to whom under ordinary conditions the active practice of surgery might have been restricted in many instances to the narrowest limits, or even avoided with studious precaution.[7]

There were differences between military and civil surgery: at the front the age of the patients and the nature of the wounds were of a more limited range; also, in the Army the surgeon had the full might of military discipline to back him up in his decisions, whereas in civil life questions of treatment could not always be so easily determined. Doctors wishing to pursue a career in surgery based on their wartime experience would have to be aware of the need to adapt to meet the different conditions of civilian work; and the process would not be as easy as they might have imagined. Nevertheless, Makins believed that due to experience gained in the RAMC 'the foundations of many successful surgical careers have been laid'.[8]

Sir Geoffrey Keynes acknowledged the impact of military surgery on his career. He remembers being 'able to practice surgery on a huge scale in casualty clearing stations in France', and that for 'eighteen months [he] was engaged in this exciting and often rewarding work, gaining extraordinary surgical experience from thousands of operations of all types from minor injuries and fractures to abdominal, thoracic, cranial, and even cardiac emergencies'.[9] He recognized that there was a downside to the training, in that the urgency of the work made it easy to drift into bad technical habits, but this was far outweighed by the advantages. Keynes was actively involved in promoting the use of blood transfusions and developed the transfusion apparatus that became standard in Britain during the 1920s.[10] By the end of the War he had become a fully-fledged surgical specialist with the rank of major.

The War also gave a boost to other areas of medicine such as pathology and psychiatry. However its impact on the medical profession was less profound than might have been expected. The majority of doctors resumed their careers with remarkable ease. Wartime opportunities for female practitioners proved short-lived, and the profession remained a largely male bastion in the inter-war period. The War's influence can be seen in the development of teamwork and in proposals for the establishment of primary healthcare centres,[11] but in many other respects the practice of medicine remained unaltered. Moreover, whilst certain aspects of medicine grew in status during the conflict the role of war as an engine of medical progress should not be exaggerated. Many of the developments in surgery, for example, actually involved the popularizing of techniques that had already been developed prior to 1914.

Possibly the most significant fact was the failure of the War to radically transform opinion within the profession about the means for delivering civilian health care. Most doctors, having served the State during wartime, did not wish to be employed by the State in peacetime. There was widespread hostility to a salaried service which was testimony to the plentiful opportunities available to doctors. Had the War been followed by a period of significant hardship and upheaval in the profession, then it is possible more doctors might have regarded the security of a salary as outweighing their fears of excessive bureaucracy and of a loss of medical independence. Instead, the BMA was able to lead the profession in successfully resisting a salaried service, seemingly at the expense of its interest in the wider questions of medical reform. This combined with growing division and disinterest in the Government, and the demands for economic stringency, to disappoint those who had hoped that the War, and the formation of the Ministry of Health, would lead to major reform of the nation's medical service. The War raised the status of preventive medicine and during the 1920s and 1930s legislation broadened the scope of the public health services. But the opportunity for radical reconstruction was missed.[12] Thus, whilst the War clearly had an impact on the course of some individual careers, its impact on the profession as a whole, and upon civil medical provision, was more limited.

The glowing tributes paid to the RAMC's achievements might suggest that the War had finally transformed the reputation of the Corps. Certainly the record on the Western Front suggested that the disasters of the Crimean and Boer campaigns had been left far behind. Unfortunately the medical history of other theatres revealed that much remained to be done to ensure that the professional skills and potential of MOs were fully recognized. According to the BMJ, the task facing the RAMC at the end of the War was to create a system capable of 'using the talent available to the best advantage, and in the most suitable types of work'.[13]

Evidently service in the RAMC did little to alter doctors' perceptions of military medicine as a career. When the War ended most doctors wished to return as quickly as possible to civilian employment. However the rapid demobilization of MOs caused difficulties for the RAMC because its work with the Armies abroad continued to demand a large medical personnel. Referring to the situation in France in March 1919 the *Lancet* feared that the pace of demobilization might have been too quick 'since even now there is an obvious shortage of doctors for the existing hospitals'.[14] The influenza epidemic had placed a great strain on the hospitals in France, where there were also large numbers of wounded men requiring prolonged treatment. Similar difficulties were experienced on other fronts. This situation prompted the War Office to make an appeal for young doctors (including those still in service, and those recently demobilized) to accept new terms of temporary commissions. The contract was to last for a year, or until the officers' services were no longer required, whichever was the sooner, and the rate of pay was set at £550 per annum.

Response to this appeal was poor.[15] An uncompetetive pay rate partly accounted for the unattractiveness of the offer. But according to the BMJ, suspicion of the War Office was an influential factor. Officers serving, or recently demobilized, had reacted unfavourably to the appeal; and it was felt that their opinion 'must greatly influence young men who have not yet served'.[16] Particularly significant were the views of Territorial and Special Reserve MOs, few of whom were willing to consider re-enlistment. They remained bitter about the poor terms under which they had served, compared with Temporary Commissioned officers. It was claimed that only by making up this deficiency could the Government expect to win over the support of these men and dispel the distrust of those who had yet to serve.[17]

The freedom of the War Office to terminate the contract whenever it chose also contributed to the lack of appeal, as the arrangement was considered to be too one-sided. In any case the commitment of Winston Churchill, the Secretary of State, to a rapid demobilization of the forces, encouraged medical men to believe that their services would be required for no more than a few months. Most doctors therefore preferred to take their chances immediately in the civil profession, rather than risk missing out on professional opportunities by signing up to this temporary contract.

However the problems facing the RAMC were not simply short-term. Service in the Corps had left most doctors with the impression that administrative skill was valued above professional expertise. The RAMC on the Western Front had recognized the valuable contribution to be made by specialists, yet opportunities for promotion on grounds of

258

medical ability remained limited. This contributed to a general impression that the AMS remained a professional backwater. As the figures below demonstrate, this was a perception that continued to impact upon the recruitment of MOs:[18]

DATE	ESTABLISHMENT (RAMC Officers)	STRENGTH (RAMC Officers)
1 October 1922	1,069	1,066
1 October 1923	959	898
1 October 1924	918	850
1 October 1925	888	813
1 October 1926	876	798
1 October 1927	872	802
1 October 1928	851	774
1 October 1929	848	771
1 October 1930	823	730

In May 1931, a committee was appointed under the chairmanship of Sir Warren Fisher to determine the causes of this shortage. The perceived lack of professional opportunities emerged as the principal factor. According to the civilian representatives on the Committee,[19] the opportunities available were more extensive than was generally believed, but conditions of service continued to restrict professional advancement.[20] The Committee made the following recommendations for the broadening of professional opportunity:

> a) eliminating from the establishment to the greatest degree possible parts which provide insufficient professional opportunity, and thus increasing the proportion of an officer's career spent in posts which give interesting professional work, and particularly in hospital posts;
> b) adopting an organization allowing of a larger proportion of officers specializing, and of their spending a larger period of their career in specialist work;
> c) improving the opportunity of continuing in professional, as distinct from administrative, work as an officer rises to the higher ranks.[21]

These points were accompanied by suggestions for improving the economic position of Medical Officers, which had again fallen well behind the financial opportunities available in civil life. The reforms, consequent upon the Warren Fisher Report, contributed to a revival of recruitment on the eve of the Second World War.

Thus, in the aftermath of the Great War, the RAMC began to recognize the importance of giving priority to medical skill as a means of advancement, and of ensuring that opportunities for professional improvement were widened. Throughout its history the AMS has been unable to compete with the financial and professional rewards available in civilian life.[1] However, the advances made between the wars demonstrated that the Corps could attract enough doctors of a sufficiently high calibre if it maximized an MO's medical work, and provided regular opportunities for further study and specialization.

The medical profession could look back on its record during the First World War in the knowledge that this had been a doctor's war, in a way that no previous conflict had been. The achievements of British medicine on the Western Front were matched by the medical services of other belligerent powers. Britain, however, was less accustomed than most of her European neighbours to the management of a citizen army. She had successfully expanded her military medical organization, and had managed to mobilize the medical profession without causing substantial disruption to civilian medical care. On the whole the Army had capitalized on the improvement in its relations with the profession which had begun in the Edwardian period. Meanwhile the conduct of the medical war had benefited from closer co-operation between civilian and military doctors. The latter assisted the on-going process of professionalization in the RAMC, as seen in the better prospects for specialization in the post-war service. The War also provided doctors with opportunities to gain experience of techniques which became standard in civilian practice.

However, the War did not lead to a revolution in the delivery of health care in Britain. The attitudes and practices that characterized the profession in the inter-war period showed a marked continuity with those prior to 1914. Nothing revealed this more clearly than the profession's views concerning the RAMC. Generally speaking, doctors accepted that they had performed vital military work, and had been prepared to accept the constraints that military discipline had placed upon their professional freedom. In peacetime most wished to reassert their professional independence, and to escape from what they regarded as the excessive bureaucracy of the AMS. Thus their war experiences had helped to reinforce the opposition of many doctors to a State medical service.

Notes

1   'The End Crowns All', BMJ, 1918, (II), p. 550.
2   'The Fifth Year', BMJ, 1918, (II), p. 138.
3   L.W. Batten, LC, Papers: letter to son, 18 March 1970.

4   Arthur S. MacNalty, *The History of State Medicine in England*, The Royal Institute of Public Health and Hygiene, 1948, p. 64.
5   McLaughlin, *The Royal Army Medical Corps*, Leo Cooper, 1972, p. 35.
6   President of the Royal College of Surgeons of England.
7   George H. Makins, 'Introductory', BJS, VI, 1918–19, p. 1.
8   *Ibid*, p. 10.
9   Sir Geoffrey Keynes, LC, Papers: Recollections entitled A Doctor's War, pp. 197–9.
10 Sir Geoffrey Keynes, LC, Tape recordings 556 & 557.
11 See Roger Cooter 'War And Modern Medicine', in W.F. Bynum & R. Porter (eds), *Companion Encyclopaedia of the History of Medicine*, London & New York, Routledge, 1993, p. 1547.
12 For a detailed discussion of medical developments in the inter-war years, see Honigsbaum, *The Division in British Medicine*, chapters 8–15.
13 'The Fifth Year', BMJ, 1918 (II), p. 138.
14 'France – Medical Demobilisation', *Lancet*, 1919 (I), p. 477.
15 'Recruiting for the RAMC', BMJ, 1919 (I), p. 803. MacPherson, 'General History', I, p. 230.
16 'RAMC Contracts', BMJ, 1919 (II), pp. 144–145; letter from 'Ex-Service Man', p. 189.
17 'RAMC Contracts', letter from Captain RAMC T, BMJ, 1919 (II), p. 155; letter from J.G. Bennett, p. 189.
18 *The General Annual Reports on the British Army*, 1922, cmd. 2114, 1924, IV, p. 637; *1923*, cmd. 2272, 1924, XIV, p. 777; *1924*, cmd. 2342, 1924–25, XVII, p. 891; *1925*, cmd. 2582, 1926, XVIII, p. 905; *1926*, cmd. 2806, 1927, XIV, p. 905; *1927*, cmd. 3030, 1928, XIV, p. 911; *1928*, cmd. 3265, 1928–29, XI, p. 913; *1929*, cmd. 3498, 1929–39 XIX, p. 895; *1930*, cmd. 3800, 1930–31, XIX, p. 879.
19 Professor G.E. Gask, Surgeon and Director of the Surgical Unit, St Bartholomew's Hospital; Professor of Surgery in the University of London; Member of the Radium Commission; Consulting Surgeon, King Edward VII's Convalescent Home for Officers. Dr A.M.H. Gray, Physician in Charge, Skin Department, University College Hospital; Dean and Lecturer on Dermatology in University College Hospital Medical School; Physician for Diseases of the Skin, Hospital for Sick Children, Great Ormond Street.
20 *Warren Fisher Report*, cmd. 4394, 1932–33, XI, pp. 10–12.
21 *Ibid.*, p. 45.
22 For references to the RAMC's difficulties in the 1950s and the 1970s see: General Sir Neil Cantlie, WIHM, RAMC 465, Papers: draft of a letter to the *Daily Telegraph*, 28 October 1953. Ministry of Defence, *Report of the Defence Medical Services Inquiry Committee*, HMSO, 1973.

Appendices

APPENDIX A: SCHEMES FOR THE PROTECTION OF ABSENTEES

AGREEMENT DRAWN UP IN HOLLAND (LINCS) AREA*

1. Each of the practitioners at home hereby promises and agrees with each of the practitioners on service that if any persons who are ordinarily patients of any of the practitioners on service shall consult him during the absence of such practitioner on service the practitioner at home will not attend such patients, or arrange for their being attended, except on the terms hereinafter mentioned, and further, that he will refuse to act as the medical attendant of such persons on his own behalf from the date of the return of the practitioner on service until at least twelve calendar months have elapsed, and will in every way do all in his power to safeguard the interests of the practitioner on service in such patients, and to induce them to return to him when he resumes practice.

2. The fees actually received by any practitioner on service shall be divided between the person receiving the same and the practitioner on service to whom such patients belong in the following proportions:

a) Where the practice is a mixed town and country practice three-eighths shall belong to the practitioner on service and five-eighths to the practitioner at home doing the work and paying all expenses.

*Source: BMJ, 1916 (II), Supplement, pp. 29–30.

b) Where the practice is a country practice one-fourth shall belong to the practitioner on service and three-fourths to the practitioner at home doing the work and paying all expenses.

c) Where the professional service is rendered in respect of an appointment held by a practitioner on service, including panel work, one-half shall belong to the practitioner on service and one-half to the practitioner at home doing the work and paying the expenses.

d) In the case of confinements the whole fee shall go to the practitioner at home doing the work and paying the expenses.

3. In the event of the death of a practitioner on service his practice shall be carried on for one year after that date or until his representatives give notice to one or more of the practitioners at home that they have disposed of the practice, whichever shall first happen, and in the meantime the representatives of the deceased practitioner shall be entitled to receive, and shall be paid, the same remuneration as the deceased practitioner would have been entitled to if he had during such time continued to be a practitioner on service.

4. Nothing in these presents shall be held to compel any practitioner at home to treat any patient or patients of any practitioner on service.

5. During the continuance of this agreement no practitioner at home shall engage a locumtenent or qualified assistant in his practice for a period exceeding fourteen consecutive days until a locumtenent or assistant shall have signed this agreement or a similar agreement embodying the terms comprised therein.

6. If any person in the First Schedule hereto shall hereafter during the continuance of this agreement obtain a temporary commission in the Royal Army Medical Corps, or in any other branch of the Army or Royal Naval Medical Service, his practice shall, during his absence, be carried on by the remaining practitioners at home on the terms above set forth, and this agreement shall be construed in all respects as though such person had originally been a person mentioned in the Second Schedule hereto, and if any person in the Second Schedule shall not be called upon to leave his practice he shall be deemed to be a practitioner at home, and he shall have the same rights and be under the same obligations as though he had originally been a party mentioned in the First Schedule hereto.

SCHEME OF DR T. CAMPBELL OF WIGAN*

1. Any medical man deciding to take up a commission or being called up for ordinary military service (hereinafter referred to as the absentee) to at once give notice to the Committee referred to in paragraph 18 hereof, and such notice shall signify whether the absentee has made arrangements with a medical practitioner or practitioners (hereinafter called the deputy) to carry on his practice in his absence and, if arrangements have been so made, the name or names or address or addresses of such practitioner or practitioners.

2. If at the date of the said notice the absentee has not made arrangements with a deputy, he should as soon as he has so done forward to the said Committee the name and address of the deputy.

3. If the absentee fails to appoint a deputy, then the said Committee on the request of the absentee or his wife or other authorized representative, can make an appointment. The authorized representative of the absentee shall be given power of attorney to act on his behalf.

4. The remuneration of the deputy to be agreed as by the absentee, but in case no arrangement as to remuneration is made, or in case of an appointment by the said Committee, the remuneration to be on the following scale – namely:

> £1 1s. per week for every £100 gross receipts of the practice during the twelve months ending December 31 immediately preceding the deputy's appointment, with a maximum weekly remuneration of £12 12s. and a minimum of £3 3s.

The said remuneration to be readjusted every six calendar months in accordance with the scale fixed by this paragraph on the gross receipts for the twelve months preceding the date of readjustment. Any fees payable by the army authorities to the absentee for any appointment held by him shall not be included in the gross receipts of the practice during the preceding twelve months unless the work of such appointment be taken over and carried out by the deputy.

5. The deputy to defray out of his remuneration all the working costs and expenses of the absentee's practice except the rent, rates, and taxes of the absentee's main and branch surgeries.

*Source: BMJ, 1916 (II), Supplement, p. 30.

6. The deputy to keep each day a strict account of his visits, consultations, dressings, operations, and medicines, with the name and addresses of the patients on whom attendance is made, by entering same up in absentee's day book, differentiating between private patients and panel patients (if necessary) and to leave such day book open to inspection of the absentee's wife or other representative, who must enter same into ledger at least once a week.

7. The record cards of panel patients to be accurately kept by the deputy.

8. The deputy to keep an accurate account of all moneys received by him on account of the absentee's practice, and to hand such moneys to the absentee's wife or his other representative on the first of each calendar month. Any clerical work connected with the absentee's practice other than that necessitated by paragraphs 6, 7, and 8 hereof to be done by the absentee's wife or other representative at the absentee's expense.

9. Cards to be exhibited in the surgeries (main and branch) of both deputy and absentee clearly stating that the absentee is away on active service and that the deputy is attending to absentee's practice, and requesting the patient to inform the deputy that he is a patient of the absentee.

10. As far as conveniently possible, the patients of the absentee to be seen at the surgeries of the latter, and the deputy to hold a surgery daily at the absentee's main surgery.

11. The absentee before leaving his practice to make out a list of his private patients, with their addresses, and to submit such list to the deputy, and such list, unless questioned within fourteen days by the latter, to be final evidence that the patients whose names appear on that list are the private patients of the absentee. A copy of such list to be forwarded by the absentee to the said Committee.

12. Proper and accurate accounts of the absentee's practice to be sent out by the absentee's wife or other representative in the name of the absentee with a request that cheques be drawn in favour of the absentee.

13. All accounts of the gross receipts of the absentee's practice to be kept by the absentee's wife or other representative, and to be open to the inspection of the deputy or his representative on request at any reasonable hour of the day.

14. The absentee should be indemnified against all claims, demands, or actions arising out of the negligence or wrongful act or default of the

deputy. (It is deemed advisable that absentee and deputy be members of a protection society and be insured against damages.)

15. Subject to the provisions of the next clause the deputy to give six calendar months' notice of his intention to resign to the absentee's wife or other representative, and also to the said Committee, whereupon, in the absence of an appointment being made by the absentee or his wife or other representative, of a fresh deputy, the said Committee to make an appointment.

16. In case the absentee die or be killed, or return home but incapable of attending to his practice, the deputy to continue to attend to the absentee's practice for at least a period of twelve months after the date of such death, or of such return home, as the case may be, or until the absentee's practice is disposed of by sale, the deputy during this period to continue to receive remuneration as provided in paragraph 4. The deputy to give every facility and information to an intending purchaser.

17. The deputy shall not attend or otherwise professionally advise or treat any of the patients on the list referred to in paragraph 11 hereof for a period of one year after the deputy has ceased to carry on, or otherwise to be associated with, the practice of the absentee.

18. A committee to be formed by the practitioners of the district (or, if thought advisable, the Local Medical War Committee), and to have relegated to it by the agreement entered into by the absentee and deputy such powers as will permit it to deal with all disputes of whatsoever nature arising between the absentee and the deputy in regard to any question affecting the absentee's practice or the carrying on of the same by the deputy, and the decision of such committees to be binding on both parties.

APPENDIX B: C.M.W.C. PROCEDURE FOR SAFEGUARDING THE PRACTICES OF ABSENTEES*

1. On a new patient presenting himself he should be asked the name of the doctor who last attended him. If his doctor is absent on service and has left a locum tenens an attempt should be made to induce the patient to go to the locum tenens.

*Circular addressed to all members of the medical profession. Source: BMJ, 1916 (II), Supplement, p. 141.

2. If the last doctor who attended be on military service it should be explained to the patient that attendance will willingly be given *on behalf of that practitioner* and on no other terms.

3. Any attendances on behalf of such patients should be carefully and separately recorded, and a list of such attendances sent at regular intervals to the representative of the absentee.

4. An attempt should be made to ascertain the fees charged by the absentee, and a charge not less than this should be made on his behalf.

5. Accounts rendered on behalf of the absentee (if sent in by the deputy) should mention the absentee's name, and moneys received should be divided according to the scheme adopted by the Local Medical War Committee.

6. The rule of dividing the fees should apply to all kinds of work. No exception, for example, should be made as regards operations, inquests, consultations, and anaesthetics, unless some special arrangement has been arrived at as regards particular services by the Local Medical War Committee after consulting the local profession.

7. New patients introduced by the patient of an absentee should be regarded as belonging to the absentee's practice.

8. In cases in which the patient's frequent change of doctor leads to doubt as to who should be regarded as the regular attendant, the absentee should be given the benefit of the doubt.

9. No patient attended on behalf of an absentee should be attended by the deputy for at least one year after the absentee's return.

10. The greatest discretion should be used as to the introduction of a partner or assistant or in commencing a new practice in an area from which men are absent on service.

11. Great care should be taken in the buying and selling of practices. Newcomers to a district should be doubly scrupulous in regard to the practice of absentees and should at once ascertain and join in any arrangements that have been made for the protection of absent practitioners.

12. The honour of the profession is specially involved where a vacancy occurs through the death of a practitioner on service. Definite arrangements have been made to meet such a contingency in some areas and should be made in all. Every assistance should be given in enabling the

successor to the practice to have such a fair start as will enable the dependants on the practice to expect a fair price for it. The local practitioners should carry out the same procedure with regard to the successor as they had undertaken with regard to the man who has fallen while on service – namely, refuse to attend the patients of the practice, except on behalf of the successor, for a period of at least a year after the practice has been taken over.

13. In all cases of doubt as to what is the right course of action as regards an absentee the practitioner should consider what he would like his neighbours to do if he were absent on military service. The Local Medical War Committee will always be glad to advise.

APPENDIX C: MOBILIZATION OF THE MEDICAL PROFESSION.

MANCHESTER REPORT ON THE NEED FOR COMPULSION.*

[DETAILS OF THE WORKING OF THE SYSTEM]

[1. *Provision of Medical Officer for the Forces.*]

When a call is made by the Central Committee or an application for a commission submitted, the medical needs of the particular section of the area, or public appointment, are considered before a decision is made.

The disabilities under which the Committee labours in this respect are (a) that candidates otherwise suitable cannot be selected because the result would be depletion in a particular neighbourhood; (b) that doctors who can be spared are found unfit for service or fit for home service only; (c) that the Committee in selecting whole-time officers for service is over-ruled by Government departments; and (d) that the Committee has no means of dealing with conscientious objectors.

[2. *Conservation of Practices.*]

This is carried out under terms of a signed agreement by which patients of practitioners on service are attended by signatories, records of non-panel work are forwarded, on cards provided, to the honorary

*Source: BMJ, 1917 (I), Supplement, pp. 9–10.

accountants, who send out accounts and apportion the sums received between the practitioner on service and the home practitioner in equal shares. Cash payments are accounted for on special cards. Insurance work in Manchester being carried out on the principle of free choice of doctors, pooling the money due and dividing periodically in accordance with work done, insured patients of practitioners on service can get attention from any signatory; panel doctors being credited with the attendance and being paid in the ordinary way, and non panel doctors sending in a record, on a special card, to the honorary accountants, who pay for the attendance at a fixed rate and recover the amount from the insurance pool. Panel doctors have agreed to deductions being made from the gross pool to allow of these sums being paid and to ensure payment to panel practitioners on service of an annual sum equal to half that earned during the last complete insurance year prior to taking up a commission. Printed notices to patients are hung up in all consulting and waiting rooms.

The disabilities of the Committee in this respect are: (a) That 20 per cent. of practitioners have not agreed to work the official scheme, and are thus outside the control of the Committee; this tends to confuse the public. (b) That there is difficulty in obtaining information as to the manner in which those who have signed the scheme fulfil their obligations. (c) Dilatoriness of the profession in entering up the cards and sending them to the honorary accountants. (d) Omission to ask a new patient who last attended him.

[3. Co-ordination of Civil Work.]

Part-time service is supplied from amongst those who have specified the work they can undertake. Full-time service is provided in certain instances by part-time men working on a rota. Co-ordination is effected by dividing the work amongst those best suited by qualification and ability to spare the time.

The disabilities of the Committee in this respect are as follows: (a) No power to make a doctor live at his surgery should a district become depleted. (b) No power to release a practitioner eligible for military service by substituting one who is ineligible. (c) No control over those who obtained temporary part-time appointments before mobilisation and who have since refused to fall into line. (d) No power to make use of conscientious objectors. (e) No power to prevent doctors undertaking work without sanction from the Committee. (f) No power to transfer a doctor from a non-depleted district to a depleted district.

269

1. To obtain any particulars from medical men which may be considered by the Committee as necessary to carry out its objects.

2. To compel every general practitioner to act in accordance with the scheme for conservation of practices already accepted by a large majority in the area.

3. To transfer for long or short periods any medical man unsuitable for military service from an area or section of an area which could spare him to another area or section of an area where his professional services are urgently needed. These doctors could be guaranteed payment by Government at the army rate for temporary commissions in the RAMC, ready cash from and accounts of work done for private patients being booked up on the proper cards and sent in to the War Committee's accountants, and money earned on account of insured patients being credited to the War Committee, less deductions for absent practitioners' fund. Payment could be made by the War Committee, the home practitioners' share of money earned being credited to the guarantor up to the amount of salary paid. The practices of those doctors could be conserved as in the case of those on military service. It would also be advisable for long-period substitutes to do this work outside their own area if powers are made general.

4. To order, when necessary, any doctor to reside at the place where he practises.

5. To decide generally how the services of civil practitioners, including conscientious objectors, can best be utilized for national purposes.

6. To control the making of temporary part-time appointments and to revise such when necessary or advisable. This revision would forward the Committee's policy of finding as much paid work as possible for doctors returning from service.

7. To obtain notification of the hearing of any case of conscientious objection, and to be represented at the local tribunal in such cases.

8. To prevent Government departments vetoing decisions on eligibility for service of whole-time medical officers engaged on executive work or as assistants to administrative medical officers.

9. To make a monetary grant to meet administrative expenses and salaries paid to transferred practitioners.

10. To make provision for dealing with breaches of regulations summarily, with a right of appeal to a central body.

[CONCLUSIONS]

1. Every registered medical practitioner should be deemed to be a member of the medical military forces of the kingdom as from a given date.

2. The control of the medical profession for war purposes should be vested in a Central Committee attached to the Department of National Service, and consisting of the Presidents of the Royal Colleges of Physicians and Surgeons respectively, and five members elected by the profession.

3. Whilst better co-ordination of existing medical manpower in the Army might be distinctly advantageous, there is no doubt that the alleged shortage would be remedied to an appreciable extent by the granting of Home Service Commissions to those certified as physically fitted for such.

4. Any scheme for regulating medical service at home should be promulgated with a view to obtaining the highest amount of efficiency, which would prove an impossible task if saddled with the voluntary principle.

5. 'Voluntary mobilisation' could not remove the present deadlock, created on the one hand by the demand of the Insurance Commissioners for efficient panel medical service, and on the other hand by the refusal of Government departments to release eligible young doctors.

6. The Manchester system of 'mobilization' could be adapted to every area in the country, and would prove a success if properly organised and local committees were given power, subject to appeal, to decide all local adjustments and arrangements.

APPENDIX D: SCHEME OF MEDICAL ADMINISTRATION OF AN ARMY OF THE B.E.F. FRANCE, 1916.*

General Headquarters

DGMS
ADGMS DDGMS
Inspector of drafts ADMS Consulting Surgeon
DADMS Consulting Physician
DADMS

Headquarters Lines Of Communication

DMS
DDMS ADMS Sanitation
ADMS DADMS Adviser in Pathology
DADMS Ambulance Trains

Headquarters of Army
DMS
ADMS
Consulting Surgeon
Sanitary Officer

CorpsHQ	*Corps HQ*	*Corps HQ*
DDMS	DDMS	DDMS
DADMS	DADMS	DADMS

Divisional HQ	*Divisional HQ*	*Divisional HQ*
ADMS	ADMS	ADMS
DADMS	DADMS	DADMS

* Source:MacPherson, *General History*, II, p. 13. For a full description of the development of the administration on the Western Front see pp. 1–14. Similar dispositions were made in armies on other fronts. For further details about the administration in Egypt see **MacPherson**, *General History*, III, pp. 368–72; for Italy see **MacPherson**, *General History*, III, pp. 335–8.

APPENDIX E: FIRST ARMY SCHOOL OF INSTRUCTION CURRICULUM*

SYLLABUS FOR REGIMENTAL OFFICERS AND OTHER RANKS

DAY ONE:

9.00–9.30 a.m.	Physical drill
10.00–10.30 a.m.	Address and practical demonstration 'Arrest of haemorrhage'
10.30–11.00 a.m.	Practical demonstration (given by Major O'Hagan)
11.00 a.m.	Practical demonstration 'sanitary appliances' (Captain Jacobs)
Noon:	Lecture 'The Care of Feet. The Prevention of Trench Foot' (Captain Price)
2.00–3.30 p.m.	Practical demonstration 'Thomas Splint' (Captain Cowell)
3.30–4.30 p.m.	Construction of sanitary appliances (sanitary orderlies only)

DAY TWO:

9.00–9.30 a.m.	Physical drill
10.00–11.00 a.m.	Practical demonstration 'First Aid': i) wound shock ii) Blanket packet (Captain Cowell)
11.00 a.m.	Lecture 'Prevention of Disease' (Captain Moss Blundell)
Noon:	Practical demonstration 'Care of Water Carts' (Captain Jacobs)
2.00–3.30 p.m.	Practical demonstration 'Thomas Splint' (Captain Cowell)
3.30–4.30 p.m.	Construction of sanitary appliances (sanitary orderlies only)

DAY THREE:

9.00–9.30 a.m.	Physical drill
10.00–11.00 a.m.	Practical demonstration: triangular bandage and rifle splint

*Source: **Major General Ernest Cowell**, Papers, WIHM., RAMC 466.

11.00 a.m.	Lecture 'Conservancy in the Field' (Captain Jacobs)
Noon:	Lecture and demonstration: 'First Aid'; Specimens; Xrays (Captain Cowell)
2.00–3.30 p.m.	Practical demonstration 'Thomas Splint' (Captain Cowell)
3.30–4.30 p.m.	Construction of sanitary appliances (sanitary orderlies only)

DAY FOUR:

9.00–9.30 a.m.	Physical drill
10.00–11.00 a.m.	Practical demonstration: triangular bandage (Captain Cowell)
11.00 a.m.	Competition: 'Thomas Splint'. Address, inspection parade, march past.
2.00 p.m.	Return to units.

COURSE FOR OFFICERS AND OTHER RANKS RAMC

DAY ONE:

8.30–9.30 a.m.	Physical drill
9.15–9.45 a.m.	[NCOs and men] Lecture: Duties in camp
10.00 a.m.	Opening address (DMS First Army). General lecture on surgery (Surgeon General Wallace)
11.00 a.m.	Practical demonstration: Thomas splint (Captain McDonald)
Noon:	General lecture: War medicine (Surgeon General Sir W. Herringham)
2.00 p.m.	Squad company drill
3.00–4.30 p.m.	Riding for half the officers. Practical sanitation for the remainder

DAY TWO

8.30–9.30 a.m.	Physical drill
9.15–9.45 a.m.	[NCOs and men] Lecture: Relation of NCOs to other ranks
10.00 a.m.	Lecture: Prevention of sick wastage (Captain Parkinson)
11.00 a.m.	Practical demonstration: Thomas splint (Captain McDonald)
Noon:	Diseases of the War (Colonel Saltau)

| 2.00 p.m. | Squad company drill |
| 3.00–4.30 p.m. | Riding for half the officers. Practical sanitation for the remainder. |

DAY THREE

8.30–9.30 a.m.	Physical drill
9.15–9.45 a.m.	[NCOs and men] Lecture: Relation of NCOs to other ranks
10.00 a.m.	Lecture: Conservancy in the field (Captain Jacobs)
11.00 a.m.	Practical demonstration: Thomas splint (Captain McDonald)
Noon:	Lecture: Gas gangrene (Major Wallace)
2.00 p.m.	Squad company drill
3.00–4.30 p.m.	Riding for half the officers. Practical sanitation for the remainder.

DAY FOUR [*Sunday*]:

8.30–9.30 a.m.	Physical drill
9.15–9.45 a.m.	–
9.45 a.m.	Church parade
11.00 a.m.	Lecture: Medical organisation (Colonel Young)
Noon:	Lecture: War surgery (Surgeon General Sir A. Bowlby)
2.00–4.30 p.m.	–

DAY FIVE:

8.30–9.30 a.m.	Physical drill
9.15–9.45 a.m.	[NCOs and men] Lecture; Duties of NCOs
10.00 a.m.	Lecture: Surgery of the War (Surgeon General Wallace)
11.00 a.m.	Practical demonstration: Triangular bandage (Captain McDonald)
Noon:	Lecture: War neurology (Lieutenant Colonel Gordon Holmes)
2.00 p.m.	Squad company drill
3.00–4.30 p.m.	Riding for half the officers. Practical sanitation for the remainder.

DAY SIX:

| 8.30-9.30 a.m. | Physical drill |
| 9.15–9.45 a.m. | [NCOs and men] Lecture: Duties of NCOs |

10.00 a.m.	Lecture: Pathology of medical diseases in War (Major McNee)
11.00 a.m.	Practical demonstration: Triangular bandage and use of the rifle splint (Captain Cowell)
Noon:	Lecture: Pyrexia Unknown Origin (Colonel Saltau)
2.00 p.m.	Squad company drill
3.00–4.30 p.m.	Riding for half the officers. Practical sanitation for the remainder
4.30 p.m.	Medical discussion

DAY SEVEN:

8.30–9.30 a.m.	Physical drill
9.15–9.45 a.m.	[NCOs and men] Lecture: Offence reports
10.00–10.30 a.m.	Address and practical demonstration 'Arrest of Haemorrhage'
10.30–11.00 a.m.	Practical demonstration (Major O'Hagan)
11.00 a.m.	Lecture: Surgery of the War (Surgeon General Wallace)
Noon:	Practical demonstration: Thomas splint (Captain Cowell)
2.00 p.m.	Lecture: Horsemanship (Colonel Saunders)
3.00–4.00 p.m.	Riding for half the officers. Practical sanitation for the remainder
4.00–4.30 p.m.	Map reading

DAY EIGHT

8.30–9.30 a.m.	Physical drill
9.15–9.45 a.m.	[NCOs and men] Lecture
10.00 a.m.	Lecture: Gas poisoning (Captain Douglas)
11.00 a.m.	Demonstration: Saddle-filling etc. (Major Saunders)
Noon:	Lecture: Wound shock (Captain Cowell)
2.00 p.m.	Squad company drill
3.00–4.30 p.m.	School of Cookery
4.30 p.m.	Discussion

DAY NINE

| 8.30–9.30 a.m. | Physical drill |
| 9.15–9.45 a.m. | [NCOs and men] Lecture: Duties on the line of march |

10.00 a.m.	Lecture: Indenting etc. (Lieutenant Colonel Goodwin)
11.00 a.m.	Practical demonstration: Thomas splint (Captain Cowell)
Noon:	Lecture: Gunshot Wound of the Chest (Colonel Saltau)
2.00 p.m.	Squad company drill
3.00–4.30 p.m.	School of Cookery
4.30 p.m.	Discussion on shock

DAY TEN

8.30–9.30 a.m.	–
9.15–9.30.a.m.	–
10.00 a.m.	Lecture: Military Law (Captain Thorpe)
11.00 a.m.	Competition: Thomas splint. Address by DMS First Army. Inspection parade and march past.
2.00 p.m.	Return to units.

APPENDIX F: THE DISTRIBUTION OF MEDICAL UNITS IN THE FIELD

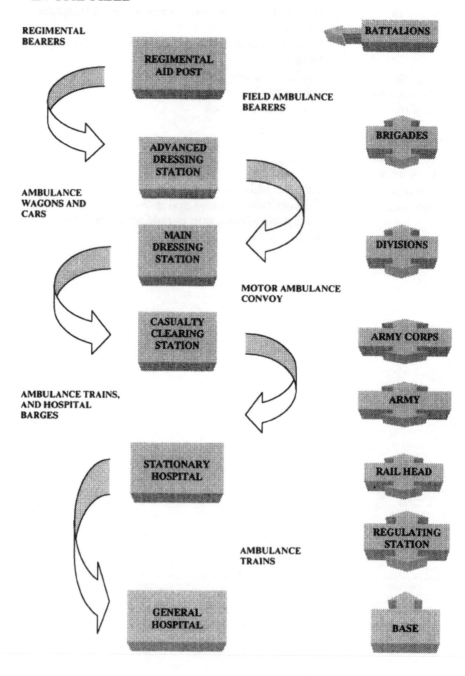

APPENDIX G: TABLE OF PREVENTIVE MEASURES TAKEN IN THE VARIOUS ARMIES AGAINST CONTRACTION OF VD. *

	British (in France)	British (UK scheme)	French	American	German
Lectures on VD and preventive measures	Given in several instances, but not under official instruction or sanction	MO of unit is to impress on men the great importance of making full use of early treatment room after exposure to infection	To be given by MOs to all soldiers, illustrated if possible by lantern slides or cinema	To be given frequently by MOs	Instruction by MO to all ranks; lectures by officers and chaplains
Provision of recreation rooms to keep men pleasantly occupied	Plenty are provided by various organizations	Not mentioned	Not mentioned	These are to be established	Reading and recreation rooms provided
Inspections of men	Nil	Not mentioned	To be carried out fortnightly; men to be examined separately and with greatest discretion. Men going on and returning from leave to be examined	To be carried out twice a month	Everybody, including voluntary aid personnel to be examined twice a month and on going and returning from leave
Inspection of women	Only where a woman is identified as being the cause of an infection and then by French authorities	Not mentioned	Registered prostitutes outside brothels to be examined twice a week	Not mentioned	Bi-weekly examination of prostitutes and of women from whom disease has been contracted
Inspections of brothels	Placed out of bounds to all troops	Not mentioned	All women inspected daily	Placed out of bounds to all troops	Women inspected twice weekly
Early treatment rooms – where established	At all bases except Étaples, Boulogne, Trouville, Marseilles and Abancourt	Medical inspection rooms in depots etc.	Not mentioned	At all camps and depots	At all regimental inspection rooms
Early treatment rooms – supervision of	An orderly not necessarily RAMC in attendance only	Under the charge of an MO	Not mentioned	Treatment to be carried out under actual supervision of a trained orderly	Not mentioned

Early treatment rooms – measures adopted	Syringing with Potassium Permanganate and application of Calomel Cream. In Paris men may take these materials away and disinfect in private	As with British troops in France	Not mentioned	Injection and ointment. Actual drugs not stated	Calomel ointment. 10% solution of Protargo. Viro, Samariter, etc.
Early treatment rooms – general	Orderlies are forbidden to take names	Not mentioned	Not mentioned	A careful register is kept which is strictly confidential	Not mentioned
Disciplinary action	Hospital stoppages. Restrictions on leave. Identification of infective women	Not mentioned	No leave for men likely to be contagious. Identification of infective women.	All ranks who contract VD to be court-martialled unless they have been to an early treatment room; they are ordered to go to these rooms within 3 hours of connection. Patients with the disease to work as far as possible and be denied all privileges. Brothels and infected women out of bounds. Drunken soldiers returning to camp to be seized by the guard and if necessary forcibly treated in the prophylactic centres.	Not mentioned except that careful military supervision of brothels will be carried out and compulsory treatment of infected women.

* In addition the Germans had the following measures in force: 1. Issue of certificates to prostitutes showing date of last examination; 2. Issue of preventatives to prostitutes for use of clients; 3.Giving employment to women and young girls to enable them to earn an honourable livelihood; 4. Wassermann Test of all, who, for their own satisfaction, wish it to be applied. Source of table: WO 95/47, PRO, DGMS Diary, 18 May 1918.

Bibliography

PRIMARY SOURCES

MANUSCRIPT SOURCES

Bodleian Library, Oxford
Sir Henry Burdett papers

Imperial War Museum, London
Papers of the following:

Dible, J.H.

Esler, M.S.

Gameson, L.

Gill, J.G.

Greaves, S.S.

Habgood, A.H.

Hamilton, E.S.B.

Henderson, P.H.

Hind, J.E.

Hughes, G.W.

Johnson, F.W.

Lodge Patch, C.J.

MacKenzie, M.D.

Mayne, W.J.F.

McTavish, G.B.

Murphy, R.W.

Owens, H.B.

Stack, E.H.

Liddle Collection, University of Leeds

Papers of the following:

Adair, G.S.	Deane, N.S.	Moor, F.
Ashton, W.W.	De Grolian, J.	Moore, G.
Atkinson, A.	Escritt, F.K.	Newton, O.
Auger, E.	Fairley, G.D.	Nicholls, H.H.
Banks, A.	Fenwick, P.C.	Osmond, T.
Banks-Smith, S.R.	Fraser, Sir J.	Plumridge, J.H.
Barnett, J.	French, A.W.	Pullinger, B.D.
Batten, L.W.	Fry, H.J.B.	Roe, F.
Benson, B.	Gainsborough, H.	Rossdale, G.H.
Bewley, W.F.	Gardner, A.D.	Rowell, H.A.
Blackley, F.J.	Gould, A.L.P.	Ruthuen, F.
Blyth, J.B.	Greenwood, A.A.	Rycroft, E.C.
Bonnet, E.T.S.	Halkier, James	Seward, C.
Boyd, A.M.	Hartsilver, J.	Sharrard, W.
Boyd, Sir J.	Henry, L.M.	Sidebottom, J.R.
Bray, W.	Hickey, P.	Spackman, C.L.
Brayley, C.E.W.	Keynes, Sir G.	Stokes, W.A.
Brown, W.	King-Wilson, N.	Storrs-Fox, D.
Brown, W.A.D.	Lathbury, E.B.	Sykes, K.A.H.
Bruce, N.	MacDonald, J.R.	Symonds, Sir C.
Buxton, St.J.D.	MacKay, M.K.	Verney, R.
Cameron, E.H.	MacKenzie, W.	Wand, S.
Campbell, M.W.M.	Magrath, D.	Weaver, S.W.
Catford, E.	Manton, L.	Webb-Peplone, M.
Chavasse, N.G.	McAlpine, D.	West, C.H.
Chavasse, F.B.	McKerrow, C.	Whiting, M.
Chesterman, C.	McLachlan, J.M.	Willcox, W.H.
Courtauld, E.	Miall-Smith, G.	Wilson, R.E.
Cumberland, T.D.	Milburn, C.H.	Wright, H.
Davidson, E.	Miller, G.	
Deane, E.C.	Mitchell, J.E.	

Public Record Office, Kew

The following papers:

FD 5	WO 123
MH 10	WO 138
MH 48	WO 158
NATS 1	WO 159
PRO 30	WO 162
WO 32	WO 163
WO 95	WO 293

Royal College of Surgeons, London

Bowlby, Sir A.
Buxton, St J.D.
McLellan, S.W.

Wellcome Institute for the History of Medicine, London

i) *BMA papers*:
SA/BMA/286
SA/BMA/288

ii) *Contemporary Medical Archive*:
Elliott, T.R. (GC/42)
Turner, E. Grey (PP/GGT/B1)

iii) *Medical Women's Federation papers*:
SA/MWF/C 10
SA/MWF/C 157
SA/MWF/C 158
SA/MWF/C 159
SA/MWF/C 160
SA/MWF/C 161

SA/MWF/C 162
SA/MWF/C 163
SA/MWF/C 164
SA/MWF/C 165

iv) *RAMC Collection*:
Anon, *Six Weeks Active Service as MO to an Infantry Bn.*
Bell, J.G.
Bowlby, Sir A.
Burtchaell, Sir C.
Cantlie, Sir N.
Cowell, Sir E.
Croker, W.P.
Donovan, Sir W.
Fell, Sir M.

Gibbon, T.E.
Glyn-Hughes, H.L.
Harris, H.
Harland, W.C.F.
Holt, M.P.C.
Kaye, H.W.
Lelean, P.S.
Lynch, J.R.
Report of Commission on Medical Establishments
Shields, H.J.S.

Silver, J.P.
Sloggett, Sir A.
Swindell, G.H.
Upcott, H.
War Diary of 26 General Hospital
Webster, W.J.

vi) *Western Manuscript Collection*:
Cheyne, William Watson

ORAL SOURCES

Liddle Collection, University of Leeds

Recordings of the following:

Adair, G.S.
Allan, H.
Baker, P.N.
Ball, H.C.J.
Boyd, Sir J.
Bray, W.
Brown, A.W.
Brown, W.A.D.
Bruce, N.
Bruce-Crafts, A.J.
Cameron, E.H.
Campbell-Smith, W.
Escritt, F.K.
Fairley, G.D.
Fisher, A.
Gamm, F.

Gilruth, J.G.
Halkier, J.
Hickey, P.
Husbands, R.
Huxtable, C.
Jacob, G.
James, F.
MacDonald, J.R.
MacKenzie, W.
Maingay, H.C.
Moor, F.
Moore, G.
Osmond, T.
Whiting, M.
Young, T.

PRINTED AND PUBLISHED SOURCES

Annual Reports of the Medical Research Committee, 1914–1918.

Annual Returns of the Territorial Force 1908–1913.

Correspondence between the Honorable Member for Ilkeston and the War Department in relation to Medical and Sanitary Arrangements at the Cape, cmd. 279, 1900.

Final Report of the Dardanelles Commission, cmd. 371, 1919.

Further Correspondence relative to the Status of Medical Officers of the Army, cmd. 6312, 1890–91.

General Annual Reports of the British Army, 1900–1930.

Interim Report of the War Office Commission on the Provision of Officers (a) For service with the Regular Army in War, and (b) For the Auxiliary Forces, cmd. 3294, 1907.

Letter, dated 17 January 1891, from Sir Andrew Clark, Bart. M.D., F.R.S., to the Secretary of State for War, relative to the Status of Medical Officers of the Army, and the Secretary of State's Reply, dated 2 February 1891, cmd. 6282, 1890–91.

Manual of Injuries and Diseases of War, HMSO, 1918.

Memorandum of the Secretary of State Relating to the Army Estimates for 1909–1910, cmd. 4495, 1909.

Memorandum on Army Reorganisation, cmd. 2993, 1906.

Memorandum on the Treatment of Injuries in War, HMSO, 1915.

Ministry of Defence, Report of the Defence Medical Services Inquiry Committee, HMSO, 1973.

Notes for Sanitary Officers – BEF in France 1917, HMSO, 1917.

Report, dated 18 July 1908, by the Director General of the Army Medical Service, as to the progress made in constituting the Medical Service of the Territorial Force, cmd. 4056, 1908.

Report of a Committee appointed by the Secretary of State for War to inquire into the Organisation of the Army Hospital Corps, Hospital Management and Nursing in the Field, and the Sea Transport of Sick and Wounded, cmd. 3607, 1883.

Report of the Commission appointed to inquire into the Military preparations and other matters connected with the War in South Africa, cmd. 1789, 1904.

Report of the Commission of the Medical Research Committee and the American Red Cross on Trench Fever, OUP, 1918.

Report of the Committee on the Medical Branches of the Defence Services, cmd. 439, 1932–33.

Report of the Committee on the Reorganisation of the Army Medical Service, cmd. 791, 1902.

Report of the Committee to Enquire into the Causes which Tend to Prevent Sufficient Eligible Candidates from Coming Forward for the Army Medical Department, cmd. 2200, 1878–79.

Report of the Committee Appointed to Enquire into the Pay, Status and Conditions of Service of Medical Officers of the Army and Navy, cmd. 5810, 1889.

Report of the Committee appointed to inquire into the Military preparations and other matters connected with the War in South Africa, cmd. 1789, 1904.

Report of The Mesopotamia Commission, cmd. 8610, 1917–18.

Report of the Royal Commission on the Care and Treatment of the Sick and Wounded in the Military Hospitals during the South African Campaign, cmd. 453–455, 1901.

Report of the War Office Committee of Enquiry into Shell Shock, HMSO, 1922.

Report of the War Office Reconstitution Committee, cmd. 1932, cmd. 1968, cmd. 2002, 1904.

Report on the Health of the Army for 1911, cmd. 6287, 1912–13.

Reports by the Joint War Committee and the Joint War Finance Committee of the British Red Cross Society and the Order of St John of Jerusalem in England, HMSO, 1921.

Telegram of Mr Burdett-Coutts to Lord Wolseley, Secretary of State for War, cmd.230, 1900.

NEWSPAPERS AND PERIODICALS*

American Journal of Surgery
Annals of Surgery, 1914–1918
Blackwoods Magazine
British Journal of Clinical Practice
British Journal of Surgery, 1914–1918
British Medical Journal, 1900–1930
Canadian Defence Quarterly
Edinburgh Medical Journal, 1914–1919
Guy's Hospital Reports

*Where extensive use of these periodicals has been made, the relevant dates are given. Only substantive authored articles in these periodicals are listed separately in the bibliography.

Glasgow Medical Journal, 1914–1919
Hansard
Journal of the American Medical Association, 1914–1918
Journal of the Medical Women's Federation
Journal of the Royal Army Medical Corps, 1913–1930
Journal of the Royal Society of Medicine
Lancet, 1914–1920
Medical Annual, 1914–1918
Medical Directory
Medical History
Medical Journal of Australia, 1914–1918
Medical Officer
Medical Record, 1914–1918
Medical Register
Minutes of the Medical Council, 1914–1918
New Scientist
New York Medical Journal, 1914–1918
Nineteenth Century And After
Proceedings of the Royal Society of Medicine
Public Health
Punch
The Nation
The Practitioner
The Times, 1914–1919

SECONDARY SOURCES

PRINTED BOOKS

Abel-Smith, B., *The Hospitals, 1800–1948*, Heinemann, 1964.
Abraham, J. Johnston, *Surgeon's Journey*, Heinemann, 1958.
Ahrenfeldt, R.H., *Psychiatry in the British Army in the Second World War*, 1958.
Babington, A., *For the Sake of Example*, Leo Cooper, 1983.
Banks, H.W. & Hughes, B., *War Surgery from Firing Line to Base*, Baltimore, Wood, 1919.
Barnett, C., *Britain and Her Army 1509–1970*, Allen Lane, The Penguin Press, 1970.
Barrett, J.W., *A Vision of The Possible: What the RAMC Might Become*, H.K. Lewis, 1919.

Bartrip, P.W.J., *Mirror of Medicine: A History of the British Medical Journal*; Oxford, British Medical Journal & Clarendon Press, 1990.

Bayly, H.W., *Triple Challenge: War, Whirligigs and Windmills, A Doctor's Memoirs*, Hutchinson, 1935.

Baynes, J., *Morale*, Leo Cooper, 1987.

Bean, C.E.W., *The Official History of Australia in the War of 1914–18*, Volumes II & III, St Lucia, University of Queensland Press, 1981.

Beckett, I. & Simpson, K. (eds), *A Nation in Arms*, Manchester, Manchester University Press, 1985.

Bell, E.M., *Storming the Citadel*, Constable, 1953.

Berrios, G.E. & Freeman, H.L., *150 Years of British Psychiatry, 1841–1991*, Gaskell & Royal College of Psychiatrists, 1991.

Blunden, E., *Undertones of War*, R. Cobden Sanderson, 1929.

Bond, B. & Robbins, S. (eds), *Staff Officer, The Diaries of Walter Guinness, 1914–18*, Leo Cooper, 1987.

Bond, B. & Roy, I. (eds), *War and Society*, Croom Helm, 1977.

Bourne, J., *Britain and the Great War*, Edward Arnold, 1989.

Brand, J.L., *Doctors and the State*, Baltimore, The John Hopkins Press, 1965.

Brereton, F.S., *The Great War and the RAMC*, Constable, 1919.

Brown, M., *Tommy Goes To War*, J.M. Dent, 1978.

Bynum, W.F. & Porter, R. (eds), *Companion Encyclopaedia of the History of Medicine*, London & New York, Routledge, 1993.

Cable, Boyd, *Between the Lines*, John Murray, 1917.

Carrel, A. & Dehelly, G., *The Treatment of Infected Wounds*, University of London Press, 1917.

Carrington, C., *Soldier from the Wars Returning*, Hutchinson, 1965.

Cartwright, F.F., *A Social History of Medicine*, New York, Longman, 1977.

Castiglioni, A., *A History of Medicine*, New York, Alfred A. Knopf, 1958.

Cecil, H. & Liddle, P.H. (eds), *Facing Armageddon*, Leo Cooper, 1996.

Clayton, A., *Chavasse – Double VC*, Leo Cooper, 1992.

Colebrooke, L., *Almroth Wright, Provocative Doctor and Thinker*, Heinemann, 1954.

Cooter, R., *Surgery and Society in Peace and War*, Macmillan, 1993.

Currie, J.R., *The Mustering of the Medical Services in Scotland, 1914–1919*, Edinburgh, Royal College of Physicians, 1922.

Cushing, H., *From a Surgeon's Journal, 1915–1918*, Constable, 1936.

Dearden, H., *Medicine and Duty, a War Diary*, Heinemann, 1928.

Dearden, H., *Time and Chance*, Heinemann, 1940.

Deeping, W., *No Hero This*, Cassell, 1936.
Dolbey, R.V., *A Regimental Surgeon in War and Prison*, John Murray, 1917.
Drew, Sir R., *Medical Officers in the British Army, 1660–1960, Volume II, 1898–1960*, The Wellcome Historical Medical Library, 1968.
Dunn, J.C., *The War the Infantry Knew, 1914–1919*, Jane's Publishing, 1987.
Edmonds, Brigadier Sir J.E., *History of the Great War Based on Official Documents, Military Operations, France and Belgium, 1915, II*, Macmillan, 1948.
Ellis, J., *Eye-Deep In Hell*, Glasgow, Fontana, 1977.
Falls, C., *History of the Great War Based on Official Documents – Military Operations, Egypt and Palestine, from June 1917 to the End of the War, Part I*, HMSO, 1930.
Fenton, N., *Shell Shock and its Aftermath*, St Louis, Mosby, 1926.
Fifty Amazing Stories of the Great War, Oldhams Press, 1936.
Gervis, H., *Arms and the Doctor, Being the Military Experiences of a Middle Aged Medical Man*, Daniel, 1920.
Gibbs, P., *Realities of War*, Heinemann, 1920.
Gilbert, Martin, *Winston S. Churchill, Volume IV, 1916–1922*, Heinemann, 1975.
Glubb, J., *Into Battle*, Book Club Associates, 1978.
Gosse, P., *Memoirs of a Camp Follower. Adventures and Impressions of a Doctor in the Great War*, Longmans, 1934.
Grieves, K., *The Politics of Manpower*, Manchester, Manchester University Press, 1988.
Guthrie, Douglas, *A History of Medicine*, Thomas Nelson, 1945.
Haber, L.F., *The Poisonous Cloud, Chemical Warfare in the First World War*, Oxford, Clarendon Press, 1986.
Hankey, Donald, *A Student in Arms*, Andrew Melrose, 1917.
Herringham, Sir W., *Physician in France*, Edward Arnold, 1919.
Holmes R., *Firing Line*, Jonathan Cope, 1985.
Honigsbaum, F., *The Division in British Medicine*, Kogan Page, 1979.
Honigsbaum, F., *The Struggle for the Ministry of Health*, G. Bell, 1970.
Hughes, B. & Banks, H.S., *War Surgery from Firing Line to Base*, Baltimore, Wood, 1919.
Hull, A.J., *Surgery in War*, Churchill, 1916.
Hurst, Sir A., *Medical Diseases of War*, Baltimore, William & Welkins, 1944.
Jacobs, M., *Reflections of a General Practitioner*, Johnson, 1965.
Laffin, J., *Surgeons in the Field*, J.M. Dent, 1970.

Leed, E.J., *No Man's Land: Combat and Identity in World War One*, Cambridge, Cambridge University Press, 1979.

Lelean, P.S., *Sanitation in War*, Churchill, 1917.

Lewis, Thomas, *The Soldier's Heart and the Effort Syndrome*, London, Shaw & Sons, 1918.

Liddle, P.H. (ed.), *Passchendaele in Perspective*, Leo Cooper, 1997

Liddle, P.H., *The Soldier's War, 1914–1918*, Blandford, 1988.

Little, E.M., *History of the British Medical Association*, British Medical Association, 1932

Lloyd, L.L., *Lice and their Menace to Man*, Hodder & Stoughton, 1919.

Lovegrove, P., *Not Least in the Crusade*, Aldershot, Gale & Polden, 1952.

Lutzker, E., *Women Gain a Place in Medicine*, New York, McGraw–Hill Book Company, 1969.

MacDonald, L., *The Roses of No Man's Land*, Penguin, 1993

McIntosh, J., *Studies in the Aetiology of Epidemic Influenza*, HMSO, 1922.

McLaren, B., *Women of the War*, Hodder & Stoughton, 1917.

McLaughlin, R., *The Royal Army Medical Corps*, Leo Cooper, 1972.

MacNalty, A.S., *The History of State Medicine in England*, Royal Institute of Public Health and Hygiene, 1948.

MacPherson, W.G., *Official History of the War – Medical Services – General History, Volumes I–IV*, HMSO, 1921–1923.

MacPherson, W.G., *Official History of the War – Medical Services – Hygiene of the War, Volumes I & II*, HMSO, 1923.

MacPherson, W.G., *Official History of the War – Medical Services – Surgery of the War, Volumes I & II*, HMSO, 1923.

Martin, A.A., *Surgeon in Khaki*, Arnold, 1915.

Marwick, A., *The Deluge, British Society and the First World War*, Methuen, 1965.

Marwick, A., *Women at War, 1914–1918*, Fontana, 1977.

Miller, E., *The Neuroses in War*, London, Macmillan, 1940.

Mitchell, A.M., *Medical Women and the Medical Services of the First World War*, Authors offprint.

Mitchell, T.J. & Smith G.M., *Official History of the War – Medical Services – Casualties and Medical Statistics*, HMSO, 1931.

Moore, W., *See How They Ran*, Leo Cooper, 1970.

Moore, W., *The Thin Yellow Line*, Cooper, 1974.

Moran, Lord, *The Anatomy of Courage*, Constable, 1945.

Mowat, Charles Loch, *Britain between the Wars*, Methuen, 1956.

Muir, W., *Observations of an Orderly*, Simpkin, Marshall, Hamilton, Kent & Co. Ltd., 1918.

Murray, F., *Women as Army Surgeons*, Hodder & Stoughton, 1920.

Myers, C.S., *Shell Shock in France, 1914–1918*, C.U.P., 1940.

Newman, B. & Evans I.O., *Anthology of Armageddon*, Greenhill Books, 1989.

Paget, S., *Sir Victor Horsley*, Constable, 1919.

Pakenham, T., *The Boer War*, Weidenfeld & Nicholson, 1979.

Penhallow, D.P., *Military Surgery*, H. Frowde, 1916.

Pickstone, J.V., *Medicine and Industrial Society*, Manchester, Manchester University Press, 1985.

Plowman, Max, *A Subaltern on the Somme in 1916*, J.M. Dent & Sons, 1927.

Richards, F., *Old Soldiers Never Die*, Faber & Faber, 1933.

Rorie, D., *A Medico's Luck in the War*, Aberdeen, Milne & Hutchison, 1929.

Rutherford, N.J.C., *Soldiering with a Stethoscope*, Stanley Paul, 1937.

Rutherford, N.J.C., *Memories of an Army Surgeon*, Stanley Paul, 1939.

Simkins, P., *Kitchener's Army*, Manchester, Manchester University Press, 1988.

Skelley, A.R., *The Victorian Army at Home*, Croom Helm, 1977.

Souttar, H.S., *A Surgeon in Belgium*, Edward Arnold, 1915.

Spiers, E.M., *The Army and Society*, Longman, 1980.

Squire, J.E., *Medical Hints for the Use of Medical Officers Temporarily Employed with Troops*, Milford, 1915.

Stevens, R., *Medical Practice in Modern England*, New Haven, Yale University Press, 1966.

Swinton, Major General Sir E. (ed.), *Twenty Years After (Supplementary Volume)*, G. Newnes, 1938.

Taith, B. & Thornton, T., (ed.), *War*, Stroud, Alan Sutton, 1998.

Teichman, C., *Diary of a Yeomanry M.O., Egypt, Gallipoli, Palestine and Italy*, Fisher Unwin, 1921.

The Times History of the War, Volume IV, The Times, 1915.

Thompson, A. Landsborough, *Half a Century of Medical Research, Volumes I & II*, HMSO, 1973.

Thompson, E., *These Men Thy Friends*, MacMillan, 1933.

Treves, F., *The Tale of a Field Hospital*, Cassell, 1901.

Trombley, S., *Sir Frederick Treves: The Extra-ordinary Edwardian*, Routledge, 1989.

Tubby, A.H., *A Consulting Surgeon in the Near East*, Christophers, 1920.

Vaughan, P., *Doctors Commons: A Short History of the British Medical Association*, Heinemann, 1959.

Wallace, C.S., *War Surgery of the Abdomen*, Blakiston, 1918.

Wallace, C.S. & Fraser, J., *Surgery at a Casualty Clearing Station*, MacMillan, 1919.

Wilson, H.W. & Hammerton, J.A., *The Great War*, Volume 4, The Amalgamated Press, 1915.

Wilson, T., *The Myriad Faces of War*, Cambridge, Polity Press, 1988.

Winter, J.M., *The Great War and the British People*, MacMillan, 1987.

Woodham-Smith, C., *Florence Nightingale*, Constable, 1950.

ARTICLES

Ainsworth, Major R.B., 'Sanitation in War', *Journal of the Royal Army Medical Corps* (JRAMC), XXIV, 1915, pp. 353–8.

Armstrong, Dr G.E., 'Surgery and War: Address of the President at the Opening of the Session of the American Surgical Association, June (1915)', *Annals of Surgery*, LXII, 1915, p. 137.

Baker, R.A. & Bayliss, 'William John Ritchie Simpson (1855–1931), Public Health and Tropical Medicine', *Medical History*, 31, 1987, p. 463.

Ball, C.B., 'An Address on the Reorganisation of the Army Medical Service', *British Medical Journal* (BMJ), 1902 (I), pp. 437–9.

Bennett, J.D.C., 'Medical Advances Consequent to the Great War, 1914–18', *Journal of the Royal Society of Medicine*, 83, 1990, pp. 738–42.

Beveridge, Major General W.W.O., 'A Brief Review of the Progress of Military Hygiene since the War', JRAMC, XLII, 1924, p. 187.

Bowlby, Sir A. 'The Work of the Clearing Hospitals during the Last Six Weeks', BMJ, 1914 (II), p. 1053–4.

Bowlby, Sir A. & Rowland, S., 'A Report on Gas Gangrene', BMJ, 1914 (II), p. 913.

Chase, C., 'Notes on Service in the French Army Medical Corps', *Annals of Surgery*, 66, 1917, pp. 1–12.

Childs, C., 'Prevention of Typhoid in our Home Camps', BMJ, 1914 (II), p. 1087.

Coates, J.B., 'On the Utilisation of Medicomilitary History', *American Journal of Surgery*, 1959, 97, pp. 687–9.

Cohen, D., 'A War of Nerves', *New Scientist*, 9 March 1991, pp. 42–4.

Cope, Sir Z., 'The Treatment of Wounds through the Ages', *Medical History*, 2, 1958, p. 171.

Cree, Colonel G., 'Medical Narrative of the Arrangements of the First Division at the Battle of The Aisne', JRAMC, 1915, XXIV, p. 201.

Crile, G.W., 'Standardization of the Practice of Military Surgery – The Clinical Surgeon in Military Service', JAMA, LXIX, 1917, pp. 291–2.

Culpin, Lieutenant M. & Fearnsides, Dr E.G., 'Frostbite', BMJ, 1915 (I), pp. 84–5.

Cumston, C.G., 'Some Reflections on the Surgery of the War, Viewed after Three Years', Medical Record, 1917, pp. 283–4.

Davy, Sir H., 'Some War Diseases', BMJ, 1919 (II), pp. 837–40.

Downes, Colonel R.M., 'The Tactical Employment of the Medical Services in a Cavalry Corps', JRAMC, 47, 1926, pp. 328–34.

Drennen, W.E., 'Experiences in Military Surgery', JAMA, LXV, 1915, pp. 296–300.

Drew, R., 'Medicine's Debt to the Army: A Review of the Army's Contribution to Medical Science', JRAMC, 110, 1964, pp. 5–12.

Drew, Major General W.R.M., 'The Challenge of Tropical Medicine', JRAMC, 110, 1964, pp. 77–83.

Eastes, Captain G.L., 'A Sanitary Section at the Front', JRAMC, XXVI, 1916, p. 228.

Ensor, Brevet Colonel H., 'The RAMC Services of a Division on Active Service', JRAMC, XLII, 1924, pp. 241, 331, 424.

Evans, B., 'A Doctor in the Great War – An Interview with Sir Geoffrey Marshall', BMJ, 285, 1982.

Fairfield, L. et al. 'Medical Women in the Forces', Journal of the Medical Women's Federation (JMWF), 49, 1967, pp. 99–107.

Farrell, P.H.J., 'The Military Surgeon on the Firing Line', NYMJ, CI, 1915, pp. 1062–4.

Fischer-Homberger, E., 'The First World War and the crisis of Medical Ethics', International Congress of the History of Medicine, Twenty-third, London, 1972. Proceedings, 1974, Vol. I, pp. 268–73.

Fraser, L.E., 'Diary of a Dresser in the Serbian Unit of the Scottish Women's Hospital', Blackwoods Magazine, 197, 1915, pp. 776–97.

Fulton, J.F., 'Medicine, Warfare and History', JAMA, 153, 1953, pp. 482–8.

Goodwin, T.H., 'Medical Service in the British Area on the Western Front', JAMA, LXIX, 1917, p. 120.

Goodwin, T.H., 'The Army Medical Service' (An Address to the Cornell Medical College Faculty and Students about to Leave for the Front', NYMJ, CVI, 1917, pp. 1–2.

Grattan, Colonel H.W., 'Medical Organisation, with Special Reference to the Transportation of Wounded in Open Warfare', JRAMC, XXXIX, 1922, p. 30.

Gray, H.M.W., 'Surgical Treatment of Wounded Men at Advanced Units', NYMJ, CVI, 1917, pp. 1013–21.

Haller, J.S., 'Gas Warfare: Military-medical responsiveness of the Allies in the Great War, 1914–1918', *New York State Journal of Medicine*, (NYSJM), Vol. 90, No. 10, 1990, pp. 499–510.

Haller, J.S., 'The Great War: Its impact on the British and American medical communities', NYSJM, 1991, vol. 91, pt. 1, pp. 19–28.

Haller, J.S., 'Treatment of Infected Wounds during the Great War, 1914 to 1918', *Southern Medical Journal*, (SMJ), 1992, vol. 85, no. 3, pp. 303–15.

Haller, J.S., 'Trench Foot – A Study in Military-Medical Responsiveness in the Great War, 1914–1918, *Western Journal of Medicine*, June 1990, 152, 6, pp. 729–33.

Hamilton, Surgeon General J.B., 'Reform in the Army Medical Service', BMJ, 1902 (II), pp. 1033–4.

Hannay, Colonel R.S., 'Medical Arrangements of an Infantry Division in Open Warfare', JRAMC, XXXIX, 1922, p. 348.

Harman, N. Bishop, 'Some Practical Points in Medical Reconstruction', BMJ, 1919 (I), p. 313.

Harrison, M., 'The Medicalization of War – The Militarization of Medicine', *Social History of Medicine*, 9, 1996, pp. 267–76.

Hatch, W.K., 'Gas Gangrene and Tetanus', BMJ, 1915 (I), p. 545.

Hopson, M.F., 'Dental Surgery and the War', *Guy's Hospital Reports*, LXX, 1922.

Humphreys, Lieutenant Colonel H.F., 'Diary of a D.A.D.M.S. on the Jerusalem Campaign, Palestine, November–December 1917', JRAMC, 50, 1928, p. 96.

Humphreys, Humphrey, 'Some Medical Memories of two World Wars', JRAMC, 101, 1955, pp. 237–43.

Ivens, M.H.F., 'The Part Played by British Medical Women in the War', BMJ, 1917 (II), pp. 203–8.

Lankford, N.D., 'The Victorian Medical Profession and Military Practice: Army Doctors and National Origins', *Bulletin of the History of Medicine*, vol. 54, 1980, pp. 511–28.

Leneman, L., 'Medical Women at War, 1914–1918', *Medical History*, 38, 1994, pp. 160–77.

MacDonald, A.T.I., 'Medical and Surgical Work as a Prisoner of War', BMJ, 1919 (I), pp. 367–9.

MacKenzie, Major D.F., 'A Few Subjects for Consideration Affecting the Corps', JRAMC, XLIV, 1915, pp. 103–5.

Makins, G.H., 'Introductory', *British Journal of Surgery (BJS)*, VI, 1918–19, pp. 1–11.

Makins, Sir G., 'The Part of the Consulting Surgeon in War', BMJ, 1919 (I), pp. 789–92.

Massac-Buist, H., 'Ambulance Work at the Front', BMJ, 1914 (II), p. 642.

Melville, Colonel C.H., 'Military Hygiene and Sanitation: a Retrospect', JRAMC, 48, 1927, pp. 25-9.

Morrison, R.J.G. *et al.*, 'Centenary of the Royal Army Medical College', JRAMC, 107, 1961.

Neal, J.B., 'The History of the Royal Army Medical College', JRAMC, 1957, 103, p. 163.

Noble, R.E., 'The Medical Corps of the Army as a Career, JAMA, LXVIII, 1917, pp. 955–7.

Oldfield, Major J., 'Regimental and Field Ambulance Training in the Territorial Force', JRAMC, XX, 1913, pp. 439–41.

Oldfield, Major J., 'The Scope of the Field Ambulance as a Training School', JRAMC, XXII, 1914, pp. 685–93.

Ormsby, Sir L.H., 'The Prospects of Medical Officers in the Army', BMJ, 1906 (II), p. 1134.

Osler, Sir W., 'Bacilli and Bullets', BMJ, 1914 (II), pp. 569–70.

Parish, H.J., 'Some Reflections of an Octogenarian Army Medical Service: Balkans and Caucasus', JRAMC, 125, 1979, p. 164.

Pike, Captain E.B., 'Field Sanitation', JRAMC, XXVI, 1916, pp. 330–48.

Pike, Colonel W.W., 'Regimental Medical Aid in Trench Warfare', JRAMC, XXV, 1915, pp. 233–6.

Reed, Major G.A.K.H., 'Some Notes on the Tactical Handling of Field Ambulances in Mobile Warfare', JRAMC, XXXV, 1920, pp. 300–7.

Renburn, E.T., 'Physiological Problems of the Soldiers in Tropical Warfare: an Operational Approach', JRAMC, 105, 1959, pp. 172–82.

Richards, O., 'The Development of Casualty Clearing Stations', *Guy's Hospital Reports*, LXX, 1922, pp. 115–23.

Ritchie, Major M.B.H., 'The Training of RAMC Officers for War, JRAMC, XLII, 1924, pp. 267–74.

Sachs, A., 'The Centenary of British Military Pathology', JRAMC, 101, 1955, pp. 100–21.

Scharlieb, Dr M., 'The Medical Woman – Her Training, Her Difficulties and Her Sphere of Usefulness', *The Nineteenth Century and After*, 78, 1915, pp. 1174–85.

Simpson, W.J., 'War and Disease', *The Nation*, XV, p. 861.

SKIA, 'A Hospital in France', *Blackwoods Magazine*, 204, 1918, pp. 613–40.

Smith, J.W., 'Clinical Notes on the Wounded in South Africa', BMJ, 1901 (I), p. 947.

Stafford, Major A.H., 'A Note on Camp Sanitation', JRAMC, XXV, 1915, p. 229.

Stephen, G.N., 'Recent Developments in Royal Army Medical Corps Front Line Education', JRAMC, XXXI, 1918, pp. 153–61.

Thompson, Colonel H.N., 'An Account of my Capture and my Experiences in Germany', JRAMC, XXIV, 1915, pp. 122–4.

Thompson, Sir W., 'Some Surgical Lessons from the Campaign in South Africa', BMJ, 1901 (II), pp. 265–70.

Thurston, L.V., 'A Criticism and Some Comments and Memories of Front Line Evacuation', JRAMC, 52, 1929, p. 260–9.

Tomkins, S.M., 'The Failure of Expertise: Public Health Policy in Britain during the 1918–1919 Influenza Epidemic', *Social History of Medicine*, vol 5, no 3, 1992, pp. 435–54.

Tooth, H.H., 'Enteric Fever in the Army in South Africa, with Remarks on Inoculation, BMJ, 1900 (II), pp. 1368–9.

Towers, B.A., 'Health Education Policy 1916–1926: Venereal Disease and the Prophylaxis Dilemma', *Medical History*, 24, 1980, pp. 73–7.

Turner, G., 'Typhoid Fever in South Africa: its Cause and Prevention', BMJ, 1902 (I), pp. 381–2.

Turner, W.A., 'The Bradshaw Lecture on Neuroses and Psychoses of War, JRAMC, XXXI, 1918, pp. 399–413.

Tyndale, W.F., 'An Assistant Director of Medical Services in War Time'
– JRAMC, XXXVI, 1921, pp. 401–16.
– JRAMC, XXXVII, 1921, pp. 23–39.

Vella, E.E., 'The Development of Pathology in the RAMC', *Proceedings of the Royal Society of Medicine*, 68, 1975, pp. 321–6.

Waggett, Major E.B., 'Medical Problems of the Mobilised Territorial Force', BMJ, 1913 (I), p. 1163.

Watson, C.G., 'Trench Frost-Bite, BMJ, 1915 (I), pp. 413–16.

Webb-Johnson, C., 'The Soldiers Feet and Footgear', BMJ, 1914 (II), pp. 702–5.

Wettenhall, R.R., 'Dermatology on Active Service with the RAMC', MJA, 1917 (I), pp. 181–3.

Wildey, Deputy Surgeon General A. Gascoigne, 'The Medical Officer and the Fighting Man', *The Medical Annual*, 1916, pp. 650–67.

Wilson, Colonel, 'Problems of Mobilisation Specially Affecting the RAMC', BMJ, 1913 (II), p. 1095.

UNPUBLISHED THESES
Elston, M.A.C., 'Women Doctors in the British Health Service: a Sociological Study of their Careers and Opportunities', University of Leeds, Department of Sociology, 1986.
Whitehead, I.R., 'Medical Officers and the British Army during the First World War', University of Leeds, School of History, 1993.

Index

Ambulance, 159; 1st SW Mounted Brigade Field Ambulance, 159; Number 5 General Hospital, 210; Number 8 General Hospital, 238; Number 13 General Hospital, 210; Number 26 General Hospital, 209, 211, 238; Number Seven Mobile Bacteriological Laboratory, 142; Number 9 Stationary Hospital, 152; Number 11 Stationary Hospital, medical society at, 171

British Colombia, 50

British Dental Association, 243

British Empire, 50

British Expeditionary Force, *see also* British Army; 43, 126, 218–19, 243

British Infantry,
Artists Rifles, 92; 9th Bn. Border Regiment, 223; 5th Bn. Black Watch, 77; 17th (Service) Bn. Northumberland Fusiliers, 152; 2nd Bn. Royal Marine Light Infantry, 223; 2nd Bn. Royal Welch Fusiliers, 184; 1st Bn. Wiltshire Regiment, 184

British Medical Association, 6, 8, 10–12, 15–20, 22–5, 32, 34–7, 40–2, 54–5, 68, 73, 113, 117, 221, 252, 257

British Medical Journal 8, 12, 15–17, 19, 21, 23, 38, 42, 44, 70, 75–6, 78, 85, 92, 98–9, 130–1, 146, 162–3, 165, 169, 187, 227–8, 230–1, 239, 253, 257

British Red Cross Society, 1, 33–4, 107, 134

British Union for the Abolition of Vivisection, 221

Brodrick, St. John, 16, 18–19, 22

Brown, A.W., 102

Brown, Malcolm, 226

Brown, W., 224

Bruay, 197

Bruce, Major General Sir David, 166

Burdett-Coutts, W.L.A.B., 12–13

Burghard, Colonel F.F., 128

Burtchaell, Sir Charles, 162, 202

Cable, Boyd, 194

Calais, 127

Cambridge Military Hospital, 159

Cambridge University, 120

Campbell, Dr Margaret, 117

Canada, 50

Canadian Army Medical Corps, 50, 138, 200

Cannon, Professor W.B., 143–4

Cantlie, General Sir Neil, 153–4

Cardwell, Edward, 10

Carrell, Alexis, 207

Carrell-Dakin method, 165, 207, 210

casualties, 77, 182, 184–5

Casualty Clearing Stations, 4, 35, 43, 127, 129, 132–3, 141–2, 155, 165–6, 182, 189–90, 192–3, 195–211, 233, 238–42; 129

Central Medical War Committee, 34, 49, 54–5, 60–6, 72–80, 82–3, 85, 95, 266–8

cerebro-spinal fever, 143, 164

Chamberlain, Neville, 73–4, 79

Charnwood, Lord, 129

Chavasse, Noel, 152

Cheltenham, 12

chemical advisers, 168

chemical warfare, (*see* gas)

Chevasson, Major, 204

Cheyne, Sir William Watson, 206

Chocques, 197

Chodak Gregory, Dr Hazel, 121

Churchill, Sir Winston S., 115–16, 258

Lewis, Thomas, 245
Liberal Party, 40, 54
lice, 166, 232-3
Lillers, 197
Limerick, 158
Linton, Dr F.C., 45-6
Lister, Colonel W. T., 128
Littlewood, Lieutenant Colonel, 63
Llandridrod Wells, 158
Lloyd George, David, 1st Earl, 73-4, 85-6
Local Government Board, 44-6, 71
locum-tenentes, 32, 47-9, 62, 107, 118, 120
London sanitary companies, 163
London School of Medicine for Women, 118, 120
London University, 101, 119-20
Loos, Battle of, 197-9

MacAlister, Sir Donald, 83, 92
McAlpine, Douglas, 159, 186
MacCormac, Sir William, 13
McKenzie, M.D., 52, 161
McKerrow, Charles, 52, 77, 186-7, 189, 224-6, 230
McLachlan, J.M., 39-40, 42, 49, 53, 152, 194-5
McLellan, S.W., 223
MacPherson, Ian, 1st Baron Strathcarron, 160
MacPherson, W.G., 197
Maghull Hospital, 169
Main Dressing Station, see also Field Ambulance; 190, 192-3
Maitland, Dr Peggy, 117-18
Makins, Sir George, 128, 131-3, 205, 256
malingering, 223-5, 242
Malta, 112, 116
Manchester High School for Girls, 119
Manchester Medical War Committee, 72, 268-71

Manchester University, 91-2, 94
Mann, Ida, 120
manpower, see also recruitment; 4, 23, 33-43, 50-1, 53, 74-86, 91-2, 95-103, 107-8, 133, 161, 182, 187-8, 242-3, 253, 258
Manual of Injuries and Diseases of War, 164
Manual of Military Hygiene, 219
Marseilles, 127
Martin, A.A., 129, 154, 157, 186, 222
measles, 233
Medical Advisory Board, 18
medical education, 91-101, 108, 119-20, 151-2, 157-8, 174
Medical Inspector of Drafts, 243
Medical Officers, see also Field Ambulances; Regimental Medical Officers; Royal Army Medical Corps; 2-4, 7-18, 24-5, 33, 35-8, 40-3, 55, 60-1, 63, 66-8, 70, 75-85, 96, 107-17, 121-2, 128-39, 142, 145-7, 151-74, 184-8, 194-5, 210, 218-20, 222-8, 230-2, 235-7, 240-1, 244-6, 252-5, 258-60
Medical Officers of Health, 44-6, 71, 163
medical profession, 1-3, 7, 9-10, 11-12, 17-25, 32-4, 36, 40-2, 44, 46-7, 49, 51-3, 55, 60, 63-86, 95, 97, 107, 109-11, 113, 115, 117-22, 170, 206, 238, 252-4, 259-60, 262-71
medical reciprocity, 50, 92
Medical Register, 72, 92, 97, 102
Medical Research Committee, 140-7, 164, 238, 245
medical staff college, 18
Medical Staff Corps, see also Army Hospital Corps; 10
medical students, 3, 12, 24, 91-103, 108, 119-21